The Case Against Christian Nationalism

An Expository Commentary on Stephen Wolfe's Book

Blake Callens

This work is licensed under a Creative Commons Attribution-NoDerivatives 4.0 International License.

Quotations from *The Case For Christian Nationalism* © 2022 Canon Press

Copyright Disclaimer under section 107 of the Copyright Act 1976, allowance is made for "fair use" for purposes such as criticism, comment, news reporting, teaching, scholarship, education and research.

Unless otherwise indicated, all Scripture quotations are from The ESV® Bible (The Holy Bible, English Standard Version®), copyright © 2001 by Crossway, a publishing ministry of Good News Publishers. Used by permission. All rights reserved.

Scripture quotations from the Legacy Standard Bible, Copyright ©2021 by The Lockman Foundation. Used by permission. All rights reserved.

v1.1.0
ISBN-13: 979-8-9890180-2-4

Table of Contents

Foreword..7
Introduction: The Great Renewal..15
    I. The Storm..15
    II. Definition...17
    III. Explicating the Definition..20
    IV. Method..25
    V. Summary of Argument..28
    VI. Foreword...35
1. Nations Before the Fall..37
    I. A Rational Animal..37
    II. The Ends and Dignity of Man..40
    III. Civil Fellowship...44
    IV. Civil Order and Civil Virtue...48
    V. Conclusion...52
2. Redeemed Nations..55
    I. State of Sin..55
    II. State of Grace..59
    III. Dominion and the Divine Image...71
    IV. Conclusion..73
3. Loving Your Nation..75
    I. Method..75
    II. People, Place, and Things...79
    III. Nation...83
    IV. Loving the Neighbor...94
    V. Nationalism..100
    VI. Conclusion..104
4. Perfecting Your Nation..113
    I. The Christian Nation...113
    II. Christian Nationalism..119
    III. Objections..126
    IV. Excluding Fellow Christians...135
    V. Conclusion...141
5. The Good of Cultural Christianity...145
    I. Mode of Religion..145
    II. Definition and Explication..149
    III. The End of Cultural Christianity..157
    IV. Celebrating Decline...160
    V. Preparation and Hypocrisy..166
    VI. Final Considerations...172
    VII. Conclusion..181
6. What Laws Can and Cannot Do...185

- I. Law in General..185
- II. Civil Law..191
- II. Civil Law in a Christian Commonwealth..............198
- IV. Modern Theonomy...203
- V. Disobeying the Law...207
- VI. Conclusion..213
- 7. The Christian Prince..215
  - I. Introduction..215
  - II. The Prince...216
  - III. The Origin of Civil Power................................218
  - IV. A Divine Office..222
  - V. The Christian Prince..228
  - VI. The King and Kingdom of God........................240
  - VII. Conclusion..246
- 8. The Right to Revolution.......................................249
  - Introduction..249
  - I. Definition and Explication................................253
  - II. Statement of the Question..............................257
  - III. Just Revolution...258
  - IV. Conditions for Revolution...............................264
  - V. Lesser Magistrates...274
  - VI. Romans 13..275
  - VII. Conclusion..281
- 9. Liberty of Conscience...285
  - I. Statement of the Question..............................285
  - II. Principle...288
  - III. Prudence...295
  - IV. Specific Groups..301
  - V. Conclusion..304
- 10. The Foundation of American Freedom................307
  - I. Introduction..307
  - II. Puritan New England and Free Expression........309
  - III. Religious Liberty in the Founding Era..............314
  - IV. Conclusion...327
- Epilogue: Now What?...333
  - Introduction..333
  - I. The New America..334
  - II. Gynocracy..346
  - III. Universalism..352
  - IV. Dominion...358
  - V. America is Not Lost..366
- Afterword...369

For my children.
Seek Christ first, no matter the situation (Luke 9:23).

Foreword

I was initially made aware of Stephen Wolfe's *The Case for Christian Nationalism* shortly after it was published in November 2022, through Christian apologist Neil Shenvi's live-tweeting of sections of note while he read the book. Though first struck by Wolfe's unorthodox theological claims about man before the fall and his use of infant baptism as a civil induction ceremony, it was a quote Shenvi shared about a "Christian Prince"[1] that gave me immediate pause. For years, I have been heavily interested, to a point of preoccupation, with the seemingly unrelated subjects of Reformed theology and the history and philosophy of totalitarian governments. What I saw in that quote, calling for a national strongman to "suppress the enemies of God and elevate his people" and to "restore masculine prominence in the land," was something far closer to what one would find in a speech by Benito Mussolini than in John Calvin's *Institutes of the Christian Religion*. Seeing a subject that potentially sat at the center of the Venn diagram of my interests, I immediately ordered the book, watched interviews Wolfe gave to promote it, and began investigating his social media posts and other writings.

What I found was nothing less than a nationalist political theory similar to that championed by early-20th century authoritarian rightists, including ethno-nationalist elements, being laundered through Calvin's "two kingdoms" theology to a Christian audience. His theory includes:

- An appeal to a mythologized cultural past, used not just as an emotional appeal, but as a point of personal identity. For Wolfe, these appeals come as:
  - a Scripturally unsound theory of ethnically distinct, and potentially warring, nations even if had Adam not fallen.
  - a selection of 16th and 17th century Reformed theologians and their form of theocratic government.

---

1 https://twitter.com/i/status/1593335175441678340
Neil Shenvi: "we should pray that God would raise up [a Christian prince] from among us: one who would suppress the enemies of God and elevate his people; recover a worshiping [sic] people; restore masculine prominence in the land and a spirit for dominion; affirm and conserve his people and place, not permitting their dissolution or capture; and inspire a love of one's Christian country." - Wolfe, The Case for Christian Nationalism, p.323

- a mythologized account of early-American colonies, chartered along religious lines.
- Blaming the core ideas of liberal democracy for most of society's current ills and naming it as the utopian state's greatest enemy. The epilogue of the book is a manifesto against Western liberalism and what he calls the "gynocracy," an expression taken from Aristotle and Calvin.[2]
- An openly expressed desire to fully eradicate the opposition. According to Wolfe, once his ideal nation is established, "atheism will be crushed" using "scripture, tradition, and Plato."[3]
- A desire to enact law, whether through executive fiat or a stacked legislature, that aims to control the day-to-day lives of individuals and shape them towards a national purpose. Wolfe argues for an official state religion, the outright banning of public worship of other religions, and civil punishment of heretics.[4]
- The installation of a figurehead, whose main purpose is to serve as the ideological director of the nation. For Spain and Italy this was *el Caudillo* (Franco) and *il Duce* (Mussolini), respectively; for Wolfe it is a play on the Erasmian "Christian Prince".

I did not originally seek to write a book on Wolfe's philosophy. I am a software engineer by trade, and though I am a voracious reader of academic material on the two aforementioned subjects, I have no degree in political theory, and my only formal training in Reformed theology has come through church discipleship. Nevertheless, the reviews for Wolfe's book came and went, and his form of authoritarian Christian Nationalism steadily gained in popularity in highly conservative, Reformed circles (and is gaining still). In the many reviews promoted by Christian publications, I found no one who addressed the details of his political theory *as political*

---

2 Stephen Wolfe, *The Case for Christian Nationalism* (Moscow, Idaho: Canon Press, 2022), 448–54.
3 https://twitter.com/PerfInjust/status/1594354335131074564
   Stephen Wolfe: "Yes, atheism will be crushed. And we'll do it citing scripture, tradition, and Plato."
4 Wolfe, *The Case for Christian Nationalism*, 387–93.

theory; instead, they focused on theology. These reviews critiqued his Scripturally dubious claims on ethnicity, his admitted lack of exegesis in his theory, and his contradictions to the *Westminster Confession of Faith* and sometimes provided a short take on how his proposed government would be impractical and/or oppressive. I highly recommend Shenvi's very thorough theological rebuttal[5], which covers all of these points.

It is understandable why none of these reviewers picked up on the traditional ethno-nationalist themes of Wolfe's book – their area of interest and expertise is theology, rendering them predisposed to counter any "Christian" theory from that angle. I quickly came to the conclusion that I may be one of a very small group of people well-read and passionate about both Reformed theology and totalitarian ideology and that I am perhaps the only person interested in writing a rebuttal along both lines. I began studying for this task in mid-December 2022. The goal of this was primarily to bolster my knowledge on the subjects of American Nativist movements of the 19th and early-20th centuries, the history and political philosophy of Falangist and Francoist Spain, which I believe is closest to Wolfe's Christian nation and is not often written about in English[6], and the historical application of Calvin's political theology in Geneva and elsewhere. The first product of this continuing study is this expository commentary on *The Case for Christian Nationalism*.

This project was originally intended to be my reference notes for a planned book describing the larger genus that Wolfe's political theory belongs to, which I had begun referring to as *Christian Authoritarianism*. This subset of self-described Christian Nationalists includes Gab CEO Andrew Torba and pastor Andrew Isker, authors of *Christian Nationalism: A Biblical Guide for Taking Dominion and Discipling Nations*. Also of note is William Wolfe (no relation), a former Assistant Deputy Secretary under

---

5   "Of Gods and Men: A Long Review of Wolfe's Case for Christian Nationalism, Part I – Book Summary," *Neil Shenvi - Apologetics* (blog), November 22, 2022, https://shenviapologetics.com/of-gods-and-men-a-long-review-of-wolfes-case-for-christian-nationalism-part-i-book-summary/.

6   I rely heavily on Georgia Priorelli's *Italian Fascism and Spanish Falangism in Comparison: Constructing the Nation,* Paul Preston's highly detailed biography of Francisco Franco, and a pro-fascist, independently published biography and collection of quotes from the Falangist leader, José Antonio Primo de Rivera.

the Trump administration, and former seminarian at Southern Baptist Theological Seminary, who worked directly with its president, Albert Mohler. He is a very vocal, and often antagonistic, proponent of both Christian Nationalism and Stephen Wolfe, regularly integrating ethnicity into his antagonistic comments.[7]

Perhaps that book on Christian Authoritarianism will eventually be written, but instead, as I began to compile my notes in early February 2023, I decided to make them public on Substack,[8] with the idea that it would allow others to reference these authoritarian and ethno-nationalist correlations and to give people the opportunity to challenge my rebuttals, to ultimately help me harden them. This public note-taking forced me to be more thorough and coherent in my thoughts than I had originally envisioned, and the project quickly took on a life of its own. I determined that these posts would be most effective if they were compiled into a standalone book, the volume which now rests before you.

The Format and Goals of This Commentary

Though it can be read on its own, this book is formatted to be a companion of deliberate contradiction to *The Case for Christian Nationalism*. My hope is that you will read a single subsection of a chapter and then refer to that subsection's rebuttal in this book. When I agree with an assertion by Wolfe, I briefly make note of it, but there is such a large quantity of disagreement I hold with his theology and political theory that I purposefully focus on them.

This commentary references not only Wolfe's book but also his social media postings, his blog posts and essays, and articles about him to add context to assertions in the book and to paint a holistic picture of his worldview. When possible, I reference original social media postings by Wolfe but will occasionally refer to an archive of a post because he has

---

[7] William Wolfe on Twitter: "If you can muster up strong words for your mostly white Presbyterian brethren to correct their theology… But walk on eggshells around minorities and women and refuse to correct their CRT and egalitarianism. You're not calibrated rightly for the fights of today." https://twitter.com/William_E_Wolfe/status/1677744945216512001

[8] https://christiannationalismnotes.com

deleted it on the original platform. It will become apparent as you read this book that Wolfe is far more bold in his online assertions regarding ethnicity and, most likely, deliberately reigned those thoughts in for his official exposition on Christian Nationalist political theory. Still, *The Case for Christian Nationalism* contains many assertions, turns of phrase, and quotations regarding ethnicity that most readers will conclude ethically compromises his theory.

I have avoided all direct reference to Nazism in this commentary because of its cultural connotations. The last thing I would want is for someone to be turned off by this book, because they perceive I am yet another person who does not understand what *fascism* actually is and is calling his opponent a "Nazi" for political effect. Besides, as stated above, I find Wolfe's theory, save for its ethno-nationalist elements, to be closest to those of the Spanish authoritarian variants of *National Syndicalism* and *National Catholicism*.

What About the Left?

In his book, *Live Not By Lies*, named after an essay written by the author of *The Gulag Archipelago*, Aleksandr Solzhenitsyn, Rod Dreher correctly identified a system of *technocratic soft-totalitarianism* that is spreading across the West, one that is analogous to the faceless, bureaucratic communism described in Czech playwright Václav Havel's 1978 masterpiece of *samizdat* (underground dissident literature), *The Power of the Powerless*. Like Havel's hypothetical "greengrocer," we have become accustomed to perpetual self-censorship, living in a society increasingly unfriendly to disagreement with the conclusions of the last three centuries of humanist philosophy. Some conservative Christian commentators today see this left-wing threat as so immediate and existential that they argue right-wing extremism should be outright ignored by Christians in order to present a unified front towards this adversary. This feeling has coalesced around a phrase, *no enemies to the right*, which may sound plausible until one thinks it through to the inevitable, common-sense ends of exactly who will make it into the coalition under these parameters.

There is a real threat from the left, one that is certainly more immediate and ubiquitous than any from the right, but that is exactly why I am *more concerned about the right-wing threat* and see this Christian political hyper-focus on left-wing excess as being born from an ignorance of history. Nearly every right-wing authoritarian-nationalist government in the 20th century came into power on the heels of excessive leftist action that caused a *crisis of legitimacy* in the government. In 1919, the Partito Socialista Italiano gained a significant stake in the parliament and immediately began forceful labor action in an attempt to nationalize industry that ultimately failed. Three years later, the Partito Nazionale Fascista swept into power, in no small part due to the popularity of its squadrist forces' willingness to use violence to remove socialist activists from the public square.[9] In Spain, nearly sixty years of right-wing military dictatorship, which had overthrown a briefly-lived constitutional republic in 1874, resulted in liberal democratic republicans allying themselves with communists and anarchists to form a coalition government in 1931. The rule of law was upended as a blind eye was increasingly turned towards leftist extremists, while the organs of the state were turned more fiercely on monarchists and fascists, leading to an ultimate crisis of legitimacy and civil war in 1936.[10]

The left in the United States is similarly overplaying its hand. The Democratic Party, after abandoning the middle class during the Obama years, has maintained a false image of *defender of the proletariat* by allying itself with far-left elements. The party has begun leveraging state power towards radical social and economic changes that a monumental portion of Americans are not interested in adopting – not the least of which was the attempt in 2021 to use executive orders and regulatory agencies to make medical compliance a requirement for employment nationwide. After spending years promoting the notion that Donald Trump was put into office by Russians to be their secret asset, they now seem aghast that his supporters would play the same game by pushing the accusation that Joe Biden was illegitimately elected. Half of all Americans believe there will

---

9 Philip Morgan, *Italian Fascism: 1919 - 1945*, 1. publ, The Making of the 20th Century (New York, NY: St. Martin's Pr, 1995), 3–59.

10 Paul Preston, *Franco: A Biography* (New York, NY: BasicBooks, a division of HarperCollins, 1994), 69–119.

soon be a civil war in the United States.¹¹ Nearly half of those who voted for Biden and just over half who voted for Trump believe it is time to divide the country along political lines; over half from each group strongly believe that the opposition party is a "danger to American democracy."¹² A significant portion of conservative America has already outright rejected any and all left-wing politics and is looking for potential solutions, including authoritarian methods. Millions of people on both sides are becoming increasingly belligerent towards those they deem existential threats. There has never been a more ripe time for right-wing authoritarian nationalism to sweep into power in the United States, and it is decidedly gaining ground within the conservative Reformed church through writings like Stephen Wolfe's *The Case for Christian Nationalism*, but he is not alone. Generalissimo Francisco Franco, assisted by Hitler and Mussolini, let his Moroccan troops literally rape and pillage their way through Spain,¹³ and then reigned over that nation with an iron fist for almost forty years, including outlawing the promotion of any religion other than Catholicism.¹⁴ That did not stop Christian political commentator, self-styled "Maximum Leader," and promulgator of "no enemies to the right" Charles Haywood from giving Franco's legacy a "positively glowing" review.¹⁵ Like Wolfe, he couches secular philosophy and plainly authoritarian-nationalist political theory in Christian terms, though he, as with Wolfe, rarely uses his platform to promote the actual person or work of Jesus Christ.

---

11 Garen J. Wintemute et al., "Views of American Democracy and Society and Support for Political Violence: First Report from a Nationwide Population-Representative Survey" (medRxiv, July 19, 2022), https://doi.org/10.1101/2022.07.15.22277693.
12 UVA Center for Politics, "New Initiative Explores Deep, Persistent Divides Between Biden and Trump Voters – Sabato's Crystal Ball," September 30, 2021, https://centerforpolitics.org/crystalball/articles/new-initiative-explores-deep-persistent-divides-between-biden-and-trump-voters/.
13 Preston, *Franco*, 164, 166.
14 Giorgia Priorelli, *Italian Fascism and Spanish Falangism in Comparison: Constructing the Nation*, Palgrave Studies in Political History (Cham, Switzerland: Palgrave Macmillan, 2020), 149, https://doi.org/10.1007/978-3-030-46056-3.
15 Charles Haywood, "On Francisco Franco • The Worthy House," *The Worthy House* (blog), April 16, 2019, https://theworthyhouse.com/2019/04/16/on-francisco-franco/.

I am witnessing this rapid shift towards the promotion of overreaction first-hand as people in my church family, layman and minister alike, are increasingly drawn to political pundits who speak in the same language of *power dynamics* as their "woke" adversaries. The Apostle Paul unmistakably instructs us, "See that no one repays anyone evil for evil, but always seek to do good to one another and to everyone" (1 Thessalonians 5:15). Yet, some of the most popular conservative Christian commentators say we should "fight fire with fire" as a response to those who "arrest their political opponents and throw them in jail,"[16] while few conservative Christians bat an eye. How can we Bible-believing Christians in the West lecture leftist secular humanists on the importance of the mortification of sin if we cannot control our own worldly urges for revenge and power?

Acknowledgments

I thank my former shepherding and teaching elder, Jeff Smith, for being my primary theological sounding-board during this process. His insight has been invaluable and has, on multiple occasions, caused me to temper my critique, which is always a good thing for a Christian to do. Along these lines, I thank the Christian journalists who have given me similar private critique.

I thank my wife, Jen, who, outside of being a fantastic mother and wife, has also put up with innumerable hours of rants on this subject, which she is far less interested in than I am. On this same note, I thank my discipleship pastor and mentor, Bill Voorhes, for our Wednesday night conversations. Lastly I thank my editor, Brady Bush, who has made my arguments far more coherent, and your reading experience far more enjoyable, than it would have otherwise been.

---

16 https://twitter.com/MattWalshBlog/status/1637172061452869633
    Catholic political commentator Matt Walsh (retweeted by Protestant political commentator Josh Daws): "Conservatives lecture their own side for being too rude and mean while Democrats arrest their political opponents and throw them in jail. If you haven't learned by now that we have no choice but to fight fire with fire, you're hopeless."

Introduction: The Great Renewal

I. The Storm

From the back cover

> Evangelical elites and the progressive media complex want you to think that Christian nationalism is hopelessly racist, bigoted, and an idol for right-wing Christians. Is Christian nationalism the golden calf of the religious right – or or is it the only way forward?

Beginning of commentary

> With weakness of will and self-abnegation, Western Christians gaze at the ravishment of their Western heritage, either blaming themselves or, even worse, reveling in their humiliation.[17]

After using the storming of the Bastille as a tongue-in-cheek comparison to the January 6 riots, Stephen Wolfe opens his book with a false dilemma for Western Christendom, one that speaks to his placement of personal identity in a worldly "Western heritage" and a potential lack of a Christian eschatology in his worldview. The Christian can both lament his nation's steady decline into sin and still place his trust in God's providence and his primary directive to share the gospel and make disciples. To stand in the face of revilement (or worse) and say, "I will not do what you tell me to, nor will I hurt you," is the exact opposite of "weakness of will."

Following this, Rousseau's denouncement of worldly inaction by Christians is likened to a modern "Stockholm syndrome theology" that uses Christianity as "a coping device for inaction, even when under tyranny and slavery."[18] This further explicates one of the many false dilemmas posed in Wolfe's book. The Christian has to be careful that he is truly driving a spoke into the wheel of injustice (as Dietrich Bonhoeffer put it)

---

17 Wolfe, *The Case for Christian Nationalism*, 3.
18 Wolfe, 3–4.

and not, through knee-jerk reactions, simply replacing another entity's crushing wheel with his own.

Wolfe adds "anti-nativism" to a list of movements lauded by Christians who have embraced the dogmas of "civil religion."[19] Nativism has a sordid, violent history in America, particularly towards Catholics, including multiple convent and church burnings and bombings,[20] an attempted murder of a papal nuncio by a mob in 1853,[21] and as the foremost policy of the (second) Ku Klux Klan during its height in the 1920s.[22] Wolfe's political theory promotes a "peculiar love for the people of own race and country,"[23] therefore anti-nativism represents a natural adversary to his movement.

> The problem we face today is not simply the absence of arguments but the lack of will for our political objectives. I hope to enliven in the hearts of Christians a sense of home and hearth and love of people and country out of which springs action for their good.[24]

This is very similar to how an early-20th century authoritarian would put it – harnessing the will of the people towards an ultimate purpose dictated by their shared heritage more than any higher ethic. This will be far from the only parallel that can be drawn between Wolfe's political theory and that of early-20th century authoritarian nationalists.

---

19 Wolfe, 5.
20 Michael Williams, Shadow of the Pope (New York: Whittlesey House, McGraw-Hill Book Company, 1932), 29, 64–65, 84–85; Ray Allen Billington, The Protestant Crusade, 1800-1860, First Paperback (Chicago, Illinois: Quadrangle Books, 1964), 74–75, 220–31.
21 Williams, *Shadow of the Pope*, 82–83.
22 Williams, 128, 133; Kenneth C. Barnes, *Anti-Catholicism in Arkansas: How Politicians, the Press, the Klan, and Religious Leaders Imagined an Enemy, 1910-1960* (Fayetteville: The University of Arkansas Press, 2016), 109, 117, 171.
23 Wolfe, *The Case for Christian Nationalism*, 87.
24 Wolfe, 5.

II. Definition

> Since anti-nationalism is a social dogma, connecting "Christian" and "nationalism" is effective for wielding social power or the public ire against dissident Christian groups – whether these groups are real or imagined.[25]

Anti-nationalism is a social dogma, because 20th-century authoritarian nationalists were only exceeded in their murder of innocents by communists. He is correct that the term, *Christian Nationalism*, is a "plastic word" that has "tremendous weight in rhetoric" and is used more for its political effect than for accurately describing a phenomenon. It is the confusion sown by the various groups using "Christian Nationalism," with both positive and negative connotations, that not only serves to demonize orthodox Christians, but, conversely, allows for the laundering of authoritarian dogmas to that same, orthodox audience.

> Indeed, there were self-described Christian nationalists. For example, William Henry Fremantle, a well-respected and accomplished Anglican priest, published a lecture in 1885 on Christian nationalism. He affirmed the belief in the "divine character of political rule, and in the unity of the sacred and the secular in the Christian nation."[26]

It is ironic that Wolfe would paint W.H. Fremantle in a positive light, for a conservative Christian audience, to make a case for long-standing Christian Nationalist thought. Fremantle embraced a critical interpretation of Scripture, including denying a literal interpretation of Christ's divinity, miracles, and resurrection.[27] In Stephen Wolfe's Christian nation, Fremantle would face civil penalty as a heretic. Fremantle was unorthodox enough

---

25 Wolfe, 6.
26 Wolfe, 6.
27 William Henry Fremantle, "Theology Under Its Changed Conditions," in Popular Science Monthly Volume 31 June 1887.

that his 1916 obituary noted his "political Liberalism" and "ecclesiastical latitudinarianism."[28]

> In 1972, Albert Cleage published *Black Christian Nationalism* in which he calls for a **redefinition of salvation** along black Christian nationalist lines: "Black Christian nationalism… calls men to a rejection of individualism, and offers a process of transformation by which the individual may divest himself of individualism and submerge himself in the community life of the group". (emphasis mine)[29]

It is shocking that Albert Cleage is presented uncritically as a voice of previous Christian Nationalist thought. Cleage also wrote in *Black Christian Nationalism*, "Today if you advance the thesis that all people are the same, Black people will reject it, saying that we could not do the bestial things that white people do. We possess human qualities commonly called soul which white people cannot even understand. We are creative because we can feel deeply and we can respond to the feelings of others. White people cannot grasp the meaning of love, music, or religion because they exist on a lower, bestial level of violence, materialism, and individualism."[30] This quote could be compared to one from an article Wolfe wrote for *IM—1776*: "For complex reasons, blacks in America, considered as a group, are reliable sources for criminality, and their criminality increases when constraints diminish."[31]

---

28 "Death of Dr. W.H. Fremantle, The Times, December 26, 1916.," *The Times*, December 26, 1916.
Latitudinarianism was a theologically liberal movement, beginning in the seventeenth century, that argued for a loosening of liturgical restrictions in worship. By Fremantle's time, the term was also synonymous with a heterodox elevation of human reasoning in matters of doctrine.

29 Wolfe, *The Case for Christian Nationalism*, 8.

30 Albert B. Jr. Cleage, *Black Christian Nationalism: New Directions For The Black Church* (New York: William Morrow & Company, 1972), 94, https://archive.org/details/blackchristianna0000clea/mode/2up.

31 Stephen Wolfe, "Anarcho-Tyranny in 2022," *IM—1776* (blog), March 18, 2022, https://im1776.com/2022/03/18/anarcho-tyranny/.

Introduction: The Great Renewal

> [Philip Gorski and Samuel Perry's] definition [of Christian nationalism] is a "constellation of beliefs," which is technically not a definition, and the unstated point of the book is certainly to secure the term's negative connotations by associating it with heretical social views.[32]

Wolfe is correct on both points. This is the calling card of the mainstream, anti-Christian nationalism genre, which regularly attempts to paint the majority of conservative evangelicals as deplorables. The most popular book of this genre, Kristen DuMez's *Jesus and John Wayne*, painfully and repeatedly attempts to squeeze everyday conservative theology into the category of *militant white masculinity* and unashamedly attempts to take the most extreme, Independent Fundamentalist Baptist ideologies and misrepresent them as mainstream evangelical thought.[33]

> This is a work of Christian political theory, not sociology. If the social scientists wish to critique my book, they must step out of social science, suspend their belief in social dogma, and enter rational inquiry.[34]

On its face, this is an incredibly elitist and fallacious statement, which reads as a preemptive buffer against criticism of his blind spots. Political theory without an understanding of social science produces *utopianism*. This is akin to a Marxist demanding that any critique of his book must not include behavioral economics. If he meant pseudo-scientific "lived experience" then he should have been explicit here.

> Christian nationalism is a **totality of national action**, consisting of civil laws and social customs, conducted by a Christian nation as a

---

32 Wolfe, *The Case for Christian Nationalism*, 8.
33 Kristin Kobes Du Mez, *Jesus and John Wayne: How White Evangelicals Corrupted a Faith and Fractured a Nation*, First edition (New York, NY: Liveright Publishing Corporation, a division of W. W. Norton & Company, 2020).
34 Wolfe, *The Case for Christian Nationalism*, 8.

Christian nation, in order to procure for itself both earthly and heavenly good in Christ. (emphasis mine)[35]

It is the well-documented history of fallen man's rapidly devolving civility, when he deems it necessary to direct the "totality of national action," including "social customs" – a project that has never succeeded – that concerns me most about this definition, and the thesis as a whole. One would expect someone who began his book with the storming of the Bastille to understand that, and to avoid this type of language. To fail to do so predisposes his philosophy to the same type of power struggles and mutual denunciations that befell the Montagnards and Girondins. It will soon become apparent that Wolfe's *totality* is synonymous with the common definition of *totalitarian*.

III. Explicating the Definition

Wolfe defines *Christian nationalism* as a species of the genus of *nationalism*. He defines the genus as "a totality of national action, consisting of civil laws and social customs, conducted by a nation as a nation, in order to procure for itself both earthly and heavenly good."[36] It's quite interesting that he retains "heavenly good" in a definition otherwise completely stripped of religion (he will explain this in more depth later in the chapter as nationalism being conducive to orienting the nation towards general revelation), which points towards nationalism being seen as a divinely ordained mode of government. The continued use of "totality" in these definitions is very much inline with the wording of Italian fascist political theory; Mussolini used the word "totalitarian" in a positive context. Historian Philip Morgan wrote that the Italian fascist philosopher Giovanni Gentile's "use of the term 'total' conveyed Fascism's claim to ubiquity and a comprehensive, all-encompassing outlook on life, like a religious faith inspiring all facets of existence. Individuals only found full self-realisation through unity and identification with the state, which was not a neutral umpire of society but an 'ethical' authority embodying moral

---

35 Wolfe, 9.
36 Wolfe, 11.

values and inculcating them in society."³⁷ A similar "full self-realisation" through the supreme authority of the state, what Wolfe calls the "complete good" and the "nation perfected," will be a major theme of his book.

> Nevertheless, the Gospel does not supersede, abrogate, eliminate, or fundamentally alter generic nationalism; it assumes and completes it.³⁸

This is a troublesome order of logic (Nationalism + Gospel = Complete Nationalism) in that it does not start with the gospel, and assumes the (incomplete) goodness of nationalism *apart from the gospel*. Would this not be better defined as *Nationalist Christianity*? There is very much a difference to be parsed here, and Wolfe will have much to say later about aspects of nature and humanity not altered by the gospel.

> Whether my conclusions classify Christian nationalism under "ideology" has no relevance as to whether those arguments are sound...

> The reader will also have to keep in mind that I am not necessarily affirming any supposed connotations of nationalism, whatever those might be, and thus they cannot be ascribed to my definition of positions prima facie.³⁹

Preemptively negating critique solely based on the label of "ideology" is fair, because many would likely dismiss his arguments through an appeal to emotion and genetic logical fallacy, claiming that "ideologies" are bad, in of themselves. The second argument about "nationalism" is not a fair point, because the word has nearly a century's worth of negative connotation that cannot be dismissed so easily. This is proven by how Wolfe felt he needed to write this sentence in the first place. Wolfe follows this up by saying that he is not "trying to justify or explain away any

---

37 Morgan, *Italian Fascism*, 79.
38 Wolfe, *The Case for Christian Nationalism*, 11.
39 Wolfe, 11.

historical example of nationalism,"⁴⁰ but by expecting the reader to accept his definition of nationalism, and ignore the long list of historical examples, he is putting forth a *no true Scotsman* fallacy, and a nationalist version of the meme, "that wasn't *real* communism." As will be shown, Wolfe's definition of *Christian Nationalism* is no different than the popular connotation of nationalism – but for the grafting on of Two-Kingdoms Theology, justified by a Scripturally ignorant theory of pre-fall man – rendering this protest irrelevant.

We are given an explanation of "a totality of national action", which, simply put, is any collective initiative that "strengthens, supports, or makes possible other actions to form an organic whole."⁴¹ This national action can be benign, until it reaches the level of *totality*. Issues have historically arisen, and atrocities have been committed, when a small group of individuals take it upon themselves to forcefully shape a totality of national action in a direction even partially at odds with the national consensus. How would the totality of national *Christian* action be practically achieved when, as cultural researcher George Barna concluded, only 6% of Americans "possess a Biblical worldview, and demonstrate a consistent understanding and application of Biblical principles"?⁴² We are here breaking Wolfe's desired rules of engagement, by referencing social science – from a conservative Christian – to question the practicality of his political theory. I hope this proves how absurd his supposed prerequisite for debate is.

> Now, since the end of Christian nationalism is the nation's good... rules of action are proper only if they conduce to the nation's good... **Being a totality of action**, law and custom form an interrelated and oftentimes redundant web of obligation that orders everything ultimately to the national good. (emphasis mine)⁴³

---

40 Wolfe, 11.
41 Wolfe, 11–12.
42 George Barna, "What Does It Mean When People Say They Are 'Christian'?," *Cultural Research Center, Arizona Christian University*, American Worldview Inventory 2021, no. 6 (August 31, 2021): 9.
43 Wolfe, *The Case for Christian Nationalism*, 13.

Introduction: The Great Renewal

This is the inversion and elevation of nation over individual so common of early-20th century authoritarian-nationalist and fascist thought. As Georgia Priorelli wrote in *Italian Fascism and Spanish Falangism in Comparison: Constructing the Nation*, "In the opinion of the theorist of the Partito Nazionale Fascista [the Italian Fascist Party]... Fascism had the merit of having turned the relationship between society and the individual on its head. It replaced the liberal-democratic and socialist formula 'society for the individual' with the formula 'the individual for society' – **The change of perspective was total** since, if the former raised the problem of individual rights, the latter prioritised the state's right and the duties of the people and the classes towards it" (emphasis mine).[44] This cannot be emphasized enough; in the introduction to his book, Wolfe has defined *Christian Nationalism* along the very same lines that Italian Fascists described their preferred nation.

> Thus, the entity that causes Christian nationalism is chiefly the people, not Christian magistrates, though magistrates are necessary to direct the will of the people into concrete action.[45]

This is not terribly different from what a theonomist[46] would write about a Christian nation, but Wolfe's claim that the people legitimize the Christian nation flies in the face of his later justification of violent revolution to achieve it. In Western representative government, the majority will of the people for an explicitly Christian nation would result in such a nation coming to fruition through peaceful, democratic means.

> Had Adam not fallen, the nations of his progeny would have ordered themselves to heavenly life.[47]

---

44 Priorelli, *Italian Fascism and Spanish Falangism in Comparison*, 4.
45 Wolfe, *The Case for Christian Nationalism*, 14.
46 Theonomy is the belief that all Old Covenant moral and civil laws are still applicable to Christian societies today, save for where they have been altered or negated by the New Covenant.
47 Wolfe, 15.

"Nations," plural, is an assumption not based on Scripture, and could very much be seen as unscriptural, in that Jesus Christ, the Last Adam (1 Corinthians 15:45), will rule over a single redeemed nation for eternity (Revelation 21:9-27). So it would go that a hypothetical, never-having-fallen world would likely have a similar polity. This idea of nationalism being a prelapsarian ideal will be the focus of chapter 1 and will serve as the ethical basis for his nationalist theory. Wolfe has made public comment on the goodness of "cultural/ethnic preservation" of nations, through social pressure to restrict intermarriage, that cannot be separated from anything he may have to say on how these unfallen, and therefore godly, nations would perceive themselves.[48]

> Thus, the totality of Christian national action orders the nation to procure the complete good in Christ...
>
> As a concise summary, we can think of Christian nationalism as a Christian nation acting as such and for itself in the interest of the nation's complete good.[49]

Whose interpretation of Christ (and his commandments) will be enforced? Wolfe will elaborate on this later, including an appeal for an official, paedobaptist state church, which would go against the doctrine of the largest Christian denomination in America, the Southern Baptist Convention. There will also be much to discuss about his notion of the "complete good," which has its first mention here.

This section closes with another appeal to collectivism, with no distinguishing characteristics from previous nationalist theorists, whom he has asked us not to compare him to. He will later argue that this national interest requires a divinely ruling monarch, the banning of public worship of other religions, and the civil punishment of heretics. Wolfe's hyper-

---

48 https://twitter.com/PerfInjust/status/1582018840799547392
Stephen Wolfe: "I think that, for example, an American Indian tribe can have a reasonable expectation that their people marry other American Indians in the interest of cultural/ethnic preservation. They should not forbid any marriage in particular but still seek a certain group-level outcome."

49 Wolfe, *The Case for Christian Nationalism*, 15, 16.

priority for a homogeneous nation, above the individual, cannot be rectified with the Christian faith, where the disciple's relation and responsibility to the nation must first pass through the individual, Jesus Christ. He distinctly calls us to place Him above all worldly relational obligations, markedly saying that someone who "finds his life" in those obligations will lose the *true life* we can have in Him (Matthew 10:34-39). A Christian church and nation are not healthy due to the power of their collective will, but because of the meekness of the individual believer's commitment to demonstrate the singular will of Christ's perfect love to others, one person at a time. To replace "society for the individual" with "the individual for society" is to consciously set up a form of "Christian" government that will inherently disfavor "the least of these my brothers" (Matthew 25:36-40).

IV. Method

> This is a work of Christian political theory. It is not, overall, a work of political theology... Some readers will complain that I rarely appeal to Scripture to argue for my positions. I understand the frustration, but allow me to explain: I am neither a theologian nor a biblical scholar. I have no training in moving from scriptural interpretation to theological articulation.[50]

Again, *Nationalist Christianity* seems a better title for his theory, under these conditions, or perhaps *Nationalism with Western Christianity as the cultural identity*. This setup opens the door for him to back out of theological rebuke of his theories, much in the same way comedian Jon Stewart will make a belligerent and controversial political statement and retreat into, "Hey, I'm just a comedian." If one aims to put forward a thesis, entitled *Christian* [anything], then he should have a strong, first hand understanding of Scripture, and not primarily rely on an intermediary, in this case the "Reformed exegetal tradition" of the "16th and 17th centuries," to give his ideas Scriptural gravitas. Wolfe goes on to say that "some of [his] conclusions are expressed differently than this tradition." At

---

50 Wolfe, 16.

the very least, to remain intellectually honest, he would need to exegete Scripture in those instances to justify his different conclusions. To do otherwise would be to implicitly admit that he is cherry-picking theological statements that fit his preconceptions.

> And, of course, I would certainly welcome any work of political theology **in favor of** Christian nationalism that can stand side-by-side with this work of Christian political theory. (emphasis mine)[51]

An intellectually honest position – and one that places our Lord at the center – would also clearly welcome political theology that can stand on its own but that *disagrees* with Christian Nationalism. The footnote to this section says that the reader is free to cite Scripture to counter this theory, but then presents another escape hatch with an unconvincing explanation of how "too often" these arguments lack coherence – how would he know if he cannot sufficiently exegete for his own arguments? Wolfe dismissed Neil Shenvi's multiple theological refutations as "Neil did not deal with my argument," including one where it was solidly proven that Wolfe's view of the fall is out of line with the Westminster Confession and Heidelberg Catechism (and, therefore, not consistent with the Reformed exegetical tradition of the 16th and 17th centuries).[52] This is a consistent pattern of rebuttal to critics from Wolfe and, until proven otherwise, it should be questioned whether there is a dissenting argument that he will accept in good faith.

Wolfe then explains that his theory is very Thomistic, not because it is necessarily Scripturally sound, but because 16th and 17th century Reformed thought was "very Thomistic and catholic."[53] Never mind the strong push-back he would get from modern, Reformed theologians for

---

51 Wolfe, 17.
52 "Of Gods and Men."
https://twitter.com/PerfInjust/status/1595089179385421827
Stephen Wolfe: "Another example where Neil did not deal with my argument, or perhaps didn't understand it. The state of integrity is different than the state of glory, even though there is an earthly element to 'heavenly life.' Adam would have looked forward to the state of glory."
53 Wolfe, *The Case for Christian Nationalism*, 17.

relying on Aquinas; by framing its use in this way, Wolfe has made the *Christian* in his "Christian nationalism" appeal to authority (Reformed thought) and appeal to consensus (catholic) logical fallacies. The reformers would certainly rebuke this as failing the *Sola Scriptura* test.

> The primary reason that this work is political theory is that I proceed from a foundation of natural principles. While Christian theology assumes natural theology as an ancillary component, Christian political theory treats **natural principles as the foundation**… (emphasis mine)[54]

Thus begins a section on "natural principles" that has a murky epistemic basis. He claims that "civil leaders ought to order the people to the true God" is a natural principle that is correctly "applied and fulfilled by means of [the] supernatural truth" of the Triune God.[55] Scripture tells us that man, apart from special revelation, suppresses the truth of general revelation (Romans 1:18-20). Therefore, man cannot rely on apparent "natural principles" for revelation of a correct horizontal relationship with other men, without *first* having his vertical relationship with the Creator revealed to him. In other words, special revelation is the *foundation* by which general revelation is no longer suppressed. Even the reprobate greet their brothers (Matthew 5:47) and can form governments that are "not a terror to good conduct" (Romans 13:3), but, in Reformed theology, this is due to the restraint of the Spirit (2 Thessalonians 2:7), and not fallen man's natural inclination. It will be shown that Wolfe's insistence on assumed natural principles as his foundation for good *Christian* government breaks with the doctrine of his own church. If he were to respond that this is the difference between *theology* and *political theory*, the denial of a foundation of special revelation would still call its *Christian* credibility into question. This strikes me as Kantian as much as it is Thomistic. He will rely heavily on it for his thesis, using it to claim that many questionable principles are "natural" and therefore good.

---

54 Wolfe, 18.
55 Wolfe, 19.

Following this, he makes a ham-fisted attempt at elevating his own methodology above his peers', by claiming that modern authors rely on devices, such as "tweetable shibboleths"[56] – an ironic complaint, considering Wolfe has no problem using Twitter in an antagonistic, otherizing way, towards his ideological opponents.[57] This section is then closed with a further classification of his theory as "Presbyterian Christian nationalism."[58] This is nothing of note yet, but it will present interesting conundrums later on, especially when baptism serves as a civil induction ceremony and turns the body politic into the visible "people of God," a notion that has drawn strong dissent from credobaptists.

V. Summary of Argument

The remainder of the chapter is a summary of arguments that the brunt of the book will handle in depth, so I will comment on individual statements that I find of note and summarize planned counter arguments.

> Adam's original task, his dominion mandate, was to bring the earth to maturity, which served as the condition for eternal life.[59]

We should pause when we come across the word "dominion" in Christian Nationalist writings, because it often is used in a militaristic fashion. Adam's "dominion… over all the earth" (Genesis 1:26) is the proper categorical description of his sum position as image-bearer and garden-tender. But perfect obedience to God *in all things*, not just successfully exercising dominion, served as the condition for eternal life under the covenant of works. In Scripture, the condition is expressed in the negative, when God commands Adam not to eat of the fruit of the tree of the knowledge of good and evil (Genesis 2:16-17). This could be dismissed as a simple misunderstanding or uncertain phrasing if *taking dominion* was

---

56 Wolfe, 19.
57 https://twitter.com/PerfInjust/status/1619391549888135169
    Stephen Wolfe: "Joel [Berry of the Babylon Bee] is enjoying the euphoric high of ethno-masochism."
58 Wolfe, *The Case for Christian Nationalism*, 20.
59 Wolfe, 21.

Introduction: The Great Renewal

not a major theme of this book – it is what Wolfe considers man's secondary *telos*.⁶⁰ Wolfe's idea of multiple pre-fall nations returns, and the main rebuttal will be saved for later, but it is of note that he seems to build his whole hypothesis forgetting that *God walked among prelapsarian man* (Genesis 3:8).

> The instinct to live within one's "tribe" or one's own people is neither a product of the fall nor extinguished by grace; rather, it is natural and good.⁶¹

Wolfe has a history of not only promoting his "tribe," but also denigrating other "tribes," which colors everything he says on the subject and may be a motivation for his conclusions. For example, here is how he treats the subject of crime among white and black people:

> **A tweet from Wolfe on Dec 18, 2021:** Anyone have the percentage of violent crime committed by white evangelicals?⁶²

> **A tweet from Wolfe on Jul 28, 2021:** Consider how absurd it is to elevate bl*ack men when they far exceed all non-bla*cks in just about every negative indicator, including in sex crimes. What is astonishing is that seemingly seriously people can't recognize how ridiculous they've become. The fact is that if there was serious racial oppression since the civil rights era, they have handled it very poorly. This is obvious if you get past the ideology. There is nothing heroic in it, given the level of violent crime and sexual assault (of underage girls).⁶³

---

60 Wolfe, 21.
  The Westminster Shorter Catechism's very first question defines man's telos as "to glorify god and enjoy him forever." I will later argue that a *caring* dominion over the earth is a *means to that telos*, not the telos itself.
61 Wolfe, 23.
62 https://twitter.com/PerfInjust/status/1472191380403683330
63 https://twitter.com/PerfInjust/status/1420385874492203015
  Note how he places an asterisk to break up the word "bl*ack," showing he knows his tweet will be picked up, and likely shadowbanned, by the Twitter algorithm.

He later bolsters his *goodness of tribes* claim with the statement that "there is no universal language."[64] Scripture tells us that, several generations after the flood, "the whole earth had one language and the same words," and that God purposefully separated man into disparate languages and cultures to limit his attempts to place himself on par with Him (Genesis 11:1-9). Thus Wolfe's theory of the prelapsarian good of tribes has already broken with Scripture before he has begun to explicate it.

> ... much good would result in the world if we all **preferred our own** and minded our own business. (emphasis mine)[65]

This is the *exact* phraseology a Klan member would use, and if Wolfe does not want to be seen in that light, then he should either not write in this way or go to great lengths to explain exactly what he means here (he does not). Though, when pressed, Wolfe promoted a heterodox definition of *ethnicity* as culture more than genetics[66], that definition would still fall under the bounds of "our own." That means, with this sentence, his theory has unequivocally become *ethno*-nationalist – and notably similar to the Falangist view of cultural *Spanishness* under their political theory of *unidad de destino en lo universal* (unity of destiny in the universal), where collectivist calls had more to do with the cultural remains of the Catalonian empire than with any region's ethnicity.[67] It is worth questioning, given what Wolfe has said about intermarriage in the past,[68] whether he thinks of

---

64 Wolfe, *The Case for Christian Nationalism*, 24.
65 Wolfe, 25.
66 https://twitter.com/PerfInjust/status/1596690471904067584
Stephen Wolfe: "Looking through old tweets and found this one. I've been publicly separating 'ethnicity/nation' and 'race' since 2020. I talk about this at length in the book."
67 Priorelli, *Italian Fascism and Spanish Falangism in Comparison*, 144.
68 https://web.archive.org/web/20220209153748/https://twitter.com/PerfInjust/status/1491434865421524993
I provide a link to the archive of the tweets, because Wolfe deleted two that mentioned black people. In this exchange he argues that, since black people often discuss interracial marriage in a negative light, "discussing whether interracial marriage is right or wrong can be acceptable, depending on the circumstances around the discussion." This is similar to his argument about Native Americans having a right to implicitly restrict intermarriage by means of social pressure.

Introduction: The Great Renewal

white and black American cultures as potentially different ethnic nations under his theory. That he followed his podcast co-host's explicitly white-nationalist, anonymous accounts on both Twitter and Facebook, where racial slurs were flung multiple times, serves as more circumstantial evidence to that end,[69] as do Wolfe's writings on the role of black Americans in "anarcho-tyranny."[70]

Continuing on the theme of *preferring our own*, Wolfe gives an endorsement for "complacent love," the "pre-rational preference we have for our own children, family, community, and nation."[71] That this love of nation is *pre-rational* and built-up from genetic relations immediately calls his online claims of primarily *cultural* ethnicity into question (something that I will prove in chapter 3). Most of note, in nearly a page on supposedly "Christian" love, is the total absence of the person of Jesus Christ. Rather than encouraging us to lean into our natural love feelings, He challenges us to turn our conception of love on its head (Matthew 5:43-45), and requires us to eschew our "pre-rational preference" in order to love Him first and foremost (Matthew 10:37).

> A supernatural conclusion can follow from a natural principle when it interacts with supernatural truths.[72]

Given God's sovereignty over His creation, the natural principle is inconsequential in this equation. Many well-functioning nations have striven to direct people towards what they believed was the true religion, when it was actually false religion. The pagan empire that Peter instructed Christians to be subject to was one of the largest and best-functioning nations the world had ever seen (1 Peter 2:13-14). Supernatural truths are not pantheistic properties waiting to be interacted with, should we collectively orient ourselves in the proper direction. It is only those to

---

69 Alastair Roberts, "On Thomas Achord," *Alastair's Adversaria* (blog), November 27, 2022, https://alastairadversaria.com/2022/11/27/the-case-against-thomas-achord/.
70 Wolfe, "Anarcho-Tyranny in 2022."
71 Wolfe, *The Case for Christian Nationalism*, 25.
72 Wolfe, 27.

whom God has chosen to reveal Himself that have any hope of applying natural principles towards *heavenly* good (Ephesians 1:11). Saul was working *against* the principle of "[directing] people to the Christian religion" when he was confronted with, and redirected by, supernatural truths (Acts 9:1-5). From Whom do natural principles come, and how/where would we confirm them as natural principles, outside of Scripture? Wolfe may somewhat agree with all of this, and it may seem like splitting hairs, but our utter dependence on God is not a small, theological matter. Continued insistence on a *foundation* of natural principles that orient us towards God minimizes the necessary epistemological starting point of God revealing His will to fallen man.

Following this, Wolfe praises the goodness of a cultural Christianity that has the under-girding of genuine faith,[73] an assessment that is hard to disagree with. Even today, our highly polarized society is held together by the shadow of the Overton window of the Christian ethic; it is that powerful and beneficial. Wolfe will take this concept too far in his defense of cultural Christianity in chapter 5.

> Laws can also penalize open blasphemy and irreverence in the interest of public peace and Christian peoplehood. The justification for such laws is not simply that God forbids these things in the First Table of the Ten Commandments, but that they cause public harm, both to the body and the soul.[74]

I will argue, when this case is made in depth, that the New Covenant explicitly tells the Christian to leave blasphemers in peace (2 Timothy 2:24-26, 2 Corinthians 10:3-6), and since, as Wolfe admits, man is only bound by (and the government can only enforce) God's moral law as revealed, a Christian government would violate the Second Table if it used the sword to punish the thoughtcrimes of "blasphemy and irreverence" (not to be mistaken with the Second Table violation of *vulgarity*). A question that must be asked of those promoting this type of First Table enforcement is, *What happens to the Mormons and Jehovah's Witnesses who won't stop*

---

73 Wolfe, 28–29.
74 Wolfe, 31.

evangelizing? Wolfe will answer that question in a way that most Western Christians will likely find unacceptable.

> Our time calls for a man who can wield formal civil power to great effect and shape the public imagination by means of charisma, gravitas, and personality.[75]

It is telling that Wolfe instructed us, in preceding sections, not to compare his theory to previous nationalist and fascist thought, when he has yet to deviate from an iota of it. Are we to ignore that he is now arguing for a Protestant *Caudillo/Duce*? There will be much more to say about this in chapter 7.

> If [a ruler's] commands harm them, they can depose or remove him and enact better arrangements. National harm can include oppression against true religion, and thus the people can conduct revolution in order to restore true religion.[76]

This is far from universal, 16th and 17th-century Reformed thought. The 16th century Swiss theologian and friend of John Calvin, Pierre Viret, considered a reliable peacemaker when these types of issues arose, wrote, "And if the magistrates do not fulfill their duty but are instead tyrants and persecutors who uphold the cause of the wicked and persecute the children of God, we must leave the vengeance of such tyranny and iniquity to God."[77]

> But there are many misunderstandings today concerning what Protestants once believed about the role of civil government with regard to false religion.[78]

---

75 Wolfe, 31.
76 Wolfe, 34.
77 Peirre Viret, *When to Disobey*, ed. Rebekah Sheats and Scott T. Brown, 1st edition (Church and Family Life, 2021), 7–9, 37.
78 Wolfe, *The Case for Christian Nationalism*, 34.

Wolfe uses this as an appeal to tradition/authority logical fallacy. Some Protestants once believed the role of civil government with regard to false religion included the burning and drowning of Anabaptists and the drawing and quartering of recalcitrant Catholics. Even then, there was far from a great consensus among the varying 16th-century Protestant city-states on how to deal with heresy, especially with Anabaptism. While Basel, Zurich and Berne regularly executed Anabaptists, the only person ever executed for heresy in Geneva was killed for publicly denying the Trinity.[79]

> Thus, chapter 9 shows that the religious toleration in the founding era was rooted, not in Enlightenment thought or liberalism, but in good Protestant principles applied in light of Anglo-Protestant experience. Early America is a Protestant resource for an American return to Christian nationalism.[80]

Wolfe touches on a subject that very few Americans know about and which he can mythologize to a general audience, as many others have. Common to colonial law was the fining of Catholics for not attending Protestant services and banning them from owning property, if not outright running them out of the territory.[81] One would be hard pressed to find modern conservative American Protestants willing to return to the colonial charter system, where the governor often had the responsibility of protecting the official state denomination by making sure no pastors of competing *Protestant* denominations were allowed to plant a church.[82]

---

79 Matthew J. Tuininga, *Calvin's Political Theology and the Public Engagement of the Church: Christ's Two Kingdoms*, Cambridge Studies in Law and Christianity (Cambridge, United Kingdom: Cambridge University Press, 2017), 78.
80 Wolfe, *The Case for Christian Nationalism*, 36.
81 Billington, *The Protestant Crusade,1800-1860*, 6; Williams, *Shadow of the Pope*, 14.
82 Charles Lee Raper, North Carolina: A Study in English Colonial Government, Library of American Civilization (New York: The Macmillan Company, 1904), 31.

VI. Foreword

The chapter ends with an appeal to a "national desire" for "our homeland and its people."[83] Of great note throughout this chapter are the ubiquitous emotional appeals to a sense of "home and hearth." Given that the ten thousand-foot view of Wolfe's philosophy, with which he is priming his audience, has not yet shown any distinguishing characteristics from previous nationalist, and even fascist, thought, these regular appeals to ethnic and cultural collectivism are especially striking.

---

83 Wolfe, *The Case for Christian Nationalism*, 38.

1. Nations Before the Fall

I. A Rational Animal

Wolfe begins the first chapter of his book with a quote about "tribal behavior" from Samuel Francis,[84] who was fired from his position at *The Washington Times* in 1995 after conservative journalist Dinesh D'Souza quoted him as blaming "humanism and universalism for facilitating 'the war against the white race'" and saying that country music star Garth Brooks was "'repulsive' because 'he has that stupid universalist song, in which we all intermarry.'"[85] Writings by Francis are popular among white nationalists, including the former Grand Wizard of the Ku Klux Klan, David Duke, who says Francis showed "how Jewish supremacists invented the word [racist] used to describe negatively those of us who love our heritage and want to preserve it."[86] Wolfe gets his idea of "anarcho-tyranny," that of a tyrannical state purposefully demoralizing its citizens by condoning anarchy, from Francis;[87] in chapter 3, I will highlight an article Wolfe wrote on the subject, which he centered around a longstanding white nationalist trope. Following this quote, the section begins with the question, "What can we say of man's animality?"[88] This leads Wolfe to the correct, general-revelation conclusion that man is a social creature, but his pattern of seeking to first define man's rough *telos* from nature and then to refine it with special revelation will present problems when he attempts to map post-fall social behaviors to pre-fall man. Simply put, if this were the apparent order of operations to understand man's purpose, then secular philosophy would not be in such complete disagreement with Scripture.

---

84 Wolfe, 39.
85 Dinesh D'Souza, "Racism: It's a White (and Black) Thing," *Washington Post*, September 24, 1995,
https://www.washingtonpost.com/archive/opinions/1995/09/24/racism-its-a-white-and-black-thing/46284ab5-417c-4c0c-83e1-029d51655d91/.
86 "By Sam Francis — Why 'Racist' Is Not What We Are!," *David Duke.Com* (blog), February 17, 2005, https://davidduke.com/why-racist-is-not-what-we-are/.
87 https://twitter.com/PerfInjust/status/1463536774257459205
Stephen Wolfe: "More Sam Francis on anarcho-tyranny:" (a screenshot of a Francis essay on the subject follows)
88 Wolfe, *The Case for Christian Nationalism*, 40.

> When we say that *by nature* man is social, are we assuming a state of integrity, a state of sin, a state of pre-glory redemption or a state of glorification?... Surprisingly, no Christian writer (of which I'm aware) has sought to provide a systematic treatment of human sociality that shows continuity and discontinuity between these states.[89]

The epistles provide us with plenty of understanding of the dichotomous character of human relations between the states of sin and "pre-glory redemption." As Paul wrote to Titus:

> Remind them to be submissive to rulers and authorities, to be obedient, to be ready for every good work, to speak evil of no one, to avoid quarreling, to be gentle, and to show perfect courtesy toward all people. For we ourselves were once foolish, disobedient, led astray, slaves to various passions and pleasures, passing our days in malice and envy, hated by others and hating one another. But when the goodness and loving kindness of God our Savior appeared, he saved us, not because of works done by us in righteousness, but according to his own mercy, by the washing of regeneration and renewal of the Holy Spirit, whom he poured out on us richly through Jesus Christ our Savior, so that being justified by his grace we might become heirs according to the hope of eternal life (Titus 3:1-7).

How can we hypothesize the functions of a government of and for prelapsarian man by modeling the interactions of people who are mostly still in a state of slavery to sin and who hate each other? That starting point might yield decent secular political theory, but we cannot shoehorn it into the mold of a "Christian" political theory which seeks the optimal state of redeemed man.

In the next sections, Wolfe uses a selection of 16th and 17th-century Reformed theologians to give his theories theological weight. While this is certainly better than using secular sources or personal observations, relying

---

89 Wolfe, 41.

on appeals to tradition from a biased selection of Reformed thought that fits his preconceptions, instead of direct exegetical insight, ultimately serves to further weaken his position. Out of this selection, the terribly wrong assumption that certain aspects of fallen man's interrelations are preserved remnants of prelapsarian society – including the potential for violent action and the need to protect against it – will also be presented as the basis of his theory.

A note on Wolfe's theory of life without a fall

Claiming knowledge of how earthly society would be structured should man never have fallen, producing a sinless humanity to populate the earth, is a position of such immense hubris that I must remain conscious to not become either overly didactic or dismissive in my dissent.[90] Here, on this side of the fall, we have no conceivable notion of what it means to exist in the direct presence of the Creator. We know that when we once again are able to stand in his presence, and not instantly die (Exodus 33:20), our condition will be so different that we will, in some way, be "like angels in heaven" (Mark 12:24-25). Can anyone living (other than Christ himself) claim to know what it truly means to have had, or to regain, access to the river and tree of life (Revelation 22:1-5)?

---

90 This position from Wolfe alone is enough for me to be shocked that Douglas Wilson's Canon Press published this theory, as is. Though I, like many people, often take umbrage with Wilson's positions on practical application of Scripture, his doctrinal positions are mostly orthodox. I am far from the only person to notice the poor doctrine that serves as the basis of this theory. As Kevin DeYoung wrote in his review, Wolfe's theory is "built upon a weak and speculative foundation about how people would have formed distinct nations even without the fall, it gives too much credence to our own fallen inclinations, and it gives too little consideration for how our desire for 'similarity' has been tainted by sin." Kevin Deyoung, "The Rise of Right-Wing Wokeism," The Gospel Coalition, November 28, 2022, https://www.thegospelcoalition.org/reviews/christian-nationalism-wolfe/. Neil Shenvi writes, "... it is pure speculation that humanity would have formed distinct nations even if the Fall had never happened... It seems at least as plausible to argue that Adam himself, as the human race's covenant head, would have served as a normative cultural, linguistic, and familial anchor for all humanity across the globe. In this case, we might just as well argue that globalism is natural and good, a conclusion which Wolfe surely wants to avoid." "Of Gods and Men."

This subject must be treated with awe and humility. Sadly, Wolfe will not do that, and he will display a lack of understanding of fallen man's radical corruption that, when combined with his foundation of *natural principles*, will become something akin to semi-Pelagianism.[91]

II. The Ends and Dignity of Man

> Indeed, the maturation of [pre-fall] earthly life would likely intensify one's desire for something higher, as earthly life is disclosed as lower, even uncanny, and unable to fully satisfy. People would increasingly feel like strangers and aliens in this world.[92]

We know of no state God revealed to Adam other than to "work and keep" the garden (Genesis 2:15). Is Wolfe claiming that *dissatisfaction* with the station plainly given man by God is a good and natural thing? Geerhardus Vos, in his *Biblical Theology*, wrote of Adam's state as probationary and that the tree of life served to point to a later "eternal life to be secured by obedience throughout [Adam's] probation."[93] Thus, the probationary test is actually whether man will *remain satisfied* with God's commandments as they are, the implication being that man would stay satisfied with his station, even should it later be elevated. There is also no great consensus among Protestant theologians as to whether "a new heaven and a new earth" (Revelation 21:1-4) constitutes an eternal earthly or heavenly existence, though the common, Reformed view is that it will be earthly. Calvin often referred to the temporal and spiritual kingdoms as "earthly" and "heavenly," and this may be what Wolfe is referring to, but Calvin also saw this as the proper "outward" and "inward" expressions of redeemed humans. It would not make sense for Adam to be unfulfilled by

---

91 "Full" Pelagians denied original sin and claimed that man could potentially effect his own salvation. Semi-Pelagians affirmed original sin, but claimed that man still retained faculties that allowed him to work in cooperation with God's grace of his own free will.
92 Wolfe, *The Case for Christian Nationalism*, 46.
93 Geerhardus Vos, Biblical Theology: Old and New Testaments (Grand Rapids, Mich. : Eerdmans, 1975), 27–28.

his station, should he have passed the probationary period, as it would include "heavenly" existence. Wolfe's picture of Adam rightly dissatisfied with his *lower existence* seems more Promethean than Scriptural.

This is one of the arguments that Wolfe claimed Neil Shenvi did not deal with or understand.[94] I agree with Shenvi that, in actuality, Wolfe misunderstands the core conditions of Adam's prelapsarian state and the covenant of works.[95] This condition of obedience and satisfaction with station would have necessarily carried over to a successful, post-probationary life. Instead of acknowledging this, Wolfe injects fallen man's sinful desire for stationary advancement into a hypothetical prelapsarian society.

> The natural gifts are constitutive to man *as man* and include **knowledge of what is good**... (among other gifts). They are essential to man, meaning that without any one of them, the thing ceases to be a human being. Calvin says that these gifts pertain to "earthly" things, enabling man in "matters of policy and economy, all mechanical arts, and liberal studies." (emphasis mine)[96]

John Calvin, in the section of the *Institutes of the Christian Religion* referenced, states that the natural gift is *reason*, "by which man discerns between good and evil."[97] The "knowledge of what is good" (and evil) is a product of man's disobedience to God. When the first man and woman partook of the fruit of the tree of the knowledge of good and evil their "eyes were opened" to that knowledge (Genesis 3:7). Clearly, man's original, natural gift was not this knowledge. Vos postulated that the tree was "the God-appointed instrument to lead man through probation to that state of religious and moral maturity wherewith his highest blessedness is connected."[98] In this view, the ability for man to understand morality, apart from it being the "unexplained, unmotivated demand of God" was only to

---

94 See footnote 35.
95 Wolfe, *The Case for Christian Nationalism*, 21.
96 Wolfe, 47.
97 Jean Calvin, *Institutes of the Christian Religion* (Peabody, Mass: Hendrickson Publishers, 2008), sec. 2.2.12.
98 Vos, *Biblical Theology*, 31.

be granted after man proved himself mature enough to possess it. In this way, even if that knowledge was meant to be a gift, it is one we have unceremoniously plundered, and that we wield like a child who has rummaged through his father's toolbox and discovered something dangerous.

> In ordering the soul, [spiritual gifts] ensure that one follow the proper internal principle, mode and end of action... performed to God's glory as the ultimate end.[99]

It is good to see the glorification of God recognized as the ultimate *telos* of man. We have no secondary purpose that is not wholly subordinate to that end and which God, in His sovereignty, could not repurpose at will (Romans 9:21) – something that Wolfe will seemingly deny, later in this chapter. What sets the Christian apart from others is his recognition of that end (1 Corinthians 10:31); this understanding served as the basis for the Puritans' vision of *vocation as worship*. My chief concern with Wolfe's interpretation of *telos* is his overzealous interpretation and elevation of the secondary purpose of *dominion* in what could be described as a *horizontal privilege* to be taken more than a *vertical responsibility* to be nurtured (more on this later).

> Reformed theologians universally agreed that the natural law was not eliminated at the fall of man, nor was it abolished, superseded, added to, or modified by the Gospel.[100]

Wolfe's defense of a foundation of natural law is essential to his later arguments of civil restriction of religious thought. On one hand, it is true that 16th and 17th-century Reformers used it as the basis for civil punishment of heresy. As Matthew J. Tuininga says of the execution of Michael Servetus, "That heresy should be punished by death was embedded in the Justinian Code, which was the basis for European civil law for a thousand years and was commonly seen as a reliable reflection of

---

99 Wolfe, *The Case for Christian Nationalism*, 48.
100 Wolfe, 50.

natural law."¹⁰¹ Yet, Tuininga also notes that Calvin, who condoned the execution of Servetus, "condemned the persecution of non-Christians, such as Muslims and Jews, and he maintained that it is unjust to punish heretics or apostates in societies with religious diversity."¹⁰² Thus, we see the need for ethno/cultural homogeneity of the nation, if it is to adopt Calvin's understanding of natural law for civil punishment of heretics. From this need comes Wolfe's justification of violent revolution, because no nation in the modern West can become ethnically, culturally, or ideologically homogeneous in a generation without it – nor could it maintain such a state without an iron fist.

Comparison must also be drawn to Wolfe's previous statement that "the Gospel does not supersede, abrogate, eliminate, or fundamentally alter generic nationalism."¹⁰³ What, *if anything,* in Wolfe's view of the Christian civil magistrate is modified by the gospel? We are fifty pages into a case for *Christian* nationalism, and there has been no mention of the gospel yet, other than *what it does not have power over.*

> **Taking dominion** is not an adventitious duty or a divine positive command. It proceeds from the very nature of man, and so **it cannot be rescinded, even by God**, without violating the fundamental nature of man. (emphasis mine)¹⁰⁴

Firstly, Wolfe's language of what God can or cannot do, as if he is legally locked into his decisions and not simply perfect in his ways (Deuteronomy 32:4), is incredibly troublesome. God *will not* rescind his perfect works – though *cannot* and *will not* may seem like semantics, it is worth pointing out the doctrinal difference, because the former can give a falsely elevated view of man, which comes through in this sentence from Wolfe. Secondly, "dominion" is generally expressed in four ways in Scripture:

---

101 Tuininga, *Calvin's Political Theology and the Public Engagement of the Church*, 78.
102 Tuininga, 2.
103 Wolfe, *The Case for Christian Nationalism*, 11.
104 Wolfe, 53.

- The dominion God gave man "over the fish of the sea and over the birds of the heavens and over every living thing that moves on the earth." (Genesis 1:28)
- The dominion of an earthly king over a kingdom. (1 Kings 4:24)
- The dominion of death, defeated by Christ. (Romans 6:9)
- The dominion of God over His creation. (1 Timothy 6:16)

"*Taking* dominion", so common among more authoritarian-minded Christian Nationalists, is a mixing and confusing of man's dominion over nature with the dominion of kings, honed into a collectivist appeal towards those who see themselves as the ethnic and cultural heirs to the Reformation and/or Western Civilization. This is similarly communicated in Andrew Torba and Andrew Isker's *Christian Nationalism: A Biblical Guide For Taking Dominion And Discipling Nations*, wherein they write, "In the simplest terms, a Christian is a disciple of Jesus Christ who seeks to take dominion in all areas of life by obeying His commandment in the Great Commission to disciple all nations." In order to accomplish this task, which requires "exiting the entire system" as a precursor to "discipl[ing] our nation," they suggest "if you don't have a sword, then sell your cloak and buy one because we have a lot of work to do," referencing Luke 22:36. This work of taking dominion belligerently requires an "eschatology of victory" that is explicitly postmillennialist, calling those with other eschatologies "Doomers," though Torba and Isker strangely welcome Catholics and Eastern Orthodox into their movement, who are not traditionally postmillennialist.[105]

III. Civil Fellowship

> Since we can affirm or deny whether something would exist in the prelapsarian state (or at least conclude things above mere speculation), we might be able to construct some robust theory about prelapsarian social life... I contend that providing an

---

105 Andrew Torba and Andrew Isker, *Christian Nationalism: A Biblical Guide For Taking Dominion & Discipling Nations* (Gab AI Inc, 2022), 1, 6, 7, 44, 45, 55.

account of human society in the state of integrity is essential to Christian political theory.[106]

Can Wolfe tell us what it is like to live in the direct presence of God (Genesis 3:8)? If not, then there is no way he could achieve a "robust theory about prelapsarian social life." He claims that, since we can identify things as good (friendship) or as sinful (slavery), we can affirm the former as existing before the fall and deny the latter.[107] Yet, later he will argue for the potential of violence in a sinless world, breaking with his own logic by injecting Sixth Commandment violations into this sinless sphere of existence.[108] He claims this potential expires only in the future state of glory, but gives no explanation of how the society of glory would differ from a post-probationary, prelapsarian society, where Adam chose to obey God's moral commandments.

Though, earlier in the book, Wolfe claims others lack understanding of the doctrine of Total Depravity, his insistence on one-to-one mapping of our postlapsarian societal norms to prelapsarian man exposes his accusation as a point of projection. As the Westminster Confession of Faith says, "By this sin they fell from their original righteousness and communion with God, and so became dead in sin, and *wholly defiled in all the parts and faculties of soul and body*" (emphasis mine).[109] There is not a single aspect of our behavior that is not tainted by sin, nor which does not have the potential of being nearly unrecognizable in comparison to any prelapsarian counterpart. Again, why does direct communion with the Creator, undoubtedly the single most consequential factor in all of prelapsarian earth, not enter into every aspect of his social theory? Though it has the veneer of academic thought, in the end, Wolfe's assertions are no more accurate than a Neo-Apostolic Reformation "prophet's" claims of what he saw during a trip to heaven. In fact, one of the most common

---

106 Wolfe, *The Case for Christian Nationalism*, 56.
107 Wolfe, 56.
108 Wolfe, 75.
109 *The Westminster Confession of Faith and Catechisms: As Adopted by the Orthodox Presbyterian Church : With Proof Texts* (Lawrenceville, Ga.: Christian Education & Publications Committee of the Presbyterian Church in America, 2007), sec. 6.2.

tropes of these false prophets is to take something people see as inherently good and enjoyable in this life and place it in heaven (i.e., heaven has treehouses and rollercoasters, where you can play with Jesus).[110]

We are then given a brief explanation of prelapsarian marriage, where Wolfe accounts for the more egalitarian relationship that existed before God's curse (Genesis 3:16).[111] It would have also been worth pondering how much Jesus's explanation of post-resurrection relations (Matthew 22:30) may describe aspects of this hypothetical, post-probationary society. Instead, we jump head-first into "households combine to form distinct civil societies." Of course, that statement is absolutely true for our postlapsarian world, but Wolfe is still describing things he believes equally transfer between the two states.

> In civil fellowship, man can exercise his distinctively human faculties to love his neighbor as himself.[112]

This sentence is ironic, given the previous statement that "much good would result in the world if we all preferred our own."[113] Wolfe has certainly cast himself as the lawyer asking, "And who is my neighbor?" (Luke 10:29), and will directly delve into these ethnocentric semantics later.

We are given a long description on the natural need for variance in vocations,[114] something that is certain post-fall, and has some circumstantial Scriptural evidence for also being true in the state of glory in the Kingdom, since we may be given more responsibilities (Matthew 25:21). As with everything else in this section, there is no direct Scriptural evidence that should lead Wolfe to his *surety* that prelapsarian society would require multiple vocations, any more than it would be a world full of literal garden tenders. We can say that it is good for a postlapsarian civil society to have a diversity of vocations working together, and that this is

---

110 Kim Robinson, *Heaven Is Real and Fun* (Maitland, Florida: Xulon Press, 2016).
111 Wolfe, *The Case for Christian Nationalism*, 57–58.
112 Wolfe, 59–60.
113 Wolfe, 25.
114 Wolfe, 60–63.

naturally evident, but we cannot say its goodness is derived from it matching prelapsarian society. In fact, the curse laid upon man negatively modified vocation from the pre- to post-fall state (Genesis 3:17-19).

> Everyday interactions with others are limited by a locale, and [man] is ignorant of events and individuals in faraway places and even in the next town over. The fall did not cause this.[115]

Though one cannot wholly disagree with this statement, once again, we cannot be entirely sure how post-probationary, prelapsarian man would function, nor how direct communion with an omnipresent being would affect global interactions. These absolute claims would be of small consequence if they did not explicitly serve as the ethical foundation of his theory. He again makes the claim that prelapsarian communities would develop different languages.[116] As mentioned earlier, this goes against the Tower of Babel narrative in Scripture (Genesis 11:1-9).

> Unfallen man is benevolent to all but can only be beneficent... to some, and this limitation is based not merely in geographic closeness but in shared understanding, expectations, and culture... Even the in-group/out-group distinction is good... effectively bounding particular expectations and preserving cultural distinctives.[117]

While we certainly are, at most times, limited by our location and immediate relations, our Lord made a point to challenge his disciples to not develop an inward preference for people naturally inclined to return their affection, "For even sinners love those who love them" (Luke 6:30-36). Wolfe finishes this section by foreshadowing a later argument that "man, by his nature, requires particularity and must dwell among similar people to live well."[118] There is a fine line between *accepting* the necessity for shared language and culture, in a fallen world, and developing a conspicuous

---

115 Wolfe, 64.
116 Wolfe, 64.
117 Wolfe, 65.
118 Wolfe, 66.

preference for it. When this particularity escapes the realm of language and customs and moves into forcing others into silence by the end of a sword should they dissent with theological and doctrinal attestations, a Christian society begins to eschew its higher obligations (1 Peter 2:21-23).

IV. Civil Order and Civil Virtue

Wolfe begins this section with the dubious, implicit claim that earth's general climate would not significantly differ between pre- and postlapsarian states, ignorant of the fact that "cursed is the ground" because of the fall (Genesis 3:17) and that creation is "subjected to futility, not willingly, but because of him who subjected it" (Romans 8:20-22).

> Inequality in bodily stature, beauty, knowledge, virtue, domestic authority, and civil authority were regularly affirmed as good and not due to the fall… Aquinas states… that differences in food sources, climate, and other factors would make some "more robust… and also greater and more beautiful, and all ways better disposed." Here, he has in mind not only individual difference but also differences in groups.[119]

With this, we are taken deeper into an *ethno*-nationalist theory; an appeal to the authority of Aquinas is used to add gravitas to the claim that people born of different climates are objectively more or less beautiful and adept. Wolfe attempts to clean up this statement – or obfuscate it – with, "Of course, the inferior are not ascribed some natural defect; good things of the same class can differ in excellence."[120] This does not change the original statement that different ethic groups (people born of varying climates) are objectively more "beautiful, and all ways better disposed" than others. One must ask Wolfe which *climate* he thinks resulted in the most objectively beautiful and/or intelligent people.

---

119 Wolfe, 67.
120 Wolfe, 67.

> Hierarchy is, therefore, not some postlapsarian necessity. But neither is it morally neutral. It is good in itself, even of higher worth that [sic] egalitarian arrangements.[121]

It is certain that civil hierarchy is ordained by God (Romans 13:1), and therefore good, though not necessarily "in itself," as he claims. When we combine Wolfe's affirmation of the goodness of hierarchy with his previous claim of the inherent superiority/inferiority of different people groups, based on the geolocation of their culture, his theory becomes even more ethically compromised. The rest of this section focuses mainly on the internal hierarchy of societal functions that naturally forms within a single people group. This is not innately objectionable, but, with such hyper-focus on *natural law*, it bears asking how the *divine law* of "There is neither Jew nor Greek, there is neither slave nor free, there is no male and female, for you are all one in Christ Jesus," (Galatians 3:28) might, in any way, alter the civil hierarchies of his supposedly *Christian* nation. Beyond claims of objective ethnic superiority, it continues to be conspicuous that Wolfe, this far into the book, has failed to declare the gospel,[122] mostly utilizing his own human reasoning and what amounts to a game of theological telephone with 16th-century intermediaries.

Wolfe then brings to bear his prelapsarian theory towards the need for civil government.[123] His general argument is sound, apart from the attempt to derive civil government's goodness from the state of integrity. He could have begun his political theory with this section and Christian readers would have simply affirmed the basic need for civil government from *natural law* as it exists in a fallen world.

> As I'll argue in chapter 6, laws do not require civil penalties by definition, but such penalties are effective in a fallen world to shore up societal law-keeping.[124]

---

121 Wolfe, 68.
122 He will give a brief, but accurate, description of the gospel on pages 91-92.
123 Wolfe, *The Case for Christian Nationalism*, 70–74.
124 Wolfe, 72.

This claim directly contradicts longstanding political and legal theory. As 19th-century French economist Frédéric Bastiat noted in his treatise, *The Law*, "law cannot exist without the sanction and the support of a preponderant force."[125] Any "law" that does not carry the implied threat of potential violence is not law, but merely *suggestion*. If a citizen incurs a fine for the most benign of infractions, and refuses to pay it, the fine will steadily increase until a critical mass is reached and a warrant is issued for his arrest. This common misconception among proponents of blasphemy law, who fail to see the inevitable snowballing of their policies, will be further addressed in chapter 6.

> We can also conclude that a natural aristocracy would arise... Still, all civil rule is by consent of the ruled... Consent remains the efficient cause of civil society and is expressed when one pledges his service to the whole by participating in and benefiting from the symbiosis under the direction of government.[126]

The irony of this statement is threefold in that it would be impossible to find a modern Western nation, province, or even a city containing a plurality of people who would consent to being ruled by "Presbyterian Christian nationalism," that he will later make an argument for the stripping of the consent of the governed from nonbelievers, and that he immediately follows this proclamation with a call to repeal women's suffrage.

He next claims that prelapsarian society would have the potential for sinful, human violence, and that unfallen man's need to physically protect himself renders counter-violence a "martial virtue" and a "feature of masculine excellence."[127] What would happen to a sinless earth if one of Adam's descendants became murderous? Would only he and his progeny become fallen while God maintained direct communion with everyone else? Would only the ground in the region of earth the murderer's tribe lived in be cursed? Simply to harbor hate towards another human being is

---

125 Frédéric Bastiat, The Law (Creative Commons, 2013), 6.
126 Wolfe, *The Case for Christian Nationalism*, 72–73.
127 Wolfe, 74–76.

1. Nations Before the Fall

sin (Matthew 5:21-22), so would God allow prelapsarian man to sin in his heart long enough for it to manifest into violence? Wolfe shows he has little understanding of the absolute obedience required to continue the covenant of works, and of the true cost of man's disobedience.

As we near the end of this chapter on "nations before the fall," Wolfe concludes his main argument with a general explanation of Two-Kingdoms Theology, though not explicitly naming it as such. Of most interest is his belief that this would have been the proper mode of *prelapsarian* government, though he is unsure whether there would be an official, ecclesiastical structure to the eternal kingdom, in relation to a needed hierarchical organization of the temporal kingdom.[128] This, again, puts him in a heterodox position to his own church's doctrine. As the Westminster Confession of Faith says of Jesus Christ, the *Last Adam:*

> It pleased God, in his eternal purpose, to choose and ordain the Lord Jesus, his only begotten Son, to be the Mediator between God and man, the **Prophet, Priest, and King**, the Head and Savior of his church, the Heir of all things, and Judge of the world: unto whom he did from all eternity give a people, to be his seed, and to be by him in time redeemed, called, justified, sanctified, and glorified. (emphasis mine)[129]

It was from this position, as humanity's prophet, priest, and king, that Adam sinned against God; hence, the corruption of sin was imputed to his descendants. As Presbyterian pastor and theologian Mark Jones wrote in his modern-day catechism, *Faith, Hope, Love:*

> In the original garden, God walked with Adam (Genesis 2:15; 3:8). Adam was God's prophet, priest, and king. The Lord directed Adam to fill the earth and subdue creation, but the man failed to execute his threefold role. So another 'Adam' (i.e., Christ) was tasked with this responsibility, namely, to fill (Matthew 28:18-20) and subdue the earth (1 Corinthians 8:6; 15:25-27).[130]

---

128 Wolfe, 77–79.
129 *The Westminster Confession of Faith and Catechisms*, sec. 8.1.

Hypothetically speaking, had he not taken of the fruit, if he had passed the probationary test and populated a sinless earth, it is assumed Adam would have remained prophet, priest, and king, wielding both the eternal and temporal swords, just as Christ will in the final Kingdom.

Wolfe will further delve into his conjecture regarding the unaltered continuity between prelapsarian and postlapsarian states in the next chapter. I will only deal with them verbosely if they are relevant to other claims, since they have been conclusively shown to be a poor understanding of both Scripture and Reformed doctrine. It bears repeating that Wolfe believes his entire theory rests on his "account of human society in the state of integrity."[131]

V. Conclusion

> More could be said about the state of integrity, but this suffices to describe the nature of prelapsarian man and his potential social life.[132]

Here is a brief summation of the more notable assertions made in this chapter:

- Different regions of earth, because of variance in food sources and climate, produce disparate levels of objective beauty and adroitness in human beings at the group level. These differences, both on the micro and macro levels, produce a natural hierarchy.[133]
- The knowledge of good (and, therefore, the knowledge of what is evil) was a *natural gift* given to man by the Creator, which transfers from the pre- to post-fall state.[134]

---

130 Mark Jones, *Faith, Hope, Love: The Christ-Centered Way to Grow in Grace* (Wheaton, Illinois: Crossway, 2017), 129.
131 Wolfe, *The Case for Christian Nationalism*, 56.
132 Wolfe, 79.
133 Wolfe, 66–68.
134 Wolfe, 47.

1. Nations Before the Fall

- "Taking dominion" is a natural function of man that "cannot be rescinded, even by God."[135] For the "natural aristocracy" that would form among prelapsarian man, this dominion would not solely be above nature. These select few would "dominate and rule weaker men."[136]
- This political theory rests on an accurate account of "human society in the state of integrity,"[137] yet God's direct communion and walking with man in that state is of such little consequence that it is not even mentioned as a factor.
- Should Adam have passed the probationary test and populated a sinless earth, the people of that world would still hold the potential for murderous, warlike violence, both as "sinful individuals and groups." Man would somehow be allowed to degrade to this state yet remain in this world to war with sinless man.[138]
- Prelapsarian society would require the enforcement of distinctly separate eternal and temporal kingdoms. This would be (presumably) as envisioned by Calvin, who saw a clear distinction between the two organizations, and not in accordance with other Reformation theologians, such as Huldrych Zwingli, who pushed for much more ecclesiastical power within the civil magistrate.[139] This contradicts the common Reformed position that Adam served as humanity's prophet, priest, and king.

---

135 Wolfe, 53.
136 Wolfe, 72–73.
137 Wolfe, 56.
138 Wolfe, 75.
   Though I highly doubt that Wolfe derives his theory from *The Book of Mormon*, I am struck by how similar this postulation of prelapsarian violence is to the narrative of war between the Nephites and Lamanites.
139 Tuininga, *Calvin's Political Theology and the Public Engagement of the Church*, 41–47, 75–81.

2. Redeemed Nations

I. State of Sin

The stated intent of this chapter is "to identify the theological basis for continuity and discontinuity in social relations between the three states."[140] Wolfe begins this task with a description of the Reformed doctrine of Total Depravity, leaning on several quotes from Calvin. While it is admitted that "man's natural gifts were corrupted by sin," and that man has an "active and efficacious inclination toward evil," this section is immediately followed up with the statement that he "retains his basic instincts for social relations."[141] Yet, as Calvin notes in the *Institutes*, "Wherefore, although we grant that the image of God was not utterly effaced and destroyed in him, it was, however, so corrupted, that *any thing which remains is fearful deformity*" (emphasis mine).[142] The Apostle Paul paints a more visceral picture of our post-fall state:

> And since they did not see fit to acknowledge God, God gave them up to a debased mind to do what ought not to be done. They were filled with all manner of unrighteousness, evil, covetousness, malice. They are full of envy, murder, strife, deceit, maliciousness. They are gossips, slanderers, haters of God, insolent, haughty, boastful, inventors of evil, disobedient to parents, foolish, faithless, heartless, ruthless (Romans 1:28-31).

There is no natural gift possessed by fallen man that is not so tainted by sin as to make it utterly corrupted in relation to its prelapsarian counterpart, most especially our "instincts for social relations." As David tells us of those who deny God, "The fool says in his heart, 'There is no God.' They are corrupt, doing abominable iniquity; there is none who does good" (Psalm 53:1). If there is any seeming goodness in the social relations of the reprobate, it is due to the Spirit's restraint of lawlessness (2 Thessalonians 2:7), not of *natural goodness* passing through the fall. There is not a single

---

140 Wolfe, *The Case for Christian Nationalism*, 81.
141 Wolfe, 83–84.
142 Calvin, *Institutes of the Christian Religion*, sec. 1.15.4.

aspect of our natural reason that is not corrupted, rotten, and debased. Though God, in his mercy, has ordained (and restrained) pagan civil magistrates in the past (Romans 13:4), we cannot rely on the *natural reason* of their philosophers to form the basis of a *Christian* nation. We must start with Scripture.

> Certainly, the effects of sin are all around us: Man rebels against God and commits varieties of moral offenses against his fellow man. Polygamy was prevalent; domestic and civil tyranny is common; people defraud their fellow man; nations unjustly dominate others. But these are *abuses* of these relations.[143]

These are indeed abuses of interpersonal relations, but that is the *natural state of fallen man*. These are not simply regrettable occurrences, but the norm of our behavior. It is only those who have placed their hope in the finished work of Christ on the cross, and who are being actively sanctified by the Spirit, who have any hope of making sin the *exception* in their mortal life (Romans 8:1-8). Wolfe will affirm the need for the covenant of grace and the sanctification of the Spirit in the next section, but he will also seemingly keep the gospel subservient to nature, in the realm of government.

> As Charles Hodge wrote, commenting on Romans 9:3, "The Bible recognizes the validity and rightness of all the constitutional principles of our nature. It therefore approves of… peculiar love for the people of own race and country."[144]

Given statements from Wolfe of the superiority/inferiority of different people groups, both previously in this book and on social media, we cannot dismiss any continuing, positive reference to an innate love of one's own race as simply a benign synonym for culture. He will address "love of nation" in depth in the following chapter, but I will continue to make note of any reference to this line of thought, wherever it is found. This

---

143 Wolfe, *The Case for Christian Nationalism*, 87.
144 Wolfe, 87.

subsection is completed with a restating of the unprovable claim of multiple nations being a natural, prelapsarian good.

> The end of civil government has not changed, because its end is subordinate to the ends of human nature, **and human nature in *itself* has not changed**. (emphasis mine)[145]

As shown above, human nature has been so corrupted by the fall that "any thing which remains is fearful deformity." This is the very definition of having been changed. Wolfe's statement yet again puts him at odds with the core doctrines of his own church. As the *Westminster Confession of Faith* states, "From this original corruption, whereby we are utterly indisposed, disabled, and made opposite to all good, and wholly inclined to all evil, do proceed all actual transgressions."[146] Wolfe may claim that the only change to man was the removal of supernatural gifts, and this means natural gifts have not been changed of themselves, but that would be to deny how the return of spiritual gifts to the redeemed alters the very character of their natural gifts. These gifts do not exist as an independent ideal, separate from the knowledge of God; otherwise, what is sanctification (1 John 3:9)? Wolfe will later claim that nature is "restored" and "perfected" by grace, which contradicts his own quote here.

> If something is natural to man, then civil government must provide conditions for people to freely and harmoniously pursue it. This includes suppressing the things that hinder man in achieving his full humanity.[147]

Where can we go to discover what is natural to man, apart from Scripture? Plato, in his natural reasoning, felt that grown men having sexual relations with young boys was not only natural to man, but inherently good for society, as long as the boy was loved for his soul as

---

145 Wolfe, 88.
146 *The Westminster Confession of Faith and Catechisms*, sec. 6.4.
147 Wolfe, *The Case for Christian Nationalism*, 89.

well as his body.[148] Where should we go to confirm or deny this belief? Though he has yet to explicitly affirm Aquinas's view that man's natural reason is sufficient to enjoin him to the eternal law, enough of this comes through Wolfe's theory of civil virtue to render its lack of an exegetical foundation more than troublesome for Reformed audiences.

> Hence, crafting policy (and ethics generally) in a fallen world requires us to consider unpleasant trade-offs, and magistrates must have the fortitude to enact and enforce the greatest good, despite unfortunate costs involved, and Christians should recognize the *necessity* of such choices and shun the moralism that limits action.[149]

"Unpleasant trade-offs" and "unfortunate costs" is quite a euphemistic way to describe the inherently violent policies that Wolfe advocates for, including active suppression of other religions and civil punishment for heresy, up to and including execution. This is the type of language used by totalitarian leaders to downplay the atrocities committed to achieve their utopian vision. For Lenin, it was not that Kulaks were violently ripped from their homes and mass banished, if not outright murdered; he had merely exhibited "the fortitude" to "shun the moralism that limits action" and accept the "unpleasant trade-offs" needed to "enforce the greatest good" of converting private farms to communes. Later, when Wolfe progresses to the legislative details of his optimum state, I will show, using the example of the 1838 Mormon War in Missouri, that the likeliest outcome to his policies would be a Holodomor-like atrocity.

This section is closed with an articulation of the need for aspects of democracy to place checks on the authority of fallen men, including universal suffrage (for males alone).[150] As previously stated, one wonders where Wolfe believes he will find a Western people who would not overwhelmingly vote against his proposed civil/religious hierarchy. We do not live in a 16th-century city-state of less than 20,000 residents, with an

---

148 Plato, The Symposium, 181.
149 Wolfe, *The Case for Christian Nationalism*, 90.
150 Wolfe, 90.

overwhelming plurality of Protestants (many of whom were religious refugees and, therefore, zealous), ruled by a theocratic council of elders, whose seat of power was shaped by a millennia of cultural cachet for the Justinian Code. Even these city-state governments were anything but perpetually stable, peaceful, and of one mind. In 1538, Calvin was banished from Geneva for refusing to give the civil magistrate control over who could access the Lord's Table and would not be allowed to return until 1541.[151]

Can it be believed that the American people, a majority of whom do not even hold church membership,[152] would not violently rebel against any attempt to institute a state church and the civil enforcement of religious doctrine? Would they not be joined by a plurality of conservative American Christians? There would be no practical way for Wolfe's government to be maintained in the 21st-century West outside of a sham politburo and Stasi-like suppression of dissent, something that will become more apparent as he further details his preferred government of *theocratic Caesarism*.

II. State of Grace

This section begins with a much needed and belated stating of the gospel of Jesus Christ. Wolfe does well in briefly expressing the need for a savior, and how the redeemed are not judged by the Law, but are still bound to it as a "*rule* for duty and happiness in this life."[153] Within this description, though, is a quote of note on Adam:

> The substance of this eternal life [in the state of glory] was not introduced in the Gospel: it is the same life promised to Adam.[154]

---

151 Tuininga, *Calvin's Political Theology and the Public Engagement of the Church*, 64–66.
152 Gallup Inc, "U.S. Church Membership Falls Below Majority for First Time," Gallup.com, March 29, 2021, https://news.gallup.com/poll/341963/church-membership-falls-below-majority-first-time.aspx.
153 Wolfe, *The Case for Christian Nationalism*, 91–92.
154 Wolfe, 92.

Before delving into Wolfe's view of redemption, in which he claims Christians are returned to Adam's full state of integrity, it should be noted again that he believes the *probationary* state of Adam would be indefinite, or at least long enough for mankind to leave the garden and populate a significant portion of the earth while under probation, and this extended humanity would then potentially ascend to glory through fulfilling the covenant of works. As shown above, this produces more hamartiological and soteriological questions than answers. For example, what would happen if hundreds of thousands of people populated the earth, and Adam, the covenantal head, *then* decided to eat the fruit? Would the rest of humanity, who have been faithfully obeying the covenant, still be thrust into sin and death? It is doubtful that Wolfe has given the ramifications of his *goodness of prelapsarian nations* theory much soteriological thought – at least not along these lines – which undoubtedly has an effect on his overall view of salvation.

While it is true that the commandment to fill the earth (Genesis 1:28) comes before the naming of the forbidden fruit (Genesis 2:16-17) in Scripture, both Genesis 1 and Genesis 2 are two, complimentary, intertwined accounts of the same creation. As Francis Schaeffer, a 20th century Presbyterian missionary and theologian, wrote:

> But there is a stronger case for unity [between Genesis 1 and Genesis 2] than the simple recognition of interplay and overlapping between the two accounts. Jesus himself ties them together. Hence, in order to set this unity aside, we would have to deny the way Jesus approached the two chapters. In answering the Pharisee's question concerning divorce, Jesus said, "Have ye not read, that he which made them at the beginning made them male and female..." Jesus is alluding here to Genesis 1:27. But he continues: "And [God] said, For this cause shall a man leave father and mother, and shall cleave to his wife: and they twain shall be one flesh." These later words in Matthew 19:4-5 are a quotation from Genesis 2:24. So Jesus puts the passages from Genesis 1 and Genesis 2 together as a unit.[155]

---

155 Francis A. Schaeffer, Genesis in Space & Time: The Flow of Biblical History, A Bible Commentary for Layman (Glendale, Calif: Regal Books, 1972), 40.

2. Redeemed Nations

Thus we cannot unequivocally declare the commandment to be fruitful and multiply a prerequisite of the probation, any more than we can say God made man, male and female (Genesis 1:27), and then later made female again from man's rib (Genesis 2:21-22). What is revealed in Genesis 1 through Genesis 3 is a condensed, unfathomably weighty revelation from the infinite Creator, containing both *literal* and *metaphysical* truths about a state of humanity vastly different from our own. It must be treated with cautious reverence. We are given no explicit confirmation that Adam's probationary period would extend beyond the garden, or that man was to greatly multiply and share in the probationary state. To build an entire ethical and political system from the assumption of an indefinite probationary period, that would apply to innumerable humans, is the result of a very poor hermeneutic – or lack of one altogether, if this is one of the points of theology that Wolfe is completely relying on intermediaries for.

This theory begins to take on new dimensions in the definition of sanctification that follows. Though well stated in some ways, it contains highly questionable assertions about holiness shared between unfallen Adam and the redeemed. Wolfe claims that, "The restored image [of God in the redeemed] is the same in substance as that which Adam possessed before his fall, which oriented his heart to heavenly life... The believer is a complete human being, restored to integrity." The proper assessment that, "The sanctified on earth are not perfect," is followed up with, "but all the gifts that were either eliminated or corrupted by the fall are restored." We are also told, "Reformed theologians of the 17th century were not scared of the term *inherent righteousness*."[156]

The statement about the "restored image" in redeemed man is categorically false. Those who have the gift of the person of the Holy Spirit have their spirits rightly oriented towards God, but they are still corrupted by sin. While Adam's spirit, pre-fall, was oriented towards God, and he was capable of sinning, he was not yet corrupted. Secondly, it is the same image of God between the redeemed and reprobate that makes the latter fully culpable for their sin (Romans 2:14-16). Paul told the church at Corinth to

---

156 Wolfe, *The Case for Christian Nationalism*, 93–96.

imitate him as he imitated Christ (1 Corinthians 11:1), yet he also had this to say about his behavior as a *born again* Christian:

> For I do not understand my own actions. For I do not do what I want, but I do the very thing I hate. Now if I do what I do not want, I agree with the law, that it is good. So now it is no longer I who do it, but sin that dwells within me. For I know that nothing good dwells in me, that is, in my flesh. For I have the desire to do what is right, but not the ability to carry it out. For I do not do the good I want, but the evil I do not want is what I keep on doing. Now if I do what I do not want, it is no longer I who do it, but sin that dwells within me. (Romans 7:15-20)

And as Calvin noted in the *Institutes*:

> The command of the law is, "Thou shalt love the Lord thy God with all thine heart, and with all thy soul and with all thy might" (Deuteronomy 6:5). To accomplish this, the soul must previously be divested of every other thought and feeling, the heart purified from all its desires, all its powers collected and united on this one object. Those who, in comparison of others, have made much progress in the way of the Lord, are still very far from this goal. For although they love God in their mind, and with a sincere affection of heart, yet both are still in a great measure occupied with the lusts of the flesh, by which they are retarded and prevented from proceeding with quickened pace toward God.[157]

Sanctification is a process that begins when a believer is justified and that continues throughout their life. No one will be completely sanctified before their death (or, for a few, the return of Christ in their lifetime), and they will continue to sin until then. Wolfe affirms that he does not believe in complete holiness among the redeemed when he says "the sanctified on earth are not perfect," but the way he describes a "restored image" and "inherent righteousness" in the children of God paints a rosier picture than exists in reality. This is concerning when we consider that much of his

---

157 Calvin, *Institutes of the Christian Religion*, sec. 3.19.4.

2. Redeemed Nations

audience may be people who do not fully understand these very important points of doctrine. It could breed a sense of *Christian superiority* that, when combined with Wolfe's championing of love of one's own ethnicity and culture, could facilitate disastrous spiritual outcomes, especially when also mixed with his next topic of the *dominion mandate* among the redeemed.

The mandate is explained mostly through a critique of Westminster Seminary California professor David VanDrunen's claim that redeemed man is not to continue Adam's original work. Wolfe is correct that "Christians cannot bring heaven to earth, for Adam never had that ability in the first place" and that Adam's dominion mandate was to "order earthly life." But, as shown above, he has no Scriptural proof that the *probationary* mandate was to order that earthly life "to the promised heavenly life" any more than ordering would instead, or also, be an *element of* Adam's "heavenly" existence.[158] In fact, the author of Hebrews tell us that the *world to come* will be subjected to man, in his state of glory (Hebrews 2:5-9). Therefore, it can be equally contested that this was the original "life promised to Adam" and his eventual progeny, should he have passed the probation in the garden.

> [VanDrunen] fails to recognize that heavenly life was the gracious end of Adam's obedience, not the natural end of it. Maturing the earth by his labor was natural to him, according to his nature, and this was natural to him even when considering Adam apart from the covenant of works.[159]

What was *natural* to unfallen man that, itself, was not a *grace* from the Creator? Wolfe here continues with his Promethean elevation of man's nature as something seemingly self-contained. He says that "Grace perfects nature"[160], but must we not first admit that *grace repairs our corrupted nature*? He will later say that grace *restores* nature, but, without acknowledging *brokenness*, this word also paints a mental picture of something mostly working as designed and simply being cleaned up. With

---

158 Wolfe, *The Case for Christian Nationalism*, 96–98.
159 Wolfe, 98.
160 Wolfe, 101.

so many facets of redeemed man not altered by the gospel, as Wolfe will continue to argue, would there be any significant difference between a revolutionary government formed on the basis of the Enlightenment value of man's *natural reason* and one centered on claims of his *natural mandate*? As Timothy Tacket says of the disastrous pinnacle of the French Revolution, "The Terror arose… through a concatenation of developments emerging out of the very process of the Revolution itself," a process born of "the profoundly humanistic faith in the ability of individuals to use their own good sense, their 'reason' to solve problems of all kinds."[161] It is quite reasonable to imagine a revolutionary National Assembly, of various political factions, denouncing each other as traitors for professing different practical interpretations of "taking dominion." I believe that this is why Wolfe, who is well knowledgeable in political theory, requires his proposed government have a *Caudillo*, a *Duce*, a *Christian Prince* to "mediate the national will"[162] and mitigate this inevitable political devolution. His theory's adherence to a foundation of *Thomasian natural reason* paints him into that corner, and negates any claims he may make regarding democratic checks.

> Since grace restores nature and natural law contains all the moral principles concerning social relations, **the Gospel does not alter the priority and inequality of loves amongst those relations**. (emphasis mine)[163]

Thus begins another section of flawed epistemology and Christology. It is true that the natural law, the work of the law written on our hearts (Romans 2:15) and through *general revelation*, contains all the moral principles concerning social revelations. But even the redeemed, in this life, are so attached to the lusts of the flesh that they require regular, repeated contact with *special revelation* (Scripture) to stop suppressing the

---

161 Timothy Tackett, The Coming of the Terror in the French Revolution (Cambridge, Massachusetts: The Belknap Press of Harvard University Press, 2015), 342, 343.
162 Wolfe, *The Case for Christian Nationalism*, 276.
163 Wolfe, 101.

knowledge of that natural law. Wolfe quotes the Anglican Divine Richard Hooker:

> The general perpetual voice of mankind is as the judgment of God Himself, since what all men at all times have come to believe must have been taught to them by Nature...[164]

If all the moral principles concerning social relations have been taught to all men at all times by nature, and they are not altered by the gospel, then why bother, as Wolfe argues several paragraphs later, with the "Christianization of civil institutions and laws"?[165] Should we Americans not accept the neo-pagan/secular government currently instated as one properly ordained by God, one that must inherently understand the *natural law* and obey it just as Paul and Peter instructed the early church to peacefully obey the Roman authorities (Romans 13:1-7, 1 Peter 2:13-17)? This is the inherent contradiction of an argument for a revolutionary, *Christian* civil government founded on natural law that does not first, and repeatedly, affirm Christ's full dominion over both kingdoms (1 Peter 3:22) and the supremacy of God's inerrant, revealed word over man's errant reason. *We must start with Scripture.*

It is through this faulty elevation of nature that Wolfe, once again, tells us what the "gospel does not alter," in this instance the "priority and inequality of loves amongst [social] relations. A Christian should love his children over other children, his parents over other parents, his kin over other kin, his nation over other nations."[166] Again we are treated to an explanation of supposedly "Christian" love which, at no point, gives even passing mention to *the love of God displayed through Christ Jesus*. It is highly suspect that ἀγάπη (agapé) love is only first alluded to here – and in a negative light, as a sentiment that liberals make an idol of – for this imparted love is the very first fruit of the Spirit listed (Galatians 5:22-23) and the most important (1 Corinthians 13:13). Though this love is best exhibited within the spiritual kingdom, there is no filter that removes it

---
164 Wolfe, 104.
165 Wolfe, 105.
166 Wolfe, 101.

from the temporal; it should pour out from the disciple's every interaction. Where also does Christ's commandment to love Him above all others (Matthew 10:37) factor into the equation? It has yet to be mentioned.

It is certainly true that the Christian has a stronger bond of love with his relations, one that is equally enmeshed with duty (1 Timothy 5:7-9), but this is not an exclusive love. A disciple of Christ does not only exist within *two kingdoms*, but also *two families*, one temporal and the other spiritual:

> And stretching out his hand toward his disciples, he said, "Here are my mother and my brothers! For whoever does the will of my Father in heaven is my brother and sister and mother." (Matthew 12:49-50)

We should also question how much of this preference is due to the flesh; certainly this preferential love is *corrupted by sin*, even in the redeemed, preventing them from fulfilling the commandment to completely love Christ more than their immediate family. To treat this preference uncritically, as Wolfe does – to champion its *naturalness* as not altered by the gospel – is a mistreatment that rises to the status of Third Commandment violation. Every natural love we have is radically corrupted by sin, and it is only the good news of Jesus Christ's crucifixion and resurrection that gives any of us hope to combat that corrupted nature in this lifetime. The Christian is called to – some would say required to – approach every natural preference in the same way David cried out to God:

> Search me, O God, and know my heart!
>   Try me and know my thoughts!
> And see if there be any grievous way in me,
>   and lead me in the way everlasting! (Psalm 139:23-24)

As for the elevation of *love of nation* to the status of being unaltered by the gospel, Wolfe's lack of distinction between most nations, which are bound by shared ethnicity, and the few that are bound by shared ideals leaves us to assume that he means the former, especially since he places it in relation to the subsumed units of kith and kin. The love of a nation for its

2. Redeemed Nations

ideals would also not qualify as *pre-rational*. Returning to the earlier quote from Charles Hodge, regarding Romans 9:3 and the goodness of "peculiar love for the people of own race and country,"[167] let us examine the greater context of how Paul's love for the people of Israel manifested itself:

> I am speaking the truth in Christ – I am not lying; my conscience bears me witness in the Holy Spirit – that I have great sorrow and unceasing anguish in my heart. For I could wish that I myself were accursed and cut off from Christ for the sake of my brothers, my kinsmen according to the flesh. They are Israelites, and to them belong the adoption, the glory, the covenants, the giving of the law, the worship, and the promises. To them belong the patriarchs, and from their race, according to the flesh, is the Christ, who is God over all, blessed forever. Amen. (Romans 9:1-5)

Paul does not wish that he would be cut off from the temporal kingdom of Israel, so that his kin may release themselves from the bonds of Rome and re-institute an independent, temporal, Messianic kingdom that would orient the people towards heavenly good. He wishes himself cut off from Christ's *spiritual kingdom* so that, by the truth of the gospel, the chosen people of Israel would be admitted to that eternal nation – a kingdom of *ideals* that does not distinguish between ethnicity or gender. Though temporal nations naturally form around geography, and there is often a primary ethnic group within geographical regions, Scripture does not explicitly support the creation of a temporal *New Covenant* kingdom built on a foundation of *natural love of one's ethnicity, unaltered by the gospel*. It is important to make this distinction now, because the rest of this chapter is dedicated to priming the reader for the proceeding chapter, *Love of Nation*.

Two-Kingdoms Theology, as presented in the *Institutes*, is now expressly named, and immediately misrepresented for ethno-nationalist ends. Calvin is quoted regarding the wide separation of the kingdoms, and then this quote is manipulated to serve Wolfe's vision of "natural order." It bears repeating that he has previously stated that this natural order renders

---

167 Wolfe, 87.

people superior or inferior to each other both on the micro, individual level and the macro, ethnic/cultural level.

> The two [kingdoms] are "widely separated" in the sense that the spiritual leveling and unifying consequences of the Gospel have their own place and are **kept from mixing up nature and thereby subverting the natural order**. (emphasis mine)[168]

It is not "the nation and affections of nationhood [that] are natural to man as man"[169] that Calvin gives as the reason for the separation of the kingdoms in the quoted section; it is the dual, opposing threats of those who would take their "Christian liberty" outside of the spiritual kingdom and use it as an excuse to reject all civil authority, and those in civil office who would declare power over the church. Calvin is not concerned with protecting man's *naturalness*, but with protecting *God's supernaturally ordained civil order*, which restrains sin among the reprobate, and protecting the body of Christ from those who would claim it an area of their *natural dominion*. It is worth quoting this section at length:

> Having shown above that there is a twofold government in man, and having fully considered the one which placed in the soul or inward man, relates to eternal life, we are here called to say something of the other, which pertains only to civil institutions and the external regulation of manners. For although this subject seems from its nature to be unconnected with the spiritual doctrine of faith, which I have undertaken to treat, it will appear as we proceed, that I have properly connected them, no, that I am under the necessity of doing so, especially while, on the one hand, frantic and barbarous men are furiously endeavoring to overturn the order established by God, and, on the other, the flatterers of princes, extolling their power without measure, hesitate not to oppose it to the government of God. Unless we meet both extremes, the purity of the faith will perish.[170]

---

168 Wolfe, 107.
169 Wolfe, 106.
170 Calvin, *Institutes of the Christian Religion*, sec. 4.20.1.

2. Redeemed Nations

Wolfe acknowledges the former concern, mostly presented by Anabaptist dissidents in the Reformers' time,[171] by correctly likening it to today's theologically and politically liberal "gospel politics,"[172] what is often little more than a ecclesiastical facade to a Hegelian-Marxist eschatology. Conspicuously absent from his modern analysis is the other extreme threat to "the purity of the faith," perhaps because this is where his camp and its obsession with natural hierarchy not altered by the gospel, a reactionary *sans-gospel politics*, resides.

> Christians should affirm the nation and nationality and even seek to order their nations to heavenly life.[173]

Should Christians "seek to order their nations to heavenly life" through overturning a magistrate's *disordering* rule by force, as Wolfe will later argue? This is certainly the dilemma for 21st-century Protestant Christians in the West, all of whom live under governments that do not champion Christian ethics and, more often than not, expressly work against them. Greg L. Bahnsen, perhaps the most prominent theonomist author of the late-20th century, did not think so. As he wrote, "The morally proper way for Christians to correct social evils that are not under the lawful jurisdiction of the state is by means of voluntary and charitable enterprises or the censures of the home, church, and marketplace – even as the appropriate method for changing the political order of civil law is not violent revolution, but dependence upon regeneration, re-education, and gradual legal reform."[174] It is the duty of members of the spiritual kingdom to work towards the reordering of a pagan, or doctrinally-unsound, temporal nation, not by exuding physical force in the temporal realm, but through peacefully executing the Great Commission and trusting in the

---

171 Tuininga, *Calvin's Political Theology and the Public Engagement of the Church*, 47–53.
172 Wolfe, *The Case for Christian Nationalism*, 107–8.
173 Wolfe, 108.
174 Gary Scott Smith, *God and Politics: Four Views on the Reformation of Civil Government : Theonomy, Principled Pluralism, Christian America, National Confessionalism* (Phillipsburg, N.J.: Presbyterian and Reformed Pub. Co., 1989), 24.

work of the Spirit. "For the weapons of our warfare are not of the flesh but have divine power to destroy strongholds" (2 Corinthians 10:4).

Next, a mostly orthodox description of Reformed theology's distinction between the *visible catholic church* and the true *people of God* is presented. This distinction is necessary for Wolfe's later advocacy of paedobaptism as an initiation rite into the body politic. But Wolfe again makes the false claim that it is the redeemed who are "fully human, having been sanctified and having received the divine image."[175] As shown above, both the reprobate and redeemed have the *imago Dei*, and there is no new image imparted upon the latter, but instead the gift of the person of the Holy Spirit is given to illuminate the hearts and minds of believers.

This section is completed with a good, general description of the differing purposes of the two "civil and ecclesiastical administrations." However, Wolfe's later arguments for civil enforcement of Christian doctrine have been irreparably damaged due to his insistence, up to this point, that the temporal kingdom's foundation is not "altered by the gospel" – there is some confusion around restored/perfected nature, but the vast majority of the book thus far has been dedicated to expressing what aspects of nature the gospel does not change. Logically, if the temporal kingdoms of men rest wholly on *natural principles* (general revelation), apparent to pagan and Christian alike, and those principles are not altered by the gospel (special revelation), in order for the civil enforcement of Christian orthodoxy to be an apparent *natural good* – as opposed to the civil enforcement of Buddhism, Zoroastrianism, Islam, or any other religion that *natural man unaltered by the gospel may choose* – those principles must be altered by *something* that would orient them towards Christianity and its ethics. Otherwise, how does this hypothetical government justify outlawing behaviors that are often condoned by the natural reason and religions of men outside of Christendom, such as polygamy and pederasty? With only the gospel-improved human interpretation of "natural principles" at hand, by what standard would Christian men rightfully claim others are working against natural law and not themselves? Wolfe's ethical foundation is enough to build a government that meets the bounds of Romans 13, in that

---

175 Wolfe, *The Case for Christian Nationalism*, 109–11.

it could *potentially* not be a terror to good conduct, but, by keeping special revelation at arm's length, he has failed to lay an ethical foundation for the civil enforcement of religious orthodoxy, as he will later argue for.

If Wolfe's constant is removed from the equation these logical dilemmas quickly disappear. His theory requires the existence of a categorical imperative[176], altered by neither the gospel nor man's total depravity, to contort behaviors that Christians inherently know are corrupted by the flesh into *pre-gospel natural goods*. On the other hand, men who have had their *corrupted nature* repaired by the gospel, not merely improved, and who no longer *suppress general revelation*, create nations and laws based upon that repaired human nature, guided first and foremost by God's inerrant word and His Spirit. They have a base of absolute Christian ethics from special revelation to govern by, and the motivation to let the true faith flourish by protecting its institutions and allowing them the freedom to operate. They can still build nations that care for and protect the citizenry while appealing to shared, spiritual ideals instead of a collectivism of fleshy ethnic/cultural identity.

III. Dominion and the Divine Image

Wolfe finishes his chapter on redeemed nations by using his claim of a "restored divine image" to build a case for special, supernaturally ordained *civil* dominion among Christians. Quoting 17th-century Puritan minister Samuel Willard, he rightly states that the Christian should not "usurp the possession of his ungodly neighbor" simply for being "pagans, idolaters, or strangers to the gospel covenant," though only as long as they "keep within the bounds of civil righteousness."[177] This raises the question, *What constitutes exiting the bounds of civil righteousness?* For instance, in rural regions of Afghanistan, it is not uncommon for well-aged men to marry

---

[176] A categorical imperative, in the philosophy of Immanuel Kant, is a rule of conduct that does not require a statement of validity, based on the acting or affected party's desire for outcome. Kant's one categorical imperative was "Act only according to that maxim by which you can at the same time will that it should become a universal law." Wolfe's claim that man's dominion is his universal law that "cannot be rescinded, even by God," functions in a similar capacity.

[177] Wolfe, *The Case for Christian Nationalism*, 113–14.

prepubescent girls. Would that constitute a violation of civil righteousness that gives Christians leave to conquer that nation? What of religious persecution? Do Christian nations have supernatural dominion over communist nations that persecute the true faith? What of our own nation, where multiple states have legalized infanticide through laws that give unfettered access to abortion at any phase of gestation, including fully viable fetuses? What of states that allow children to receive sterilizing, cross-sex hormones from government-funded organizations without notifying their parents? Do these violations of civil righteousness give Christians the same dominion over America that Joshua had over Canaan?

Wolfe avoids these questions for now and even alludes to an answer in the negative, quoting Calvin on the difference between the reprobate's *use of good things* versus the redeemed's *right to them*.[178] But chapter 8 will be wholly dedicated to affirming such a religious revolution in the West. Again, one wonders how Wolfe believes a Christian revolution to be remotely viable in the modern West, where the majority would outright reject its premise. Perhaps Wolfe knows a successful rightist revolution would require a coalition force, and one of the potential, unstated purposes for a *Christian Prince* would be to either slowly marginalize his potential coalition rivals, as Franco did,[179] or, that failing, outright purge them, as Lenin did with the Mensheviks. It is also possible that he has no idea what he is advocating for, something I will make the case for in that chapter.

> Finally, Christian nations should regard themselves as nations of true dignity, being a people of the true God on earth. This status should give them confidence and even boldness in their national and international affairs.[180]

Let us contrast this with how Paul and Peter instructed Christians to engage others, both inside and outside the body of Christ:

---

178 Wolfe, 114–15.
179 Preston, *Franco*, 295–96; Priorelli, *Italian Fascism and Spanish Falangism in Comparison*, 185.
180 Wolfe, *The Case for Christian Nationalism*, 115.

> Put on then, as God's chosen ones, holy and beloved, compassionate hearts, kindness, humility, meekness, and patience, (Colossians 3:12)
>
> Clothe yourselves, all of you, with humility toward one another, for "God opposes the proud but gives grace to the humble." (1 Peter 5:5b)

There is a difference between boasting in the cross of Jesus Christ (Galatians 6:14), and being bold about the superiority of your real or imagined nation to others because it is formed of a sense of *special dominion*. It is with this type of dominion-oriented "boldness" that President George W. Bush made the incredibly reductionist statement that Islamists "hate our freedoms,"[181] kicking off a *War on Terror* that lasted twenty years and took nearly a million lives.[182] If there ever is to be another Christian nation in the West, it should learn from history and collectively seek to be a humble emissary of Christ.

IV. Conclusion

> Grace does not destroy what is natural but restores it. Grace also perfects nature, and thus nations can be Christian nations and commonwealths can be Christian commonwealths.[183]

As shown above, Wolfe is mistaken about the level to which fallen man's nature is corrupted and needs to be "restored" by grace. As has also been shown, there is no natural principle that passed through the fall unscathed and which is clearly visible to men who do not have the gospel.

---

[181] "Text: President Bush Addresses the Nation," *The Washington Post*, September 20, 2001, https://www.washingtonpost.com/wp-srv/nation/specials/attacked/transcripts/bushaddress_092001.html.

[182] "Costs of the 20-Year War on Terror: $8 Trillion and 900,000 Deaths," Brown University, September 1, 2021, https://www.brown.edu/news/2021-09-01/costsofwar.

[183] Wolfe, *The Case for Christian Nationalism*, 116.

A hypothetical Christian nation is certainly one of *repaired nature,* but the knowledge of grace should cause that nation to act as a corporate Christian, and seek to order its policies by the same "kindness, humility, meekness, and patience" as the individual believer. Let the boldness be saved for declaring *Christ's work* to the world.

3. Loving Your Nation

I. Method

> One of the conclusions from the previous chapter is that neither the fall nor grace destroyed or abrogated human natural relations. The fall did not introduce the natural instinct to love one's own, and grace does not "critique" or subvert our natural inclinations to love and prefer those nearest and most bound to us.[184]

Here is the fulcrum of Wolfe's entire theory. As has been proven, he has no Scriptural basis to make this absolute claim, which is required for his theory to be remotely plausible for a Christian audience (nor does he attempt to present one). To make matters worse, he has now disqualified his theology by saying that "grace does not 'critique'… our natural inclinations… The fall introduced the *abuse* of social relations and *malice* towards ethnic difference."[185] Again, the *Westminster Confession of Faith*, the doctrinal standard of Wolfe's own church, the Presbyterian Church in America, states that fallen man is "wholly defiled in all the parts and faculties of soul and body."[186] Critiquing what we *wrongly perceive as natural to us* is exactly what grace does, and turning our notion of "natural instinct to love one's own" on its head is exactly what Christ does (Matthew 10:37). That Wolfe does not even attempt to wrestle with these basic notions of what it means to be Christian is heavy evidence of rotten spiritual fruit.

He then lays out his objective of making readers aware of their *pre-rational preference* for those similar to them. He embraces his genetic ethnicity that is "rooted ancestrally in Western Europe," accepts that he is primarily addressing a "Western European male audience," and states his ultimate aim to "reinvigorate Christendom in the West." The false dilemma from the introduction is then restated:

---

184 Wolfe, 117–18.
185 Wolfe, 118.
186 *The Westminster Confession of Faith and Catechisms*, sec. 6.2.

"Which way, Western Man – the suicide of the West or its revitalization?"[187]

In the companion book to his 1976 film series, *How Should We Then Live*, an exposition on the rise and fall of Christendom, Francis Schaeffer described the near-ubiquitous modern values of *personal peace* and *affluence*:

> Gradually, that which had become the basic thought form of modern people became the almost totally accepted viewpoint, an almost monolithic consensus. And as it came to the majority of people through art, music, drama, theology, and the mass media, values died. As the more Christian-dominated consensus weakened, the majority of people adopted two impoverished values: *personal peace* and *affluence*.
>
> *Personal peace means just to be let alone, not to be troubled by the troubles of other people, whether across the world or across the city – to live one's life with minimal possibilities of being personally disturbed. Personal peace means wanting to have my personal life pattern undisturbed in my lifetime, regardless of what the result will be in the lifetimes of my children and grandchildren. Affluence means an overwhelming and ever-increasing prosperity – a life made up of things, things, and more things – a success judged by an ever-higher level of material abundance.*[188]

The desire to create – by violence if necessary – an ethnically, culturally, and religiously homogeneous nation for the purpose of protecting one's own praxis is the ultimate exercise of *personal peace* and *affluence*. Wolfe is not referring to any gospel principles in the naming of the supposed existential threat, but is instead appealing to his audience's

---

187 Wolfe, *The Case for Christian Nationalism*, 118–19.
 Which Way Western Man? was a book written by white supremacist, William Gayley Simpson, in 1978.
188 Francis A. Schaeffer, *How Should We Then Live? The Rise and Decline of Western Thought and Culture* (Old Tappan, N.J: F. H. Revell Co, 1976), 205.

fear of losing the *personal peace* of cultural dominance and the *affluence* of not having to interact with vocal dissent to one's religion. Our Lord tells us:

> If you were of the world, the world would love you as its own; but because you are not of the world, but I chose you out of the world, therefore the world hates you. (John 15:19)

Though some have been blessed to have been born in times and places where the true faith was genuinely shared and practiced by a plurality of their immediate physical neighbors, most have not, including 21st-century Christians in the West. For those with a proper eschatology, this is not the existential threat Wolfe makes it out to be. Though I cannot say for certain whether I will die peacefully with my family by my side, or by the hands of my countrymen, who seem increasingly interested in physically persecuting me for my faith, I know that, either way, I will be greeted by Christ on the other end. This is why the prime directive has been, and will always be, the peaceful application of the Great Commission (Matthew 28:19-20). For Western Christians to eschew this, in order to violently seek their *personal peace* and *affluence* in a supposedly Christian nation, is nothing short of abandoning the commandment of Christ.

An account from *Foxe's Book of Martyrs* on the fourth Roman persecution of Christians under Marcus Aurelius, who, ironically, is often quoted by modern Christians as a pagan who rightly interpreted *natural law*, puts this predicament in perspective. The fourth persecution included the execution of the early-church bishop Polycarp, reportedly discipled by the Apostle John himself.

> The cruelties used in this persecution were such that many of the spectators shuddered with horror at the sight, and were astonished at the intrepidity of the sufferers. Some of the martyrs were obliged to pass, with their already wounded feet, over thorns, nails, sharp shells, etc. upon their points, others were scourged until their sinews and veins lay bare, and after suffering the most

excruciating tortures that could be devised, they were destroyed by the most terrible deaths.[189]

I ask the reader, "Which way, Christian Man – will you honor the suffering of your Lord, and that of your *spiritual ancestors*, or will you retreat into your *personal peace* and *affluence*?"

Wolfe now moves to an argument that is terribly similar to that of early-20th-century fascist political theory, the naming of liberal democracy, the "creedal nation," as the enemy of the proper "intimate connection of people and place."[190] Like Wolfe in the beginning of this section, fascists identified this enemy of the true nation as an immediate, existential threat. Also like him, they often presented this threat under the terms of *suicide or revitalization*. Priorelli, quoting the Falangist leader, José Antonio Primo de Rivera, notes his belief that Spain, through its democratically elected republic, "had been reduced to the 'farce of the ballots in a glass urn' that decided 'at any instant if God existed or did not exist, if the truth was the truth or not the truth, if the fatherland had to live or if it had to commit suicide.'"[191]

This section is closed with an admission that not all political and social creeds are bad in of themselves and that "the statement 'Jesus is Lord,' which is a universally true statement, certainly serves to unite the people of a Christian nation."[192] What of the creed that "All human beings are made in the image of God?" The real trouble with Wolfe's incorrect belief that the redeemed receive a different "restored image," mixed with the now-repeated claim that "the nation is rooted in a pre-reflective, pre-propositional love for one's own," begins to take shape.

---

189 William Byron Forbush, ed., *Fox's Book of Martyrs* (United States: The John C. Winston Company, 1926), 8–9.
190 Wolfe, *The Case for Christian Nationalism*, 119.
191 Priorelli, *Italian Fascism and Spanish Falangism in Comparison*, 41.
192 Wolfe, *The Case for Christian Nationalism*, 120.

II. People, Place, and Things

Wolfe lays out an agreeable explanation of how "the space we inhabit is invested with meaning."[193] When he moves into how socialization transfers this meaning through generations, he stumbles into a statement that challenges his previous epistemological and hamartiological assertions:

> Knowing that our children are not machines or computers but creatures of habit, we train them to have a cautious disposition toward the street. We want them to feel something in relation to it, to have a sort of habitual, pre-rational response of caution. The tone of our voice in denying them access to a street communicates the seriousness of that place.[194]

Why must we change to a serious, perhaps even stern, tone of voice to communicate the danger of the street to a child? Why, as any parent knows, do we have to repeat this warning multiple times? Shouldn't the *natural law* of the dangerous street be apparent to our children through a combination of their own observation and our gentle, logical instruction? Wolfe has unknowingly touched upon the real problem of sin, the actual *totality* of which he doubts. We must use a serious tone of voice, multiple times, to properly instruct our young children to not run into the street, not just because they are "creatures of habit," *but because of their inherent selfishness*. Children often do not pay attention to their parents' instruction, because they lack *executive function* and are preoccupied with the things they want to do at any given moment. They will willfully test boundaries to see what they can get away with, again, trying to do whatever they want at any given moment.

This does not significantly change in man until his broken nature is repaired by the gospel. Fallen man perpetually drives ten miles per hour over the speed limit, slyly undercuts his professional colleagues for his own career advancement, and slips terms for his own advantage into the fine print of contracts (even redeemed man can still wrestle with this). In other

---

193 Wolfe, 122.
194 Wolfe, 123.

words, he never stops testing and pushing boundaries to try to do what he wants at any given moment. What seems like recognition of absolute morality in the average adult has less to do with an understanding of *natural law* than with self-preservation within the bounds of acceptable behavior they have received through a lifetime of the type of socialization Wolfe describes in this section. Even the Stoic and Buddhist goal of attaining perpetual self-control and a detached benevolence is for the selfish purpose of *personal growth*. This is the effect of *total depravity*.

> [Sacred spaces] are unique in that one can disrespect and desecrate them.[195]

Some initial groundwork for the later argument for civil punishment of blasphemy and irreverence is being laid here. Detailed rebuttals to that proposition will be saved for chapter 9, but it is worth discussing here how a civil magistrate's view of "sacred spaces" applies to the broader subject of the subjectivity and objectivity of sacredness in civil and religious law.

In the United States, the primary charge for willfully defacing or destroying a federal monument is *Code 16, Subsection 426i, Protection of monuments, etc.*, a misdemeanor, where the perpetrator "shall for each and every such offense be fined not less than $5 nor more than $100."[196] On the other hand, the primary charge for defacing or destroying everyday government property is *Code 18, Subsection 1361*, where "if the damage or attempted damage to such property exceeds the sum of $1,000, [the perpetrator will be punished] by a fine under this title or imprisonment for not more than ten years, or both."[197] Though, in a just society, someone who severely defaces a public monument would likely be charged with violations of both of these codes, that the former is much less severe is a good example of how our *creedal nation* understands the *subjectivity of sacredness* in the civil sphere.

---

195 Wolfe, 124.
196 https://www.law.cornell.edu/uscode/text/16/426i
197 https://www.law.cornell.edu/uscode/text/18/1361

3. Loving Your Nation

The *eternal kingdom* of the church must consider certain *ideas* and *spaces* objectively sacred and protect the communion of saints by punishing openly-expressed sinful thought and behavior through the practice of peaceful church discipline. As Calvin wrote in the *Institutes*, "Wherefore, all who either wish that discipline were abolished, or who impede the restoration of it, whether they do this of design or through thoughtlessness, certainly aim at the complete devastation of the church."[198] While public blasphemy can, by itself, be damaging to order within the religious sphere, the same cannot be said of heterodox thought and irreverence in the civil sphere, where speech must first cross into the *threat of action* before *civil order* is truly challenged. A civil magistrate that properly protects the independent functioning of the church allows it to handle blasphemy though its own discipline. It need not involve itself in the fine details of spiritual matters (Wolfe will later argue for this overreach when he gives his Christian Prince veto power over doctrinal decisions from a synod). More so, in a religiously diverse society, sacredness must be considered subjective and, but for crimes committed with the intent to intimidate, demands leniency. Wolfe will make a later argument for "prudence" in punishment, but he does not extend that prudence to allowing the public evangelizing of other religions. While this is considered extreme by many modern Christians, it puts him in line with Calvin's public thoughts on the duties of civil magistrates, which took on a stricter character after he regularly dealt with Anabaptists during his three year exile from Geneva.[199]

We are next given a description of sentiment towards people and places that have been involved in our most cherished life experiences.[200] There is nothing wrong or unproductive in a sense of sentiment or nostalgia, by itself, and it can be a source of loving action. But, just as it is with other forms of love promoted in Wolfe's book, *sentiment* is something explicitly required by Jesus to be wholly secondary to the disciple's focus on Him.

---

198 Calvin, *Institutes of the Christian Religion*, sec. 4.12.1.
199 Tuininga, *Calvin's Political Theology and the Public Engagement of the Church*, 228–29.
200 Wolfe, *The Case for Christian Nationalism*, 125–26.

Yet another said, "I will follow you, Lord, but let me first say farewell to those at my home." Jesus said to him, "No one who puts his hand to the plow and looks back is fit for the kingdom of God." (Luke 9:61-62)

In the same vein are the following sections on *intergenerational love* and *familiarity*.[201] There is nothing inherently wrong with caring for your long-term posterity or having a sense of duty to your city, state, and nation, but these are *secondary obligations* for Christians. We are citizens of a higher nation, through Christ, which must always take precedence:

> But you are a chosen race, a royal priesthood, a holy nation, a people for his own possession, that you may proclaim the excellencies of him who called you out of darkness into his marvelous light. Once you were not a people, but now you are God's people; once you had not received mercy, but now you have received mercy. (1 Peter 2:9-10)

> After this I looked, and behold, a great multitude that no one could number, from every nation, from all tribes and peoples and languages, standing before the throne and before the Lamb, clothed in white robes, with palm branches in their hands, (Revelation 7:9)

Throughout all three of these sections, Wolfe fails to even give passing mention to how Christ plays into any of these earthly obligations; he genuinely believes that the gospel does not alter certain aspects of the Christian's life. Appealing to an obligation towards *kin* or *homeland*, without, in every instance, purposefully filtering it through our primary obligation to Christ, is the very definition of *idolatry*, for it is serving the creature rather than the Creator (Romans 1:25). As Dietrich Bonhoeffer wrote in his seminal work, *The Cost of Discipleship*, "[Discipleship] is nothing else than bondage to Jesus Christ alone, completely breaking through every programme, every ideal, every set of laws. No other significance is possible, since Jesus is the only significance. Beside Jesus

---

201 Wolfe, 127–34.

nothing has any significance. He alone matters."[202] Again, that Wolfe has not yet even attempted to address the person of Jesus Christ, nor his teachings, within the context of his *Christian* political theory, is highly suspect. America has a long history of organizations and publications that promoted the "preservation" of what Wolfe has elsewhere called "Anglo Protestantism,"[203] but that rarely, if ever, actually mentioned the person and work of Christ. As an anonymous correspondent wrote to journalist Stanley Frost in the early 1920s, the Ku Klux Klan believed "that Protestantism as a religion must be made as militant as the Klan is in its political activities, and that it should appeal to all men who are teachable and aspiring, who measure themselves by ideals of loyalty."[204]

III. Nation

> I do not argue here for the sort of 19th-century nationalism that homogenized the socio-economic classes of peoples. My principal interest is a reinvigoration of a collective will that asserts and stands up for itself. Prerequisite to such a self-regard, at least today, is a conscious articulation or sense of one's people as distinguished from others.[205]

Much can be said about this section, wherein the ethno-state begins to be defined, but this is probably the best place to attempt to first answer the question, *How does Stephen Wolfe view his "people as distinguished from others"?*

On March 1, 2023, Jason Truett Glen, a professor of ethics at Liberty University, tweeted that Wolfe's "writings & social media posts have been

---

202 Dietrich Bonhoeffer, *The Cost of Discipleship*, 1st Paperback ed (New York: Macmillan, 1963), 63.
203 Stephen Wolfe on Twitter: "Anglo Protestantism is the US norm. Everything normalizes off of it or defines themselves against it." https://twitter.com/PerfInjust/status/1470203620796911616
204 Williams, *Shadow of the Pope*, 134.
205 Wolfe, *The Case for Christian Nationalism*, 135.

clear enough on his thoughts on interracial marriage" for him to be considered an ethnocentrist.[206] Wolfe responded to this tweet with:

> Maybe not [sic] believe every lie told about my "writings & social media posts". From CCN pg. 139.[207]

A picture from *The Case for Christian Nationalism*, provided by Wolfe in his tweet, contained a quote from the current section on nations:

> We should not, however, disregard the work of intermarriage over time in creating bonds of affection, as Aristotle argues.[208]

Conspicuously cropped from Wolfe's picture of the book is the immediately preceding sentence, on the same page, which would serve to significantly undermine his claim that Glen is lying about him.

> Blood relations matter for your ethnicity, because your kin have belonged to *this people* on *this land* – to this nation in this place – and so they bind you to that people and place, creating a common *volksgeist*.[209]

Also, as was earlier noted, Wolfe has publicly championed the limiting of intermarriage through social pressures. He could argue with Glen about the *severity* of his views on intermarriage, but he cannot argue that Glen was lying when he said Wolfe was "clear enough" on them that they can be legitimately seen as *ethnocentric*. Secondly, his use of *intermarriage* is nondescript in a practical context. For example, this section mentions that the Israelites and Moabites were *blood relations*, through Abraham; Wolfe

---

[206] https://twitter.com/TruettGlen/status/1630934100746948613
Jason Truett Glen: "John, I'm pretty sure you know enough people to suggest otherwise. Is the left attempting to capitalize on the fire in the house? Sure, but the fire is in our house. Stephen Wolfe's writings & social media posts have been clear enough on his thoughts on interracial marriage."
[207] https://twitter.com/PerfInjust/status/1630946183873978377
[208] Wolfe, *The Case for Christian Nationalism*, 139.
[209] Wolfe, 139.

also notes a lack of cultural ties to his "Italian, German, and English" ancestry, though he earlier described his ethnicity as rooted in "Western Europe."[210] Would Wolfe see an ethical or practical difference between Israelite marrying Moabite versus Israelite marrying Ethiopian, between German marrying Italian versus "Western European" American marrying African American? Though his book does not answer that question, as Glen correctly observed, his other public writings can help one make an educated guess.

The Anti-Defamation League defines 13/52 as:

> The number 13 used in conjunction with either the number 52 or the number 90 is a shorthand reference to racist propaganda claims by white supremacists against African Americans to depict them as savage and criminal in nature.
>
> In this numeric shorthand, the number 13 refers to the purported percentage of the U.S. population that is African American. The number 52 refers to the alleged percentage of all murders committed in the U.S. that are committed by African Americans. Some white supremacists use the number 50 instead of 52…
>
> White supremacists typically employ references to 13 (by itself), 13/50, 13/52 or 13/90 in response to social media posts, and in the comments sections of news stories about crimes in which the suspected perpetrator is African American. In some instances, white supremacists use the numbers as a purported police radio code, using language like, "We have a 1390 in progress."[211]

This very particular type of characterization of ethno-cultural enemies as predisposed to violent criminal behavior is nothing new in American Nativism. An anonymous leaflet (likely from the Klan) disseminated during the 1928 presidential election, where the Democrats ran the Catholic Governor of New York, Al Smith, contained the following:

---

210 Wolfe, 118–19, 136, 138.
211 https://www.adl.org/resources/hate-symbol/1352-1390

> In 90 per cent of the cases where criminals are executed for crimes committed, the victims of the execution have a priest at their elbow to administer the last sacrament.
>
> Over 65 per cent of the prison convicts of all grades and of all kinds of prisoners are Roman Catholics, while less than 5 per cent are graduates of our public schools.
>
> These statements are astounding when we remember that only about 12 1/2 per cent of the entire population of the United States are Roman Catholics, while the other 87 1/2 per cent are not.[212]

In March of 2022, Wolfe wrote an article for *IM—1776*, an online and print magazine that publishes some of the more academically-minded authors within the *anti-left* "meme war" movement,[213] entitled *Anarcho-Tyranny in 2022*.[214] Running the nationwide riots of the summer of 2020 through political theory from white nationalist author Sam Francis, he makes the claim that "the Regime uses disorder (anarchy) to terrorize its opponents and uses state power to protect the anarchical element and to crush any resistance to disorder (tyranny)."[215] As for whom they utilize for this anarchy, he writes:

---

212 Williams, *Shadow of the Pope*, 233–34.
213 I realize that "meme war movement" may be an insufficient description, but I believe it works better than "alt-right" or "MAGA", which has a myriad of connotations and could calumniate some of the authors. On the other hand, the magazine's website has several thumbnail images of Pepe frogs and a 2022 article entitled, The Power of Meme Magic.
214 Wolfe, "Anarcho-Tyranny in 2022."
215 Roberts, "On Thomas Achord."
Alastair Roberts's investigation into Wolfe's podcast co-host, Thomas Achord, and his anonymous Twitter and Facebook accounts revealed that they were "almost entirely followed by Achord's close friends," including Wolfe. On September 3, 2020, Achord tweeted, "Meanwhile the perpetrators of these crimes go undocumented, unrecognized, exonerated, justified, applauded. Anarchy for them. Tyranny for you. Don't rise up, white man. Keep your head down. That's the message."
https://twitter.com/TuliusAadland/status/1301493286373404673

3. Loving Your Nation

> In the United States, this anarchic element is composed largely of black Americans. For complex reasons, blacks in America, considered as a group, are reliable sources for criminality, and their criminality increases when constraints diminish. Despite being around **13% of the US population**, blacks have consistently committed **over 50% of the homicides** for decades, and it is getting worse. In 2020, according to the FBI stats, blacks committed nearly 57% of all known murders. (emphasis mine)

Later in the article, he states:

> There is more to the story of black criminality, but what is important here is that black Americans, considered as a group, are more willing to conduct certain types of public disorder (violence, petty theft, vandalism, looting, rioting, etc.) when constraints are reduced. For this reason, they serve as the anarchic element of anarcho-tyranny in the United States.

One would imagine that someone who has *socially acceptable* reasons for claiming that black Americans are "reliable sources for criminality" would be eager to share them, so as to dispel any notion of harboring unacceptable prejudices. Yet, at no point in the article does Wolfe attempt to explain how he came to this conclusion. When questioned about these comments on Twitter in November of 2022, he gave the following excuse across four terse tweets, posted within eight minutes of each other:

> Nothing I said can be logically construed to mean that any group is inherently more violent.
>
> The people I criticize in article [sic] are *white liberals*.
>
> The whole point is that white liberals exploit the factually obvious problems in black communities for their own purposes.
>
> You can find this in the work of Thomas Sowell.[216]

---

[216] https://twitter.com/PerfInjust/status/1587637263890014208

Wolfe is most likely referring to Sowell's essay, *Black Rednecks and White Liberals*, where the economist claims that "ghetto" behavior in black people is actually culturally appropriated from their former Celtic neighbors in the American South.[217] Therefore, it would seem that Wolfe believes the reason black people are "reliable sources for criminality" is that it has been ingrained in them culturally, over multiple generations. This means that it meets his definition of being an integral part of their *ethnicity*.

This article is not the only place where he has expressed the principles of 13/52. As mentioned before, Wolfe tweeted the following in July of 2021:

> Consider how absurd it is to elevate bl*ack men when they far exceed all non-bla*cks in just about every negative indicator, including in sex crimes. What is astonishing is that seemingly seriously people can't recognize how ridiculous they've become. The fact is that if there was serious racial oppression since the civil rights era, they have handled it very poorly. This is obvious if you get past the ideology. There is nothing heroic in it, given the level of violent crime and sexual assault (of underage girls).[218]

On December 8, 2020, the anonymous Twitter account Woke Preacher Clips, known mainly for highlighting the poor doctrine and political idolatry of theologically liberal pastors, shared a video of Reformed Seminary Chancellor Ligon Duncan saying, "It's gonna take us 100 years to overcome the trust issues...My very best black friends have trouble trusting me, for really good reasons. Because people like me have been doing awful things to them and to their families for four centuries."[219] Stephen Wolfe responded to Duncan's statement with:

> Just think about the principle at work & affirmed here. If one group disproportionately does awful things (say, violent crime and

---

217 Thomas Sowell, *Black Rednecks and White Liberals* (New York: Encounter Books, 2006).
218 https://twitter.com/PerfInjust/status/1420385874492203015
219 https://twitter.com/WokePreacherTV/status/1336343036926816257

property crime) to another group, then the victim group has "good reasons" to distrust all members of the offending group.[220]

Working this sentiment of 13/52 from Wolfe into his definition of nations, it is reasonable to infer that he considers white and black Americans to be distinct, ethnically disparate peoples. We can also reasonably infer that he would likely be indisposed to joining his family to a people whom he sees as having a higher group propensity for "violent crime and sexual assault (of underage girls)" than his own.

Moving to the specific content of this section of his book, Wolfe's assertions on ethnicity lead to several observances of note in regard to his views on the importance of both *genetic relations* and *mythologized history* in his ideal nation.

> My intent here is not to discount or dismiss the importance of blood ties in ethno-genesis – a dismissal that is fashionable, politically correct and could save me some trouble. It simply is the case that a "community of blood" is crucial to ethnicity. But this should not lead us to conclude that blood ties are the sole determinate of ethnicity, as if all we need are DNA tests.[221]

In the average ethno-nationalist state, being of the correct ethnicity is nothing more than a physical sign of one's citizenship, although, in more extreme states, there were degrees of bureaucratic access based upon how far back one could trace his ethnic purity. What is truly required of the status-minded citizen is his willingness to go along with state-sanctioned ideology, foundational to which is an official account of the nation's "heroic past, great men, [and] glory" that seeks to affirm that the "nation is a soul, a spiritual principle" (as Wolfe quotes from the 19th century, French philosopher and historian, Ernest Renan).[222] This mythologized history of

---

220 https://twitter.com/PerfInjust/status/1336689996330307587
221 Wolfe, *The Case for Christian Nationalism*, 140.
222 Wolfe, 140.

the nation serves as a point of personal identity and pride for true-believers in the state, men who often lack similar accomplishments of their own. As Priorelli writes, "Both [Italian and Spanish fascists] identified the nation as the instrument to rebuild people's identity. For them, it embodied the ideal weapon against the political, social, cultural and moral crisis caused by modernity, which liberal democracy, despite its best efforts, had failed to overcome." Italian fascist intellectuals saw the nation as having an "authentic spiritual dimension that went beyond liberal individualism."[223]

By quoting Renan, as with W.H. Fremantle, Wolfe is building his case for an ideologically homogeneous, Christian nation utilizing selected quotes from a heretic who, if he lived in Wolfe's ideal nation, would be crushed by the organs of the state. In 1862, Renan was elected to the chair of Hebrew studies at the Collège de France, but when his opening lecture was published it was revealed that he had referred to Jesus as "an incomparable man" and the founder of "the eternal religion of humanity, the religion of the spirit, disengaged from everything sacerdotal, from all rights and observances." Within days he was suspended from his post. In his official protest he wrote, "The supernatural has become a sort of original defect, of which one is ashamed; even the most religious want no more than a *minimum* of it; one seeks to make it play as small a part as possible; one hides it in the corners of the past." He then went on to write *Vie de Jésus* (Life of Jesus), a historical account which omitted all supernatural events.[224]

> Members of ethnic groups share similarities that are distinct to them. They possess similarities not only with regard to their common humanity but also in particulars. By "particulars," I refer to what one cannot ascribe to all mankind; or, to put it positively, it refers to features (e.g., culture) that can be ascribed only to *some* people…

---

223 Priorelli, *Italian Fascism and Spanish Falangism in Comparison*, 25, 56.
224 Wardman, Harold W., "Ernest Renan," in *Brittanica*, February 24, 2023, https://www.britannica.com/biography/Ernest-Renan; review of *Review of Vie de Jésus; The Life of Jesus, Ernest Renan*, by Ernest Renan et al., *The North American Review* 98, no. 202 (1864): 195–233.

> The human instinct to socialize and dwell with similar people is universal, though for many today, especially Westerners, this instinct is understood as evil or pathological.[225]

Socializing with others who like the same pastime as you, or who share similar cultural interests, is not considered evil or pathological in the West, nor is purposefully marrying someone who is *culturally, ideologically,* or *temperamentally* similar to you. Even the most dedicated critical theorist aims to socialize with people of similar disposition. Wolfe has overplayed his hand, because the only thing in this ethno-cultural vein that is considered taboo in Western culture is to purposefully seek to surround yourself with people of the same *"race."* One might argue that seeking similar *sexual ethics* has risen to that same level of taboo, but that has nothing to do with a pre-rational love for ethnic similarity. He has sunk his claim that ethnicity is as much cultural as it is genetic. He goes as far as to say that seeking this similarity is "universally good,"[226] in other words, that the gospel does not touch it. An attempt is made to obfuscate or ease this statement with, "The clearest example of this enablement is having a common language."[227] But seeking to order your everyday social relations along the lines of language is not at all considered "evil or pathological" in the West. He then moves to discussing the inverse urge.

> Exclusion follows not necessarily from maliciousness or from the absence of universal benevolence, but from a natural principle of difference that recognizes for oneself and for others the goods provided by similarity and solidarity in that similarity.[228]

This is a rephrasing of his earlier sentiment that "much good would result in the world if we all preferred our own and minded our own business,"[229] but we now have a much clearer idea of along what lines Wolfe sees these societal groupings. I am reminded of the many

---
225 Wolfe, *The Case for Christian Nationalism*, 141, 142.
226 Wolfe, 142.
227 Wolfe, 143.
228 Wolfe, 145.
229 Wolfe, 25.

documentaries and news specials I have watched over the years on white nationalist organizations, where an interviewed member inevitably says something to the effect of, "We don't hate other races, we just think everyone should stick to their own kind." Though Wolfe continues to pepper his description of ethnicity with references to "culture," to make it more palatable, from here on I will address the term from the conclusion that he is *primarily* concerned with *genetic similarity* and sees culture as downstream from that.

Wolfe then moves to a distinction between citizen and foreigner which, from the general standpoint of any sovereign nation, is ethically sound.[230] But, taking an already diverse nation and trying to form a new citizen/foreigner dichotomy along ethnic lines is anything but moral. He affirms his openness to this when he later states that he is "not saying that ethnic majorities today should work to rescind citizenship from ethnic minorities, though perhaps in some cases amicable ethnic separation along political lines is mutually desired."[231] This raises the immediate question of what those conditions would be, but he conspicuously makes no effort to elaborate on his statement. One wonders how he would accomplish *amicably* moving the millions of people not of his ethnicity who have lived in almost every region of the West for generations.

Nearly a page and a half towards the end of this section is given to a Rudyard Kipling poem on the citizen/foreigner distinction.[232] In and of itself, this is nothing of great note except that, almost 150 pages in, the book has not given so much as a paragraph to *Scripture*. This is doubly insulting to his Christian audience, because, immediately following the poem, Wolfe appeals to Aristotle's use of κοινωνία (koinōnia), to promote a *community* based on pre-rational preference for one's own ethnicity. This is the Greek word in the New Testament that is translated as *fellowship* and *communion*. That he would use it to justify the following statement to Christians is disturbing.

---

230 Wolfe, 145–47.
231 Wolfe, 147, 149.
232 Wolfe, 147–48.

> People of different ethnic groups can exercise respect for difference, conduct some routine business with each other, join in inter-ethnic alliances for mutual good and exercise common humanity… but **they cannot have a life together** that goes beyond mutual alliance. (emphasis mine)[233]

The absence of Christ from Wolfe's political worldview has been made painfully apparent through his description of the ethno-nation. In stark contrast stands the Christ-centered writing of Bonhoeffer, in the first chapter of his aptly titled book on deliberate Christian community, *Life Together*. It serves to remind the reader what *genuine Christian writing* on our interrelations looks like.

> Because Christ stands between me and an other, I must not long for unmediated community with that person. As only Christ was able to speak to me in such a way that I was helped, so others too can only be helped by Christ alone. However, this means that I must release others from all my attempts to control, coerce and dominate them with my love. In their freedom from me, other persons want to be loved for who they are, as those for whom Christ became a human being, died and rose again, as those for whom Christ won the forgiveness of sins and prepared eternal life.[234]

After examining such a displeasurable section of Wolfe's book, the Apostle John's use of κοινωνία stands out to me as the best rebuke:

> If we say we have fellowship (κοινωνίαν) with him while we walk in darkness, we lie and do not practice the truth. (1 John 1:6)

---

233 Wolfe, 149.
234 Dietrich Bonhoeffer, *Life Together* (Fortress Press, 2015), 17–18.

IV. Loving the Neighbor

> Christians will ask, "Aren't we called to love all equally?" assuming the affirmative answer is obvious.[235]

It is not that we are constantly called to love all equally, but that at any given moment we may be called to love someone fully, *as Christ loved us*, though that person may be unfamiliar to us, or even if he hates us.

> "You have heard that it was said, 'You shall love your neighbor and hate your enemy.' But I say to you, Love your enemies and pray for those who persecute you, so that you may be sons of your Father who is in heaven. For he makes his sun rise on the evil and on the good, and sends rain on the just and on the unjust. For if you love those who love you, what reward do you have? Do not even the tax collectors do the same? And if you greet only your brothers, what more are you doing than others? Do not even the Gentiles do the same? You therefore must be perfect, as your heavenly Father is perfect. (Matthew 5:43-48)

It is right that, after reading this, we should feel the bar is set higher than we can practically achieve, because this statement from Christ is not only to set an ideal behavior, but to remind us of the holiness of a perfect God and our inability to meet His standard by our own actions. *But the standard is still there*. Those who aim to follow Christ's example cannot purposefully attempt to shape their physical world into a configuration that would ease their responsibility in this regard. For "I have been crucified with Christ. It is no longer I who live, but Christ who lives in me" (Galatians 2:20).

> No one questions that we ought to love our own children over other children and our own family over other families and **our own church over churches**. (emphasis mine)[236]

---

235 Wolfe, *The Case for Christian Nationalism*, 149.
236 Wolfe, 150.

No one questions whether they are more duty-bound, under regular conditions, to materially provide for their own church more than others. Neither do they question whether they are called to share life more frequently, and with greater everyday intimacy, with their church more than others. Yet, Christ specifically prayed that all His disciples would share a *universal love* for each other, one that reaches beyond the bounds of familiarity.

> "I do not ask for these only, but also for those who will believe in me through their word, that they may all be one, just as you, Father, are in me, and I in you, that they also may be in us, so that the world may believe that you have sent me. The glory that you have given me I have given to them, that they may be one even as we are one, I in them and you in me, that they may become perfectly one, so that the world may know that you sent me and loved them even as you loved me. (John 17:20-23)

Would anyone be considered a true disciple of Christ if, after hearing of the immediate and severe needs of another church, he reserved his giving and personal sacrifices to save them for his own church, because he loves them more? Would he be truly following Christ if he held back some of his love and care for those people, because they "believe in the gift of tongues," "believe in apostolic succession," or even because they "believe in justification by works"? Christ challenges us to be *perfect in our love, just as our heavenly Father is perfect*. We will fail, but we cannot *accept failure* or, even worse, embrace it as a "universal good."

> As I argued above, a community of similar people provides the best social conditions for the communication of gifts and achieving collective goals. Dissimilar people together can achieve the basic goods of humanity, **but not the complete good**. (emphasis mine)[237]

---

[237] Wolfe, 151.

In sparkling clarity, Wolfe shows that he has his heart set on worldly things, in that he believes physical and ideological similarity is where "complete good" is found. In his view, can the missionary traveling in foreign lands, where Christ's name has yet to be spoken, find *complete good*? Can a person in Taliban-controlled Afghanistan who has discovered Christ through a Bible app on his phone, has given his life to Him, and now has to practice in secret or be shot, find *complete good*? Can our brothers and sisters in communist China, locked away in prison for proclaiming Christ, find *complete good*?[238] Complete good is in Jesus Christ alone and can be found by the disciple in any physical situation. Anyone who seeks to place another condition between the disciple and his complete good in Christ should be rejected outright.

Wolfe may protest that this is not the type of "complete good" he is referring to, but *physical comfort* and *familiar relations* are not what constitutes *complete good* to the disciple. It is when we are taken out of our comfortable, daily existence that Christ often uses us to share the gospel with those who do not know Him. We 21st-century Christians in the West have been born into a hostile mission field. As stated before, to retreat from it, to seek to exclude those who are belligerent towards us in order to preserve a sense of *personal peace* and *affluence*, is to abandon Christ's commandment of the Great Commission.

> The Christian tradition recognized three types of love: benevolence, beneficence, and complacence.[239]

Before examining Wolfe's description of these three loves it is worth pointing out that Scripture provides us a better understanding of differing types of love than "the Christian tradition." The following examples are only from the Gospel of Matthew, to provide extra clarity on how a single author viewed different loves (emphases mine).

---

238 Olivia Enos, "Chinese Christians Face Intensifying Persecution Ahead Of Christmas," Forbes, December 20, 2018, https://www.forbes.com/sites/oliviaenos/2018/12/20/chinese-christians-face-intensifying-persecution-ahead-of-christmas/.
239 Wolfe, *The Case for Christian Nationalism*, 151.

3. Loving Your Nation

- ἀγαπάω (agapaō), used 142 times in the New Testament.
  - But I say to you, *Love* your enemies and pray for those who persecute you, (Matthew 5:44)
  - And he said to him, "You shall *love* the Lord your God with all your heart and with all your soul and with all your mind. This is the great and first commandment. And a second is like it: You shall *love* your neighbor as yourself. (Matthew 22:37-39)
- φιλέω (phileō), used 25 times in the New Testament.
  - Whoever *loves* father or mother more than me is not worthy of me, and whoever *loves* son or daughter more than me is not worthy of me. (Matthew 10:37)
  - Now the betrayer had given them a sign, saying, "The one I will *kiss* is the man; seize him." (Matthew 26:48)

The more frequently used ἀγαπάω is closest to what Wolfe describes as *benevolence*, though it is greater and more pure than "love for all people simply on account of shared humanity."[240] It is the higher, sacrificial love of Christ, the ideal which we should aim to exhibit in our every interaction. Wolfe correctly links benevolence to a requirement of *self-love*, but, in his narrow focus on worldly benefit, he fails to mention the potential negatives of self-love that Christians must always be wary of. This pitfall of placing oneself or one's group above others, that Wolfe falls into through his promotion of *13/52*, is succinctly presented by Paul in the book of Romans:

> Do you suppose, O man – you who judge those who practice such things and yet do them yourself – that you will escape the judgment of God? (Romans 2:3)

What Wolfe goes on to describe as "complacent love" is closer to the common use of φιλέω, a *horizontal, brotherly love* based on personal experience with someone. Like his description of complacent love, φιλέω is the love the Father has for Jesus (John 5:20), but so is ἀγαπάω (John 3:35). While the former can meet the definition of *"a kind of self-love in*

---

240 Wolfe, 151.

which one delights in the totality of himself – a totality that extends to people and place,"[241] it can also describe the brotherly love that two men of completely different backgrounds share as *brothers in Christ*. As a Christian, I am not my (ethnic) relations, as Wolfe explicitly claims here.[242] The person who primarily saw himself along those lines died years ago, and was raised with Christ to be adopted into *His family*. My ethnic relations are now a wholly secondary, or even tertiary, aspect of my self-identification, which begins with Christ. Similarly, a Christian's "delight in [his] wife or children" also must first pass through his delight in Christ. To allow it to exist separately in the "background," as Wolfe argues for,[243] is to want to hold it apart from Christ, to be unwilling to sacrifice it for Him, turning it into an idol.

The same goes for the next section on "action and extending the self," which, like all appeals to *nation* yet in the book, has no phraseology or call-to-action that differs from the philosophy of early-20th-century authoritarian nationalists (whom Wolfe has requested we not compare him to). By themselves, these sorts of appeals may not seem disagreeable to the average, Reformed Christian reader, but to those who are studied in traditional fascist thought, the language and concepts conveyed by Wolfe are nearly identical to their century-old counterparts. As individual examples, these congruences do not point to a shared political theory, just as a single reference to "power dynamics" does not make someone a postmodernist. But, if a text continually refers to concepts such as "metanarratives," "hegemony," and "synthesis," the overarching, postmodern worldview of the author can be reasonably ascertained. There has yet to be a section of Wolfe's book, wherein he discusses his view of *nation*, that cannot be directly correlated to the political theory of Italian and Spanish fascists. In fact, his theory is *more ethnocentric* than theirs. The Falangists accounted for a wide genetic diversity among the citizens of the former Spanish empire, with the hope that they could be united under a

---

241 Wolfe, 155.
242 Wolfe, 156.
243 Wolfe, 157.

new *fascist* empire, through a shared cultural Catholicism originally spread by the Conquistadors and Jesuits.[244]

Wolfe continues to give a Falangista/Fascista-like spiritual dimension to *the fatherland* in this subsection when he writes, "We have intense connection with the land on which we and our natural relations have labored... Out of [interaction with this land], we come to a sense of ownership – of owned space – and come to see the objects of our activity as images of ourselves..."[245] Likewise, in a speech given in Madrid on May 19, 1935, Primo de Rivera said, "Property is the direct projection of man upon his goods; it is an elementary human attribute. Capitalism has been replacing this property of man by the property of capital, by the technical instrument of economic domination."[246] To criticize capitalism may seem like a major difference between Primo de Rivera and Wolfe, but what the former is describing is what 21st-century man would call *globalism*. In the epilogue of the book, Wolfe describes a "globalist American empire" which serves to "advance international liberalism" through an "allure of liberal decadence" and whose opponents are "marked for elimination."[247] The pattern is one and the same: the *man of the nation* who, along with his forefathers, has deposited his essence into the soil of the fatherland, faces the existential threat of bureaucratic, international elites.

Rightly anticipating the accusation of idolatry, Wolfe now moves to negate it, correctly stating that "the term is lazily deployed against those who love something 'too much.'"[248] This is why I have taken care to properly define idolatry as the desire to *worship creature rather than Creator*, to desire that one's affection for something need not first be

---

244 Priorelli, *Italian Fascism and Spanish Falangism in Comparison*, 144.
245 Wolfe, *The Case for Christian Nationalism*, 159.
246 Nick W. Sinan Greger, Jose Antonio Primo de Rivera: The Foundations of the Spanish Phalanx (o.A: Independently published, 2018), 62.
 Since this is the first time I have referenced this book, I should note that it is a self-published, pro-fascist biography of Primo de Rivera, and a collection of various quotes, organized by topic. Objective sources on the Falangist leader are practically impossible to acquire in English; most books on him are printed by openly white nationalist publishers. This volume's author bills himself as "Ambassador for the Arab & Muslim world of the Italian Fascist Party MFL-PSN."
247 Wolfe, *The Case for Christian Nationalism*, 440–41.
248 Wolfe, 161.

mitigated by one's affection for Christ. This is exactly what Wolfe's *pre-rational love* is, a "pre-reflective familiarity" that he claims is not a "product of the fall"[249] or altered by the gospel. Anything in the Christian's life not altered by the gospel of Jesus Christ is an idol, doubly so if he consciously advocates for such a distinction. As Bonhoeffer wrote during the height of European fascism:

> But since we are bound to abhor any deception which hides the truth from our sight, we must of necessity repudiate any direct relationship with the things of this world - and that for the sake of Christ. Wherever a group, be it large or small, prevents us from standing alone before Christ, wherever such a group raises a claim of immediacy it must be hated for the sake of Christ. For every immediacy, whether we realize it or not, means hatred of Christ, and this is especially true where such relationships claim the sanction of Christian principles.[250]

V. Nationalism

> Given its 20th-century manifestations, theorists in favor of nationalism have an uphill battle, often having to repeatedly and tiresomely disclaim and denounce any hint of "xenophobia" and "racism"...
>
> Though I favor [Yoram] Hazony's account over others, nationalism in this book follows conceptually from my account... I have no need to celebrate or defend or or denounce past "fascist" regimes or "populism" and other socio-political phenomena.[251]

Here are some of the claims Wolfe has made in the book, thus far, before he has even explicated the *specific policies* of his brand of nationalism:

---

249 Wolfe, 163.
250 Bonhoeffer, *The Cost of Discipleship*, 108.
251 Wolfe, *The Case for Christian Nationalism*, 163, 164.

- That his ideal government would, in a "totality of action," prioritize nation over individual.[252]
- That preferring to live with those genetically similar to oneself (and, downstream from that, culturally similar) is "natural and good," not "a product of the fall," and grace "affirms and completes it."[253]
- That "much good would result in the world if we all preferred our own."[254]
- That "Our time calls for a man who can wield formal civil power to great effect and shape the public imagination by means of charisma, gravitas, and personality."[255]
- That the Christian nationalist, who has received a "restored image" of the Creator, rightly interprets his natural purpose of "taking dominion."[256]
- That the "in-group/out-group distinction" is a prelapsarian good that "preserves cultural distinctives."[257]
- That "differences in food sources, climate, and other factors" produce on the macro, ethnic level a natural variance in which some people groups are objectively "more beautiful, and all ways better disposed."[258]
- That hierarchy is of inherently greater worth than egalitarian arrangements and, based on natural variances within humans, an aristocracy would arise in his nation.[259]
- That this natural aristocracy will need to weigh "unpleasant trade-offs" and have the "fortitude to enact and enforce the greatest good, despite unfortunate costs involved" by "shun[ning] the moralism that limits action."[260]

---

252 Wolfe, 13, 16.
253 Wolfe, 23, 117–18.
254 Wolfe, 25, 145.
255 Wolfe, 31.
256 Wolfe, 53, 113–14.
257 Wolfe, 65.
258 Wolfe, 67.
259 Wolfe, 68, 72–73.
260 Wolfe, 90.

- That the eternal and temporal kingdoms are separated so that the former (Christ's spiritual kingdom) is prevented from "subverting the natural order."[261]
- That "the Gospel does not alter the priority and inequality of loves" among one's genetic relations.[262]
- That "Western Man" faces a binary, existential crisis of *suicide* or *revitalization* (an idea he reiterates to close this chapter).[263]
- That a deliberate, focused affection and sentiment for ethnic relations and inter-generational property is a *universal, natural good* (though Christ directly commands us to make any such sentiment wholly secondary to Him).[264]
- That, though some intermarriage is acceptable, "blood-ties" are integral to "ethno-genesis," and "a 'community of blood' is crucial to ethnicity."[265]
- That the "nation is a soul, a spiritual principle," and the nationalist views the physical land of his nation as a projected *image of himself*.[266]
- That "the human instinct to socialize and dwell with similar people is universal, though for many today, especially Westerners, this instinct is understood as evil or pathological."[267]
- That "perhaps in some cases amicable ethnic separation along political lines is mutually desired."[268]

---

261 Wolfe, 107.
262 Wolfe, 101.
263 Wolfe, 118–19.
264 Wolfe, 125–26.
265 Wolfe, 139–40.
266 Wolfe, 140, 159.
267 Wolfe, 142.
 Using logical deduction, it was concluded that the only social taboo that qualifies for this statement is consciously working to surround oneself with members of the same "race." Wolfe's disagreement with the belief that such behavior is "evil or pathological" speaks volumes on his views of ethnicity, and is likely an unintended exposure of them.
268 Wolfe, 149.

3. Loving Your Nation

- That people of different ethnic groups, including ethnically differing Christians, "cannot have a life together that goes beyond mutual alliance."[269]
- That no people, including Christians, can find "complete good" outside of communities of similar ethnicity.[270]

One is left to wonder exactly why Wolfe is so averse to having his political theory compared to 20th-century fascism, given that his prima facie statements, viewed as a whole, paint a near-identical picture to that philosophy. His theory even contains an implicit claim of the ethnic superiority of at least one unnamed group, due to differences in food and climate, making him *more explicitly ethnocentric* than Spanish and Italian fascists. Someone who holds a doctorate in political theory, as he does, is most likely fully aware of these similarities – that he has at multiple times made a conscious effort to shield himself from such comparisons is strong circumstantial evidence to that end.

The remainder of this section serves as a summary and justification of his nationalist views, and is mostly not of great note when compared to these earlier statements, with the exception of two claims.

> But hospitality is subordinate to higher duties: **no individual**, family or nation is duty-bound to welcome strangers to the detriment of the good of those most near and bound it. (emphasis mine)[271]

Wolfe's hubris of placing appeals to "natural law" on par with (nonexistent) exegesis once again exposes him to a direct rebuke from our Lord, who said in the Sermon on the Mount, "And if anyone would sue you and take your tunic, let him have your cloak as well. And if anyone forces you to go one mile, go with him two miles. Give to the one who begs from you, and do not refuse the one who would borrow from you" (Matthew 5:40-42). There certainly could be a nuanced discussion on what would

---

269 Wolfe, 149.
270 Wolfe, 151.
271 Wolfe, 167.

constitute the *bounds of our duty*, but his claim that *no individual is duty-bound*, in this regard, is categorically false.

> Aquinas, following Aristotle, suggested that newcomers should not receive citizenship until the second or third generation of residence.[272]

This is not only a Thomasian and Aristotelian argument, but also a traditional Nativist one. As Ray Allen Billington writes of Nativist thought on immigration in 1850s America, "Propagandists who pointed out these supposed evils [brought to America by Catholic foreigners]... suggested... that laws of the various states be changed to limit voting to naturalized immigrants, rather than allowing any alien who had lived in the state for six months or a year to enjoy the privileges of the ballot box... countless other Americans were convinced that their nation would be saved only if voting were limited to naturalized citizens who had lived for twenty-one years in the United States and if all foreign-born were denied political office."[273] This *twenty-one year* rule later became an official policy position of the secretive Know-Nothing party. While the general topic of immigration and naturalization, and Wolfe's comment on it, are benign in and of themselves, it is again of note that the *overall picture* he is painting is in no way contradictory to the historical types of destructive, ethno-culturally obsessed nationalism he wishes us to not compare his theory to.

VI. Conclusion

Much can be said about the first paragraphs of Wolfe's conclusion on what constitutes *nation*, but one quote stands head and shoulders above the rest:

> The object of [Western man's] regard is the non-Westerner at the Westerner's expense – a bizarre self-denigration rooted in guilt and malaise. Loss and humiliation is the point, however. It is euphoric

---

272 Wolfe, 168.
273 Billington, *The Protestant Crusade,1800-1860*, 327.

3. Loving Your Nation

to him; his own degradation is thrilling. This is his **psycho-sexual etnho-masochism**, the most pernicious illness of the Western mind. (emphasis mine)[274]

There can be legitimate discussion about some of what he is first presenting here; there is definitely an aspect of "self-denigration" in the leftist American worldview, such as presented in books like Robin DiAngelo's *White Fragility*. But Wolfe takes this complaint to another level when he describes it as "psycho-sexual ethno-masochism." Stripped of its academic-linguistic obfuscation, what he is claiming is that Westerners gain a perverse, sexual gratification playing the cuckold to foreigners.[275] That he would make such a statement in his book and then attempt to later claim, on Twitter, that his views on ethnicity discussed in the current chapter are "following a much older nationalist tradition," and are not synonymous with contemporary connotations of "race," is patently ridiculous.[276]

I challenge the reader to take this section as a whole, replace "Western man" with "white man," and see if there is any ideological difference between what Wolfe promotes and the ideas that one would expect to hear in a speech from a local Exalted Cyclops at an average Klan meeting. They certainly do not correlate if you change "Western" to "black" or "latino." Wolfe has even admitted, in now-deleted posts on Twitter, that black Westerners do not fall under this rubric.[277]

---

274 Wolfe, *The Case for Christian Nationalism*, 169.
275 Wolfe has accused Joel Berry, a writer for the Babylon Bee, of harboring this sentiment, because he pointed out that Western Civilization began in the Mediterranean and not Northern Europe.
https://twitter.com/PerfInjust/status/1619391549888135169
Joel Berry: "Western Civilization was invented by the Greeks and Jews while white Europeans were still naked savages dancing around campfires."
Stephen Wolfe: "Joel is enjoying the euphoric high of ethno-masochism."
276 https://twitter.com/PerfInjust/status/1581986035919360000
Stephen Wolfe: "Since some people are asking and subtweeting, I discuss 'ethnicity' in Ch. 3 of my book (and I distinguish it from 'race', following a much older nationalist tradition). Most of your questions are answered there (the chapter is over fifty pages long)."
277 https://web.archive.org/web/20220209153748/https://twitter.com/PerfInjust/status/1491434865421524993

Thus, Western (white) man, whose birthrates have plummeted, creates well-ordered spaces and civil institutions not for himself and his natural progeny but for his replacements.[278]

Repeatedly, in the face of ethnic identity politics, we see Western (white) man retreating to this universality – to the universal values of the Declaration of Independence, for example – not realizing that those values come from the collective experience of a cluster of European nations.[279]

Most left-wing social movements exploit Western universality and Western (white) guilt, leveraging the bizarre tendency of Western (white) man to out-group himself.[280]

You would think that Western (white) man would come to his senses. But universality is so ingrained in him and is so strongly enforced that he psychologically cannot reject it, even in the face of its absurdity.[281]

Western (white) man blames himself; he reaffirms the promise; he offers restitution or reparation at his own expense; he receives more immigration;[282]

The Western (white) mind needs to be critiqued in order to free it from exploitation and self-disparagement… Indeed, you must critique and deliberately decline to act on certain mental habits

---

Joshua (Bread of Life Eater): "A Lutheran Facebook group is having 'interracial marriage' discourse because some other Facebook page posted 'arguments' for it and I can't help but be reminded that 'we need to find biblical evidence for this or else its wrong' seems like a very Calvinist way of thinking anyway."
Stephen Wolfe: "Seems to be a very common and open discussion among black people."
Joshua (Bread of Life Eater): "Where that does happen is due to multiple factors ranging from sociology, nationalism, and racism, not Scriptural debate."
Stephen Wolfe: "So you agree that black people often discuss whether interracial marriage is right or wrong?"

278 Wolfe, *The Case for Christian Nationalism*, 169.
279 Wolfe, 170.
280 Wolfe, 170.
281 Wolfe, 170.
282 Wolfe, 170.

designed to extinguish this discomfort, such as accusations... like "racist" or "fascist" or "xenophobe";²⁸³

That is, we tend to impute Western (white) altruism to all people, concluding that their first love is humanity, not their ethnicity.²⁸⁴

Again, would it make sense to say that "left-wing social movements" exploit Western *Latino* guilt? Would it make sense to say that a Western *Asian* man blames himself for not perpetuating affirming ethnic universality, resulting in him offering "reparation at his own expense"? Does a Western *black* man have to free his mind from accusations like "racist" or "fascist" because he critiques appeals to ethnic universality, such as the Declaration of Independence? These statements only make sense from a perspective of *antagonistic white ethnocentrism*.

Further evidence is that, in a review of Jake Meador's book, *What are Christians For?*, Wolfe discussed one of the above points in an explicitly white context, writing, "Meador – a white male – can 'prove' his assertions only by out-grouping himself and by speaking ill of his civilization," and, "The only way for white people to contribute to Protestant 'social doctrine' is by out-grouping themselves in order to offer credible assertions."²⁸⁵ One can reasonably conclude that Wolfe's *Western Man* is primarily a stand-in for *white man*.

On November 27, 2022, Alastair Roberts (whom Wolfe mentions earlier in this chapter²⁸⁶), a teaching fellow at the conservative Christian Davenant Institute, published an exposé on Wolfe's podcast co-host, Thomas Achord.²⁸⁷ In the article, published several days after he made a public

---

283 Wolfe, 170.
284 Wolfe, 171.
285 Stephen Wolfe, "An Unhelpful Review of 'What Are Christians For?' By Jake Meador," Sovereign Nations (blog), March 2, 2022, https://sovereignnations.com/2022/03/02/unhelpful-review-what-are-christians-for/.
286 Wolfe, *The Case for Christian Nationalism*, 166.
287 Roberts, "On Thomas Achord."

accusation, Roberts conclusively proved that Achord had long kept anonymous "alt" accounts on both Twitter and Facebook, where he regularly expressed explicitly white nationalist sentiment, including:

- Calling Congresswoman Cori Bush the female derivative of the n-word.[288]
- Claiming that all Antifa are Jews.[289]
- Promoting "a robust race realist white nationalism" as a counter to wokeism.[290]
- Writing that the takeaway from the same type of "Anarcho-Tyranny" that Wolfe discussed in his article for *IM—1776* was, "Don't rise up, white man. Keep your head down. That's the message."[291]

Though Achord initially denied that the account was his, he later admitted to being the account holder in a since deleted blog post, where he said he had "trouble recollecting tweets (and the entire account)" and that it was the product of a "period of [his] life [that] was a spiritually dark time marked by pessimism and anger and strained relationships."[292] One

---

288 https://twitter.com/TuliusAadland/status/1431209937477189636
Tulius Aadland (Thomas Achord): "Ngress squaring on lawn, demands money and power"

289 https://twitter.com/TuliusAadland/status/1301657368359510016
Tulius Aadland: "What a coincidence that a random shooting of Antifa members hit 100% jews and 100% pedos!"
https://twitter.com/TuliusAadland/status/1269747784728686598
Tulius Aadland: "Jews admit they are behind Antifa."

290 https://twitter.com/TuliusAadland/status/1269689804486254592
Tulius Aadland: "Anyway, a robust race realist white nationalism can be antifragile regarding cultural Marxism, critical race theory, wokism, BLM, etc. by accepting their premises of standpoint epistemology, systemic racism, white privilege etc."

291 https://twitter.com/TuliusAadland/status/1301493286373404673
Tulius Aadland: "Meanwhile the perpetrators of these crimes go undocumented, unrecognized, exonerated, justified, applauded. Anarchy for them. Tyranny for you. Don't rise up, white man. Keep your head down. That's the message."

292 Thomas Achord, "Thomas Achord Admits to Being Tulius Aadland in a since Deleted Medium Post," *Medium* (blog), November 28, 2022, https://web.archive.org/web/20221128221320/https://medium.com/@thomasachord/from-the-start-of-this-controversy-i-have-tried-to-find-the-truth-of-the-matter-and-i-have-an-e18b7e6f560e.

wonders how someone has "trouble recollecting" regularly posting racist tweets on an anonymous account only a year prior. Before Roberts posted his evidence and Achord made his admission, Wolfe claimed in a lengthy Twitter thread that Roberts, out of his "obsession with [him]," and "with total disregard for anyone but his tribe," "unleashed the twitter animals on [his friend] right before Thanksgiving."[293]

Roberts's investigation revealed that the anonymous "Tulius Aadland" accounts on both Twitter and Facebook had roughly thirty followers each, mostly people whom Achord was personally acquainted with – all but two of the Facebook account's twenty-seven followers were in Achord's friend list on his public account. The small list of followers of the accounts, on both Twitter and Facebook *included Wolfe*. The most reasonable conclusion to draw from this is that Achord told his personal acquaintances to follow these anonymous accounts, likely with the expressed intent to post things he wouldn't say on his public account, and Wolfe did so.

Wolfe engaged with the Aadland accounts at least once, liking a tweet that read, "I'm back on this account just to meme."[294] A meme posted on the account just a day later (and two years before Wolfe's book was published) is a picture of an attractive white woman in a sun dress holding a baby, with a caption nearly identical to the question Wolfe asked in the beginning of this chapter, "Which way, Western Woman?"[295] The book *Which Way Western Man?* was written by a white nationalist author, William Gayley Simpson, in 1978. Its last official printing was in 2003 by National Vanguard Books, the publishing arm of the white supremacist organization National Alliance. The phrase has become moderately popular in right-wing memes, used in a similar, dichotomous vein to the far more common *Reject Modernity, Embrace Tradition*, a consistent, though unwritten, theme of the "Tulius Aadland" Twitter account, which often

---

293 https://twitter.com/PerfInjust/status/1596176463589433345
  Stephen Wolfe: "Alastair's obsession with me has led him to this. After failing to find evidence that I'm a secret racist, he allegedly doxxed my friend & unleashed the twitter animals on him right before Thanksgiving. Why? for no reason but to discredit me. He destroyed a guy to get at me."
294 https://twitter.com/TuliusAadland/status/1333243359004127232
295 https://twitter.com/TuliusAadland/status/1333618307195432961

shared images highlighting traditional aesthetics. Perhaps this history of the phrase explains why, in a footnote to that question, Wolfe went out of his way to contend that his was "not a 'white nationalist' argument" before continuing to use *Western Man* as this chapter's protagonist.[296] It beggars belief, when a Google search shows the clear origin of the phrase (as does the *knowyourmeme* page[297]), that he benignly chose it as the call-to-action for his chapter on the nation's "ethno-genesis", and as an expression of a central theme of his theory.

Despite the evidence, and after Achord admitted to being the account holder, Wolfe claimed that he did not remember seeing these posts, that he did not know it was Achord's account, nor did Achord ever confirm to him that it was his.[298] The day after Roberts published his evidence, Douglas Wilson, the pastor behind Canon Press, who published *The Case for Christian Nationalism*, ran cover for Wolfe in a blog post sardonically titled, *My Part in a Delightful Little Proxy Row*, where he chose to focus on Roberts's probable motive to impugn Wolfe, whose book had just been published, more than Achord.[299] To my knowledge, he has yet to address any of the actual evidence that Wolfe likely knew the account was his co-host's. On March 1, 2023, Wolfe announced on Twitter that their podcast, *Ars Politica*, would be returning.[300] Since restarting, the podcast has only been hosted by Wolfe.

---

296 Wolfe, *The Case for Christian Nationalism*, 119.
297 "Which Way, Western Man?," Know Your Meme, August 13, 2021, https://knowyourmeme.com/memes/which-way-western-man.
From the website: "Which Way, Western Man?, also misquoted Which Way, White Man?, is a catchphrase originating from the name of a 1978 book by white nationalist author William Gayley Simpson."
298 https://twitter.com/PerfInjust/status/1597351612816953344
Stephen Wolfe: "I do not recall seeing any of these tweets now made public, and I now know that he regularly changed his twitter name. He at no time confirmed to me that it was his account, and it took me a while to suspect that it was his. I knew Thomas Achord, not the pseudonym Tulius Aadland."
299 Douglas Wilson, "My Part in a Delightful Little Proxy Row," *Blog & Mablog* (blog), November 28, 2022, https://dougwils.com/books-and-culture/s7-engaging-the-culture/my-part-in-a-delightful-little-proxy-war.html.
300 https://twitter.com/PerfInjust/status/1631043873576300544
Stephen Wolfe: "returning next week…"

3. Loving Your Nation

I see no core ideological disagreements between what Wolfe promotes in his book, on social media, and through his articles and the thoughts presented by his podcast co-host on his anonymous Twitter and Facebook accounts. Wolfe publicly disavowed Achord's racism after he admitted to it, but the *philosophy of nation* presented in his book would in no way disagree with or be considered too light-handed in the worldview of "Tulius Aadland." Wolfe is more reserved and coded in his language, but so was Thomas Achord in his public discourse. Two steps forward into a "community of blood" and one step back towards "culture" still ultimately leads to the ethno-state.

4. Perfecting Your Nation

I. The Christian Nation

The chapter in which the distinguishing attributes of a Christian nation are described begins with a quote from the 18th-century German philosopher and theologian Johann Herder: "The Christian religion was only ever able and meant to permeate everything."[301] Considering that Wolfe has thus far made repeated references to a myriad of behaviors that the "gospel does not alter," he should learn from Herder's instruction.

> The Christian nation is a species of nation, meaning that the "Christian" qualification does not destroy, eliminate, or **preclude** the features of the nation described in the previous chapter. (emphasis mine)[302]

Wolfe's order of operations is again laid out through this statement; his "Christian Nationalism" is *nation* first and *Christian* second. If his perspective was properly *Christ first*, he would know that his utter dependence on the Son of God would have the potential to preclude anything, especially civil organizations. We are again presented with the necessary conclusion that Wolfe is proposing something better described as *Nationalist Christianity*.

> A Christian nation... has been ordered to heavenly life in Christ, having been perfected by Christian revelation as **grace perfects nature, without undermining that particularity** but rather strengthening it so that the people might achieve the complete good. (emphasis mine)[303]

Again, grace does not perfect an already properly functioning nature, one that simply needs a touch-up; it *repairs a broken nature* where the

---

301 Wolfe, *The Case for Christian Nationalism*, 173.
302 Wolfe, 173.
303 Wolfe, 174.

reprobate are *slaves of sin*. As a *slave of God*, I want His grace to fully "undermine" every particularity from my former, sinful existence:

> For when you were slaves of sin, you were free in regard to righteousness. But what fruit were you getting at that time from the things of which you are now ashamed? For the end of those things is death. But now that you have been set free from sin and have become slaves of God, the fruit you get leads to sanctification and its end, eternal life. For the wages of sin is death, but the free gift of God is eternal life in Christ Jesus our Lord. (Romans 6:20-23)

Wolfe's continual reference to a grace that *improves* and *perfects* nature, when it even has the ability to alter nature *at all*, reads as Semi-Pelagianism – the belief that sin is a corrupting force that requires grace in order to be *fully* conquered, but that the power of one's individual will is enough to take the initiative to repair it. Given the frequency at which this belief has been repeated, and that Wolfe has described his theory as built upon the work of Thomas Aquinas, it can be reasonably concluded that the Catholic theologian is the source of these views. Aquinas believed that, though the good of "original justice" was destroyed by sin, our "natural inclination to virtue is only "diminished by sin," and the "good of nature is neither destroyed nor diminished by sin."[304] Wolfe's Thomasian view is at direct odds with his own church's confessional document, the *Westminster Confession of Faith*, and the common understanding of sin among most Reformed Protestants.

Wolfe then goes on to reiterate that the redeemed "possess all the native gifts once given to Adam," "they can achieve all that Adam was commanded to do with those gifts," and are "complete in dignity."[305] Do you, Christian, when on your knees in a private room of your house, asking the Father's forgiveness for yet another sin you have committed, feel as if you are "complete in dignity"? Though we have been justified through Christ's finished work on the cross, and though He is sanctifying us

---

304 Thomas Aquinas, Summa Theologica, I-II Q. 85.
305 Wolfe, *The Case for Christian Nationalism*, 174.

through the Spirit, unlike Adam before the fall, we are still corrupted by sin and will not be *complete* until the resurrection. It is true, as Wolfe states, that Christians can "relate to each other as fellow human beings *and* as God's children," but we fail to achieve this as much, if not more, than we succeed. No explicitly Christian country has ever been "the nation perfected," as he next claims; in their zealousness, many have descended into atrocity. That should be the prevailing caution of anyone attempting to order a nation "to heavenly life."

The remainder of the subsection is an explanation of how his Christian nation does not undermine the *pre-rational love* described in the preceding chapter. The nation receives an "infusion of Christianity" in a way that makes identity in the religion synonymous with citizenship.[306] This character of Wolfe's nation is inline with what was discussed in the last chapter about status in the totalitarian state being tied to public championing of official state ideology. Wolfe then correctly notes that modern Christian nations are not neo-Israels, bound by the same covenant, and then posits that the "complete Christian nation comes into being *synergistically*" when it explicitly names itself as Christian. He incorrectly states this as a prerequisite for the nation to "look upon national prosperity as a divine blessing and national troubles as divine displeasure."[307] God blesses and curses all nations as he pleases (Job 12:23), therefore an *implicitly* Christian nation (one that has an overwhelming plurality of Christians, but no state church) can also rightfully look at its condition in the same way.

> Likewise, the people may look upon the architects of these laws [of an explicitly Christian nation] as great men, **inspired by God** as instruments of God's will for his people's good. (emphasis mine)[308]

This is very dangerous ground to tread, from both a theological and political perspective. Firstly, to what degree would Wolfe say that these

---
306 Wolfe, 175–76.
307 Wolfe, 177.
308 Wolfe, 178.

hypothetical men are *inspired by God*? Secondly, how can he be sure they are inspired by God, when the principles of this nation are found almost entirely in *natural law*? Thirdly, to what degree are we to revere these men? Will monuments be built for them and be considered sacred national ground? If so, and these men are considered inspired, would that be any different than erecting a statue of a saint? This may seem ridiculous to an American reader, but think about how many autocratic nations deify their leaders. Is it out of the question to imagine portraits of the *Christian Prince* on the side of public buildings, hung in every classroom, and marched around during parades? This sort of cult of personality starts with claiming your founding politicians are "inspired by God."

> The place of a Christian people is a Christian land... Being a place of their activity and of their ancestors, this land is *their* Christian country, their Christian homeland. Their Christian ancestry speaks through it, as a mode of discipleship in Christian faith and life, and only they can hear it. Their Christian homeland is not suitable for all Christians, let alone all mankind.[309]

In the early 1830s, a reportedly "escaped nun" from the Ursuline Convent in Charlestown, Massachusetts, Rebecca Theresa Reed, began publicly sharing dark tales of her supposed convent life. These calumnious stories of concubine nuns, in which they were the sexual playthings of lecherous priests, and where the offspring of their liaisons were born, baptized, and immediately murdered, were commonplace among Nativist tracts, most famously in 1835's *The Awful Disclosures of Maria Monk*. Primed by Reed's stories, the mostly Protestant citizens of Charlestown concluded the worst when, on July 28, 1834, a nun from the convent, Elizabeth Harrison, had a mental breakdown and ran to the home of one of her students, seeking refuge. After regaining her senses, she returned to the convent several days later.

Rumors quickly spread all over the Boston area. It was "generally believed that she had been forced to return and had been cast into a deep

---

309 Wolfe, 179.

dungeon in the cellars of the convent building as punishment."[310] Boston newspapers, such as the *Mercantile Journal, Morning Post,* and the *Commercial Gazette,* printed a false claim that Harrison's friends were unable to find her when calling on her at the convent.[311] On August 9, spurred on by the citizens of Charlestown, leaders of the city visited the convent building and found Harrison in sound mind and good physical condition. Edward Cutter, the father of the student she had sought refuge with, was with the group and "satisfied himself that she was contended with the lot and not languishing in a hidden dungeon."[312]

Despite this, a Congregationalist divine, the Reverend Lyman Beecher, sought to whip the citizens of Boston into an anti-Catholic frenzy, giving three sermons at three different churches on the night of August 10, "exhorting overflowing audiences to action against Popery."[313] It was not uncommon in those days for Protestant ministers to earn a side-income through verbal and print exhortation of "No-Popery." Beecher is considered the main ideological instigator of what happened the next night. Historian Ray Allen Billington's description of the event is worth quoting at length:

> A mob had begun to gather in the school grounds at nine o'clock on the night of August 11, carrying banners and shouting "No Popery" and "Down with the Cross." One Charlestown selectman was present and others were notified but they insisted that the town's one police officer could handle the situation adequately. While the crowd was milling about, a group of forty or fifty men, evidently well organized and more or less disguised, approached the building and demanded that they be shown the nun who was secreted there. They were told to return the next day when the children would not be awakened and retired, seemingly satisfied. But at eleven o'clock a pile of tar barrels was lighted in a neighboring field, evidently a pre-arranged signal. Fire bells were set ringing and crowds of people began pouring into Charlestown. Fire companies appeared but stood helplessly by as the mob began

---
310 Billington, *The Protestant Crusade,1800-1860*, 72.
311 Billington, 72.
312 Billington, 74.
313 Billington, 72–73; Williams, *Shadow of the Pope*, 65.

the attack. The Mother Superior vainly tried to appeal to the throng, first by pleading, then by threatening that "the Bishop has twenty thousand Irishmen at his command in Boston." This only infuriated the crowd. Led by the same forty or fifty organized men who had been active from the first, they burst open the doors and entered the convent building as the dozen sisters present hurried the sixty pupils through a rear door and to a nearby place of refuge. At a little after midnight the torch was applied to both the school and a neighboring farmhouse belonging to the Ursulines. The large crowd stood by until both buildings were consumed by the flames.[314]

We are the same fallen people the Protestant citizens of Boston were in 1834. They believed that they lived in an explicitly Christian nation, and that the Irish Catholics who had emigrated were a foreign horde, bringing the scourge of "Roman Popery." Well into the 20th century, it was common among Protestants to believe that the Pope was the beast of Revelation. The people who burned down the Ursuline convent school, including the fifty disguised vigilantes, likely believed they were doing what God would want them to, that they were protecting the *true religion* and the *state sanctioned church*. They likely believed that Boston was "a place of their activity and of their ancestors," that Massachusetts was "their Christian country," and that their "Christian homeland [was] not suitable for all Christians," as Wolfe writes.

This would not have been an unreasonable estimation. As journalist Michael Williams wrote of the anti-Catholic interpretation of Massachusetts civil law regarding religion at the time, "In 1800 the Rev. Mr. Cheverus, later to become the first Bishop of Boston, had married two Catholics in Maine, then a part of the state of Massachusetts. Father Cheverus was arraigned and prosecuted for violation of the law on the charge that he was not a 'settled minister' of the state… The judges were divided as to his guilt, and the criminal prosecution collapsed."[315] This indecent happened nine years after the Bill of Rights was ratified, yet the

---

314 Billington, *The Protestant Crusade,1800-1860*, 74–75.
315 Williams, *Shadow of the Pope*, 56–57.

judges were still divided. Can it be truly believed that a nation built upon Wolfe's theory, thus far, would not easily fall into the same excesses? He will argue for the goodness of such theocratic states in the early American republic in chapter 10.

On January 25, 2023, Neil Shenvi tweeted, "Today, my timeline was filled with 'Christian nationalists' who think Hindu temples should be illegal (not sure how they feel about mosques/synagogues/Catholic churches)." A former Trump administration deputy secretary, now a Southern Baptist Theological Seminary student and vocal proponent of Christian Nationalism, William Wolfe (no relation), wrote, "This is bait. Don't take it. He is setting up a motte and bailey." Shenvi replied, "No, it's not a motte-and-Bailey. [Christian Nationalists] need to decide what limiting principle (if any) would permit non-Christian religious expression. This is clearly an open question for lots of Christian Nationalists." William Wolfe went on to deflect from the topic of self-described Christian Nationalists promoting hard-line enforcement of the First Table of the Ten Commandments (shutting down Hindu temples for promoting a false religion), by appealing to Second Table violations, writing, "No, it is, because there are plenty of limiting principles in place now. Satanists can't perform child sacrifice. Mormons can't practice polygamy. You are repackaging an entirely mundane and ongoing question – the limits of religious liberty – into a scary-sounding talking point."[316] William Wolfe has since deleted the tweets.

II. Christian Nationalism

Wolfe repeats his order of operations of "nation, nationalism, and the Christian nation," then restates his definition of *Christian nationalism* from the introduction:

> Christian nationalism is a totality of national action, consisting of civil laws and social customs conducted by a Christian nation as a

---

[316] https://web.archive.org/web/20230208134949/https://twitter.com/William_E_Wolfe/status/1618369643466612736

Christian nation, in order to procure for itself both earthly and heavenly good in Christ.[317]

Given all that we have learned about Wolfe's views on the fall and generic nationalism, I propose an alternate definition:

> Christian Nationalism is a totalitarian political ideology, based upon a faulty understanding of prelapsarian man and the nature of sin, which seeks to create a "Christian" nation that is genetically and ideologically near-homogeneous, and looks to procure, by the exclusion of other peoples through the process of "taking dominion," what it perceives as the earthly and heavenly "complete good."

Wolfe correctly states a key component of orthodox *Two-Kingdoms Theology*, that "Civil power cannot legislate or coerce people into belief." He then goes on to express another belief of Calvin, that the civil authorities are responsible for the "suppression of public blasphemy, heresy, and impious profanation" and "obligating Sabbath observance."[318] When Wolfe goes into detail in chapter 7, I will contend that such action is precluded by the New Covenant. This will not only put me at odds with him, but with many theonomists as well. I am confident that my Scriptural reference of New Testament commandments that negate Old Covenant enforcement of the First Table, as well as its application within the realm of *natural law*, will force both groups to at least admit that the issue is not as black-and-white as they would have us believe. I will also show that any attempt to enforce blasphemy law in the 21st-century West would likely result in crimes against humanity.

The faulty claim that a "supernatural application can follow from a natural principle" is repeated and affirmed as "crucial for [his] argument."[319] As mentioned earlier, this belief fails to account for the sovereignty of God, rendering the statement worthless. Supernatural

---

317 Wolfe, *The Case for Christian Nationalism*, 180–81.
318 Wolfe, 182.
319 Wolfe, 183, 185.

application *can* follow from a natural principle, but it can just as easily follow from working *against nature*. God decides when supernatural application happens, not us. Believing that certain behaviors result in supernatural application is no different than a charismatic Christian believing they can prophesy on demand. Wolfe uses his rule to state the following:

> (1) Civil government ought to direct its people to the true religion.
> (2) The Christian religion is the true religion.
> Therefore, (3) civil government ought to direct its people to the Christian religion.[320]

There is a giant hole is Wolfe's logic, in that he has provided no empirical evidence that the first item is true – his later arguments for this point assume the conclusion that the only beneficial role of civil government is to proactively direct man to the *highest good*, through a false dichotomy that contains no room for a *neutral* position. These types of *either/or* dilemmas are a common trope of authoritarian political theory. For example, *suicide or revitalization* leaves no room for the legitimate, third option of thoughtful moderation and skepticism towards both extremes (Matthew 5:9, James 4:1-3).

After listing these points, and seemingly recognizing that he has put forth something akin to a categorical imperative with the first one, Wolfe immediately attempts to obfuscate it with a sidebar appeal to special revelation. Christians may want the first item, on the directive role of government, to be true – depending on how it is accomplished, I might like it to be true – but it is not necessarily *objectively* true for civil governments that are not explicitly Christian, but that are still ordained by God. It also may not be beneficial or even God's will, in general. The only way we could know for certain would be to reference it from Scripture, not our fallible interpretation of "natural principles." We cannot appeal to Mosaic law, because Israel served a specific, priestly function. One might appeal to the several times Nebuchadnezzar recognized Yahweh in the book of

---

320 Wolfe, 183.

Daniel or the king of Nineveh leading his nation to repentance (Jonah 3:5-9), but neither actually directed their people to the true religion; they only acknowledged the sovereignty of God and did not explicitly enforce the First Commandment (Daniel 6:25-28). There are many verses about the good of a king, or a people as a whole, *orienting themselves* towards God (Proverbs 25:2, Psalm 47:1), and of the government not *suppressing* the true religion (Romans 13:1-4), but these are different than the government *actively directing* its people to the true religion. I am not arguing that it is impossible for a Christian nation to direct its people towards the true religion in a beneficial manner, but that action is not a *self-apparent natural principle*. Also, through Romans 13, Scripture affirms that God may ordain leaders who do not take such actions, but who let people openly practice their religion in peace. The Reformed exegetical tradition of the 16th century overwhelmingly affirms that He may ordain tyrannical governments as well, something that will be addressed in the chapter on revolution.

Freedom of religion is not only an Enlightenment value, but was also the mode of government under the first Christian Roman emperor, Constantine. In the *Edict of Milan*, given a year after his conversion to Christianity, he set the bounds of religious direction in the empire, as required of the imperial governors:

> We thought it our duty to express this to thy Lordship in the plainest terms, so that thou knowest we give to the afore said Christians free and unlimited permission to practice their religion. Thy Lordship understands, that for the tranquility of our times the same freedom as to religion and observance is likewise expressly and liberally granted to others, so that every one may enjoy the fullest permission to worship what he chooses.[321]

Constantine believed the result of a government promoting such peaceful plurality would be God dispensing His "divine favor towards us, which... we have experienced on the most momentous occasions, [and]

---

[321] Francis S. Betten, "The Milan Decree of A. D. 313: Translation and Comment," *The Catholic Historical Review* 8, no. 2 (1922): 191–97.

will forever prosper our future enterprises and the happiness of our people." Certainly, many of America's material blessings in the 19th and 20th century were the direct result of its welcoming attitude towards immigrants seeking religious freedom, fueling the industrial revolution. Much of what we see now in the sharp decline in that prosperity is from the institutionalization of a domineering, state-promoted religion of ἔρως (erōs[322]) that is explicitly antagonistic towards orthodox Christianity. The answer to this problem is not for Christians to lower themselves to their postmodern adversary's game of power-dynamics, seeking to wrest control and impress our own First Table dogma on them and prosecute wrongthink, but to affirm the mode of Second Table enforcement laid out in Romans 13, social mores that a significant portion of non-Christian Americans agree with. That can be done without compromising on any of the current pre-political positions of conservative, American Christians, such as our pro-life stance, because they all concern Second Table violations.

It may surprise many Reformed readers to learn that most of Calvin's reasoning for First Table enforcement also came from his interpretation of natural law, as opposed to Scripture. Its attempted justification in the *Institutes* begins with an admission that Scripture does not teach enforcement of both tables, followed by an appeal to tradition logical fallacy, through a consensus of "profane [pagan] writers," before turning to references from Scripture that are more about maintaining Second Table order.[323]

> The Christian nation is not the spiritual kingdom of Christ or the immanentized eschaton;[324]

---

[322] ἔρως, unlike ἀγαπάω and φιλέω, is a lustful love, from which we get the word *erotic*. In 1953, the German postmodernist, Herbert Marcuse, published *Eros and Civilization*, in which he argued that a sexually unbridled society (including pederasty) would orient the people towards self-actualization and an ultimate utopia. Considered a foundational work of Critical Theory, its philosophy drives much of today's thinking on sexual ethics.

[323] Calvin, *Institutes of the Christian Religion*, sec. 4.20.9.

[324] Wolfe, *The Case for Christian Nationalism*, 186.

It is quite interesting to see that Wolfe believes that "the nation perfected," through leaders "inspired by God," which brings about "supernatural application" among the people, who "possess all the native gifts once given to Adam" and "can achieve all that Adam was commanded," orienting them to the same "heavenly life" of "complete good" promised to him, does not *immanentize the eschaton* (bring about utopian conditions that create heaven on earth). In true, totalitarian political theory fashion, it would seem to promise everything just short of that.

Wolfe then lays out an eight-point case for his first premise (civil government ought to direct its people to the true religion), using nothing but his own deduction, and not a single reference to the actual religion he would want to enforce through civil punishment.[325] The hubris of this position, that the foundational premise of a godly "nation perfected" should be arrived at from his own errant interpretation of general revelation as opposed to God's inerrant special revelation (which he has easy access to), is astounding. My counter-arguments follow:

- The people of God can "institute a civil government... that is cognizant of true religion... and is for their spiritual good," without *civil* policies that explicitly "direct them to the true religion." They are already the people of God and, through the work of the Spirit, will direct themselves and their progeny to the true religion regardless of whether the state gets involved. Civil law can protect the church and, by proxy, the true religion without *proactively enforcing it.*
- It is not true that for "any civil government that lacks in principle any knowledge of the highest good, earthly goods must be the chief and highest good of man," nor that a nation that does not actively promote the true religion "fails to meet its natural end or *telos*" (Romans 13:1). A nation can consciously choose to limit its "knowledge" to the earthly good of its citizens and protect their ability to seek higher good on their own. For example, a nation can enforce universal Sunday sabbath or it can pass a law preventing companies from forcing employees to work on *their* sabbath. The latter preserves the Christian's ability to observe the

---

325 Wolfe, 187–93.

sabbath without actively discriminating against Jews, Muslims, and Seventh Day Adventists.
- If a government made of fallible men decides it has the mandate of God to "regulate outward things for the people's heavenly good," it runs a higher risk of working against the people's earthly good, and undercutting the supposed "complete good." Looking back to the sabbath example, one would expect that enforcing a nation-wide Sunday sabbath in the 21st-century West would result in strong push-back and even civil unrest – Seventh Day Adventists would take it as a sign of the end-times tribulation. On the other hand, personal-sabbath law would still allow the people to freely seek heavenly good, while the policy would probably only receive moderate criticism from non-religious business owners.
- Wolfe's *prelapsarian nations* theory has already been conclusively disproved, so there is no need to address any further appeals to it as an example for good postlapsarian government.
- Wolfe asks, "Why, after all, would man come together to form society if not for mutual support in procuring *all* [earthly and heavenly] good things?" Firstly, societies can form for means of survival in the harsh climate of a fallen world, with no initial thought to *higher benefit*. Secondly, many societies in the third world still operate on fealty to the most powerful individual; a warlord dictates the membership and terms of his society and there is very little mutual benefit for lower caste subjects. This notion of a naturally arising "community of mutual cooperation… procuring things earthly and heavenly" is quite Rousseauian in its presumptive elevation of man's natural inclinations.
- It is true that "Well-ordered souls are made possible only by true religion," but that ordering takes place within the *eternal kingdom* of the church and by the work of the Holy Spirit (John 6:44). This is not directly connected to "administration of law, justice and good order," as that is civil enforcement of the Second Table (when not promoted through church discipline). It can be equally claimed that a government which focuses its efforts on Second Table enforcement and strictly

protects religious *freedom* will attain similar, if not greater, good order, because it understands the use of both stick *and* carrot.
- It is not the role of government (the temporal kingdom) to "encourage civic virtue," because, as Wolfe stated himself, "Well-ordered souls are made possible *only by true religion*" (the eternal kingdom). Civil law, therefore, should concern itself only with the "abhorrence of vice." For example, would it make more sense to write laws that reward parents for fulfilling their duty to care for their children, or to write laws that punish parents who neglect their children? Those who attempt to proactively legislate "civil virtue" are *socialists*.
- Wolfe again references his prelapsarian theory and Thomasian view of sin, and mimics Calvin's appeal to tradition, citing "Plato, Aristotle, Cicero, Plutarch, and others." He then takes his consistent theme to new heights with, "And thus neither grace, nor the Gospel, nor the New Testament, nor anything subsequent to creation could destroy or abrogate this principle [of nature]." Wolfe should be disciplined by his church for such impious writing. The gospel is *everything*. Jesus *changes everything*. He turns the "world upside down" (Acts 17:6). There is not a single thing that we can avoid putting completely at His disposal and still properly claim to be Christian. If He wants to abrogate anything that we *perceive as natural* to us, that is His prerogative. **He is God**.

> "If anyone comes to me and does not hate his own father and mother and wife and children and brothers and sisters, yes, and even his own life, he cannot be my disciple. Whoever does not bear his own cross and come after me cannot be my disciple." (Luke 14:26-27)

III. Objections

While Wolfe's description of the eternal kingdom's *redeeming work* versus the temporal kingdom's *restorative work* is is not entirely

4. Perfecting Your Nation

disagreeable, on the surface, his argument for a Christian nationalist application is anything but air-tight.

> Thus, the question… concerns this conception of restoration, viz., whether Christians ought to seek the Christianization of the family, civil society, and civil government.[326]

This is a false equivalence of family to government. There is specific Scriptural precedent for the explicit "Christianization of the family", as he puts it (Proverbs 14:26, Ephesians 6:4, 2 Timothy 1:5, to name a few). The same can be said for the Christianization of civil society as a work of the Spirit, through the peaceful application of the Great Commission (Matthew 28:19), but there is no explicit, Scriptural precedent for the purposeful Christianization of civil government. As was mentioned in the last section, even Calvin opened his section in the *Institutes* on First Table enforcement by admitting this. His commentary on Romans 13 also notes that "the first table of the law, which contains what we owe to God, is not here referred to at all."[327]

Wolfe then writes, "… working is no longer (for the believer) the *condition* for eternal life. But this does not rescind the work itself; ordering this world to the next remains natural to man, especially to restored man."[328] Again, Wolfe breaks with Scripture (Isaiah 24:5), the doctrine of his own church, and its 16th and 17th-century founders, when he states that the reprobate naturally order this world to the next. For the redeemed, recognizing the limits of our ability to bring about restorative change is of great concern, for we must remember that what matters most to God is *heart change* (Matthew 15:11), and that He desires mercy far more than sacrifice (Matthew 9:13) and man's acknowledgment of Him far more than performative action (Hosea 6:6). That Wolfe is so sure of what is "natural" does not give me great confidence in his ability to restrain himself. The accusation of *Pharisaical legalism* is certainly overused, but was not their sin that they became obsessed with "ordering this world" through the civil

---
326 Wolfe, 194.
327 John Calvin, Commentary on Romans, 13:10.
328 Wolfe, *The Case for Christian Nationalism*, 194.

enforcement of their interpretation of *natural principles* (John 5:9-12)? Should a Protestant Christian, especially one who relies so heavily on appeals to Reformed tradition, not tread with extreme caution, fully aware of how the Catholic church's attempt to wield *two swords* resulted in just this type of destructive, legalistic civil government?

> An earthly kingdom is a Christian kingdom when it orders the people to the kingdom of heaven.[329]

Though he previously attempted to prove the need for a government to "direct its people to the Christian religion," this is still what is known as a *genetic logical fallacy*, assuming that something is good or bad simply based upon its taxonomy (Christian). In 1693, Salem, Massachusetts was a "Christian kingdom" that thought it was ordering people to the kingdom of heaven when two-hundred people were accused of witchcraft and nineteen murdered. Most Bible-believing American Christians, if they knew the details of colonial civil law regarding religion, would recoil at the thought of returning to such a mode of civil government and would perhaps think deeper about the full ramifications of loudly proclaiming that we are a "Christian nation." Williams writes of how the explicitly Christian kingdom of England chartered the colony of New England, and how the polity of Wolfe's own Presbyterian church was prohibited by law:

> In the charter of New England granted by William and Mary in 1691, we find the provision 'That forever hereafter shall there be a liberty of conscience allowed in the worship of God to all Christians (except Papists) inhabiting or which shall inhabit or be resident without our said province or territory.' But long before this document was drawn up the Congregational Church had been established as the official religion, compulsory for all the inhabitants and supported by general taxes, and no Jesuit or spiritual or ecclesiastical person ordained by the authority of the Pope or See of Rome was allowed within the colony.[330]

---

329 Wolfe, 195.
330 Williams, *Shadow of the Pope*, 24.

4. Perfecting Your Nation

Wolfe is not initially incorrect in his proceeding assertion that restoration "is an outgrowth or secondary effect of salvific grace," but he puts forth an incredible contradiction to Scripture (and the Reformed doctrine of sanctification in the *Westminster Confession of Faith*[331]) when he next states that "It follows that restoration is a work of human will. It is a matter of striving; man cooperates with grace to restore the natural world for his good."[332] Multiple assertions from the Apostle Paul directly rebuke him:

> for it is God who is at work in you, **both to will and to work** for His good pleasure. (Philippians 2:13, emphasis mine)

> For I am confident of this very thing, that He who began a good work in you will perfect it until the day of Christ Jesus. (Philippians 1:6)

> I have been crucified with Christ, and it is no longer I who live, but Christ lives in me. And the life which I now live in the flesh I live by faith in the Son of God, who loved me and gave Himself up for me. (Galatians 2:20)

> But far be it from me to boast except in the cross of our Lord Jesus Christ, by which the world has been crucified to me, and I to the world. (Galatians 6:14)

Wolfe straw-mans his opposition with the opening to his next subsection, entitled *Exile, Sojourner, Stranger*, when he paints those who would not "Christianize civil and social institutions" with a sort of

---

331 *The Westminster Confession of Faith and Catechisms*, sec. 13.2-3.
2. This sanctification is throughout in the whole man, yet imperfect in this life: there abideth still some remnants of corruption in every part, whence ariseth a continual and irreconcilable war, the flesh lusting against the Spirit, and the Spirit against the flesh.
3. In which war, although the remaining corruption for a time may much prevail, yet, through the continual supply of strength from the sanctifying Spirit of Christ, the regenerate part doth overcome: and so the saints grow in grace, perfecting holiness in the fear of God.
332 Wolfe, "Anarcho-Tyranny in 2022," 196.

American Anabaptist brush, as if they are almost totally averse to participation in politics. He then claims their worldview is rooted in "modern notions of tolerance and legal conceptions of freedom (e.g., freedoms of religion, expression, assembly, and speech)," and that "the Reformed tradition prior to the 20th-century would not recognize it, and... it reflects the post-World War II consensus of values."[333] This statement is worth breaking down, in detail.

- As shown in the last section, freedom of religion is not just a modern, secular value, but was the rule of law for the first Christian empire under Constantine in 313 A.D.
- A plurality of the most politically active, conservative Christian Americans today would affirm the Bill of Rights, including "freedoms of religion, expression, assembly, and speech," and prohibiting the establishment of a state church. A 2022 study conducted by the Marist Poll, concluded that 62% of Americans believe that the First Amendment was inspired by God.[334] His correlation between First Amendment values and an aversion to conservative politics among Christians is patently false.
- He yet again makes a fallacious appeal to "the Reformed tradition," as if that statement, on its own, should garner immediate obedience. The actual reformers, whose authority he has so often appealed to, would demand he at least somewhat cite Scripture to back up his claims.
- We should not miss the implication that his "nation perfected" would, like other forms of authoritarian nationalism, take away one's rights of "freedoms of religion, expression, assembly, and speech." As someone who has now publicly disagreed with nearly everything written so far, under his rule I would likely be imprisoned and then banished for unrepentantly refuting his form of government. Wolfe will go as far as to

---

333 Wolfe, *The Case for Christian Nationalism*, 196.
334 Kelsey Dallas, "Many Americans Say God Inspired the Constitution ... except That Part about Guns," Deseret News, April 23, 2022, https://www.deseret.com/faith/2022/4/22/23036178/many-americans-say-god-inspired-the-constitution-except-that-part-about-guns-pew-research-marist.

argue for the execution of "arch-heretics" and those who will not cease evangelizing other religions, in chapter 9.[335]

> A Christian is a foreigner in relation to fallenness – to a world in "bondage to decay" (Romans 8:21) – **but fallenness itself is foreign to nature**. (emphasis mine)[336]

Almost two hundred pages into the book, Wolfe finally cites Scripture, but he unfortunately cites it poorly. I believe he probably relied on Aquinas for this reference and did not properly look at the full context and at other areas of Scripture. One might be able to overlook "fallenness" and "foreign" as semantics issues, if Wolfe had not spent the entire book thus far repeatedly stating how nature, in and of itself, is properly functional in its present condition, and if Aquinas was not explicit in his view that "the good of nature" is not "diminished by sin." Scripture directly rebukes these claims.

> For the creation waits with eager longing for the revealing of the sons of God. **For the creation was subjected to futility**, not willingly, but because of him who subjected it, in hope that the creation itself will be set free from its bondage to corruption and obtain the freedom of the glory of the children of God. For we know that **the whole creation has been groaning together** in the pains of childbirth until now. (Romans 8:19-22, emphasis mine)

> And to Adam he said, "Because you have listened to the voice of your wife and have eaten of the tree of which I commanded you, 'You shall not eat of it,' **cursed is the ground because of you**; in pain you shall eat of it all the days of your life; (Genesis 3:17, emphasis mine)

> The earth mourns and withers; the world languishes and withers; the highest people of the earth languish. **The earth lies defiled**

---

335 Wolfe, *The Case for Christian Nationalism*, 391–92.
336 Wolfe, 197.

under its inhabitants; for they have transgressed the laws, violated the statutes, broken the everlasting covenant. **Therefore a curse devours the earth**, and its inhabitants suffer for their guilt; therefore the inhabitants of the earth are scorched, and few men are left. (Isaiah 24:4-6, emphasis mine)

Only two verses back from his reference, we can see that creation is not just subject to decay, as Wolfe claims, but also *futility*. The Greek word is ματαιότητι (mataiotēti), which means *devoid of truth, frail*, or *perverse* (at any rate, certainly diminished to some level). Paul also uses this word in his letter to the Ephesians, when he describes the *futility* of the reprobate mind (Ephesians 4:17). Genesis and Isaiah remind us that the earth is defiled by our sin and cursed by God. Paul tells us that the hope for creation is to obtain the same freedom of glory promised to us, that will come with Christ's return. Creation shares our fate and, thankfully, we both have a redeemer in the Son.

Wolfe closes this subsection by repeating the unfounded claim that, "Even Adam in the state of integrity, as he grew in maturity, would have felt as if he were a stranger in this world…"[337] As shown in chapter 1, God revealed no prelapsarian state to Adam but to "work and keep" the garden (Genesis 2:15), and there is no Scriptural reason to proclaim that his probationary state would extend indefinitely and to his progeny.

> I suspect that people will label my position a "triumphalist" theology or a "theology of glory" as opposed to a "theology of the cross". I'll simply say that I've laid out my premises and my argument, and I welcome anyone to refute them or demonstrate my argument's invalidity. Simply labeling my view a "theology of glory" proves nothing. If you want to claim that the cross and the resurrection revealed new universal and binding principles of outward human action, then explain their place theologically. Explain how these principles of grace cohere with those of nature. Explain how adventitious heavenly duties conduce to natural

---

337 Wolfe, 197.

4. Perfecting Your Nation

earthly goods. That is to say, do more than assert disparate ethical principles; provide a coherent system.[338]

The monumental narcissism of this statement is breathtaking, which is why I quoted it in its entirety; I am genuinely shocked that he would be so bold as to state that any opposition to his theory must be limited to his rules of engagement, and would likely be incoherent in its argument. I will leave it to the reader to determine whether, thus far, I have successfully refuted his premises and argument and demonstrated their invalidity. I will now take on each of his individual challenges.

- I would not call his a "theology of glory," because I have seen next to no *theology* from him at all. Theology requires one to be able to at least minimally exegete Scripture. What Wolfe has presented is *doctrine*, faulty at that, because his views of God and creation are derived through a game of telephone with 16th and 17th-century intermediaries. I believe he relies so heavily on Aquinas, not because it comports with what he has read in Scripture, but because it fits into his worldly, political preconceptions.
- Here is a universal and binding principle of outward human action that the cross and resurrection revealed: *Jesus Christ is the only begotten Son of God and no one comes to the Father but through submission to Him*. I know this doesn't meet Wolfe's requirement, but I felt it needed to be stated anyway. His question is based on the false premise that he has properly interpreted nature, and thus constitutes a loaded question fallacy. Jesus came to "fulfill the Law" (Matthew 5:17), and so did not alter universal principles, but He did so in a way that no one anticipated. That is the lesson to learn here, that *our interpretation of nature is faulty* and must be tested against the special revelation of God. I believe I have already conclusively proven, in previous chapters and even just above, that Wolfe has a very Scripturally unsound understanding of nature, and of the "principles of outward human action" that he builds upon that defective understanding.

---

338 Wolfe, 198.

- Requesting an explanation of how "principles of grace cohere with those of nature" is again a loaded question that assumes his interpretation of *natural principles* is correct and is also a burden of proof logical fallacy. He must prove how his view of nature coheres with Scripture, not the other way around. I doubt Wolfe would publicly say that God's word is errant; therefore, he must confirm it as the only infallible rule in this comparison. General revelation *cannot* contradict special revelation, therefore, he must exegete Scripture to prove every one of his claims about nature's relation to the gospel. He has failed miserably on this front. He may claim, because of all his supposed aspects of nature that are not altered by the gospel, that I would be forcing him into making an argument from silence. But, as I have shown above, his base premises about creation, fall, and redemption are not congruous with Scripture, so he would first have to exegetically prove his version of the three before worrying about how the gospel does or does not interact with creation.
- His purported theology proves its brokenness when he assumes a universal principle of "adventitious heavenly duties conducive to natural earthly goods." Christ could not have been more explicit when He said, "If anyone would come after me, let him deny himself and take up his cross daily and follow me" (Luke 9:23). We are given no guarantee of the type of "earthly goods" through obligation to "heavenly duties" that Wolfe requires to reach his nation's "complete good." It is *possible* that we will have earthly prosperity, but it is just as possible that our dedication to Christ will require a life of poverty and physical suffering. Paul tells us to *rejoice in those sufferings* (Romans 5:3-5), because they produce the real *complete good*. Certainly, "blessed is the nation whose God is the Lord" (Psalm 33:12), but Christian nations are not under the same Mosaic covenant that Israel was (as Wolfe also affirms). The guaranteed blessings of a modern people oriented to God are spiritual fruit (Galatians 5:22-23), not any special "natural earthly goods" beyond what non-Christian nations seek after (Matthew 6:31-33). In the end, how is the human-initiated "supernatural application" Wolfe is proposing any different than a "health and wealth" prosperity gospel on the national level?

- It is not my goal to present an alternative political theory in this book, or elsewhere. I am only concerned with proving that Wolfe's theory is not inline with Scripture, and that it is little more than repackaged authoritarian nationalism, with significant ethno-nationalist elements, laundered through Two-Kingdoms Theology to a Christian audience. I pray this work will be of assistance to Christ's body, and has been to the reader, thus far.

IV. Excluding Fellow Christians

After spending copious amounts of ink on the "blood-ties in ethno-genesis", the necessity of a "community of blood," that "blood relations matter for your ethnicity," that they create a "common *volksgeist*," that there is group-level variance in beauty and other immutable characteristics between ethnicities, and that the instinct to gather in such groups is a prelapsarian, universal good that is completed by grace, Wolfe now attempts to gaslight the charitable reader into thinking his call for segregation is primarily about common language – as if first-generation immigrants cannot learn the common tongue, and as if the nation's language and culture would not be native to the second generation. He acknowledges that Christians of all ethnic groups "share in the highest good... and thus have a spiritual brotherhood," but says this is "wholly inadequate as to its kind for cooperating to procure the full range of goods necessary for living well in this world."[339] He presents no statistical evidence for his argument, because studies show the exact opposite of what he claims. As noted by the Harvard Business Review:

> A study in 1996 from the Alexis de Tocqueville Institution (AdTI) used the issuance of new patents to measure immigrants' inventiveness and spirit of enterprise. Examining 250 recently-issued U.S. patents chosen at random, AdTI found that over 19% of them were issued to immigrants alone, or to immigrants collaborating with U.S.-born co-inventors. These patents generated

---
339 Wolfe, 199.

more than 1,600 jobs. A 2011 study by Partnership for a New American Economy found that 76% of patents awarded to the top 10 patent-producing U.S. universities that year had at least one foreign-born inventor.

According to another study, more than 40% of Fortune 500 companies operating in 2010 were founded by immigrants or their children – including some of the most well-known brands, from Apple and IBM to Disney and McDonald's. The companies noted in this study had combined revenues of $4.2 trillion – more than the GDP of most countries.[340]

A 2021 study published in the *American Economic Review* found that, over the last two centuries, children of immigrants have had a higher upward mobility than those of native born parents.[341] Immigrant families, even those who do not share our faith, contribute more per capita to the economic prosperity of the nation than native-born citizens. When you add in Wolfe's hypothetical filter of immigrants being professing Christians, the biggest potential multi-generational ideological barrier is removed, showing his assertion to be even more ridiculous.

With no empirical evidence to stand on, he resorts to a red herring when he writes, "Thus, it is a categorical error to make unity in Christ the sole basis of civil fellowship."[342] It is fine to list this as a hypothetical "categorical error," but he goes on to write, "It simply doesn't work, no matter how much modern sentiment you place on spiritual unity," implying he has opposition arguing for this. There is no serious movement – if any at all – calling for immigration and naturalization based solely on a profession of faith in Christ; it makes no sense to structure a society larger than a primitive tribe based on *any* single factor. That being said, a different *creedal unity* has been the predominant basis for citizenship within the

---

[340] Glenn Llopis, "Adopt an Immigrant Mindset to Advance Your Career," *Harvard Business Review*, August 24, 2012, https://hbr.org/2012/08/adopt-an-immigrant-mindset-to.

[341] Ran Abramitzky et al., "Intergenerational Mobility of Immigrants in the United States over Two Centuries," *American Economic Review* 111, no. 2 (February 2021): 580–608, https://doi.org/10.1257/aer.20191586.

[342] Wolfe, *The Case for Christian Nationalism*, 200.

4. Perfecting Your Nation

United States for two centuries. Despite our religious and cultural differences, it was a creedal common thread of a *brotherhood of ideals*, based on the Christian truth that all men are created equal, that held us together when we were "engaged in a great civil war, testing whether that nation, or any nation so conceived and so dedicated, can long endure."[343] Therefore, a successful, *primarily* creedal, nation in Christ without genetic homogeneity is hypothetically possible.

> Culturally distinct groups of Christians could, of course, start their own churches, and this would solve one problem. But it remains the case that cultural diversity harms civil unity, for it undermines the ability for a community to act with unity for its good.[344]

Cultural diversity does not harm civil unity, significant *ideological diversity* does. Many of the most prosperous and well organized empires in history had high levels of cultural diversity (i.e., the Persian, Roman, and Mongol Empires). Logic would dictate that having neighbors who only religiously vary in their particular sect of Christianity, as long as they have no standing animosity, would result in *more* societal cohesion than these empires. Wolfe appeals to "a common language" as a "bare minimum" requirement,"[345] which, yet again, highlights the weakness of his argument. All nations and empires naturally settle on a *language of business* that becomes the common tongue. The New Testament is written in just such a language (Koine Greek), though the words of Christ and the Apostles, in the Gospels and Acts, were primarily spoken in Aramaic.

Wolfe presents another red herring when, mid-paragraph, he switches the subsection's stated intent of "excluding fellow Christians" with the wholly different topic of secular multiculturalism and its "injection of diversity… on a mass scale."[346] This is the *false dichotomy of the authoritarian proposition* (i.e., suicide or revitalization); we have more options to choose from than to a) acquiesce to all the demands of secular

---

343 Abraham Lincoln, The Gettysburg Address.
344 Wolfe, *The Case for Christian Nationalism*, 200.
345 Wolfe, 200.
346 Wolfe, 200–201.

humanist globalization or b) develop a genetically and ideologically homogeneous nation that civilly punishes heterodoxy. We must remember that both fascists and communists have long been each other's greatest enemy and that they spend much of their propaganda efforts attempting to convince the majority, who have other options, that there is a black-and-white, existential crisis requiring them to put aside their principles for extreme measures.[347]

> ... the chief practical argument against Christian nationalism in Western countries, especially in the United States, is that cultural diversity renders it politically impossible.[348]

I argue that the chief practical argument against Christian Nationalism in Western countries is that *ideological diversity* renders it *morally reprehensible*. Bible-believing Christians are in an extreme minority in the West – depending on how that is categorized, we make up as little as 6% of the population in the United States[349] – which presents multiple issues for Wolfe's argument and ultimate vision:

- The vast majority of people who belong to the same genetic ancestry and wider culture as him would oppose such a government. This would include many of his fellow *orthodox Presbyterians of Western European descent*, who are probably not interested in his hierarchical ethnology,

---

347 This is best highlighted in the phrase "no enemies to the right", which is gaining in popularity among self-described Christian Nationalists. Logic would dictate that adherents to this principle would join forces with, or at least turn a blind eye to, ethno-nationalists, something explicitly stated by the most notable proponent of the phrase, Charles Haywood, when he used it regarding Wolfe's podcast co-host, Thomas Achord.
https://twitter.com/TheWorthyHouse/status/1597416017583812609
Journalist Rod Dreher: "So now the truth comes out, but Achord claims he 'forgot' a year's worth of racist, sexist, Jew-hating tweets -- and Stephen Wolfe says ppl were mean to attack his pal, and now it's time to move on. This is the opposite of moral courage, from both of them."
Charles Haywood: "Who cares? No enemies to the Right."
348 Wolfe, *The Case for Christian Nationalism*, 201.
349 Barna, "What Does It Mean When People Say They Are 'Christian'?," 9.

once laid bare, and who often ascribe to Neo-Calvinism or general equity theonomy, both of which argue for peaceful, democratic change through the Great Commission.
- Due to the extreme minority of adherents to his theory, a violent revolution would be required to accomplish its goals, which would constitute a collective Sixth Commandment violation. The *exegetical tradition of the 16th and 17th centuries* agrees that such a revolution would be sinful. As Tuininga writes of the 1536 version of the *Institutes*, "That the Israelites had to obey the very Babylonian king who destroyed Jerusalem and took them into exile is compelling for Calvin. Like Augustine before him, he invokes the prophet Jeremiah's instructions to the exiles to seek the peace of Babylon."[350]
- A successful revolution would require continued, collective violations of the Sixth, Eighth, and Tenth Commandments. There is no area in the West that is not heavily populated by people who have extreme ideological disagreements with Wolfe's position. He would be forced to banish a massive amount of people, usurping their property in the process. These types of policies have historically resulted in the perpetration of great evils. In chapter 7, I will describe how such actions by the state of Missouri in 1838 against the Mormons resulted in multiple atrocities, such as the murder of eighteen initially-unarmed civilians by the state militia, including a young boy who was shot, point-blank, in the head after fighting had ceased.

Wolfe then describes issues with the integration of religious refugees in various cities in the 16th century, unwittingly undermining his own case when he cites Cristina Garrett's claim that troubles were "due in a part to native distaste for foreigners."[351] That issue would be solved today by not inculcating the population with Wolfe's brand of ethnocentrism in the first place. The second reason given, of there being a lack of common tongue, is an issue of *mass migration* under special circumstances. Naturally

---
350 Tuininga, *Calvin's Political Theology and the Public Engagement of the Church*, 241.
351 Wolfe, *The Case for Christian Nationalism*, 201–2.

occurring, legally restricted immigration (of the type conservatives usually argue for) would not present nearly as much of an issue in this regard, especially with the educational and technological resources available in the modern West.

He next claims that "Reformation history is replete with examples of Christian refugees in foreign Christian countries causing public disturbance, civil strife, and social segregation."[352] As mentioned earlier, this would include the reformer whose political theology he is most utilizing, John Calvin, a French refugee to Geneva, who caused so much civil strife that the city banished him in 1538. The true irony of this statement is completely lost on Wolfe; he is *also* looking to cause "public disturbance, civil strife and social segregation," with the only difference being that he is not a refugee. Wolfe then returns to the straw-manning of his opposition as people who advocate for unfettered immigration, as if that would be the standard, conservative Christian rebuttal to the ethnic segregation of his authoritarian Christian Nationalism, and not controlled, legal immigration.

He closes this section by once again demonstrating his broken hamartiology and soteriology when he states, "It is not due to sin that dissimilar people cannot (ordinarily) achieve together what similar people can achieve... those who want to be **radically selfless** should **return to their instincts** lest they harm people for generations" (emphasis mine).[353] As mentioned earlier, sin is the very reason we have different languages and culture (Genesis 11:1-9), so his first statement is totally false. Wolfe cannot deride *radical selflessness* in others, and still claim to be a disciple of Christ, without at least addressing the concept in the context of Jesus's perfect example that can be described with those exact two words. Otherwise, what are we to do with Paul's instruction to, "Be imitators of me, as I am of Christ" (1 Corinthians 11:1)? As a pastor friend of mine likes to say, "We're not called to judge someone's salvation, but we *are* called to be fruit inspectors." There is a distinct, rotten odor to what Wolfe

---

352 Wolfe, 202–3.
353 Wolfe, 203–4.

brings forth; genuine disciples of Christ would rather die than "return to their instincts," which are nothing but sin and rebellion.

V. Conclusion

In the next chapter, Wolfe will move to his definition of *cultural Christianity* and its societal good, something that, when left to the most basic of terms, I agree with. He will also begin to lay the groundwork for some of the specific policy points regarding cultural enforcement in his Christian nation, most of which I wholeheartedly disagree with. Therefore, this is a good juncture to present my sum assessment of the doctrinal, ethical, and sociological foundations of his theory.

First and foremost, Wolfe has completely disqualified himself as an expositor of Reformed theology and doctrine. He has previously identified himself as a member of the Presbyterian Church in America on Twitter[354] and, until recently, his profile listed him as "Presbyterian," so it is safe to assume that he is at least currently a member of a conservative Presbyterian denomination. As a former member of the PCA, I am versed in its doctrine, based primarily in the *Westminster Confession of Faith and Catechisms* (I have a hard copy of the official PCA version in my personal library, which I have referenced in this book). I have identified three points of incongruity or outright disagreement with core PCA doctrine which, though it would not necessarily disqualify him from membership, would at least preclude him from holding the position of deacon or elder in the church; both require a good-faith subscription to the confessional standards in a way that does not violate core tenets. This would mean, from his own church's perspective, he is *unqualified to teach doctrine*. These doctrines are so core to Reformed belief that they make up three of the five main points by which most characterize that Calvinistic theological tradition to which orthodox Presbyterianism belongs (Total Depravity, Irresistible Grace, and Perseverance of the Saints).

---

354 https://twitter.com/PerfInjust/status/1470417449011097601
Stephen Wolfe: "I've lived in several places in the US. I'd say that my PCA church in Baton Rouge and the church I attend in New Jersey would seamlessly integrate in a political/cultural setting."

- Though he claims others lack understanding of the doctrine of *Total Depravity*, Wolfe wrongly believes in prelapsarian aspects of our nature that are "not altered by the gospel," meaning they are fine just as they are. This is a direct disagreement with his church's core teaching that we are "wholly defiled in all the parts and faculties of soul and body" (6.2), and that "we are utterly indisposed, disabled, and made opposite to all good, and wholly inclined to all evil" (6.4).
- He disagrees with more non-negotiable church doctrine when he says that man, by the striving of his human will "cooperates with grace." This is totally incompatible with our radically corrupted condition described in chapter 6 of the *WCF*, as well as with the doctrines of *Irresistible Grace* and *Perseverance of the Saints* found in chapters 3 and 17, respectively. God actively dispenses His Spirit to not only bring about belief in Christ, but to continually cause the redeemed to "will and work for His good pleasure" (Philippians 2:13). This "depends not upon their own free will, but upon the immutability of the decree of election" (17.2). As shown above, we are "utterly indisposed" to do so on our own.

If Wolfe was to agree with these core doctrines of his church, the entire basis for his theory would fall apart, because it stands and falls on his postulations on prelapsarian man and certain natural goods not being altered by the fall (he has admitted this himself). His doctrinal justifications for a civilly enforced Christian nation are dead on arrival. This would not necessarily be the case if he were arguing from a Methodist or Catholic perspective, but he has explicitly titled his theory "Presbyterian Christian nationalism."

As for ethics, the case I laid out in chapter 3 proves that, at the very least, Wolfe is not disclosing his full private views on ethnicity in his book and that he is using "culture" and "language" as a sort of *get out of jail free card* whenever he brings up the topic of forging communities primarily on genetic similarity. He has exposed those views, likely unintentionally, through his promotion of *13/52*, his concept of "psycho-sexual ethno-masochism," his statement that society finds "the instinct to socialize and

4. Perfecting Your Nation

dwell with similar people... evil or pathological," and his listed issues with "Western Man" that only make sense when applied in a context of *white ethnocentrism* (also as a phrase used in a white nationalist context by his podcast co-host). Due to the apparent connotations of these views, it is fair to wonder if he seeks out community based on what the average American would describe as "race." Despite what some liberal works on the topic of Christian Nationalism might say, I believe that the majority of conservative, American Christians would reject Wolfe's views of ethnicity, now that the scattered pieces have been put together and his academic-linguistic cover has been removed. I have shown his theory's core ideological similarities to traditional American variants of Nativism and ethno-nationalism, and the themes of *harnessing the will of a middle-class under threat of losing dominance* and *using spiritual terms to discuss private property and homeland* found in National Syndicalism (a component of Spanish and Italian fascism derived from the concepts of earlier proletarian labor movements).

Lastly, his sociological assertions on the benefits of excluding the other are not only refuted by Scripture but by scientific inquiry as well. While the idiom of *too much of a good thing* can be applied to modern left-wing notions of globalism and the purposeful breaking down of societal norms, that does not abrogate the truth that our 21st-century society sits on the benefits of at least two centuries of the deliberate tearing down of culturally exclusionary walls. His theory rests on the same fallacious belief held by 20th-century authoritarian nationalists that the excesses of Marxism and Bolshevism are not endemic to a particular extreme strain of liberal democratic theory, rooted in the philosophy of Jean-Jacques Rousseau and first applied in the French Revolution, but that they are endemic to liberal democracy *as a whole*. Like his predecessors, he will now begin to make a case for throwing the baby out with the bath-water.

5. The Good of Cultural Christianity

I. Mode of Religion

> The primary mode of religion is found in the instituted church... But in a Christian nation there are two *supplemental* modes of religion: the *civil power* of civil magistrates and the *social power* of cultural Christianity.[355]

Though I have previously voiced my disagreement with using the civil magistrate to enforce the First Table, and will continue to do so as it comes up, I fully agree with Wolfe that there is a positive social power to cultural Christianity. That agreement will end at the very beginning of the next section, when he takes the concept too far and claims that it includes the power "to make the earthly city an analog of the heavenly city" (only real heart change does that), but it is worth highlighting what is likely the only section of the book where he and I can find near-complete agreement.

Because he will immediately take the topic in an authoritarian direction and cite Scripture only once, in a questionable manner, to argue for cultural Christianity blending the visible church into the body politic, I would like to prime the reader with the *Biblical perspective* on how Christians are to "engage the culture" by quoting Scripture at length. Firstly, the most powerful witness of Christians is not our enforcement of God's moral standard through social pressures, but our ability to remain peaceful and loving when others break that standard:

> And the Lord's servant must not be quarrelsome but kind to everyone, able to teach, patiently enduring evil, correcting his opponents with gentleness. God may perhaps grant them repentance leading to a knowledge of the truth, and they may come to their senses and escape from the snare of the devil, after being captured by him to do his will (2 Timothy 2:24-26).

---

355 Wolfe, *The Case for Christian Nationalism*, 207–8.

> But even if you should suffer for righteousness' sake, you will be blessed. Have no fear of them, nor be troubled, but in your hearts honor Christ the Lord as holy, always being prepared to make a defense to anyone who asks you for a reason for the hope that is in you; yet do it with gentleness and respect, having a good conscience, so that, when you are slandered, those who revile your good behavior in Christ may be put to shame. For it is better to suffer for doing good, if that should be God's will, than for doing evil (1 Peter 3:14-17).

When applied on the societal level, this explicit direction to remain peaceful in the face of verbal revilement of our faith negates the argument for civil enforcement of doctrinal orthodoxy. Those who argue for blasphemy law (Christian nationalist and theonomist alike) often claim this to be the difference between individual and governmental responsibility, but this is a categorical error. While civil government has extra leeway to enforce morality (i.e., after the fact determination of guilt and punishment), it does not have an *extra set of morals to enforce*. If the individual Christian is not to respond to blasphemy with anger or violence then neither is a Christian government – civil punishment is state violence, regardless of whether or not it is justified. This will be explicated and defended in detail in chapter 6, *What Laws Can and Cannot Do*.

Peter, continuing on this theme, reminds us of the extent to which we are expected to bear witness to the suffering of the Messiah, which he saw with his own eyes. We must accept that we may be called to share in His physical suffering for the sake of the gospel:

> For what credit is it if, when you sin and are beaten for it, you endure? But if when you do good and suffer for it you endure, this is a gracious thing in the sight of God. For to this you have been called, because Christ also suffered for you, leaving you an example, so that you might follow in his steps. He committed no sin, neither was deceit found in his mouth. When he was reviled, he did not revile in return; when he suffered, he did not threaten, but continued entrusting himself to him who judges justly. He

himself bore our sins in his body on the tree, that we might die to sin and live to righteousness. By his wounds you have been healed. For you were straying like sheep, but have now returned to the Shepherd and Overseer of your souls (1 Peter 2:20-25).

Most American Christians living within the common connotation of "cultural Christianity," that of the *personal peace* and *affluence* made possible by the post-war consensus, have forgotten to just what extent they may be expected to suffer for Christ. Wolfe's theory is predicated on a negative, guttural reaction to this Scriptural requirement and even promotes a right to violent resistance under our present condition, one that pales in comparison to what the early church endured; he goes as far as to say we lack "the spirit to drive away the open mockery of God and to claim what is ours in Christ."[356] Does that comport with *anything* the Apostles, inspired by the Holy Spirit, wrote on the subject? The acceptance of peacefully suffering under tyranny is not an easy concept for Christians of any generation to digest and, like most Scriptural directives, it can be taken too far. But it must be seriously contended with as a *key component of our cultural witness* by any political theory that wishes to be seen as substantively "Christian." Lastly, our cultural Christianity must be grounded in humility, fully aware of whom we are in relation to a holy God:

> I thank him who has given me strength, Christ Jesus our Lord, because he judged me faithful, appointing me to his service, though formerly I was a blasphemer, persecutor, and insolent opponent. But I received mercy because I had acted ignorantly in unbelief, and the grace of our Lord overflowed for me with the faith and love that are in Christ Jesus. The saying is trustworthy and deserving of full acceptance, that Christ Jesus came into the world to save sinners, of whom I am the foremost. But I received mercy for this reason, that in me, as the foremost, Jesus Christ might display his perfect patience as an example to those who were to believe in him for eternal life. (1 Timothy 1:12-16)

---

356 Wolfe, 352.

> Remind them to be submissive to rulers and authorities, to be obedient, to be ready for every good work, to speak evil of no one, to avoid quarreling, to be gentle, and to show perfect courtesy toward all people. For we ourselves were once foolish, disobedient, led astray, slaves to various passions and pleasures, passing our days in malice and envy, hated by others and hating one another. But when the goodness and loving kindness of God our Savior appeared, he saved us, not because of works done by us in righteousness, but according to his own mercy, by the washing of regeneration and renewal of the Holy Spirit, whom he poured out on us richly through Jesus Christ our Savior, so that being justified by his grace we might become heirs according to the hope of eternal life (Titus 3:1-7).

Here is a key paradox of our faith: though we can rationalize our current moral predilections compared to non-Christians – what Wolfe will describe as *reason perfected by a pre-reflective prejudice*[357] – we must perpetually regard ourselves as the *foremost of sinners*. We are required to be ever cognizant of this and ensure that it permeates every aspect of our cultural witness. The true power of cultural Christianity is not found in collective ritual, like the prayer before a Little League baseball game that Wolfe will appeal to in this chapter[358] or in the social and legal pressures of a Second Table Overton window, though these all have some benefit, especially the latter in the soft restraint of sin. Namely, it is the collective witness of a *community of love, trust, and forgiveness*, made up of people who were once the most condemnable of sinners, that has the greatest effect on society. The average American cannot tell you what the gospel is, in the first place, let alone knowingly reject it. The more frequently he interacts with people whom he once personally knew as consistently immoral, but who are now forever changed by the person of Jesus Christ, the more *the law written on his heart* (Romans 2:15) will testify to him of his own sinfulness and the truth of that gospel.

---

357 Wolfe, 209–10.
358 Wolfe, 213.

II. Definition and Explication

Wolfe's technical definition of *cultural Christianity* is as follows:

> *Cultural Christianity is a mode of religion wherein social facts normalize Christian cultural practices (i.e., social customs) and a Christian self-conception of a nation in order (1) to prepare people to receive the Christian faith and keep them on the path to eternal life, (2) to establish and maintain a commodious social life, and (3) to make the earthly city an analog of the heavenly city.*[359]

I slightly break with the foundation of his definition of cultural Christianity, because he is primarily concerned with normalized praxis as a form of social pressure, while I find its greatest benefit in the cultural acceptance of the public witness of the saints; it provides the eternal kingdom with more room to work in the temporal realm, for example, making it less of a social taboo to invite an agnostic neighbor to a fellowship group at your church. Also, while Wolfe's definition may seem benign on the surface, it dovetails perfectly into an authoritarian-nationalist power structure, because it is rooted in a desire for societal order though a collectivist identity – what he calls the "Christian self-conception of a nation in order".

It is true that the normalization of Christian cultural practices can "prepare people to receive the Christian faith" and that it assists in the maintenance of a "commodious social life." But only the genuine heart change that comes from the work of the Holy Spirit can even begin to "make the earthly city an analog of the heavenly city." This is an overbold assertion by Wolfe, though it once again comports with his propagandistic view of "the nation perfected." Though Christian Nationalism seems to be gaining the most ground among postmillennials, it is not my intent to directly challenge their eschatology of the world becoming Christendom before the Second Advent.[360] Still, whatever our eschatology, we must be

---

359 Wolfe, 208–9.
360 I am aware that this statement will cause many to wonder what my eschatology is. I have yet to be fully convinced of any single view on the millennial reign and return of Christ. I believe pre-, post-, and amillennials all make excellent points, and I am

cognizant of the limits of our human reach. The gate is still narrow and few still find it (Matthew 7:14); it is not within the nation-state, but the *local church*, that we find the greatest opportunity to create an "analog of the heavenly city." Even then, we regularly fail to achieve such ends on that smaller level; how often do we sin against each other and need to ask forgiveness? Knowing of that persistent battle of spirit and flesh within ourselves, how far astray will we go if we move beyond public advocacy for Second Table mores to become obsessed with forcing an entire Western nation into affirming orthodox Protestant Christian culture, especially when the majority of our fellow citizens are unfriendly to the core tenets of our religion? From a solely earthly perspective, and by pure demographics, it would be easier to get America to collectively pray the rosary.

The remainder of this subsection is a good explanation of how societal norms build a "pre-reflective judgment on particular thoughts and actions."[361] Most people, including Christians, are not predisposed to philosophical inquiry and will assume the inherent goodness of whatever customs their society promotes. Thus, social facts become a self-referential and self-propelled cultural modality. Wolfe rightly notes how abuse of this can lead to sin, which is ironic considering that one of the most widely acknowledged promulgators of this abuse are extreme identitarian nationalists. Wolfe will end the chapter by advocating for such abuse (and commit the monumental blunder of placing *supremacy* after his nationalist theory's key identity), by writing, "A Christian nation that is true to itself will unashamedly and confidently **assert Christian supremacy over the land**" (emphasis mine).[362] Again, this is not just an unfortunate turn of phrase or only a call for a more *verbal* assertiveness; he promotes violent revolution by Christians in our time and place.

Wolfe further solidifies his hyper-concern for unified outward performance with his definition of *Christian culture*, which he considers a "necessary element of cultural Christianity."

---

wary to take a firm stance on such immensely symbolic prophesy. I believe the most important eschatalogical point is that Christ will return in physical space and time to rule for eternity.

361 Wolfe, *The Case for Christian Nationalism*, 209–12.
362 Wolfe, 241.

5. The Good of Cultural Christianity

Christian culture is a public culture in which a people presume a Christian relation between themselves and adorn their collective, everyday life with Christian symbols, customs, and social expectations in order to mutually orient one another to worship God and love one's neighbor in Christ.[363]

His examples of the "symbols, customs, and social expectations" of Christian culture could be more accurately and succinctly described as a sort of *civil liturgy*. He claims that "Festivals, feast days, and civic observances – though not in themselves holy or administered by spiritual authority... can be means of faith, sanctification, repentance, and spiritual reconciliation."[364] Civil liturgy in a majority Christian country can be a normative practice by which our faith is strengthened, but it can just as easily be abused by the majority to impress their cultural dominance upon the minority. Wolfe calls for Christians to *drive away the open mockery of God* and protect orthodox doctrine using the full force of the state, up to and including execution. Thus, it is difficult to not envision a more forceful side to his Christian culture's presumption of "social expectations," one that ramps up the frequency and severity of its efforts as it gains more social power. Forceful promotion of state-sanctioned, ideological homogeneity creates a performative standard by which an *underclass of conscience* is inevitably created. The Partito Nazionale Fascista and Falange Española not only treated those who would not publicly condone their ideology as dissenters, but as betrayers, and separated them from the state community both physically and morally,[365] something that Wolfe argues for later in this section. As Priorelli writes, "Only the Blackshirts benefited from the status of authentic Italians, while those who did not embrace the PNF belief received different treatment as 'excommunicated and renegade'."[366] This type of in-group/out-group antagonism towards ideological dissent (both inside and outside the church), that is characteristic of previous authoritarian nationalists, has already been shown

---

363 Wolfe, 212.
364 Wolfe, 213.
365 Priorelli, *Italian Fascism and Spanish Falangism in Comparison*, 39.
366 Priorelli, 49.

in Wolfe's "psycho-sexual ethno-masochism." In this chapter, he will turn a similar eye towards Russell Moore, former President of the Southern Baptist Convention's Ethics and Religious Liberty Commission, now Editor-in-Chief at *Christianity Today*, whose beliefs have taken a much-noticed politically and theologically liberal turn in recent years.

Wolfe appeals to the Scripturally sound example of a father raising his children in the "discipline and instruction of the Lord" (Ephesians 6:4) to make the factually and Scripturally unsound claim that cultural Christianity "provides what no ecclesial institution can fully provide – social direction to perform Christian practices in every area of life."[367] This statement is ridiculous; if the church can not sufficiently provide "social direction to perform Christian practices" without cultural Christianity, then it would have never survived the first two and a half centuries of its existence. Secondly, Scripture provides us with two different intents and methodologies for exhibiting moral standards, depending on the target. This is best exemplified in Paul's first letter to the Corinthians, where he discusses the different approaches to sin inside and outside of the church:

> I wrote to you in my letter not to associate with sexually immoral people – not at all meaning the sexually immoral of this world, or the greedy and swindlers, or idolaters, since then you would need to go out of the world. But now I am writing to you not to associate with anyone who bears the name of brother if he is guilty of sexual immorality or greed, or is an idolater, reviler, drunkard, or swindler – not even to eat with such a one. For what have I to do with judging outsiders? Is it not those inside the church whom you are to judge? God judges those outside. "Purge the evil person from among you." (1 Corinthians 5:9-13)

When he says to not even eat with a brother who is unrepentantly living in sin, he is specifically dictating how the "ecclesial institution" of the communion of saints can provide "social direction to perform Christian practices in every area of life." The key distinction is that this type of social pressure is to remain within the body of Christ. As for people outside of the

---

367 Wolfe, *The Case for Christian Nationalism*, 213–14.

body, as shown in the last section, we are not to exert the same totality of cultural pressure, but instead demonstrate the love of Christ through our exemplary behavior and kindness to all. While the former says to the believer, "You should know better than to do the wrong thing," the latter says to the unbeliever, "Wouldn't you like to know why I do the right things?"

Wolfe would seem to acknowledge this in the end to this subsection when he writes that social pressures "provide the complete conditions that order **Christians** to perform good Christian practices and encourage them to embrace the Gospel unto eternal life" (emphasis mine).[368] But in order to genuinely be a Christian, one must have already embraced the gospel and accepted Christ as Lord and Savior. Wolfe is beginning to engage in a melding of the visible church into the body politic that he will make a core component of his political theory.

> Likewise, civil government, though arising from the instinct of man, is established voluntarily, since no man is king over another by reason of pure nature.[369]

This may seem to contradict his earlier statement that a "natural aristocracy would arise,"[370] but he likely believes that the naturally occurring better disposition of this aristocracy serves as a first-line filter, a sort of *primary election driven by nature* in a society with some democratic processes. One wonders if this aristocracy would be recognized by his nationalist state through membership in one or more state-sanctioned political parties, with the others outright banned. When people who proselytize false religions would face civil punishment, his government would obviously not allow political parties formed on the basis of defending religious freedom.

> Christian peoplehood does not refer simply to a people who are submitted to both the church and the state. In a fundamental sense,

---

368 Wolfe, 215.
369 Wolfe, 215.
370 Wolfe, 72.

the people are *prior* to both, as those who established these public administrations for their good.³⁷¹

This subsection, entitled *Christian Self-Conception*, has a very *Nietzschian will to power* feel to it, in the collectivist way 20th-century authoritarians interpreted the phrase. There are multiple references to an "antecedent Christian national will for action"³⁷² that are seemingly inline with the German philosopher's view of a similarly *pre-rational* force in all individuals that was later shoehorned into fascist political theory. In Falangist thought, Spanish "radical romantic" philosopher José Ortega y Gasset was similarly utilized, though he was publicly against the "dead ends" of both communism and fascism.³⁷³ Like Nietzsche, Ortega y Gasset also had a philosophy of an irrational force driving the ordering of life, which he gave the moniker of *ratiovitalism*. Though more of an individualist than his collectivist contemporaries, such as Martin Heidegger, and although his philosophy's version of the *Nietzschian ubermensch* is also able to create his own morality, he would have agreed, at least in philosophical principle, with Wolfe's assertion that social pressures on the state level are something the masses must accept. As political scientist Kenneth R. Hoover described Ortega y Gasset's thoughts on social self-conception, "Our circumstance is a part of us. It is not merely an external reality with which we have relations; it is something we are. This relation of mutual submersion, so to speak, of the self and circumstance implies a dependent relation between man and the state."³⁷⁴ Ortega y Gasset also shared a similar disdain for liberal modernity with the Falangist leader Primo de Rivera. Priorelli notes that he developed a "Nietzschean pessimism" with Spanish society where he believed

---

371 Wolfe, 215.
372 Wolfe, 216.
373 Oliver Holmes, "José Ortega y Gasset," in *The Stanford Encyclopedia of Philosophy*, ed. Edward N. Zalta, Summer 2022 (Metaphysics Research Lab, Stanford University, 2022), https://plato.stanford.edu/archives/sum2022/entries/gasset/.
374 Kenneth R. Hoover, "The Political Thought of Jose Ortega y Gasset," *Midwest Journal of Political Science* 10, no. 2 (May 1966): 235, https://doi.org/10.2307/2109151.

5. The Good of Cultural Christianity

"disintegrating impulses overwhelmed the anarchist and undisciplined masses."[375] This description would fit right into Wolfe's thoughts on *Anarcho-Tyranny* and the *globalist American empire;* Wolfe directly references Nietzsche's distaste for modern life in his epilogue.[376] In essence, Wolfe's belief in a *pre-rational national will* as the force that puts a *nation in order* is perfectly inline with how fascists across Europe interpreted and utilized contemporary philosophical thought to collectivist ends.

This subsection is closed with more aspects of Christian nationalist political theory that are in no way distinctive from its early-20th-century predecessors. Wolfe lauds giving homage to one's country from "a gratitude for the various modes of religion" displayed through "loyalty oaths, pledges, and other acts of national solidarity," then pushes the very common authoritarian-nationalist trope of saving the people from suffering the "indignity of perpetual humiliation."[377] Again, Scripture tells us that "if when you do good and suffer for it you endure, this is a gracious thing in the sight of God" (1 Peter 2:20). As long as we remain faithful to Christ, we can find joy and peace regardless of how the world reacts.

Wolfe then lists his first specific policy position of the book by broaching the controversial subject of who would be baptized in his state church. It is unsurprising that, as a Presbyterian, he would argue for paedobaptism as most conducive to his political theory. Unfortunately for him, credobaptists exponentially outnumber paedobaptists in America, especially among the theologically conservative.[378] It stands to reason that, unless the majority of conservative Christians in America change one of their most closely held doctrinal beliefs, Wolfe would be potentially excluded from any state church formed on our shores. To make matters worse for him, the Southern Baptist Convention's statement of faith, the *Baptist Faith and Message*, since its first adoption in 1925 has stated that

---

375 Priorelli, *Italian Fascism and Spanish Falangism in Comparison*, 32.
376 Wolfe, *The Case for Christian Nationalism*, 446, 447.
377 Wolfe, 216, 217.
378 "Religious Landscape Study," *Pew Research Center's Religion & Public Life Project* (blog), accessed March 17, 2023, https://www.pewresearch.org/religion/religious-landscape-study/.

"The church should not resort to the civil power to carry on its work," and that "The state has no right to impose penalties for religious opinions of any kind."[379] This is especially awkward for one of Stephen Wolfe's most prolific defenders online, Southern Baptist Theological Seminary graduate and former Trump official William Wolfe.

The majority of American baptists are maligned by Stephen Wolfe, when he states, "Their theology of baptism restricts Christian obligation to the credobaptized, and thus the mass of society, at least in people's formative years, do not (in principle) have Christian obligations."[380] This is a common calumny of credobaptist belief that, as with Nativist anti-Catholic sentiment of the 19th century, is often promulgated by people who have little personal experience with that tradition's polity. As someone who sees baptism as a clear liberty of conscience issue and who has been a member of both the PCA and SBC, I have seen their very similar views on the obligations of children first-hand. Baptists often perform a baby dedication that is practically identical to a Presbyterian baptism, but for the absence of water; the family and church commit to raising the child in the discipline and instruction of the Lord. These children are still raised with a sense of obligation to both their physical and spiritual families in Christ. When children make a professions of faith, they are baptized by immersion and are given official membership in the church. Likewise, Presbyterian children are catechized in the faith and, usually around age thirteen, make a public profession of faith to the congregation and are given membership in the church. Wolfe's claim that paedobaptism in a state church "makes possible a society that is baptized in infancy and thus is subject to Christian demands for all life"[381] is either a statement of near total ignorance or a purposeful calumny to bolster his claims regarding the integration of the visible church into the state. His claim that "Since [he is] not credobaptist" he does not have "any great personal interest in reconciling Baptist doctrine and Christian nationalism" points to both being factors, especially

---

379 Baptist Faith and Message (1925), sec. 18,
    https://www.utm.edu/staff/caldwell/bfm/1925/18.html.
380 Wolfe, *The Case for Christian Nationalism*, 217–18.
381 Wolfe, 218.

considering the amount of ink he spent laying out a baseless theory of prelapsarian man.

III. The End of Cultural Christianity

> Eternal life is the ultimate end of cultural Christianity... Its chief object is church attendance, where the ordinary means of grace are administered for eternal life.[382]

One can make a case that Wolfe's means and ends of cultural Christianity would ultimately lead many, if not more, people to damnation than eternal life. If a nation exerts purposeful pressure on its citizens to "at least outwardly" appear Christian or face the potential of "social separation"[383] – if people go to prison for antagonism towards the state religion – it stands to reason that a large number of people will simply *pretend to be Christian*. Feeling the need to attend Sunday services or else give away the ruse and relegate themselves to the *underclass of conscience*, they will also participate in the ordinary means of grace of the Lord's Supper. The Apostle Paul's warning, which is often repeated before the sacrament in Presbyterian churches, details the result:

> Whoever, therefore, eats the bread or drinks the cup of the Lord in an unworthy manner will be guilty concerning the body and blood of the Lord. Let a person examine himself, then, and so eat of the bread and drink of the cup. For anyone who eats and drinks without discerning the body eats and drinks judgment on himself. (1 Corinthians 11:27-29)

That Wolfe gives one paragraph to his subsection on *Eternal Life* and nearly four full pages to the next subsection on *Commodious Life* shows how little thought he has given to the soteriological effects of his government. This is the utopian ends of a political theory devoid of social science and a "Christianity" with little genuine concern for evangelism; to

---
382 Wolfe, 218.
383 Wolfe, 216.

be so convinced that the masses will fall in line with your state religion if you only exert enough social and civil pressure is sociopathic.

> In this way [of mutual expectations], the individual does not collapse into the collective, nor does the collective erode on account of excessive self-interest.[384]

This initial description of "commodious life" would sound perfectly reasonable to Christian and non-Christian alike. Mutual expectations between society and individual are the foundation of any civilization; Romans 13 told its original readers to obey the mutual expectations of the pagan empire they lived under because it was an *authority from God* that would *give approval to good conduct*. But Wolfe presents another false dilemma in an attempt to convince his reader that a civilly enforced Christian orthodoxy is the *only* way to achieve this type of commodious life. This is shown most clearly in his near-immediate invoking of the arch-enemy of authoritarian rightism, *authoritarian leftism* – in this case, the obsession of modern theological liberalism with *restorative social justice*.[385] He employs a common political trick of misdirecting the reader away from *his* more extreme measures by pitting his enemy's extremities against middle-of-the-bell-curve policies. Wolfe would have you forget that both he and his ideological enemy would enforce their personal visions of Christianity from behind the barrel of a gun.

Secondly, his appeal to tradition/authority claim of how charity-work was conducted in "medieval and early modern periods" is not entirely accurate, at least within the *Reformed tradition of the 16th century*. Calvin broke with several Swiss reformers, including Huldrych Zwingli and Heinrich Bullinger, on the role of the deaconate in relief for the poor. The first believed it to be an official office and responsibility to remain in the church, while the other two believed that such responsibility should be yielded to civil government.[386] While I agree with Wolfe, in principle, that

---

384 Wolfe, 219.
385 Wolfe, 219–20.
386 Tuininga, *Calvin's Political Theology and the Public Engagement of the Church*, 68–69.

5. The Good of Cultural Christianity

Christian charity should flow from the love of one image-bearer to another, he disfigures such love by shoving it back into his limiting framework of pre-rational love for ethnic and cultural similarity.[387] This is especially egregious in regard to charity towards the downtrodden, because looking beyond this similarity is the exact parameter of the parable of the Good Samaritan (Luke 10:25-37). Though the way leftist Westerners discuss and organize their charity work often otherizes the poor, the "'radical' command of poverty relief" demanded by them is usually for people within their own countries. Again, we are not in a binary dilemma of choosing between outsourcing our charity work to bureaucratic organizations (government or private) and only doing personal charity work among people we are similar to and familiar with. Did any of the people in Samaria who came to believe in Jesus know Him beforehand as anything more than a wandering Jewish rabbi who had reportedly prophesied to a sexually immoral woman (John 4:40-42)? Did they recognize Him as someone with whom they had "organic unity… similarity… a shared and particular civil project",[388] or did they initially view Him as a citizen of an unfriendly nation (John 4:9)? Yet He stayed with them for two days and opened the doors of heaven to them. *Whom should we seek to emulate in our charity?*

Wolfe follows this with an invocation of John Winthrop's speech at Massachusetts Bay, which provides an excellent example of how a theocratic government's call to "abridge ourselves of our superfluities" limits itself in a way that does not meet Christ's full demands.[389] I do not believe it was a coincidence that, in the Sermon on the Mount, He so closely paired "Do not resist the one who is evil," with "Give to the one who begs from you, and do not refuse the one who would borrow from you" (Matthew 5:38-42). These two things regularly coincide; people often resort to begging because an antisocial lifestyle has led them to poverty. In this same vein, our charity should not be limited to those who are ethnically or culturally similar; 21st-century Western Christians have no excuse to do

---

387 Wolfe, *The Case for Christian Nationalism*, 220.
388 Wolfe, 220.
389 Wolfe, 221.

this, as nearly every medium- and large-scale city has significant ethnic and ideological diversity. Wolfe's conscious limiting of beneficence to a "community of 'regenerates'" exposes the dark side of his poor theology of a "restored image," in that it creates a false, secondary *in-group* distinction.

Overall, dedicating the majority of this section to a Manichaeistic false dilemma shows the ultimate extremity and frailty of his position. His utopian final assertion, that his proposed government would be a "complete image of eternal life on earth" and would "provide a foretaste of heaven"[390] should be outright rejected by the people of God. In reality, his government would use collectivist social pressures and, should that fail, the threat of violent "social separation" through prison or banishment[391] to enforce an unscriptural dogma of *the work of Jesus Christ limited by the preeminent forces of nature*, while calling it "promoting cultural Christianity".

> Jesus answered, "My kingdom is not of this world. If my kingdom were of this world, my servants would have been fighting, that I might not be delivered over to the Jews. But my kingdom is not from the world." (John 18:36)

IV. Celebrating Decline

Wolfe is very much correct that a "regime-enforced moral ideology" is being forced upon us, especially our children, "as the standard of moral respectability".[392] There is genuine reason to lament the decline of Second Table morality in the West, and to vociferously advocate for its reinstatement, regardless of what an increasing majority of our countrymen believe. But, this is very different from the "Bible Belt near-Christianity" which Russell Moore derides in his blog post, *Is Christianity Dying?*,[393] and which Wolfe attempts to champion; the social pressures of Southern cultural Christianity have a very dark past, one that even Moore avoided in

---

390 Wolfe, 223.
391 Wolfe, 391.
392 Wolfe, 224.
393 Russell Moore, "Is Christianity Dying?," Russell Moore, May 12, 2015, https://www.russellmoore.com/2015/05/12/is-christianity-dying/.

5. The Good of Cultural Christianity

his post but which should not be omitted from the discussion. Wolfe should be given some benefit of the doubt here, because he is possibly not familiar with much of the history of the Southern Baptist Convention, or other ecclesial institutions in the South – although he should be, as a Christian living in the South. Aspects of this history comport, at least tangentially, with much of what he has promoted in his book.

One of the more commonly known facts of the SBC's history is that it was founded in 1845 specifically to uphold the institution of slavery[394] (Presbyterians had a similar schism[395]). During reconstruction, SBC churches continued to force black Christians to the back of the church (a direct violation of James 2:1-6) and initially attempted to prevent them from forming their own churches, fearing Northern influence would make them "uppity." They quickly changed their position, as the majority of members wanted separation, though James Clement Furman, son of the founder of then SBC affiliated Furman University, told the 1866 convention that integration was fine as long as blacks maintained a lower status within mixed congregations. Several sub-associations began adding "all-white" clauses to their constitutions, at that time.[396]

Virulent anti-Catholicism was rampant in the South well into the 20th century, and the region had a number of newspapers dedicated to anti-Catholicism, many of which were edited by active ministers. The most popular anti-Catholic paper, *The Menace*, published in Aurora, Missouri, had nearly 1.5 million subscribers at its height in 1914.[397] Arkansan Missionary Baptist pastor Joseph Addison Scarboro and his weekly *The Liberator* are a good example of the content of these papers. Regularly accused of using his publication to advocate for mob violence, he promoted such policies as government inspection of all convents, Houses of the Good

---

[394] "Report on Slavery and Racism in the History of the Southern Baptist Theological Seminary," SBTS, accessed March 20, 2023, https://www.sbts.edu/southern-project/.

[395] Elwyn A. Smith, "The Role of the South in the Presbyterian Schism of 1837–38," *Church History* 29, no. 1 (1960): 44–63, https://doi.org/10.2307/3161616.

[396] John W. Storey, "Southern Baptists and the Racial Controversy in the Churches and Schools During Reconstruction," *The Mississippi Quarterly* 31, no. 2 (1978): 211–28.

[397] Barnes, *Anti-Catholicism in Arkansas*, 69; Williams, *Shadow of the Pope*, 117.

Shepherd, and nunneries if twenty citizens signed a petition, something that was made state law in 1915 and not repealed until 1937; in the October 12, 1913 issue, he wrote, "Preacher, load your gun and go after Romanism. The hunting season is now and the game is plentiful."[398] In both the 1928 and 1960 presidential elections, where Catholics Al Smith and John Kennedy were run by the Democratic party, respectively, the SBC, made up mostly of Democrats, took an official stance against voting for Roman Catholics to public office.[399]

Many SBC congregations were openly against desegregation, and some continued to vote to remain segregated as late as 1968.[400] South Carolina's Bob Jones University, a fundamentalist, non-denominational school whose namesake was a devout segregationist, officially prohibited interracial dating between students until 2000.[401] Clearly, "Bible Belt near-Christianity" has far more implications than the "mild social norms" Wolfe attempts to make it out as.[402]

Russell Moore left his position within the SBC in 2021 over his disagreement with how allegations of racism and sexual abuse were handled by the convention,[403] something I have much agreement with him on. Since then, he has quickly made a name for himself as a foil to theological conservatives, joining an ever-growing group of former conservative Christian thought-leaders now championing "winsome" cultural engagement towards regime-promoted, relative morality. This is especially disconcerting, considering the position he resigned from was the leadership of the Southern Baptist Convention's commission responsible

---

398 Barnes, *Anti-Catholicism in Arkansas*, 18, 20, 54, 67.
399 Barnes, 182; Williams, *Shadow of the Pope*, 195.
400 "Love the Sinner," *The Economist*, October 22, 2015, https://www.economist.com/united-states/2015/10/22/love-the-sinner.
401 "Bob Jones University Apologizes for Its Racist Past," The Journal of Blacks in Higher Education, accessed March 20, 2023, https://www.jbhe.com/news_views/62_bobjones.html.
402 Wolfe, *The Case for Christian Nationalism*, 225.
403 Bob Smietana, "Russell Moore, Baptist Ethicist and Trump Critic, to Leave ERLC for Christianity Today," *Religion News Service* (blog), May 19, 2021, https://religionnews.com/2021/05/18/russell-moore-baptist-ethicist-and-trump-critic-to-leave-erlc-for-christianity-today/.

5. The Good of Cultural Christianity

for promoting absolute ethics. Still, the 2015 blog post that Wolfe takes issue with is quite different than how it is painted.

That people in the 1940s avoided divorce when, as Moore writes, "the motive wasn't obedience to Jesus' command on marriage but instead because they knew that a divorce would marginalize them from their communities," is dismissed by Wolfe as "the social benefits of cultural Christianity." Though I think it is more guided by ignorance than maleficence, the implications of this dismissal are that a not too uncommon situation, a woman with a husband who beats her and their children deciding to not speak up or leave the marriage due to social pressures, was a good thing for society. Wolfe's portrayal of the spirit of the piece is almost wholly inaccurate. For example, a quote from Moore's article that is ignored by Wolfe has a decidedly conservative character:

> Secularization in America means that we have fewer incognito atheists. Those who don't believe can say so – and still find spouses, get jobs, volunteer with the PTA, and even run for office. This is good news because the kind of "Christianity" that is a means to an end – even if that end is "traditional family values" – is what J. Gresham Machen rightly called "liberalism," and it is an entirely different religion from the apostolic faith handed down by Jesus Christ.[404]

This sentiment of secularization serving as a natural, intermediary separation of wheat from tares (Matthew 13:24-30) is something I have heard from several very conservative PCA pastors. Moore is also correct in his description of what Machen wrote of cultural Christianity in his exceptional book *Christianity and Liberalism*. In his time and place, the Presbyterian Church in the United States of America (PCUSA) had become little more than a social club, where many of the pastors did not believe the core tenets of the gospel, such as the divinity of Christ (and it has remained this way). This is likely what would happen to congregations under Wolfe's government too, with even more potential for wrongdoing. How many people, including ministers, would become more interested in maintaining

---

[404] Moore, "Is Christianity Dying?"

social order than privately working with those who struggle with sin? How many members would become legalistic terrors to their congregation, ready to denounce people who struggle with doubt to both church and state? Perhaps Wolfe glossed over this paragraph, because it derides the exact type of cultural Christianity he wants to enforce. His straw-manning of Moore as someone who "wants a society and government that actively destroy communities like Mayberry,"[405] when he was referring to small town, "nosy neighbor," performative "Christianity" for social status, is a taste of the type of unnecessary and unfair personal attacks that are commonplace on Wolfe's Twitter account. This accusation is also very leftist in its character, in that it assumes that someone who does not like the proposed solution must not care about the problem (i.e., "If you are against universal basic income then you must hate poor people.").

> But I must ask: How is the loss of cultural Christianity going for you?[406]

Considering that the disciple counts it as joy when he meets "trials of various kinds", knowing that the "testing of [his] faith produces steadfastness" (James 1:2-3), *I'm doing just fine, thank you*. As shown above, this does not mean that I am happy with the rapid moral devolution of our society, nor will I stop advocating for its reversal, but *my joy is not subject to such a reversal* (Matthew 6:19-20); and, as Moore described, I have an extended church family of people who genuinely seek Christ, and who are committed to unpretentious life together. Wolfe thinks it egregious that Moore, in his view, believes "the Gospel flourishes when the enemies of God have social power,"[407] but this is perfectly inline with early church thought. As the 2nd century Christian author, Tertullian, famously wrote in his *Apologeticus*, "The blood of the martyrs is the seed of the church." The stoning of Stephen (Acts 7) served both as a watershed moment for the

---

405 Wolfe, *The Case for Christian Nationalism*, 226.
406 Wolfe, 227.
407 Wolfe, 227.

5. The Good of Cultural Christianity

New Testament's most prolific author and as the motivation for Christians in Jerusalem to "scatter" and preach the word of God elsewhere (Acts 8:4).

What would Wolfe tell our brothers and sisters in Afghanistan, China, North Korea, and anywhere else where governments physically persecute believers? Should they resign themselves to a life of absolute misery, because they will never know the *complete good*? There is a saying in the military that, as a fellow veteran, I know Wolfe would understand the full weight of. Though he sees his aggressive stance as strong, as a Christian, his position lacks *intestinal fortitude*, because he does not fully trust in his chain of command. He is unsatisfied with the Scriptural position of *exile and sojourner*; he has outright berated such thought at several points in the book, thus far. Unfortunately for him, that is the state of a Bible-believing Christian in every generation of Christendom, including one of the sources of his appeals to tradition, 16th-century Switzerland. Reformer Pierre Viret, in a letter to Admiral Gaspard de Coligny, noted the common, unscriptural proverb among the Swiss and French, "If you act like a sheep, you'll be eaten by a wolf." He went on to discuss one of the great paradoxes of Christian life in any era:

> This is why He said to His disciples: "Behold, I send you forth as sheep in the midst of wolves" (Matthew 10:16). He Himself is the Good Shepherd who gives His life for His sheep (John 10:11). But here it doesn't seem like He's performing the office of a good shepherd. Instead, it looks like He's doing the complete opposite when He sends His sheep among the wolves instead of guarding and defending them. For, if it's contrary to the office of a good shepherd to abandon his sheep to the wolves, it's much worse for him to send them to the wolves. For, according to human reason, this is exactly the same as delivering them into their paws and giving them up as a prey.
>
> But God forbid that we should consider Jesus Christ as such a shepherd, for He bears such affection for His sheep that He didn't spare His own life for them. And He guards them in such good keeping that, just as He Himself promised and testified, not a

single one of them can be snatched from His hands by any power at all, either human or demonic…

But when He said, "Behold, I send you," we can be even more assured that, since it is He Himself who sends them, He sends them in such a way that He always maintains their care and is always right beside them and always guards and protects them in the midst of the cruelest and fiercest wolves in the world. Therefore by this He shows by effect what kind of Shepherd He is and what power and strength He possesses, since by it He works in such a way that the sheep under His protection conquer and overcome the wolves in the end.[408]

V. Preparation and Hypocrisy

I readily admit that cultural Christianity cannot save souls and that it often produces hypocrisy. As I said above, it is not a means of salvific grace. It is a supplemental mode of religion.[409]

If cultural Christianity *often* produces hypocrisy, then Wolfe has at least partially affirmed Moore's statement that "Mayberry leads to hell just as surely as Gomorrah does,"[410] even if he thinks the benefits for his in-group outweigh the costs for the out-group. He again straw-mans Moore as affirming "social power *as a hostile force* is a necessary condition for Christianity to thrive."[411] What Moore wrote was that hostility is *a better condition for revival* than normalization of cultural "near-Christianity":

Christianity isn't normal anymore, and that's good news. The Book of Acts, like the Gospels before it, shows us that the Christianity thrives when it is, as Kierkegaard put it, a sign of contradiction. Only a strange gospel can differentiate itself from the worlds we construct. But the strange, freakish, foolish old

---

408 Viret, *When to Disobey*, 126, 128–29.
409 Wolfe, *The Case for Christian Nationalism*, 228.
410 Moore, "Is Christianity Dying?"
411 Wolfe, *The Case for Christian Nationalism*, 228.

> gospel is what God uses to save people and to resurrect churches (1 Corinthians 1:20-22).[412]

True discipleship will always be more concerned with heavenly good than earthly, and will always produce a *peculiar people* (1 Peter 2:9 KJV), especially when compared to nominal, performative Christians. Even in "Mayberry," the average citizen is happy to to talk with his neighbor about nearly anything but *that one thing*; Wolfe has tacitly proven this in that, though we are over two hundred pages into his book on *Christian Nationalism*, he has only given one measly paragraph to the actual good news. His greatest error throughout this chapter is to confuse the practice of *church discipline* with that of "the normalization of Christianity in society."[413] His brand of social power is not some collective looking-down of the nose, reminiscent of Dana Carvey's Church Lady character from *Saturday Night Live* – a relatively benign force that disapprovingly nudges recalcitrants into going to Sunday service to hear the word preached. His "nation perfected" would be made manifest through a violent revolution, expressly waged to end "our shame that we sheepishly tolerate assaults against our Christian heritage."[414] His "cultural Christianity" would tell dissidents to *keep their heads down and shut up,* lest one be denounced by his neighbor and have the organs of the state unleashed upon him. He wishes to institute a Christianized cancel culture, erroneously thinking that it will demonstrate the "plausibility of the Gospel."[415] The non-negotiable truth is that loving and forgiving those who openly hate us is *how Christians demonstrate the plausibility of the gospel,* because that is what Jesus Christ did when he gave his life for us while we were his enemies (Romans 5:10).

> The preparation to believe something does not make the resulting belief inauthentic; indeed, it would seem to make the belief *more* authentic, for you feel its truth. Prejudice completes reason. At the

---

412 Moore, "Is Christianity Dying?"
413 Wolfe, *The Case for Christian Nationalism*, 228.
414 Wolfe, 352.
415 Wolfe, 229.

very least, being against the world on some issue is not a necessary condition for authentic belief.[416]

Through an on-its-face fallacious, absolutist statement that *prejudice completes reason* (as if it cannot also equally subvert reason), Wolfe again favors a Nietzschian *will to power* worldview over Scripture and his own church's doctrine. We are directly commanded to "not be conformed to this world" to such a degree that we should be seen "as a living sacrifice" to God (Romans 12:1-2). We are "wholly defiled in all the parts and faculties of soul and body" (*WCF* 6.2) and must perpetually repent and realign ourselves to the perfect example of Christ. These are not half-measures that we can hand-wave away and say, "This is all well and good, but here are a few areas where I am going to not filter the world through my relationship with Christ." At some point in every Christian's life, he will need to be "against the world on some issue" as a "necessary condition for authentic belief." To refuse this is the very definition of idolatry. That Wolfe, on the one hand, is arguing for a *totality of Christian state action*, but, on the other hand, attempts to sidestep the conditions of *total faith in Christ*, by continuing to claim that there are aspects of the Christian's life not altered by the gospel, is strong evidence of rotten spiritual fruit.

He then yet again misrepresents his opposition with, "In other words [according to Moore], hostile social conditions lead fake Christians to abandon the faith, thereby making it easy to recognize who needs to hear encouragement in the faith and who needs conversion to the faith."[417] There is a monumental error in this statement, in that "fake Christians" do not have a faith to abandon in the first place. Moore is absolutely right that allowing them to be open about their doubts give us the opportunity to minister to them in ways that would not be possible if they feared being honest with us. That Wolfe immediately moves from this into the theme of protecting Christian families from hostile social forces lays bare the self-centered sinfulness of his framework of *pre-rational love*. He would seemingly rather spend his life in a church full of people pretending to be

---

416 Wolfe, 230.
417 Wolfe, 230.

5. The Good of Cultural Christianity

Christian, letting countless people he fellowships with face the unfathomable horror of Christ telling them "I never knew you" (Matthew 7:23), than for him and his blood relations to have to live among people who are publicly unfriendly to his religion.

Though he is correct that the preaching of the word of God is an ordinary means of grace that is effectual for bringing someone to faith in Christ,[418] it is but one piece in a larger puzzle. *Who* is preaching the word, *why* they are preaching the word, and *how* they are preaching the word is monumentally important – exponentially more so when the person speaking holds institutional power over the hearer, something that would be common under Christian nationalism.

On Easter Sunday, 2004, I was stationed at Camp Anaconda, just outside of Balad, Iraq. At this point in my life, I had walked away from a weak, nascent faith in Christ and had embraced Buddhism, a religion far more congruous to my Southern California upbringing; non-Christians in major cities often only interact with Christianity through street preachers who hold annoyingly large signs and bludgeon passers-by with threats of fire and brimstone through a megaphone. The charismatic Christianity of the only people who shared the genuine gospel with me – people whom I love and am grateful for – placed such heavy emphasis on emotional experience over doctrine that I was very much the "seed in rocky ground" (Matthew 13:1-9).

That Easter morning, someone in my chain of command forced everyone to go to the battalion service, regardless of their religion. I was livid, as this was a violation of Army policy, but I knew better than to make an issue of it and face assured administrative backlash. Since I was forced to go, the word of God was not effectual for me. My anger got the better of me, and I decided after the service to grill the chaplain on all the supposed contradictions I thought disproved the Bible, such as who actually bought the *field of blood*, and why it was named as such. Rather than see someone who needed empathy and engagement in honest apologetic discourse, the

---

418 Wolfe, 231.

chaplain gave a terse answer, then walked away, and Christians in my platoon chastised me for challenging him. I responded, "You made me come here when I didn't want to."

Back at Fort Bragg, when I was later made to speak to that same conservative Protestant chaplain because I was having a severe moral crisis after killing people in Iraq, instead of using that opportunity to lead me towards the gospel of forgiveness, he gave me a *pick yourself up by your bootstraps* speech that left me feeling he was more concerned with avoiding conscientious objector proceedings than with my well-being. Another time, a Christian platoon sergeant saw "Buddhist" on my dog tags during inspection and, while holding on to them, got in my face and said, "What's the matter, don't you like Jesus?" He was about to further berate me about my religion, or worse, when he was stopped by my first sergeant who, knowing of my status, had earlier confided in me that he had been adopted and raised around Buddhists, though he was not a practitioner. This is the regular experience of non-Christians when cultural Christianity is mixed with even minimal civil, bureaucratic power.

I do not hold anything against these people; they were a part of God's providential hand in my life, giving me first-hand experience in what it feels like to be on the wrong end of aggressive cultural Christianity, ultimately strengthening my own witness. This is one reason I disagree that our current climate in which, as Wolfe puts it, "Priestesses now have regular columns in national newspapers, and 'religion reporters' generate buzz around regime-friendly churches and leaders and disparage those deemed hostile"[419] is the existential threat to evangelism he makes it out to be. In the end, 2015 Russell Moore was correct that such a climate gives us the opportunity to share the gospel as the counter-cultural truth it is, even if 2023 Russell Moore is the Editor-In-Chief of the largest regime-friendly Christian news outlet.

---

419 Wolfe, 231.

5. The Good of Cultural Christianity

> While the costliness of faith in times of persecution can reveal the authenticity of faith, it does not clearly reveal the authenticity of belief… Persecution challenges one's faith, not his assent to propositions, for one can outwardly deny what he inwardly assents to. Persecution, if directed at those who affirm orthodox beliefs, will reveal true and false faith. I acknowledge this. But this speaks only to the direct effects of the less frequent overt form of persecution.[420]

As our Lord said, "One who is faithful in a very little is also faithful in much, and one who is dishonest in a very little is also dishonest in much" (Luke 16:10). If a member of the elect outwardly denies the propositions of Christianity when ridiculed by peers, in his heart he knows he has failed more than a mild challenge of faith. It may be the greatest spiritual test he ever faces; it has real metaphysical significance, and we should not diminish what passing such a test may say about the authenticity of someone's belief. For a few in the 21st-century Western workplace – not nearly every Christian, as Wolfe will argue in his epilogue – not denying Scriptural truths when under public social pressure can result in severe economic punishment; ask a conservative Christian working for Google or Facebook with a family to support and a mortgage on a multi-million dollar home if "assent to propositions" can not be a full test of the authenticity of his belief, one that rises to the level of *refusing to sprinkle salt on Caesar's altar*. Conversely, as much as Wolfe derides those who admonish right-wing excess, being willing to be shunned as a liberal, or worse, by the growing number of Christians who see the test of true faith as adherence to a set of narrow political propositions, is also a test of authenticity of belief for theological conservatives. We are not secularists, left with only our interpretation of general revelation to judge something's "authenticity." If a fellow Christian is facing any level of social, economic, or physical persecution for affirming a plain reading of Scripture, then we can consider such a trial to reveal the authenticity of his belief.

Wolfe is not wrong when he says that "social hostility eliminates a necessary condition of faith," but, by concerning himself with disdain for

---

420 Wolfe, 232.

Christianity, he points his statement in the wrong direction. Social hostility eliminates a necessary condition of faith *in that which is being hostilely pushed.* One need only look at the many people who parrot Critical Theory talking points out of fear of not being seen as a "good ally" to know hostile ideologies create fake believers, many of whom get caught up in the sadistic power they can wield through purity tests. He is wrong that "even in its abuse, cultural Christianity prepares people to receive Christ."[421] Its abuse pushes people away from true faith in Christ towards performative, fake Christianity; he opened this section admitting that. Thankfully, it can later serve as an example for the believer of how he should not behave, after he has received and accepted the gospel from people who actually make it their daily priority to emulate the Savior, even if it should put them at odds with "socially acceptable" Christians and secularists alike.

VI. Final Considerations

> All Christians today agree that the family is a vital source for transmitting the faith to the younger generation. It is not clear, however, why the family can play this role but not civil society.[422]

As shown previously, Scripture has many forthright instructions about the Christian family's role in transmitting the faith and is equally clear that God ordains civil societies for the Christian's good that do not necessarily transmit the faith. Wolfe further builds his straw-man by writing, "No one accuses Christian families of being hypocrite-factories, sending their kids straight to hell."[423] Are there not myriad stories of fundamentalist Christian parents who, through their over-zealousness, drove their children away from the faith? Wolfe will find few conservative Christians who would not advocate for a civil society that is *friendly* towards Christianity, but he is attempting to justify far more than that.

---

421 Wolfe, 232, 233.
422 Wolfe, 233–34.
423 Wolfe, 234.

5. The Good of Cultural Christianity

Was God's plan really to subject the little family and local churches to such powerful hostile forces and give them this narrow window of time (perhaps a dozen or so years) to prepare children for faith before tossing them to the world for testing?[424]

In short answer, *probably*. At least, there are some very direct words from Jesus that lead one to conclude that to be quite plausible. Though, as Viret reminds us, "He sends [us] in such a way that He always maintains [our] care."[425]

> "Behold, I am sending you out as sheep in the midst of wolves, so be wise as serpents and innocent as doves. Beware of men, for they will deliver you over to courts and flog you in their synagogues, and you will be dragged before governors and kings for my sake, to bear witness before them and the Gentiles." (Matthew 10:16-18)

> "Do you think that I have come to give peace on earth? No, I tell you, but rather division. For from now on in one house there will be five divided, three against two and two against three. They will be divided, father against son and son against father, mother against daughter and daughter against mother, mother-in-law against her daughter-in-law and daughter-in-law against mother-in-law." (Luke 12:51-53)

As before, it would seem that Wolfe is not happy with the Christian's status in the world as plainly laid out in Scripture; perhaps this is why he is so indisposed to integrating it into his theory. His obsession with "living well in this world," to a point that he is willing to institutionalize a cultural Christianity that he admits "often produces hypocrites," is directly contradictory to the instructions of Christ to His disciples. There is no way around this; whatever Wolfe's theory is, it is not *Christ-centered*.

---

424 Wolfe, 234.
425 Viret, *When to Disobey*, 129.

At least intuitively, everyone seems to recognize that when you reject the idea of Christian civil society, some essential element of life is left unaccounted for, and so you must expand the church's function and roles in the life of a believer.[426]

The repeated use of *alleged certainty* logical fallacies in this section (*all Christians today agree, no one accuses, everyone seems to recognize*) exposes the weakness of his argument, and perhaps a lack of intellectual testing of it, on his own part. In this instance, his appeal is a blatantly false one, because every Western Christian does not recognize explicitly Christian civil society as an "essential element of life". Much of the Epistles are dedicated to how the ἐκκλησία (ekklésia), the assembly of saints we call a "church", plays an essential and primary role in the life of the believer. No such role is given to civil authority, neither ἄρχων (archón, ruler) nor βασιλεύς (basileus, king). Instead, the believer is to pray for these authorities, that they may enact their primary duty of ensuring that the ἐκκλησία can live in peace (1 Timothy 2:1-2). While we may count it a blessing when a civil magistrate is a devout Christian, this is something that must come about through the peaceful application of the Great Commission. It comes from the work of the Holy Spirit, not our worldly antagonism towards unfriendly governments.

He next takes umbrage with the variety of resources many churches provide for members, "children's ministries, schools, sports programs, family counseling, and an array of special-interest and support groups and clubs,"[427] highlighting his inability to accept the current state of the Western mission field. *Bible-believing Christians are in the extreme minority in America.* I highly doubt that he would begrudge the church in Malaysia, Japan, or India for having similar ecclesial programs. The SBC's International Mission Board considers an *unreached people* to be "any people group that is less than 2 percent evangelical Christian."[428] By this

---

426 Wolfe, *The Case for Christian Nationalism*, 235.
427 Wolfe, 235–36.
428 Zane Pratt, "Here's What We Mean by Unreached Peoples and Places," *IMB* (blog), November 22, 2016, https://www.imb.org/2016/11/22/what-do-we-mean-by-unreached-peoples-and-places/.

5. The Good of Cultural Christianity

metric, deep blue areas of America should be placed in the same category as Saudi Arabia and Nepal. Most Americans, including those in the Bible-Belt, do not attend church weekly, but there is good news that backs up Russell Moore's claims. Church attendance among Millennials and Gen-X is above pre-pandemic levels.[429] Since it would be very difficult to make a case that American society has become *more* favorable towards Christianity since 2020, this would seem to prove Moore's point that hostility helps the true faith flourish.

Wolfe is grossly incorrect in his following statement, that the church should be concerned with nothing but the liturgical worship of God[430] – strangely, only two sections back in this same chapter, he was appealing to how charity work was administered in "medieval and early modern periods" (more often than not, under the purview of the church). Again, Scripture directly rebukes him. We may decide to parse the practical application of the following verses for modern times, but it cannot be said that the apostolic church only concerned itself with "administering sacred things" and that anything else was "accidental."

> Now the full number of those who believed were of one heart and soul, and no one said that any of the things that belonged to him was his own, but they had everything in common. And with great power the apostles were giving their testimony to the resurrection of the Lord Jesus, and great grace was upon them all. There was not a needy person among them, for as many as were owners of lands or houses sold them and brought the proceeds of what was sold and laid it at the apostles' feet, and it was distributed to each as any had need (Acts 4:32-35).

He then moves on to claim that, "Having only social power, cultural Christianity cannot, **by itself**, lead anyone to act internally according to the proper spiritual motivation" (emphasis mine).[431] This statement would take on a wholly different character to the reader if it was placed *after* the

---
429 "A New Chapter in Millennial Church Attendance," Barna Group, accessed March 22, 2023, https://www.barna.com/research/church-attendance-2022/.
430 Wolfe, *The Case for Christian Nationalism*, 236.
431 Wolfe, 236.

chapters where Wolfe advocates for violent revolution, followed by execution of "arch-heretics" and recalcitrant evangelists of false religions. I have expressed this several times already, but it cannot be stated enough: Wolfe's brand of cultural Christianity does not do *anything* "by itself." It is the "Christian nationalist" version of the Junior Spies in George Orwell's *1984* – an ever-present, propagandized people ready to denounce anyone engaged in thoughtcrime, allowing the authorities to determine if their publicly-expressed, heterodox beliefs are worthy of "civil punishment." It would be inevitable that not only non-Christians in his proposed nation but also Christians who do not belong to the state church would live in constant fear of saying the wrong thing to the wrong person.

An irony, in that civil enforcement of orthodox Reformed doctrine is promoted by Wolfe, is shown in his later statement that, "But only [our children], by grace, can choose spiritual obedience; only they can adorn their virtuous habits with true piety."[432] This soteriologically hazy statement, when mixed with his previous one that "man cooperates with grace," once again casts doubt on his adherence to his church's doctrine of *Irresistible Grace* and *Perseverance of the Saints*. In the Reformed view, we do not *choose* spiritual obedience; God chooses us and effectively calls us to a spiritual obedience (*WCF* 17.1) that is in no way dependent on our own will (17.2). In fact, our fallen inclination is to run away from such grace (17.3). An orthodox Reformed version of this sentence would read more like, "Only by the work of the Holy Spirit can our children be called to spiritual obedience; we pray that God would lead them to adorn the virtuous habits we teach them with true piety." As previously mentioned, this would not be an issue if he did not define his theory as "Presbyterian Christian nationalism." If orthodox Presbyterianism were made the official state religion in Wolfe's mode of government, most of the theological assertions made in his book would put him in the position of having to explain himself to a civil doctrinal committee; not the least of these is his wildly heterodox prelapsarian theory.

---

432 Wolfe, 237.

5. The Good of Cultural Christianity

> But [secret non-Christians'] conformity is still good as to the outward action, for (1) it has led them to regularly hear the Gospel; (2) their conformity helps to sustain the cultural practices in the community, leading others to hear the Gospel – and (3) it helps to sustain civil honesty, social institutions (e.g., marriages), and civil manners that work for the common good.[433]

It would seem that, instead of having to contend with the disciple's expressly stated evangelical requirement of associating with, and not judging, sinful people in a fallen world, Wolfe would rather make his whole country an extension of the church, so he can revert to judging everyone (1 Corinthians 5:9-13). This is also implied in his injudicious assertion that his nation would "make the earthly city an analog of the heavenly city," because the *real* heavenly city has no ecclesial/civil separation and is not occupied by sinners. He closes this subsection by straw-manning his opposition's argument, claiming they believe cultural Christianity "lead[s] the unregenerate to sin." *Aggressive* cultural Christianity causes people to fear expressing their doubt, leading us to not properly minister to them, and leaving them in a position less likely to accept the gospel than if they felt free to speak openly. Jesus Christ – the One we are to emulate – does not force anyone to *pretend to believe in Him* under threat of being cut-off from earthly good in this life. These verses bear repeating:

> But I say to you, Love your enemies and pray for those who persecute you, so that you may be sons of your Father who is in heaven. For he makes his sun rise on the evil and on the good, and sends rain on the just and on the unjust. For if you love those who love you, what reward do you have? Do not even the tax collectors do the same? (Matthew 5:44-46)

Wolfe next moves to negate criticism of his aggressive methodology, writing, "One often hears that cultural Christianity harms 'Christian moral witness.' Rarely, if ever, is moral witness defined or theologically

---
433 Wolfe, 237.

grounded, but is often used to denounce the pursuit of worldly power (both social power and civil power)."[434] In the last section, I shared some specific instances in my life when a Christian's surety in his majority status and/or institutional power led him to harm his "moral witness." Wolfe's claim that such a thing is rarely defined is simply not true; agnostic and atheist Westerners often share tales of Christians being "jerks for Jesus." I do not know how he is in person, but Wolfe is one among a growing list of self-described Christian Nationalists whose social media accounts exhibit a near-perpetual state of *in-group/out-group* antagonism, flinging ad hominems towards those who disagree with them on seemingly any subject, including other Christians. There is a distinct "schoolyard bully" essence to the way Reformed Christian Nationalists act within the digital public square, often ganging up on an ideological opponent, collectively hurling childish insults that have little to nothing to do with whatever the opponent said to draw their ire.[435] In doing so, Wolfe and other Christian Nationalists show exactly what type of "social pressures" they would bring to bear in their "Christian" nation.

Secondly, it is entirely false that arguments for our "moral witness" are rarely theologically grounded, so much so that I am shocked he made such a statement. That he admitted in the introduction that he has "no training in moving from Scriptural interpretation to theological articulation,"[436] yet would now presume to tell the reader what is and is not "theologically grounded," is immensely hubristic. It is no coincidence that I will later refer to some of the following verses to argue against blasphemy law.

> Walk in wisdom toward outsiders, making the best use of the time. Let your speech always be gracious, seasoned with salt, so that

---

434 Wolfe, 238.
435 An example of this mockery: In response to an anti-leftist, Christian author and speaker, Michael Young (who uses the name Wokal Distance on Twitter), pointing out Stephen Wolfe's defense of the antisemitic writings of Christian Nationalist author Andrew Torba, online personality, and self-described Christian Nationalist, Adam "AD" Robles tweeted, "Wokal needs to add his pronouns to the bio. Its only fair."
https://twitter.com/ADRoblesMedia/status/1676746128585261056
436 Wolfe, *The Case for Christian Nationalism*, 16.

you may know how you ought to answer each person (Colossians 4:5-6).

Keep your conduct among the Gentiles honorable, so that when they speak against you as evildoers, they may see your good deeds and glorify God on the day of visitation (1 Peter 2:12).

For this is the will of God, that by doing good you should put to silence the ignorance of foolish people (1 Peter 2:15).

And the Lord's servant must not be quarrelsome but kind to everyone, able to teach, patiently enduring evil, correcting his opponents with gentleness. God may perhaps grant them repentance leading to a knowledge of the truth, and they may come to their senses and escape from the snare of the devil, after being captured by him to do his will (2 Timothy 2:24-26).

The remainder of this subsection is dedicated to using non-Christians' desire for worldly power as justification for Christians to seek the same, once again showing how little Wolfe's theory is concerned with the commandments of Christ. The primary aim of the Christian witness is to be *wholly different* in thought and deed than the world, most especially in the realm of power-seeking.

> And Jesus called them to him and said to them, "You know that those who are considered rulers of the Gentiles lord it over them, and their great ones exercise authority over them. But it shall not be so among you. But whoever would be great among you must be your servant, and whoever would be first among you must be slave of all. For even the Son of Man came not to be served but to serve, and to give his life as a ransom for many." (Mark 10:42-45)

When he writes, "Why shouldn't Christian witness include a confident socio-cultural assertion of its truth?",[437] he is holding back the true extent of his proposed *socio-cultural* action; in chapters 8 and 9, he will argue that we should do far more than just *verbally* defend our position. He yet again

---
437 Wolfe, 239.

paints his opposition with a broad, unfair brush and bolsters his all-or-nothing proposition by claiming that they "celebrate our people and place being overrun with moral chaos."[438] There are certainly some Christians, like New York Times columnist David French, who allow their libertarian absolutism to override Second Table morality and go as far as to defend the legislative protection of egregious sin as "civil liberties."[439] But there are also many conservative Christians who wish to legislate Second Table morality while not compromising their witness or the principles of republicanism. I am not referring to what has been described as "winsome third-wayism," an acquiescence to sinful cultural norms in the hope that it will open a door for later witness, nor am I advocating that we allow the state to force their worldview on our families. We should always boldly affirm Scriptural truth and refuse to participate in sinful commands from governmental authorities, but we should also *always* aim to be patient and peaceful when doing so. Wolfe may not like that, but he cannot deny it is the example set forth by Christ and the Apostles, who, Scripture and church tradition tell us, went to their deaths peacefully defending God's absolute truth.

This section is ended with a sentiment I wholeheartedly agree with, that national flags and patriotic song-singing should not be part of worship[440]; my church does this every July 4th service, and it makes me uncomfortable, especially as someone who was sent to fight a war, and killed people, over a lie of *weapons of mass destruction*. The sabbath should be the day that Christians focus on their allegiance to the nation to come and, while we can show gratitude and intercede for our earthly nation and its leaders through prayer, we should not incorporate patriotism into our liturgy. That being said, there is irony in how Wolfe then writes, "Nor must Christian politics be some extension of formal Christian ministry, organized by the instituted church." He somehow believes that giving civil

---

438 Wolfe, 239.
439 David French, "Opinion | Don't Let the Culture War Degrade the Constitution," *The New York Times*, March 12, 2023, sec. Opinion, https://www.nytimes.com/2023/03/12/opinion/newsom-desantis-walgreens-constitution.html.
440 Wolfe, *The Case for Christian Nationalism*, 239–40.

authorities the power to enforce orthodoxy of doctrine and placing the nation under the monarchy of a "Christian prince," who "mediates divine rule... by a sort of divine presence," "suppress[es] the enemies of God," and has veto power over doctrinal decisions,[441] is not letting the eternal kingdom bleed into the temporal.

VII. Conclusion

> Christians need to recover an assertive will for their good and have the spirit and resolve to exclude what is bad. We should use social power to oppose those who threaten them and who attempt to subvert our faith or exploit its moral demands. That means opposing, suppressing and excluding the very sort of people who run the American regime. A Christian society that is for itself will distrust atheists, decry blasphemy, correct any dishonoring of Christ... frown on and suppress moral deviancy... A Christian nation that is true to itself will unashamedly and confidently assert Christian supremacy over the land...
>
> A people must have spirit, self-affirmation, self-regard, and confidence in themselves. They must, in other words, become the opposite of what Western Christianity has become. The spirit to live says, "This is ours for our good," and it drives a people to endure the sacrifices to keep it.[442]

In preparation for the remainder of the book, in which he describes the near-ubiquitous repression he would unleash against his ideological enemies, Wolfe brings his rhetoric to a climax, using the *language of destiny* to unite his audience around an emotional appeal to protect their dignity from, and assert their dominance over, the enemy forces of the *liberal order*. This is textbook authoritarian-nationalist speechcraft, placing the call-to-action in absolutist, *them versus us* terms. Here are some samplings from the Falangist leader, José Antonio Primo de Rivera, and how they speak to the same means and ends:

---

441 Wolfe, 290, 313, 323.
442 Wolfe, 240–41.

The need for extra-legal measures:

The destiny of the people is to shun the democratic process and *assert their supremacy* over an opposition that actively maligns them and abuses the system (i.e., "those who threaten them and who attempt to subvert our faith or exploit its moral demands," atheists, blasphemers, moral deviants):

> In obedience to our destiny we travel from place to place, enduring the shame of appareling like a public show; obliged to shout aloud things we have thought out in the austerest silence; suffering distortion at the hands of those who do not and those who will not understand us; breaking our backs in this ridiculous sham, this procedure of winning over "public opinion" as if the people, capable as it is of love or anger, were collectively susceptible of opinion.[443]

The purity of the fatherland threatened:

The attempt to *subvert the moral order* is an existential threat from *an irredeemable other*; they should be suppressed by the *true people of the nation*, who must first regain their forgotten, ancestral qualities (i.e., "Christians need to recover an assertive will for their good", and "A people must have spirit, self-affirmation, self-regard, and confidence in themselves"):

> The "feeling" of the movement now coming to the fore is fundamentally anti-Spanish. It is hostile to the Patria. It scorns chastity by encouraging the collective prostitution of young working girls at those country festivals were [sic] every sort of impurity is practiced… Is this Spain? Is this people of Spain? You would think we were living in a nightmare, or that the ancient Spanish people – serene, courageous, generous – had been replaced by a frenzied and degenerate plebs, drugged with Communist propaganda pamphlets.[444]

---

443 Greger, *Jose Antonio Primo de Rivera*, 64.
444 Greger, 141.

5. The Good of Cultural Christianity

***The only available option*:**
Our current situation is a binary dilemma, with only a single, radical, *all-or-nothing* solution. The baby must be thrown out with the bath-water (i.e., "They must, in other words, become the opposite of what Western Christianity has become"). Through embracing this solution – the only one that was ever legitimate – the people will realize their destiny of national revival:

> There are only two serious ways of life: the religious way and the military (or, if you like, there is only one, for there is no religion that is not a militia, and there is no militia that is not quickened by a religious feeling), and the hour has now come for us to realize that it is by this religious and military interpretation of life that Spain is destined to be restored.[445]

One thing can be said with absolute certainty: the last thing that someone who has wholly given himself to following the Son of God is interested in is *asserting supremacy*. The Creator of the universe, the most *supreme* Being, condescended Himself, suffered the most horrible revilement, and was brutally murdered, *for our sake*. "When he was reviled, he did not revile in return; when he suffered, he did not threaten, but continued entrusting himself to Him who judges justly." (1 Peter 2:21-23). This is the example he expressly left us to emulate; anything short of denying our worldly desires, picking up our cross, and following him is failure (Luke 9:23). Of course, we will all fail, but the difference is whether you feel remorse and repent for your failure or build a framework of rationalization around it.

Ultimately, I find Stephen Wolfe's worldview to be one that lacks trust in the sovereignty of God. His hyper-concern for attaining what he sees as the complete material and spiritual good, in this life – his *complete good* – is directly contradictory to the teachings of Christ, who said, "Whoever loves his life loses it, and whoever hates his life in this world will keep it for eternal life" (John 12:25). So much of what I see from self-described

---

445 Greger, 157.

Christian Nationalists is little more than an inability to accept their status of sheep among wolves, or perhaps a *fear of it*. There is a seeming paradox on the surface level of the Christian experience; we are told that we will be hated by everyone and may even be murdered for His name's sake (Matthew 10:22, Matthew 24:9), yet at the same time His yoke is easy and his burden light (Matthew 11:30). But, below the surface – beyond nominal, cultural Christianity – this is not a paradox; once the disciple has wholly placed himself in the hands of God, once he has consciously committed to make all things in his heart subservient to Christ, then he is truly, in full spiritual reality, *raised with Him* and has the confidence and joy that comes with seeking the things that are above (Colossians 3:1). He knows that fretting over an earthly utopia is nothing but "vanity and a striving after wind" (Ecclesiastes 1:14), and rejects emotional appeals for the active, wholesale suppression of enemies.

We are now at the turning point of the book. Wolfe has set his "theological" stage and will now move into the realm of his expertise, political theory, but the play he has written is a *fantasy adventure* based in a world of grievance and conjecture. He has not presented a Christian worldview that supports nationalism but has instead clumsily shoehorned a quasi-Christianity into his nationalist preconceptions. It is not Christian Nationalism; it is *Authoritarian Ethno-Nationalism with Western European Christianity as the cultural identity*.[446]

---

446 I am certain that calling his theory *ethno-nationalism* will result in significant protest from Wolfe and his supporters. I would refer them back to chapter 3, where I noted multiple assertions by him, in the book and online, that directly promote white nationalist tropes or that only make sense in the context of white ethnocentrism. His driving question of the chapter, *Which Way, Western Man?*, is the title of a well-known white nationalist book, which his podcast co-host used in its full, white nationalist context on social media, at the very time Wolfe was interacting with his anonymous account. I have also noted that his requirement of "blood-ties" in the identity of the nation is *more ethnocentric* than the political theory of Spanish and Italian fascists.

6. What Laws Can and Cannot Do

I. Law in General

> That distinction which is put between the Laws of God and the laws of men becomes a snare to many as it is misapplied in the ordering of their obedience to civil Authority; for when the Authority is of God and that in way of an Ordinance, (Romans 13:1) and when the administration of it is according to deductions, and rules gathered from the word of God, and the clear light of nature in civil nations, surely there is no humane law that tends to common good (according to those principles) but the same is immediately a law of God, and that in way of an Ordinance which all are to submit unto and that for conscience sake (Romans 13:5).[447]

The chapter on civil law is opened with a quote from the preamble of the 1647 *Laws and Liberties of Massachusetts*, which references Romans 13 to justify the people's requirement to submit to the laws of that theocracy.[448] As mentioned above, most conservative American Christians would consider many aspects of these laws to be quite undesirable; this includes the law that drove the Salem Witch Trials and one where a boy who was raped by a man could face corporal punishment of up to forty stripes.

> IF any man after legal conviction shall HAVE OR WORSHIP any other God, but the LORD GOD: he shall be put to death.
>
> If any man or woman be a WITCH, that is, has or consults with a familiar spirit, they shall be put to death.
>
> If any man LIES WITH [A MAN] as he lies with a woman, both of them have committed abomination, they both shall surely be put to

---

447 The Book of the General Laws and Liberties Concerning the Inhabitants of the Massachusetts (1647).
This is the full paragraph that Wolfe quotes from to open the chapter.
448 Wolfe, *The Case for Christian Nationalism*, 243.

death: unless the one party were forced (or be under fourteen years of age in which case he shall be severely punished) That no Jesuit, or spiritual or ecclesiastical person [as they are termed] ordained by the authority of the Pope, or See of Rome shall henceforth at any time repair to, or come within this Jurisdiction: And if any person shall give just cause of suspicion that he is one of such Society or Order he shall be brought before some of the Magistrates, and if he cannot free himself of such suspicion he shall be committed to prison, or bound over to the next Court of Assistants, to be tried and proceeded with by Banishment or otherwise as the Court shall see cause: and if any person so banished shall be taken the second time within this Jurisdiction upon lawful trial and conviction he shall be put to death.[449]

Wolfe does not directly address the preamble quote, or explain its context, in this section; the only statements remotely related to it are a section on "deductions" and a reference to God-granted "types of power" in the end of the section, but neither are tied back to this colonial law. This quote also refers to several beliefs that seem contradictory to ideas Wolfe promotes in his book. It mentions the "clear light of nature in civil nations," secondary to "rules gathered from the word of God," meaning that those without special revelation are not able to properly deduce God's will through general revelation (natural law) alone; this is something that would be obvious to colonists living in close proximity to native peoples. It is especially interesting that Wolfe decided not to include the first half of the first sentence of the paragraph, because its appeal to a unity between the "[Mosaic] Laws of God and the laws of men" works slightly against his later dismissal of modern theonomy (though it works well for his arguments against *neo-Anabaptism*). He also never addresses the two references to Romans 13 in this section, though they are the driving force behind the quote he chose to open the chapter with; let us examine them in their historical context.

---

449 The Book of the General Laws and Liberties.

6. What Laws Can and Cannot Do

> Let every person be subject to the governing authorities. For there is no authority except from God, and those that exist have been instituted by God. (Romans 13:1)

> Therefore one must be in subjection, not only to avoid God's wrath but also for the sake of conscience. (Romans 13:5)

The book of Romans was written during the reign of Emperor Nero, who was anything but a friend to Christianity. Church history tells us that, approximately two years before Paul wrote these words, the Apostle Philip was scourged and crucified in Roman-controlled Phrygia. Paul would later too be martyred under Nero, who, among other tortures, also "had some [Christians] sewed up in skins of wild beasts, and then worried by dogs until they expired; and others dressed in shirts made stiff with wax, fixed to axletrees, and set on fire in his gardens in order to illuminate them."[450] We should never lose sight of the fact that Paul was martyred by the highest governing authority, the *very person* he told his readers to obey in all earthly matters, or face "God's wrath." The context of Romans 13 tells us that Christians should submit to the civil requirements of all governments, as long as they do not demand we violate the commandments of God, even if those governments are a supreme tyranny to Christians. This is not modern interpretation; Calvin was insistent, as far back as the 1536 version of the *Institutes*, that Christians must be obedient to tyrannical governments.[451] Thus, the quote that Wolfe uses to open his chapter on civil law negates his later chapter, *The Right to Revolution*, and his call, just a few pages back, for "opposing, suppressing and excluding the very sort of people who run the American regime." Wolfe will address Romans 13 in that chapter, including the context of Nero, making the incredibly theologically dubious claim that "no power ordained of God can command what is evil,"[452] using that as a way to wiggle out of God's command of

---
450 Forbush, *Book of Martyrs*, 3, 4, 6.
451 Tuininga, *Calvin's Political Theology and the Public Engagement of the Church*, 241.
452 Wolfe, *The Case for Christian Nationalism*, 359.
  This will be addressed in more detail in chapter 8, but Wolfe seems to forget that God has previously ordained violent, oppressive power over his people (Isaiah

subjection to authority. I will revisit this context when that section is reached, and break down his poor hermeneutic, which does not account for similar instructions of submission from others within the Reformed exegetical tradition of the 16th and 17th centuries, but also from the Apostle Peter *and Christ*.

> In the previous chapter, we discussed social custom... But this prejudicial ordering has limitations: it is neither centralized nor possessed and exercised by a decisional authority, nor does it permit the use of outward force to achieve compliance.[453]

The previous chapter was not about generic customs, such as holding a door open for someone or respect for elders, but was dedicated to how *cultural Christianity* can be used to force people to pretend to be Christian, which supposedly maintains the *social order*. All the talk of its effectiveness is now thrown out the window, for Wolfe has implicitly admitted, right at the outset of this chapter, that his nation would use such "social power" as little more than an implied threat of state violence for "achieving compliance" with religious doctrine. Perhaps he knows the reader is not ready for that explicit admission, and that is why he retreats into the more secularized language of "social custom," now that legal authority is being brought into the equation. But the truth is that every social pressure in his nation, laid upon religious recalcitrants by their neighbors, would come with an implied "or else."

- Are you one of the twenty percent of Americans who believe in justification by works and papal authority? Keep that to yourself, *or else*.
- Are you one of the majority of American Protestants who believe that only full immersion of a professing believer is legitimate baptism? Do not advocate against the state church's view, *or else*.

10:5, Jeremiah 21:4), and still told them to seek the good of these nations (Jeremiah 29:7). God will not personally commit evil, but people he places in power over us most certainly can commit evil against us, and we very much can still be conscious bound by Him to submit to them (1 Peter 2:18).

453 Wolfe, 244.

6. What Laws Can and Cannot Do

- Do you believe in a fringe theory, such as well-known Christian apologist William Lane Craig's belief in Molinism (that God limits his knowledge to make room for free will)? Do not even think of publicly debating your case, *or else*.

Next, Wolfe argues for the sufficiency of man's reason to "discern and understand both the laws of his nature and why those laws are good for him," then immediately disproves that argument by presenting a definition of law that was not fully reasoned:

> *Law is an ordering of reason by an appropriate lawgiver for the good of the community.*[454]

The 20th-century laws that forced black Americans and South Africans to be segregated from whites, that forced Indians to serve the monopolistic interests of the British East India Company, and that prevented Protestants in Spain from sharing the gospel were all passed by *appropriate lawgivers*, the internationally recognized governments that ruled over those people. Clearly, law is not always good for the community; it is quite often only good for the ruling class, at the community's expense. Natural law, *as interpreted by humans*, is just as fallible as we are, yet Wolfe appeals to it as if its interpretation by the reprobate carries the same absolute truth of God's revealed word; he must do this, because he cannot (or will not) exegete Scripture to confirm what is true and false in their interpretations. A self-negating lack of objective reasoning behind such faith in the human interpretation of natural law is shown in that he, on the one hand, appeals to a biased selection of assumptions from pagan philosophers, such as Cicero, Plato, and Aristotle, as *inherently good* and considers the neo-pagan assumptions of our current secular order to be *inherently bad*, without justifying such conclusions through the absolute authority of God's inerrant word.

As previously shown through his argument for pederasty as something natural, Plato would have been fine with much of the sexual immorality at

---

[454] Wolfe, 245.

the center of today's Christian politics. Since Wolfe would not concur with Plato's approval of men courting young boys, by what reasoning does he determine that other selected assessments from the philosopher were proper interpretations of "universal principles"? His lack of exegesis to define or confirm universal principles, coupled with an insistence that pagan philosophers discovered these principles as self-apparent truths, continues to come across as more Kantian than Reformed. Calvin occasionally referred to the insights of pagan philosophers, but, with few exceptions (most notably civil punishment of heretics), he completed those arguments with exegeted insights from Scripture. Wolfe fails to meet the bounds of his own argument for these universal principles of natural law being "known in themselves" and "true for all situations" when he uses modern application of Deuteronomy 22:8 (Mosaic roofing law) as the example,[455] because such ends *begin with the special revelation of God.*

By Wolfe's own definition, any law passed by a government that he, through his personal interpretation of "natural law," believes is detrimental to the polis is *not law at all* (he will explicitly say so in the next section). Thus, in practical application, he negates his argument for a *totality of state action* from others in favor of his own individuality. The only *legitimate government* is one that fully concurs with his worldview; his definition's assumption of a beneficial lawgiver is built from a subjective standpoint, the supposed good of the collectivist, authoritarian requirement of *the totality of national action over the individual.*

Bastiat, from an inverse perspective of Enlightenment individualism, defined law as "the collective organization of the individual right to lawful defense."[456] From this standpoint, he would make what is perhaps the greatest moral argument against socialism, that it is a collective form of theft, no different ethically than if a single person robbed another at gunpoint. Under the bounds of Wolfe's definition, if the "appropriate lawgiver," through what he thought was an "ordering of reason," decided that converting the nation to communism by force was for the "good of the community," that would be perfectly acceptable. Certainly, as long as such

---
455 Wolfe, 246.
456 Bastiat, *The Law*, 2.

a government did not force us to abandon God, we would be bound to obey its earthly commands, but we should not *advocate* for the foundations of our nation to be built upon a definition of law that is so open to abuse, as Wolfe's is. Neither should a raw, libertarian individualism drive us, but Bastiat's definition is still exponentially better than Wolfe's in that it at least has some built-in safeguards against tyranny.

> Since every sphere of life is under natural law and that natural law requires particular applications, it follows that every sphere of life requires a suitable authority, with suitable power, to make determinations. For this reason, God has granted specific types of power by which the authorities of each sphere make judgments... civil life has the civil magistrate with civil power;[457]

By his own reasoning, Wolfe has made the case that "God has granted" what he refers to as the "global American empire"; it is currently far less tyrannical than the *global Roman empire* was, and he begins this chapter by quoting a colonial Puritan law's reference of Paul's specific instruction to be subject to that empire. Since he will spend much of the remainder of the book arguing for the violent overturning of the "GAE," he has proven, by his own internal contradictions, that man's reasoning of natural law is insufficient for the creation of the "nation perfected." This will become increasingly apparent as he attempts to build a case that the "GAE" is not a *suitable power* by continuing the strained and unscriptural argument that only "good" law requires obeyance.

II. Civil Law

Wolfe's explanation for the need of civil law begins quite agreeably but starts to crumble when he presents two logical issues. Like he did with *nationalism* and *Christian nationalism*, he expands upon his previous definition of *law*, giving his characterization of *civil law* the same subjective "legitimate civil authority" and "good of civil communities" that

---

457 Wolfe, *The Case for Christian Nationalism*, 247.

is wide open for abuse.[458] He then presents another statement of extreme subjectivity:

> Hence, it is a derived authority, and so laws are just only if they command what proceeds from the natural law.[459]

Whose interpretation of "natural law" is correct? Christendom is full of socialists who would argue that capitalism works against natural law; one could make a case, no worse than Wolfe's, that the prelapsarian good would be to share all things in common. With no exegesis to back up his postulations, by what authority, other than his own subjective reasoning, does he dispute such a statement? He then confirms his personal, subjective claim to legitimate interpretation of general revelation, when he writes, "However, a purported law that does *not* order according to reason is no law at all. That is to say, unjust laws are not laws, properly speaking, and so they do not bind the conscience to obedience."[460] With these sentences, he confirms that he places pagan philosophy above Scripture, because both Paul and Peter tell us to be obedient to all authorities, which would include any unjust law that does not force us to violate the direct commandments of God; Wolfe and I agree as a universal principle that slavery is unjust, but twice in Scripture Paul tells slaves to obey their masters (Ephesians 6:5, Colossians 3:22).[461] Wolfe then calls supposedly correct interpretation of natural law "divine civil rule," a quality he will later transfer to the *Christian prince*.

What are the limits of this interpretation of law? If Wolfe considers taxes to be excessive, does that make it *no law at all*? Since, through his

---

458 Wolfe, 248.
459 Wolfe, 249.
460 Wolfe, 249.
461 A good historical example of when such laws rise to the level of justifiable civil disobedience would be segregation because it required the citizen to consider another human being, made in the image of God, to be of an insurmountable lower caste, based solely on their ethnicity. In our time, the attempted medical coercion from the Biden administration in 2021 also rose to this level, in that it wished to place the state over the bodies of Christians, when they are temples to God (1 Corinthians 3:16-17).

6. What Laws Can and Cannot Do

interpretation of natural law, he would enact all manner of civil punishment against those who proselytize other religions, is the First Amendment *no law at all*? He next writes of the limits of civil law and its subordination to other spheres of life (family, church, etc.) until those other spheres "cannot effectively regulate to the common good," such as the civil restraint of a "husband's abuse of his power."[462] Yet, in the preceding chapter, he chastised Russell Moore for alluding to how cultural Christianity often upheld such abuse. Again, his own internal contradictions negate his argument for the sufficiency of human reason in the creation of *fully just* law.

> Though civil command is backed by penalties for non-compliance, it is not inherently a coercive power.[463]

As previously shown, this is patently false. As Bastiat wrote, the law "is made, generally, by one man, or by one class of men. And as law cannot exist without the sanction and the support of a preponderant force, it must finally place this force in the hands of those who legislate."[464] There is no such thing as a *civil command* that is not born from the preexistence of, nor not irrevocably intertwined with, *coercive power*. Power is the difference between "you should" and "you will." If the "civil command" is to redistribute wealth, and someone refuses to give up their possessions, what happens next? Does the government say, "pretty please," and then abandon their pursuit if the person remains obstinate? No government institutes law until they first have the coercive power to enforce it. From laws against murder to the traffic ticket you get for missing a stop sign, all carry the implied threat of the preexisting governmental authorities breaking down your door, dragging you out, hog-tied, and putting you in prison if you refuse to comply. Law does not "become coercive," as he argues, but is *always coercive*, even though most people knowingly avoid being made physical examples of that coercion.

---

462 Wolfe, *The Case for Christian Nationalism*, 250.
463 Wolfe, 251.
464 Bastiat, *The Law*, 6.

Wolfe attempts to justify his backwards order of operations with, "Also, since man's private judgment concerning suitable civil action is naturally limited, public judgment is both necessary for living well and natural for him to obey. Thus, civil command is not inherently coercive, for man is naturally willing to be directed in life by a civil authority."[465] Wolfe is in an incredibly minuscule minority of Americans who wish to bring about a Protestant theocracy – most who believe this to be a "Christian country" want to stop well short of instituting a state church and enforcing doctrine; even if they did, the overwhelming majority would not choose a paedobaptist church. By his own logic, he should be at least somewhat willing to be directed by the "civil determinations" of the overwhelming majority of Americans who, even among many Republicans, have little interest in abandoning relative morality and the secularization of government, because Christians are still mostly left alone by them. He cannot live by the very rules he would subject others to, a hallmark of authoritarian political theory. This is further confirmed when he states that "most people are unable to sufficiently judge the reasons for every action required of them." He has implicitly placed himself in the class of a ruling intelligentsia, worthy of the "deference" of the masses and capable of "discerning the public good" without their input or consent.[466] In his chapter on revolution, he will explicitly say that a Christian minority has the right to violently overthrow majority non-Christian rule and "disregard the non-Christian withholding of consent."[467]

He then confuses his own argument of the inherent non-coercive nature of *civil command* through a lengthy description of *civil power* as "a power to command" through a deference to "legitimate civil authority," as if the command exists separately from the power of the authority to enforce it.[468] His example of the military chain of command further undermines this claim, because the assumption that superior commanders are making better informed judgments is buffered by the restraint of military law (in the United States the *Uniform Code of Military Justice*). The UCMJ would be

---
465 Wolfe, *The Case for Christian Nationalism*, 251.
466 Wolfe, 252, 255.
467 Wolfe, 346.
468 Wolfe, 252–55.

a worthless piece of paper if it was not backed by the coercive force of court-martials and military prison. He puts the cart before the horse, for how could a list of civil commands ever come into existence *before* the existence of a preponderant force? Those are not *commands*, but merely the *suggestions* of a political theorist; the majority of Americans can tell Wolfe to take his purported *universal principles* and pound sand, and there is nothing he can do about it until he gathers enough force to make them comply. Even God's *natural law* proceeds from His preexisting authority over all creation, and cannot be separated from it.

Wolfe has locked himself into this inversion of command and power, because without the command's inherent authority, derived from his personal interpretation of natural law, his claim to possess the right to dictate the "good of civil communities" becomes nothing more than a single, subjective position in a postmodern game of competing power-dynamics. He wishes to determine the absolutes of a Christian nation without basing its law on the only absolute, inerrant authority for Christians; he has no choice but to do this, because, as I have shown, a plain reading of Scripture contradicts the very foundations of his argument. His avoidance of Scripture is made painfully apparent in the next subsection, *Righteous and Good Laws*, which does not once refer to the revealed moral laws of our righteous and good God; though there is a later subsection in this chapter on Mosaic law, his initial defining of *good law* without mentioning *God's Law* is yet another red flag in the context of *Christian* nationalism.

There is a twisting of words at the end of this subsection that disqualifies Wolfe as an arbiter of God's natural law. Demosthenes is quoted as saying "all law is a gift of God";[469] the pagan Greek philosopher was not speaking of θεός (theos, God), but his pantheon of θεῶν (theōn, gods). The true quote, "All law is an invention and gift of the gods," that Wolfe puts in the footnote, demonstrates that Demosthenes was, in many ways, a fool "claiming to be wise" who "exchanged the glory of the immortal God for images resembling mortal man" (Romans 1:22-23), and whose deductions should not be held in equal reverence to the special

---

[469] Wolfe, 257.

revelation of God. Wolfe would likely argue that he does not do this, but his own predilection for referencing pagan philosophy exponentially more than Scripture throughout his book says otherwise.

> This might seem overly abstract, but my interest is in ensuring the preservation of individual agency and vitality.[470]

The last thing that a government engaged in prosecuting thoughtcrime does is *preserve individual agency*. He will later justify oppressing heterodox religious thought by fallaciously comparing it to suppressing the Second Table crimes of "murder, adultery, theft, and defaming character,"[471] all of which have victims who are not the all-powerful Creator of the universe, who repeatedly in the New Testament tells us to let Him judge offenses against His name (Wolfe will use a faulty claim of *spiritual harm* to get around this). For all his talk of how law cannot engender belief, Wolfe would still seek to control the minds of the people in his "nation perfected." His claim to be interested in individual agency is akin to an abusive parent who says his violent methods are for the child's own personal development.

> The scope of objects [for civil law] includes all outward things, except spiritual ceremonies and the ecclesiastical order (which are matters of divine law).[472]

How does a nation with a single, sanctioned state church, and which enforces religious doctrine through civil law, not have at least some jurisdiction over "spiritual ceremonies and the ecclesiastical order," even if only tangentially? How would such a nation not quickly become a bureaucratic commingling of church and state apparatchiks? The history of Northern European Protestantism over the last two hundred years is that of just such a mixing of concerns, where the blurred lines between state and church allowed state-sponsored seminaries to be ideologically subverted by

---

470 Wolfe, 258.
471 Wolfe, 369.
472 Wolfe, 258–59.

6. What Laws Can and Cannot Do

intellectuals more interested in earthly concerns than heavenly truths. Imagine the type of politicking that takes place today inside large denominational polities being given the power of civil enforcement. Why bother with a whisper campaign against an ecclesial rival for being too "liberal" or "fundamentalist" when you can leverage your civil political connections? Why would the *Christian Prince* allow his church's power structure to contain elders who might contradict his political aspirations when he can guarantee, through the ecclesiastical appointment of loyalists, that the people would hear his praises sung from the pulpit? Bonhoeffer's maternal grandfather, the son of one of the nation's most highly-regarded theologians, Karl August von Hase, was chaplain to the Kaiser until he was forced to tender his resignation for holding contradictory political beliefs.[473] This is how the type of unrealistic hypotheses that Wolfe promulgates play out in the real world.

When he writes, "Of course, communities that lack self-governability will require more law and more law enforcement," one cannot help but think he is referring to the demographics he considers "reliable sources for criminality." Following this, his statement that people have the *natural right* to make "a claim against others to conduct free, unhindered, and undistracted worship,"[474] without expressly specifying the limitations on which interpretation of God they are allowed to worship under his form of governance, is laughably disingenuous. Many religions beyond orthodox Protestantism – including those of Mormons, Jehovah's Witnesses, and Black Hebrew Israelites – consider evangelizing an aspect of their worship; Wolfe would have these people, at the very least, jailed and banished. Truly, he is either a man of immensely conflicting visions or an outright liar. Either way, his definition of the bounds and purpose of civil law should be rejected by Christian audiences.

---

473 Bonhoeffer, *The Cost of Discipleship*, 12.
474 Wolfe, *The Case for Christian Nationalism*, 259.

II. Civil Law in a Christian Commonwealth

> Civil government is Christian not because it declares itself Christian (whether through pomp, titles, or constitutional preambles), but because it actually orders a Christian people to their **complete good**. This includes acting for the peace and good order of the **instituted church**, which administers the chief good. (emphasis mine)[475]

Martin Luther posted his ninety-five theses over five centuries ago. Since then, hundreds of major Protestant denominations have formed, each with their own set of unique beliefs that they considered important enough to disfellowship with another group. Conservative Presbyterians make up 0.8% of American citizens, less than a quarter of the number associated with a Pentecostal denomination, less than a sixth of the number of non-denominational Christians, less than a tenth of the number of Baptists, and less than 1/28th the amount of nonreligious Americans; there are even more *liberal* Presbyterians than *conservative*.[476] Wolfe will end his chapter on revolution with another emotional appeal, using authoritarian *language of destiny* rhetoric, to call for Christians to "cultivate [their] resolve" and make use of their current "power and right to act."[477] One must conclude that he either holds the delusional belief that a) conservative Christians still have the numbers to form a formidable revolutionary coalition, b) he and his compatriots could carve out a tiny, Presbyterian nation in United States territory, or c) one of these groups could politic itself into a power-position on the right-wing side of an impending second civil war. I will address the logistical impracticality of Christian revolution, and its lack of Scriptural warrant in our place and time, when that chapter is reached, but here it is worth noting that Wolfe is not writing abstract theory. Though he will later state in this section that other Christian commonwealths might not find a

---

475 Wolfe, 260.
476 "Religious Landscape Study."
477 Wolfe, *The Case for Christian Nationalism*, 352.

6. What Laws Can and Cannot Do

state church necessary, given the opportunity here and now, he would seek to violently impose Presbyterianism on his Christian countrymen.

It should also be restated that his "complete good" is not inherently *Christian language*, but very much in line with the language of 20th-century totalitarian utopianism. Christianity tells us to seek heavenly good above earthly, and that the *true good* can be found in the most dire of circumstances (Colossians 3:2, Matthew 6:20, Philippians 1:21). As much as Wolfe says he dislikes post-war American cultural Christianity, he repeatedly appeals to its sensibilities of *personal peace* and *affluence.*

From his quotation of Franciscus Junius that "grace perfects nature; grace does not, however, abolish it,"[478] we can see where he received a bolstering of the Thomasian notion that he has repeated throughout the book. The same section of Junius's *The Mosaic Polity* also states, "*Law is the ordering of reason to the common good established by the one who has care for the community.*"[479] Wolfe has implicitly used and explicitly quoted this treatise so much in this chapter that one could call his view of law *Juniusan* as much as his view of nature is *Thomasian*. Interestingly, the French reformer contradicts Wolfe's separation of command and power and his statement that law cannot alter belief, in the same section:

> But any ordering of reason is so regulated that the reason of the one who orders influences the reason of those who are under the ordering, and in turn the reason of these would depend upon the reason of the one who orders. Only then must be it called a law. Any laws done in any other way are not laws, but must be called customs, unless perhaps someone would want to speak ομώνύμως [homonymous], or equivocally.[480]

---

478 Wolfe, 261.
479 Franciscus Junius, *The Mosaic Polity*, ed. Andrew McGinnis, trans. Todd Rester (Acton Institute for the Study of Religion & Liberty, 2015), 38.
Junius's definition is just as subjective and open for abuse as Wolfe's paraphrasing. Dictionary definitions of law are far more objective and center around the concept of *rules of conduct enforced by an instituted authority*. Unjust law is still law.
480 Junius, 39–40.

The Case Against Christian Nationalism

Though his heavy reliance on Junius for definition of law results in a reduction of doctrinal errors in this chapter, and though this section's main sentiment of the mutability of law between different peoples is correctly drawn from the reformer, Wolfe restates an error that he likely arrived at through a misapplication of Junius; he again claims that civil law "can be a supernatural *conclusion* **from** natural principles that have **interacted** with supernatural truth" (emphasis mine).[481] Junius writes, "For even if the principles and conclusions that are natural according to human reason are present in human beings by natural law, nevertheless it is necessary that other principles above nature be **inspired and infused** by God so that we may know that end beyond nature to which we have been ordered, and the truth that would certainly lead to that end" (emphasis mine).[482] As previously shown, supernatural conclusions do not flow *from* or as a *result of* man's recognition of natural principles, but, as Junius confirms, God's supernatural truth flows from Him to his elect, *free from our input*. It may seem like splitting hairs, but the difference between supernatural truths *resulting from* recognition of natural principles and them *being infused* by the self-sufficient will of God determines one's view of God's sovereignty; this difference in views strikes at the heart of Wolfe's motivations and methodologies for the creation of his "Christian nation."

> Special revelation is above reason, but it is not contrary to reason;[483]

Wolfe again has his order of operations and rules of inerrancy backwards. A properly Reformed version of this sentence would read, "Special revelation is above reason, therefore our flawed human reasoning must remain congruous with it to be true." When he follows this statement with, "A Christian body of law is the only *complete* and *true* body of law," he is stating something not wholly true, for we are still in a battle of spirit and flesh and cannot do *anything* complete and true; even if we were able

---

481 Wolfe, *The Case for Christian Nationalism*, 262.
482 Junius, *The Mosaic Polity*, 50.
483 Wolfe, *The Case for Christian Nationalism*, 263.

to do so, he has shown himself to be unqualified to determine a genuinely *Christian* body of law. Certainly, to do so at least requires the ability to exegete, but Wolfe would have us believe that his personal reasoning, informed by 16th-century Catholic and Reformed opinions on nature and Scripture, is sufficient.

> A Christian people may want to censure atheism and blasphemy through civil law, but another people may find social power sufficient to that end.[484]

Wolfe's totalitarian blinders shine through this sentence, in that he does not even give passing mention to the obvious and practical third option that a Christian people may decide that such censure is not warranted at all, even though he follows this with having no state church as a legitimate possibility. It would seem that, in his view, a commonwealth is not genuinely *Christian* unless it actively suppresses religious dissent, in one way or the other. He later disingenuously states that he does not supply a set of laws when chapter 7 is dedicated to his case for a Christian monarchy, with a "prince" who "mediates the people's national will for their good,"[485] and chapter 9 defines laws against blasphemy, heresy, and promulgation of false religions. What other body of laws would his readers be more interested in him explicating than the very structure of the nation and how it deals with dissent?

The subsection on the Law of Moses (separate from the next full section on theonomy) begins with the dubious statement, "Questions around the Mosaic law are typically more theological in nature and best left for the theologians."[486] Surely, since it contains the only civil law of divine origin, a full understanding of Mosaic law's theology and history is a prerequisite for attaining the Christian "nation perfected." If Wolfe does not understand the full context of what he admits is the "perfect application" of natural law, how can he be sure that he has not merely attained the *nation moderately improved*? Facetiousness aside, I have no doubt that Wolfe

---

484 Wolfe, 263.
485 Wolfe, 276.
486 Wolfe, 265.

came to this conclusion less out of an altruistic stream of logic than from a desire to not leave his comfort-zone or undermine his case. It speaks more than anything else, thus far, to his primary desire for authoritarian power and how "Christianity" is simply a means to that end; someone who is truly interested in *Christian Nationalism* above *Nationalist Christianity* would feel obligated, regardless of the final conclusions, to give a full chapter to the body of laws and commandments specially revealed in Scripture instead of brushing the former aside in four and a half pages, most of which are dedicated to how they are not more applicable to the Christian nation than human reasoning alone. Comparatively, he dedicates forty-six pages to the next chapter on his vision for a national, *Caudillo*-like strongman.

There is only one Scriptural reference in this subsection, Deuteronomy 19:15 (the need for multiple witnesses), used as an example of something that "one might also consider... to be a universally wise law."[487] We are given no explanation as to why it only *might* be considered universally wise; this likely unintended admission of the inherent subjectivity of individual determination of what *may or may not be a universal principle* proves them not to be inducible by human reasoning alone. *We must start with Scripture.*

There is an inherent contradiction in Wolfe's affirmation that the Mosaic civil law is "a perfect example of the law," but also that "it still belongs to the same genus as all bodies of civil law," and that it only "*can* serve as a guide or source of law for all nations."[488] Jesus Christ is a *perfect man*, one who belongs to the same genus as all men, but does that mean we can *choose* whether or not to look to him, among a group of other men, as our guide for righteous behavior, and remain *Christian*? It is Christ's *divinity* that makes him the example to emulate, just as the divine origin of Scriptural commandments, not only Mosaic civil law but also those of the New Covenant, makes them the required benchmark for the *ethical principles* of good *Christian* law; it also gives us the opportunity to appeal to something more than our own flawed reasoning. This is how 20th-century theonomists, such as Bahnsen, viewed the Mosaic civil law, not as

---

487 Wolfe, 268.
488 Wolfe, 265, 266, 268.

an immutable set of copy/paste rules that all nations should use, unaltered; Wolfe will misrepresent modern theonomy with this false claim in the next section.

IV. Modern Theonomy

The subsection on theonomy contains very little actual content on the subject, and how it describes adherents' view of Mosaic civil law is inaccurate.[489] Simply put, modern theonomy is the position that God's laws, as revealed in the Old Testament, are *morally* binding (not to be confused with *literally*) unless they have been modified or overruled by later revelation, especially that of the New Covenant. Though theonomists often do themselves no favor in how they argue their case, this is not as fundamentalist or radical a position as it may initially sound. The New Covenant overrules quite a large amount of the Mosaic law, including all of the ceremonial law (Hebrews 4:14, Matthew 27:51) and the portions of civil law regarding the cleanness of food and people (Acts 11:5-18). As Wolfe affirmed in the last section, the Mosaic civil law is a perfect application of natural law; one must logically conclude that, unless otherwise stated by God, the *moral principles* communicated in that civil law are still binding to Christians. As Bahnsen writes, "Our obligation to keep the law of God cannot be judged by an extrascriptural standard, such as whether its specific requirements (when properly interpreted) are congenial to past traditions or modern feelings and practices."[490] It is easy to see how one could read this and come to the misunderstanding that Bahnsen was looking to adopt Mosaic civil law, wholesale, but he also writes in the same essay:

> But it is theologically legitimate to make contemporary use of this biblical material on civil law. On the one hand, to deny that these revealed dictates (or at least those in the Old Testament) are unchanging moral absolutes is implicitly to endorse the position of *cultural relativism* in ethics ("They were morally valid for that

---

489 Wolfe, 270.
490 Smith, *God and Politics*, 23.

time and place, but invalid for other people and other times"); this is diametrically contrary to the testimony of Scripture (Malachi 3:6; Psalms 89:34; 111:7; 119:160; Ecclesiastes 12:13, Romans 2:11). On the other hand, to affirm that the principles for civil government found in the Bible (even the Old Testament) are binding in our day and age might suggest to some people that no differences between Old and New Covenants, or between an ancient agrarian society and the modern computer age, have been recognized. After all, in the Old Testament we read instructions for holy war, for kosher diet, for temple and priesthood, for cities of refuge at particular places in Palestine, for goring oxen and burning grain fields...

It is one thing to realize that we must translate biblical commands about a lost ox (Exodus 23:4) or withholding pay from someone who mows the fields (James 5:4) into terms relevant to our present culture (e.g., about misplaced credit cards or remuneration of factory workers). It is quite another thing altogether to say that such commands carry no ethical authority today![491]

Between the positions of Bahnsen and Wolfe, the former has the upper hand, in this respect: *If both agree that the Mosaic civil law is the divinely revealed, perfect application of natural law, even though Christian nations may use other references when forming their civil law, should they not be obligated to use God's perfect application as their primary source and moral standard?*

A Christian nation is, by definition, a corporate Christian – assuming it achieved such a status by peaceful evangelism and not through a violent revolution by an oppressive minority. Ethically, all properly functioning nations are bound by the same set of morals as individual citizens; otherwise, they become tyrannies (this is the basis for *rule of law*). As Bastiat wrote, "Collective right, then, has its principle, its reason for existing, its lawfulness, in individual right; and the common force cannot rationally have any other end, or any other mission, than that of the isolated forces for which it is substituted. Thus, as the force of an individual cannot

---

491 Smith, 31.

lawfully touch the person, the liberty, or the property of another individual – for the same reason, the common force cannot lawfully be used to destroy the person, the liberty, or the property of individuals or of classes."[492] When we apply this principle to any self-described "Christian" nation, it becomes apparent that the laws and practices of that nation must be bound by the same *Scriptural commandments* as the individual Christian, or it would lose the right to its *Christian* designation. Thus, Wolfe's definition that a Christian nation is one that orders a Christian people to its *complete good* is incorrect, because one individual outwardly directing another on how to be a good Christian does not automatically make the director also a Christian. He must also be bound by the same tenets of Christianity he is leading the other person in before he can lay claim to that title. In practical application, Wolfe's nation has no safeguards to prevent it from using doctrine it does not follow as a cudgel against Christian citizens, much like some atheists who will take a verse from Scripture out of context and attempt to manipulate the behavior of a Christian to their advantage.

A common argument against this is to refer to individual commandments, such as Christ's instruction to turn the other cheek (Matthew 5:39, Luke 6:29); surely, a nation cannot allow assault to go unhindered and unpunished. But Scripture is also very clear on the believer's duty to protect *others* from harm (Proverbs 24:10-12, Psalm 82:4, Isaiah 1:17). It is from this position that government acts against Second Table wrongdoing, just as individual Christians can protect others but do not repay evil done directly to us. Another example of how government does not possess additional moral commandments, but only extra means to enforce them, is shown through the Sixth Commandment. If someone witnesses a murder in progress, they have the moral right to stop the assailant and even kill them if necessary; the *Westminster Larger Catechism* interprets the inverse of the Sixth Commandment as a *divine command* to protect the innocent.[493] What individuals do not have the right to do is enact *after the fact vengeance*, even after receiving the evidence of

---

492 Bastiat, *The Law*, 3.
493 *The Westminster Confession of Faith and Catechisms*, sec. WLC Q. 135.

multiple witnesses. This is the sole, collective right of the nation, though it is not an extra *moral* obligation, in and of itself.

The Reformed tradition, indeed orthodox Protestantism as a whole, affirms that the final authority for all matters is Scripture. If an individual Christian wishes to know if a particular course of action conforms to God's will, or at least that it exists within his liberty of conscience, he does not rely on his own reasoning or what presses on his heart during prayer; he goes to the inerrant word of God to confirm whether or not such actions are permissible. In the same way, the corporate Christian nation must place all its actions under the authority of Scripture, part of which is the moral content of the civil law divinely revealed to Moses. Reusing Deuteronomy 22:8, a secular nation might look at that verse and consider it a *good idea* to embed proper safety standards into its law, but the Christian nation *must do so*; it cannot look to another nation that did not have such standards as an equal arbiter of good civil law.

> But ordering ourselves to God must spring in large part from self-affirmation, from an instinct of peoplehood, and from the felt need to act for our own good. We do not fight for Christian civilization in the abstract or according to a ready-made, universal set of civil laws. We do not fight according to a bare divine law but according to a law of God that inheres and enlivens our whole being.[494]

Yet again, we are presented with an emotional appeal, using authoritarian *language of destiny*. One way to test for this type of language is to take a paragraph and see if it fits into the mental picture of someone standing behind a podium, wearing pompous military garb, speaking aggressively with a raised, clenched fist, and whipping a crowd into an ecstatic frenzy. In this paragraph, that picture is accentuated by the repeating of the collectivist, aggressive call-to-action, "We do not fight"; this gives the reader/hearer a sense that they are a member of a collective waging a *just and holy crusade* against an *invading other*. By comparison,

---

494 Wolfe, *The Case for Christian Nationalism*, 271.

this mental picture would not work with any other paragraph in this section.

Wolfe's hypothetical nation, by placing the brunt of its epistemic foundations in a hubristic appeal to human instinct and reasoning instead of a humble deference to Scriptural directive, is not truly a *Christian* nation; it is a *humanist* nation that would enforce a selection of Christian mores, and the doctrine of a Presbyterian state church, via its civil law. Not bound by God's inerrant word, and placing national right over individual right, it could pass any tyrannical law contradictory to Scriptural commandments and explain it as "reasoned natural law that is good for the community." Organized protests and political movements from Christian citizens against these humanist conclusions would likely be suppressed; as previously mentioned, Wolfe is frank about his lack of concern for the consent of non-Christians; why would he not equally dismiss Christians who appeal to Scripture above his human reasoning?

V. Disobeying the Law

> The ancient maxim that "an unjust law is no law" is justified on the grounds that laws are civil commands to act according to reason in accordance with the natural law.[495]

As a *Christian*, one does not set the rule for his outward behavior based on *ancient maxims*, but by the instructions from the Creator given in His inerrant word. Here is what Scripture has to say about obeying the laws of men:

> Be subject for the sake of the Lord to every human institution, whether to a king as the one in authority, or to governors as sent by him for the punishment of evildoers and the praise of those who do good. For such is the will of God that by doing good you may silence the ignorance of foolish men. *Act* as free people, and do not use your freedom as a covering for evil, but *use it* as slaves of

---

[495] Wolfe, 271.

God. Honor all people, love the brethren, fear God, honor the king.
(1 Peter 2:13-17 LSB)

Wolfe would say that this verse communicates our obligation to the "public reason" of the civil magistrate, but that unjust laws are "laws in name only, and God does not bind one's conscience to them."[496] Unfortunately for his argument, the very next sentence from Peter destroys that notion:

Servants, be subject to your masters with all fear, not only to those who are good and considerate, but also to those who are crooked.
(1 Peter 2:18 LSB)

I referenced the *Legacy Standard Bible*, because its translation denotes the difference between the δοῦλος (doulos, slave) of God and the οἰκέτης (oiketes, household-servant) of an earthly master. The Roman domestic servant was also under the authority of a human institution, one that derived its authority from the societal hierarchy that ended with the Emperor, codified in civil laws; the master is, in essence, a domestic-level magistrate above his servant. God here binds the conscience of servants to their domestic masters, even if they are σκολιός (skolios, crooked, perverse, *unjust*). This level of deference is not given as something *separate* from a lesser level of deference required of the governmental authority, but *in addition to it*. As *slaves of God*, we are bound to "be subject for the sake of the Lord to every human institution," and are not given the freedom to disregard laws simply because we, in our subjective interpretation, find them "unjust."

Wolfe rightly references Acts 5:29 to demonstrate that we are duty bound to obey the commandments of God above *explicitly contradictory* commands of men; that is because God's authority is always higher, binding us to his expressed commandments first, not because we have been given the liberty of conscience to arbitrarily decide which human laws adhere to natural law. Note how, throughout the Apostles' ordeal with the

---

496 Wolfe, 271.

Sanhedrin, while they were unjustly being persecuted, they remained *perfectly obedient* to its earthly authority when it did not contradict God's commandments. When Paul and Silas were *unjustly* arrested in Philippi and had the opportunity to escape after an earthquake, they remained in jail and used the example of their peaceful submission to authority to convert their jailer (Acts 16:25-34).

Wolfe lays out four types of "accidentally unjust" law which he claims one can legitimately disobey,[497] all of which have questionable practical applicability. Note that the issue is not whether or not a law can actually be unjust, by these definitions, but how tenuous the supposed principle is that we can disregard subjection to authorities when we *subjectively perceive* a law to fall within these bounds.

- "Illegitimate authorities or non-authorities cannot obligate anyone to some civil action, even if the action is good." What constitutes a *legitimate authority*? How does an authority gain or lose legitimacy? If a Christian determines, by his own subjective reasoning, that his government is illegitimate, can he disobey every one of their laws? If a group of citizens are Christian socialists and believe that their capitalist government is illegitimate, because it misinterprets natural law, do they have the same right to revolution as capitalist Christians in a communist nation?
- "Legitimate authorities [cannot] demand what is beyond another's ability." Do we all now get to decide what is and is not beyond our abilities as citizens? Can a Christian business owner decide that his tax debt is "beyond his ability" and come up with his own figure, or ignore taxes outright? Can a Christian civil engineer decide that the latest safety regulations are overwrought, and "beyond his ability," and build a bridge to his preferred, deprecated specifications?
- "When the magistrate's personal good is the reason for some law, then that law is unjust, for the reason for any law is the ground of its legitimacy." Could anyone name a single law, in any republic in the history of the world, that did not benefit one of the legislator's group

---

497 Wolfe, 272.

identities more than another group of citizens? Does a Christian citizen have the right to disobey a law, because he perceives some legislators passed it for their personal gain? Since it is exceedingly rare in our time that a magistrate enacts a law and explicitly says it is for their own benefit, what is the objective metric by which this determination can be made?

- "Any law that does not conduce to the common good is unjust, for essential to any just law is the suitability to achieve the end of the law." Could anyone name a single law passed by a modern legislature that was not promoted as being for "the common good"? The Affordable Care Act, colloquially known as *Obamacare*, was sold as being for the common good, but a significant portion of Americans disagree. Can a consortium of Christian owners of medical insurance companies, who believe these regulations are not for the common good, ignore them and create their own "insurance black marketplace"?

Wolfe attempts to address the issue of when disobedience becomes warranted in the subsection, *Epistemic Limitations*,[498] but only digs himself a deeper epistemic hole. He appeals to *repeated demonstration* of unjust behavior, but that does not remove the subjectivity of "unjust." It is also not human nature to remain objective and perceive only a few laws from an authority to be unjust, without applying that distinction, part and parcel, to the authority itself. Even "repeatedly" is a *subjective determination*. The proposal that we should or should not disobey laws, based on the frequency of unjust behavior, speaks against the *universality* of his principles of justice. He correctly identifies the "lesser magistrate" as whom the individual citizen should appeal to, but says nothing of what the citizen should do if he is not assisted by the magistrate; can he then revolt? I believe he left this unanswered on purpose to maintain more room to advocate for revolution in chapter 8.

Looking back at Peter's instruction, he tells us, "For such is the will of God that by doing good you may silence the ignorance of foolish men" (1 Peter 2:15). What would more work against this instruction than a group of

---

498 Wolfe, 274–75.

6. What Laws Can and Cannot Do

Christians deciding to *go rogue* because they perceive the authorities "openly express contempt for [them] or affirm moral absurdities and a degenerate conception of the common good,"[499] while these authorities currently stop short of using their preponderant force to demand Christians actively *participate* in those absurdities?[500] Were the Roman authorities, while Peter was writing this, not openly expressing contempt for Christianity and affirming moral absurdities? Though the current American regime certainly takes an absurd moral stance, our day-to-day experience with governmental authorities is still overwhelmingly that of "punishment of evildoers and the praise of those who do good" (1 Peter 2:14); for example, law-abiding Americans do not carry extra cash with which to bribe officials, as much of the rest of the world still must do. What happens on our televisions is not what happens to most of us in our daily life, at least not yet; we are still very much allowed to practice our religion and redress our grievances in relative peace. How much would the gospel witness, which is far more important than our physical well-being (and even that of our children), be damaged by extralegal Christian action at this juncture? Think about how much those who live up to the left-wing stereotype of "Christian Nationalism," that of someone marching into Congress waving a flag-draped cross while screaming that this is a "Christian country," have enlivened the "ignorance of foolish men" as of late.

Wolfe references Christ's instruction to "turn the other cheek" and follows it with the possibility of eschewing this commandment when "harm against you" would also result in "harm to those who are dependent on you."[501] This is entirely agreeable, but while the Christian has the duty to actively protect others under physical threat, and the duty to advocate for those being maltreated in other ways, he does not, *as a Christian alone*, have the right to "confront injustice and exploitation in order 'to protect himself and his property from injury,'" no matter how badly Wolfe

---

499 Wolfe, 275.
500 Wolfe will later make the unsubstantiated claim that the authorities *are* forcing Christians to participate in degeneracy, and posit that modern America is a tyranny.
501 Wolfe, *The Case for Christian Nationalism*, 273.

attempts to misrepresent Calvin with this quotation. Here is the reformer's complete thought:

> I admit that Christ restrains our hands, as well as our minds, from revenge: but when any one has it in his power to protect himself and his property from injury, without exercising revenge, the words of Christ do not prevent him from turning aside gently and inoffensively to avoid the threatened attack.[502]

There is a massive difference between shielding oneself from physical harm and actively confronting injustice aimed at oneself. We certainly have a right *as citizens of a Western republic* to confront injustice, and a Christian citizen of such a system can attempt to, as Wolfe says, "use the full, legitimate powers of law to secure his person and property." A genuinely *Christian* nation would, of course, also imbue its law with such means of justice; one of the topics Scripture is most concerned with is seeking justice for the mistreated. But Calvin could not have been clearer in the very next verse of the same commentary (Matthew 5:40) about the Christian's requirement of subjection to authority. Wolfe again cuts off the full quote when it works against his argument:

> Christ now glances at another kind of annoyance, and that is, when wicked men torment us with law-suits. He commands us, even on such an occasion, to be so patient and submissive that, when our coat has been taken away, we shall be prepared to give up our cloak also. **None but a fool will stand upon the words, so as to maintain, that we must yield to our opponents what they demand, before coming into a court of law: for such compliance would more strongly inflame the minds of wicked men to robbery and extortion;** and we know, that nothing was farther from the design of Christ. What then is meant by giving the cloak to him who endeavors, on the ground of a legal claim, to take away our coat? If a man, oppressed by an unjust decision, loses what is his own, and yet is prepared, when it shall be found necessary, to part with the remainder, he deserves not less to be

---

502 John Calvin, Commentary on Matthew, Mark, Luke, [on Matthew 5:39].

commended for patience than the man who allows himself to be twice robbed before coming into court. In short, when Christians meet with one who endeavors to wrench from them a part of their property, they ought to be prepared to lose the whole. (emphasis is the portion Wolfe quotes)[503]

It is patently absurd, and intellectually dishonest, that Wolfe would quote Calvin, to help build a case for disobeying unjust law and set the stage for his call to revolution, when the same commentary uses the very next verse to instruct Christians to *patiently endure grievously unjust legal action*. Calvin confirms that, should the lesser magistrate not take up our cause, we should accept such injustice in peace. "For this is a gracious thing, when, mindful of God, one endures sorrows while suffering unjustly" (1 Peter 2:19).

VI. Conclusion

The conclusion of the chapter on civil law is not a summation of the chapter's arguments, but a single paragraph describing the requirement of a civil magistrate, the "Christian prince," to "mediate the national will for their good" and to be "the one to whom they look to see greatness, a love of country, and the best of men. He is their spirit."[504] Similarly, Mussolini once said, "The man of Fascism is an individual who is nation and fatherland."[505] There will be far more intense language in the next chapter, dedicated to this figure.

As for the content of the chapter just finished, we are left with the question: *What exactly is "Christian" about Wolfe's definition of civil law?* With the exception of the examples of Mosaic laws regarding roofing and witnesses, used more for their *practicality* than their *morality*, Scripture is only eisegetically used to give him the excuse to disobey *other* governments' civil laws. He has not given the indication that a single law in his "Christian commonwealth" would be based on Scriptural directive; if the few, brief sections on how his nation would vaguely enforce aspects of

---

503 Calvin, [on Matthew 5:40].
504 Wolfe, *The Case for Christian Nationalism*, 276.
505 Priorelli, *Italian Fascism and Spanish Falangism in Comparison*, 28.

"Christianity" were removed, a reader would probably not know this was a chapter from a book *for* "Christian nationalism." This sentence from the section on the Christian commonwealth is a fantastic example of this issue:

> This is precisely why I've used the word totality in my definition of Christian nationalism; it allows us to say that all national actions – whether directed by custom or law – are Christian customs and laws, even if in themselves they are not distinctly Christian or religious and are merely human and mundane.[506]

You could swap "Christian" with the name of any other religion – really any word in the English language – and this sentence would convey the same core thought. The totality of *Islamic* nationalism makes *all* national actions *Islamic* customs and laws. The totality of *cheeseburger* nationalism makes *all* national actions *cheeseburger* customs and laws. This sentence is so plastic because it does not come from a Christian worldview; it comes rather from authoritarian-nationalist political theory; "Christian" is being grafted in. Morgan describes Mussolini's similar vision for a nation that "subordinated individuals to the state and imposed no limits on the activity of the state, which educated and moralised them in conformity with its values and purposes so as to achieve the unity of the two." The dictator spoke of a "fascistisation" of the nation, which would see to it that "tomorrow Italian and Fascist, rather like Italian and Catholic, mean the same thing," just as Wolfe would seek a "totality of action" that makes all things "Christian." In the realm of state-enforced ideological homogeneity, Wolfe's *totality* is perfectly in line with Mussolini's definition of totalitarian, "Everything within the state, nothing outside the state, nothing against the state."[507]

Now this nation will be given its *Duce*.

---

506 Wolfe, *The Case for Christian Nationalism*, 261.
507 Morgan, *Italian Fascism*, 80.
Italian fascism wan inextricably intertwined with its economic vision of *productivism*; thus, this sentiment of *state-control* from Mussolini carries both an ideological and economic significance, the latter of which does not apply to our subject.

7. The Christian Prince

I. Introduction

> The national will alone cannot terminate *immediately* into national action. It must terminate upon a *mediator* – upon one who translates that national general will into specific commands of action that lead the nation to its good.[508]

This description of the mediator is worth spending extra time parsing; the national will does not *pass through* or *interact with mediation*, it "terminates upon a *mediator.*" This is the type of statement in political theory that most readers gloss over because, in its vagueness, it sounds fairly agreeable, but this is also a turn of phrase where the mind of the author peeks through. Every nation has a highest authority where decisions are final, but we would not describe our executive, legal, or judicial systems as a *terminating* authority; that is not the *telos* of the nation. Modern Western law is characterized by the checks and balances of multiple arbitrating authorities, something that Wolfe deems *nontraditional.*[509] Though it does not necessarily feel this way as of late, theoretically, should the President of the United States make an unfavorable decision against an individual citizen, that person would still have multiple levels of legal recourse. That is not the type of system that the phrase "terminate upon a *mediator*" invokes; it is very *final* and speaks more to the image of a *general* than a *legislator*. This is bolstered by Wolfe's stated vision of "theocratic Caesarism"[510]; the Roman senate very quickly became a hamstrung, lesser entity under the Caesars, so it is quite telling that he chose this reference instead of one that would more convey that the will of the people would actually be respected by the monarch (the Magna Carta, for example). He has previously stated that "all civil rule is by consent of the ruled" but will later say that he would "disregard the non-

---

508 Wolfe, *The Case for Christian Nationalism*, 277.
509 Wolfe, 278.
510 Wolfe, 279.

Christian withholding of consent,"[511] so there is definitely mixed messaging in his theory.

II. The Prince

> I cannot conceive of a true renewal of Christian commonwealths without *great men* leading their people to it.[512]

Conspicuously absent from all of this writing about what it would take for *renewal* of *Christian* commonwealths is even a passing mention of how such an act would be wholly dependent on the *will of the Father*. This is especially inexcusable for Wolfe, as a Presbyterian, because there is no other Protestant denomination more concerned with the sovereign will of God. He simply assumes it to be God's will that, after two and a half centuries of American liberal democracy, we should take extreme, potentially violent action to enact "theocratic Caesarism," a "totality of national action" where a single individual is the final arbiter of *national good*. Would not a rational *Christian* seek confirmation of this vision in God's inerrant word more than in his own interpretation of *natural law*? Would he not seek to convince other Christians with words from the only inerrant authority on the matter?

> "Prince" is a fitting title for a man of dignity and greatness of soul who will lead a people to liberty, virtue, and godliness – to greatness.[513]

The Spanish had a word for such a man: *el Caudillo*. There is no direct translation that gives its full weight, though *leader*, *chief*, or *warlord* will often be given. The Caudillo is more than just a military or political leader. He carries the very soul of the nation; he is a living, breathing rallying cry. The name evoked images of great conquerors, such as El Cid, Cortés, and

---

511 Wolfe, 72, 346.
512 Wolfe, 278–79.
513 Wolfe, 279.

7. The Christian Prince

Pizzaro. Even before Francisco Franco, the dictator of Spain from 1939 to 1975, had risen to power, he was being called "un caudillo" (*a* as opposed to *the*) by the nationalist press.[514] As the youngest general in the nation's history, he was a rising star that was considered a required asset for the legitimacy of an insurrection against the second Spanish Republic. Once the civil war began, and several potential rivals for power died, including both the presumed military dictator and the Falange Española's leader, Primo de Rivera, he quickly finagled his way to the position of *Jefe del Estado Español* (Head of the Spanish State),[515] although there was no real nationalist state yet to speak of. Though he would refer to himself by this title, the official propaganda campaign that followed referred to him as *el Caudillo*, in an effort to place him ideologically and internationally on par with the *Führer* and *Duce* (both of whom provided significant military assistance to his campaign). All newspapers in the nationalist zone had to place under their masthead, "One nation, one state, one Caudillo."[516] As a children's textbook later read, "a Caudillo is a gift that God makes to the nations that deserve it and the nation accepts him as an envoy who has arisen through God's plan to ensure the nation's salvation."[517] This is what comes to mind when I read these types of statements from Wolfe, describing "a man of dignity and greatness of soul who will lead a people," most notably the statement with which he will end this chapter:

> ... we should pray that God would raise up such a leader from among us: one who would suppress the enemies of God and elevate his people; recover a worshiping people; restore masculine prominence in the land and a spirit for dominion... In a word, pray that God would bring about, through a Christian prince, a great renewal.[518]

---

514 Preston, *Franco*, 42.
515 Preston, 184.
516 Preston, 187.
517 Preston, xvii.
518 Wolfe, *The Case for Christian Nationalism*, 323.

III. The Origin of Civil Power

> As a collective entity, a nation has a collective will for its collective good. It must have a collective will, because **the nation is a moral person, responsible for itself before God.** (emphasis mine)[519]

Wolfe is absolutely correct here, though, as previously stated, if the nation is explicitly Christian then the nation is a *Christian person*, morally responsible in the all the same ways an *individual Christian* is. This would mean that the nation is bound by all of the same moral commandments of God as the individual. For example, while a Christian nation can prevent physical harm done to others, it must abide by the moral commandment to leave blasphemers in peace, with the prayer that "God may perhaps grant them repentance leading to a knowledge of the truth" (2 Timothy 2:24-26); otherwise, it is not acting as a collective *Christian* person. The Christian nation must use Scripture as its primary and infallible source of truth; it can never pass a law that would be considered a sin if an individual performed the same action. It would have extra *responsibilities*, such as after-the-fact determination of guilt and punishment, but its *moral directives* are identical to the individual, no more and no less.

> The people lack coordination, and disorder (though unintended) will frustrate acts of good.[520]

If we apply this principle to Wolfe's argument regarding charity in chapter 5[521], then the whole subsection would be negated in favor of state-controlled action; why would the people's inability to coordinate themselves be limited to a vaguely defined *national good*? If we need a prince "through whom the people act for their own good," then should we not defer everything, including our charity organizing, to him as well? If

---

519 Wolfe, 279.
520 Wolfe, 280.
521 Wolfe, 218–23.

7. The Christian Prince

Wolfe disputes this, then the statement that the "people lack coordination" that will "frustrate acts of good" is not entirely true. As we have seen before, the inherent contradictions in this theory disprove its claim that man's subjective interpretation of general revelation is sufficient for good, consistent, *Christian* government.

Next, there is nothing inherently wrong with a people being "ordered according to both the general conception of the common good and their own particularities," but horrible atrocities have been committed in the past when the ordering force has decided that it is, as he writes, "not bound to any specific dictates of the people."[522] With a similarly questionable self-confidence and disregard of *consent*, Primo de Rivera said, "The leader should not obey the public; he should serve it, which is a different thing. To serve it means to direct the exercise of the command for the people's good, achieving the good of the people ruled, even though the people itself be unaware what its good is."[523] As has been proven several times, throughout Wolfe's book, one man's interpretation of the "moral law of God," by which he is bound, is entirely subjective. What would stop a lineage of *theocratic Caesars* from filling the highest echelons of civil and ecclesial government with sycophants who would confirm whatever their eisegetical hearts desire? This type of feedback loop has a historical precedent in what happened to the Catholic church in the four and a half centuries between the two councils of Nicea.

> Would God create something that lacks what is necessary for that thing to achieve its purpose? Would God create human society with an inherent need for an ordering agent and not provide the power for ordering? No.[524]

There is a very theologically dubious implication to this statement. Though God has a purpose for everything he creates, we are not necessarily inclined to *correctly perceive* that purpose; one example is the man born blind whom Jesus healed:

---

522 Wolfe, 280.
523 Greger, *Jose Antonio Primo de Rivera*, 83.
524 Wolfe, *The Case for Christian Nationalism*, 280–81.

> As he passed by, he saw a man blind from birth. And his disciples asked him, "Rabbi, who sinned, this man or his parents, that he was born blind?" Jesus answered, "It was not that this man sinned, or his parents, but that the works of God might be displayed in him." (John 9:1-3)

Wolfe would have us believe that, should a government not perform to his personal standards of *national good*, that it is abdicating its authority from God.[525] Again, how could he refute a similar subjective interpretation from Christian socialists? They are equally concerned with "ordering" society, just not along the lines that he finds most beneficial.

There is another seeming contradiction in the next section with what was written earlier in the book. On the one hand, he says that "no one possesses an inherent, natural superiority in relation to other men such that, by pure nature alone, natural inferiors are bound by their nature to submit to them." However, in his prelapsarian theory, he stated that, through an "unequal civil virtue by nature," a "natural aristocracy would arise in each community to rule, establishing a rule by the best."[526] Perhaps he would say that this is the difference between a *principle of submission* and *practical outcomes*, but the nature of how his aristocracy would rise brings the whole principle into question. If people are supposedly naturally (genetically) predisposed to have better civil virtue and should two of those people pair and procreate, would they not produce offspring who are equally or more virtuous by nature? When two tall people have a child, the child often grows to be even taller. Assuming this immutable characteristic of natural virtue to be true (I do not think it is), how would a nation that fosters it through intra-marriage not breed itself a *natural nobility*, born to rule? As in Aldous Huxley's *Brave New World*, why should the naturally bred *Alphas* not rule over the *Gammas*? Considering he thinks aristocracy is born of nature, would not such an arrangement be *natural law*?

> The power to order the whole must come from God; it does not inhere in or originate from any man or men in aggregate...

---
525 Wolfe, 349–51.
526 Wolfe, 281, 72.

7. The Christian Prince

One important corollary is that recognizing the true God (or Christ) is unnecessary to possess this power, for having this power is simply a natural consequence of the people's combination into human society.[527]

Is the power directly *from God* or a *natural consequence*? I suspect he would say it is *both,* as a principle of natural law, but that would be somewhat incorrect; God, through his supernatural providence, appoints all earthly authorities, whether they recognize him or not. This is why we are told "whoever resists the authorities resists what God has appointed" (Romans 13:2). Wolfe rightly recognizes Peter's instruction to "honor the [Roman] emperor,"[528] but through his later argument on Romans 13 and revolution, we can infer that he believes this statement to really mean "honor the [office of Roman] emperor"; in his view, the people can dishonor and depose the person who is currently emperor if he is a tyrant. As I have shown, that belief is not drawn from Scripture (1 Peter 2:18). Though this is a point that I have made repeatedly, it must continue to be made when the subject of deference to divinely appointed authority comes up because the supposed *right to violent Christian revolution* in our day and time is likely the key takeaway the average reader would glean from Wolfe's book. If nothing else, I would hope to disabuse the reader of that notion.

Again, the statement, "Consent is the mechanism by which divine civil power is bestowed upon the prince"[529] cannot seemingly be rectified with his later statement that Christians would likely have to "disregard the non-Christian withholding of consent." Though these two claims are contradictory, on the surface, Wolfe has a trick up his sleeve; he precedes the latter thought on disregarding consent with, "Today, those who are restored in Christ are the people of God. Thus, civil order and administration is for them."[530] Here is the insidious underbelly of his poor

---

527 Wolfe, 282, 283.
528 Wolfe, 284.
529 Wolfe, 285.
530 Wolfe, 346.

theology of the "restored image," creating an *underclass of conscience* not even worthy of giving or withholding consent for civil rule. Even the Romans did not fully withhold or revoke citizenship along these lines (Acts 16:37). This entire section, so concerned with convincing the reader that, under his civil government, the will of the people would be respected, is a bait and switch; only those who meet his set of religious qualifications will be counted as fully human, for they are the only ones with the image of God that is "same in substance as that which Adam possessed."[531] They are the ones allowed to decide if they possess the "proper motivation" and the "*rational* need" for submission, and whether it "conduces to living well." Everyone else will be disregarded and *told to submit*.

IV. A Divine Office

The doctrinal content of the description of the prince's "divine office" in this section is in line with 16th and 17th-century Reformed thought;[532] the monarch is God's appointed authority on earth and was often written of as a *little-G* god, in that context. Calvin's commentary on Isaiah 3 is quoted to make the case that "the palace of princes ought to resemble a sanctuary: for they occupy the dwelling place of God, which ought to be sacred to all."[533] This is also consistent with that era's Reformed thought, and not of great note, but something Wolfe ignores from the very same chapter of the commentary has far more significant applicability to his theory. A pattern is emerging where he selectively quotes ideas from Calvin he finds agreeable, as an appeal to authority/tradition, but ignores ideas in the same commentary that wholly contradict his philosophy; just two verses back, we find this:

> There is nothing which men are more reluctant to allow than to have a yoke laid on them; nor do they willingly submit to be governed by nobles. Feeble and cowardly, therefore, must be the minds of those who obey delicate and effeminate men, and permit

---

531 Wolfe, 94.
532 Wolfe, 286–87.
533 John Calvin, Commentary on Isaiah, [on Isaiah 3:14].

222

7. The Christian Prince

themselves to be oppressed by them; nor can it be doubted that God has struck with a spirit of cowardice those who offer their shoulders, like asses, to bear burdens. **The power of a tyrant must indeed be endured, even by men of courage**; but the reproach which Isaiah brings against the Jews is, that while they obstinately shake off the yoke of God, they are ready to yield abject submission to men, and to perform any services, however shameful or degrading. (emphasis mine)[534]

Calvin affirms that even "men of courage" *must endure the tyrannical rule* of "effeminate men"; this is very similar to the "gynocracy", first mentioned later in this section and the same as Aristotle and Calvin's *gunaikokratia*[535] (the government of women). The book of Isaiah shows us that God is the One who enacts judgment on nations, and the prophet's example is that of someone imbued with God's Spirit speaking boldly in truth, while still submitting to His appointed authorities. Calvin's beliefs on submission to tyrannical rule were based on exegetical insight. If Wolfe is not going to exegete and use Calvin's thought as his theory's most cited exegetical authority, then he must show, *with Scripture*, why he disagrees with any of Calvin's exegesis; not the least being Calvin's consistent stance on submission to tyrannical rule, a sentiment shared with Viret. Appeals to reasoning of natural law will not suffice for Wolfe, because he has made Calvin an authority on God's will. As mentioned above, when Wolfe does briefly attempt to exegete Romans 13, in chapter 8, I will show how his hermeneutic is terribly flawed; one of the tools I will use is Calvin's exegesis on the same chapter.

> The prince promotes national self-love and manly, moral liberty. He recognizes national sins but swiftly resolves them, leaving no license for exploitation or room for lingering self-doubt and the lack of national confidence. He encourages and channels the boldness and spirit of youth, while elevating the old and

---

534 John Calvin, Commentary on Isaiah, [on Isaiah 3:12].
535 John Calvin, Commentary on 1 Timothy, [on 1 Timothy 2:11].

venerating the dead. **He silences the social mammies** and countenances the spartan bootstrapper. (emphasis mine)[536]

I want to be as charitable as I can, so I spent some time trying to find another context for *mammy* than the racial epithet for a stereotype of a brash house-slave and nursemaid. It is used for "mother," without racial context, in England, but that makes no sense in the antagonistic context of Wolfe's statement. Besides, Wolfe has used the *longhouse mammies* antifeminist meme in the past, which has explicitly white nationalist origins, within the same *anti-gynocratic* context of the above quote, when he wrote on Twitter in 2021, "Rejecting 'individualism' is a mistake. There are bad forms of it, but emphasizing individual agency is good. We can't let the individual be subsumed in and submitted to the longhouse mammies or the nanny welfare state or the gynocracy."[537] Given this, I have to no reason but to conclude that Wolfe used this word intentionally and with an understanding of its racial connotations, and that "social" is likely a stand-in for "longhouse."

We are given another *Caudillo-like* description of the prince. Wolfe pulls out all the stops, even saying that he "fights foreign aggressors" with θυμός (thumos), the Greek concept of an inherent *spiritedness* that is very much inline with the Nietzschian *will to power* themes in his theory's *prerational preference*. The prince also has "a sort of divine presence or *gravitas*."[538] When one compares these descriptions to how we traditionally describe America's "great men," it becomes clear that the Christian Prince is being propped up in a very different way; there is the myth we tell children that George Washington never told a lie, but would we expect grown men to speak of him in these terms? When we hear these very same sentiments broadcast by national adversaries, we easily see through them as

---

536 Wolfe, *The Case for Christian Nationalism*, 288.
537 https://twitter.com/PerfInjust/status/1459891682380599308
   "Longhouse mammies" was first made popular by the Nietzschean white nationalist Twitter user "Bronze Age Pervert". He has acknowledged that *longhouse* is associated with him, and has used phrases similar to Wolfe's tweet, such as "longhouse bog mammy" and "longhouse gynomales".
   https://twitter.com/bronzeagemantis/status/1670089166883807236
538 Wolfe, *The Case for Christian Nationalism*, 288, 290.

7. The Christian Prince

ridiculous propaganda. Does North Korean state television not use this very type of imagery to describe the *Dear Leader*?

Also of note are the continued appeals to *manliness*; he is not only concerned with *liberty*, but "manly, moral liberty," whatever that may be; "mammies," beyond its racial context, is *negative female* language, while "spartan" is *positive male*; the prince will also "restore masculine prominence in the land."[539] This type of language is common among what may be best described as *patriarchalists*, those who take Christian male headship of the home to extreme levels. It serves to fuel the opposition rhetoric of liberal Christian writers, such as Kristin Kobes Du Mez; her book *Jesus and John Wayne* is filled with so many repetitions and derivatives of the phrase *militant white masculinity* that one might mistake whole sections for conservative satire. I believe she wrongly diagnoses a real issue in conservative Christian punditry that dovetails with Christian Nationalist circles, that of a faux *performative masculinity*.

One often sees a concerted effort from patriarchalists and Christian Nationalists to portray themselves as exceedingly manly. They will regularly talk about how *real Christian men* go to the gym and lift weights, something I agree with as a principle for good health, not because doing so will make someone more authentically conservative or Christian. Stereotypical "masculine" props, like cigars and whiskey, are common; an anonymous Christian Nationalist account on Twitter once strangely derided me by claiming that I would not "feel comfortable sitting in a room having two fingers of Bourbon or a Single Malt with Phinehas or Nehemiah."[540] This was because I had used Scripture to show it is a sin for a Christian to make fun of the physical appearance of an ideological opponent (2 Timothy 2:24), as self-described Christian Nationalist and online personality Adam "AD" Robles had just done.[541] This is the other side of this group's

---

539 Wolfe, 323.
540 https://twitter.com/Shibboleth001/status/1641921797963780096
Shibboleth01: "I very much doubt this guy would feel comfortable sitting in a room having two fingers of Bourbon or a Single Malt with Phinehas or Nehemiah. Or Peter for that matter, after he told some guy to go to hell..."
541 https://twitter.com/ADRoblesMedia/status/1641842058817163266
AD Robles Media: "Tranny Nationalism it is!" (With a picture of Westminster Seminary California professor, R. Scott Clark, clearly to make fun of his

performative manliness, the shaming of those whom the practitioner deems *unmanly*. Robles is perhaps the most prolific in this behavior[542] among his peers, but Wolfe will regularly make statements, such as, "Yes, losing the dad bod is Christian nationalism," and "Best I can tell, all PCA [teaching elders] have the same body type,"[543] something that will be echoed in his epilogue.

Performative masculinity is *fake masculinity*; it is something insecure men do to project a strength they do not truly believe they possess – it is *betas* pretending to be *alphas*. Many of the most dangerous, well trained men I have had the pleasure of knowing were incredibly meek and kind in person and often could care less about doing stereotypical "manly" things. One, whom I will call Matt, sticks out to me. He was a former Marine in a rock band in Los Angeles, well over six feet tall and probably close to three hundred pounds of mostly muscle. Because of Matt's stature, people would often challenge him to fights outside the venues we would frequent, even though he was always very down-to-earth and kind to everyone. On multiple occasions, I saw him knock out someone with very little exertion when they tested their performative masculinity on him; it was like watching a child fight an adult. One night, while we were all hanging out, sitting around a fire pit and playing guitar, I improvised a short comedy song about these encounters and how dominant he was in them, set to the tune of *Ghost Riders in the Sky*. Matt was visibly upset, and said to me, "I just wish people would see me for more than that." I do not think I could have had more respect for that man than in that moment.

I believe that Christian Nationalism, for many adherents, is a form of performative masculinity; believing themselves to be fighting a holy crusade, even if just online, makes them feel more *dominant* than they really are. This dominance (what I believe is often tied to the Christian

---

    appearance)
542 https://twitter.com/ADRoblesMedia/status/1621845266117656576
    AD Robles Media: "They always look like beetles" (Commenting on the profile picture of Daniel Darling, Director of The Land Center, a SBC affiliated think tank)
543 https://twitter.com/PerfInjust/status/1597342351428849664
    https://twitter.com/PerfInjust/status/1410308004222836737

Nationalist perversion of Biblical *dominion*) is perhaps something they wished they had in their daily lives, and joining a movement that offers a promise of a world where a civil government and state church would enforce such order – in which a "great man" will "restore masculine prominence" – gives them a sense of purpose in a West that has truly devalued men, as Wolfe next discusses. What he describes is the essence of the "longhouse mammy" meme, men required to subjugate themselves to the leadership of brash, domineering women.

> We live under a *de facto* gynocracy where masculinity is pathologized in the name of "fairness" and "equity." To achieve acceptance or relevance today, men must become female-adjacent; that is, to adjust to toxic-feminine conditions of empowerment: sameness, credentialism, risk-aversion, victimology, and passive-aggression.[544]

Like any effective meme, there is a some truth in this statement; masculinity is most certainly considered a negative trait among Western elites, and some of the most underserved demographics in our culture are boys and young men, who are often told that their natural, healthy behavior must be suppressed. But overcompensation through performative masculinity, which is what this subsection linguistically represents, is actually a *weakling's* response; it is *whiny talk* and childish *acting out*. We do not need to bombastically hearken to "heroic masculinity," the "greatness" of "powerful men," or "commit[ment] to natural hierarchy" while demonizing all things "equality"[545]; we simply need to affirm confident, Christian men. We need to *be* confident, *Christian* men; men who are not afraid to be *meek* and *kind*, because we trust ourselves and, even more, we trust our Savior; we need to be men who are confident in our eschatology, who place our treasure in the only place that matters, and who let that exude itself through our actions. We do not need *wannabe warriors*, we need *elders*.

---

544 Wolfe, *The Case for Christian Nationalism*, 290.
545 Wolfe, 291.

V. The Christian Prince

> A prince is a Christian prince only if he wields his power so that the totality of national action is Christian.[546]

In this statement one can see the vice of authoritarian power closing in on the people of the nation, coalescing around the will of a single man. One *Caesar* has the power to wield "the totality of national action" to what he and those closest to him consider "Christian." It may be possible, though highly unlikely, that a coalition of Western Christian zealots could come to an agreement on what civil enforcement of the doctrine of a state church would entail without devolving into multiple, warring factions. Perhaps, for the first several generations, this nation's definition of "Christian civil enforcement" would be in alignment with what most conservative Christians consider to be orthodox, but to remain that way, Wolfe's would have to be the first nation-state in history with this amount of intended control over its citizens' behavior to not get drunk on its own power. The 21st-century West is overwhelmingly ideologically disparate (with orthodox Christians in a significant minority), and shows no sign of changing; his nation would need to employ an iron grip to maintain what it sees as "social order"; in all of human history, only one "great Man" has had the *gravitas* to peacefully change that many hearts and minds, and yet He was still murdered by His countrymen. We Christians must recognize that we are far more like them than Him, and temper our earthly ambitions accordingly.

Quoting the Puritan minister John Cotton, Wolfe claims that the prince should not "draw his sword to compel all his subjects to the obedience of the faith of Christ and to the profession of it,"[547] but he very much envisions the prince enforcing orthodoxy in public discourse, making this a mute point. What would be the outcome for certain credobaptists who see believer's baptism by immersion to be a prerequisite for salvation? What of fundamentalist baptists who believe the *King James Bible* to be the only

---
546 Wolfe, 293.
547 Wolfe, 295.

7. The Christian Prince

authoritative English translation? What would happen to megachurch charismatics who have "prophets"? What of all the mainliners who see liberal politics in the gospel? What are the actual limits of enforced public orthodoxy in such a nation? Wolfe will later argue for "prudence," but there is such wide variance in belief among Protestants five hundred years into the Reformation that *some professing Christians* in his nation would ultimately wind up with a boot on their neck.

The majority of the remainder of this section is dedicated to the majesty of the prince's rule and how he would "Christianize civil life" by "adorning and perfecting it with true religion."[548] As with many of his other appeals to Christian culture, there is nothing distinctly "Christian" about any of these descriptions; for example, Wolfe asks us to consider the "Christian harvest festival" of fellowship and thanksgiving, as if most non-Christian, agrarian peoples do not have harvest festivals where they fellowship and give thanks to their god. Though there are many appeals to actions that vaguely "point the people heavenward," there is nothing in particular that could be tied to *Scriptural ethics*. Wolfe also claims that the military of his nation would be "soldiers of Christ," which is a designation ripe for abuse. Otherwise, there is nothing of significant note; this is mostly standard nationalist propaganda about the *greatness of the nation* under its figurehead. I would rather focus on a thought that gets its first emphatic utterance in this section:

> Punishing blasphemy would certainly solidify a culture of pious speech.[549]

Let us conduct a thought experiment regarding "punishing blasphemy" (and heresy) in the 21st-century West to see if the end result would be any different than other state actions in history that implicitly or explicitly designated a people group as "other." The Latter-day Saints hold a myriad of beliefs that are heretical to all Christian churches – Catholic, Eastern Orthodox, and Protestant – not the least of which is that Elohim was once a

---

548 Wolfe, 295–98.
549 Wolfe, 293.

man who ascended to the status of a god, receiving his own planet. Likewise, Jehovah's Witnesses do not believe in the divinity of Christ and believe that God is limited in his being. Both groups have at least ten thousand believers in every state (1 out of every 115 people in Wolfe's state of North Carolina are Latter-day Saints[550]), and both groups are *fierce evangelists*. It must be remembered that, as Christians, though we know we worship the true God, those who do not are often, *practically speaking*, just as firm in their belief as us. Those of us who are Reformed must also remember that the only reason we are not lost in false belief, just as they are, is because God, in his mercy, moved us to belief through His Spirit.

In Wolfe's nation, it would be illegal for both of these groups to evangelize in public spaces or go door to door, because such action would constitute a Third Commandment violation. Would these people stop? Would there not be at least some who obstinately continue in their belief that they are spreading life-saving truth? When missionaries are fined and forced to go home, will some not go right back out as soon as the "police of Christ" leave? Will some not refuse and be taken to jail? When released from jail, will they not continue evangelizing? When banished, will some not return? If they are executed, as Wolfe will claim as a possibility,[551] will their death not only embolden their comrades? Would a nation doing these things not quickly cut itself off from other nations, including its neighbors? Would the best and brightest not flee to places where they would be free to express their heterodox opinions? Lastly, what happens if an entire congregation or denomination of a false religion decides to peacefully disobey these laws, believing they are doing the will of God? Would tens of thousands of people, or more, need to be forcefully removed from their land and shipped out of the country? What if they decide not to go peacefully, but to stay and fight?

This last scenario actually happened in the United States when Mormons clashed with Christians in Missouri, with the resulting state action turning murderous. The story of what came to be known as the 1838

---

550 "Statistics and Church Facts | Total Church Membership," The Church of Jesus Christ of Latter Day Saints, 2023, http://newsroom.churchofjesuschrist.org/facts-and-statistics/country/united-states.
551 Wolfe, *The Case for Christian Nationalism*, 392.

7. The Christian Prince

Mormon War in Missouri is a sobering example of how a Christian nationalist state would likely see perpetual inter-group violence, insurgency, and state-sponsored persecution and atrocity.

My account of the 1838 Mormon War in Missouri is drawn from the book of that title by historian Stephen C. LeSueur, written for the University of Missouri; to my knowledge it is the only modern, detailed account not sponsored by the LDS church and, therefore, holds Joseph Smith and his compatriots well accountable for their part in the conflict. This is important, because, as will become apparent, there are two relevant angles to this story. If his theory were acted out in our time, Wolfe and his compatriots would initially play the part of the belligerent religious minority attempting to colonize areas held by people with other worldviews; should their project succeed, they would likely next take the position of the state, expelling other religious groups but unable to restrain their troops' hatred of the religious minority. LeSueur opens his account with a wonderful insight that, for our purposes, highlights how the academic "logical principles" of political theory often crash, head first, into the reality of human behavior this side of the fall:

> Perhaps more than anything else the conflict between the Mormons and Missourians reveals the many weaknesses of human nature. Most people in both groups tried to follow a peaceful and moderate course, but rumors, prejudice, fear, and a misconceived devotion to God carried the conflict beyond the control of its participants leading normally law-abiding citizens to commit numerous crimes.[552]

In 1835, Joseph Smith, the self-described "prophet-president" of the Church of Jesus Christ of Latter-day Saints, prophesied that Christ would return in fifty-six years and told his people to prepare for the Second Coming. In 1831, he had located Zion in Jackson County, Missouri, saying

---

552 Stephen C. LeSueur, *The 1838 Mormon War in Missouri*, 1. paperback print., [Nachdr.] (Columbia, Mo: Univ. of Missouri Press, 1990), 5.

that this was where the Garden of Eden had resided; Mormons began settling in the region, mostly coming from New York; some built traditional towns, while others started communes, sharing all things in kind.[553] Missourians were generally not pleased; as LeSueur writes:

> A variety of motives and fears stimulated the Missourians' opposition to the Mormons. Although most of the older settlers were not particularly religious, they regarded the Mormons' beliefs as obnoxious. They resented the Saints' claims to being God's chosen people and they considered the Mormons to be deluded fanatics, victims of the scheming designs of Joseph Smith and other Church leaders.[554]

Attempting to find a peaceful arrangement, a new county was created, and a gentleman's agreement was made with the Mormons that they would settle there. Toleration of Mormonism from Missourians now "rested primarily upon the Missourian's belief that the Mormons would confine themselves to Caldwell County." Though their main settlement, Far West, was in Caldwell, they very quickly broke the arrangement, spreading into several other counties, including Daviess, where they started the settlement Adam-ondi-Ahman, which Smith claimed was the place where Adam and Eve settled after the fall and whose name meant "the place where Adam dwelt." This name was based on his claim to have received from an angel named Moroni golden tablets containing a set of hieroglyphics which related a new testament of Jesus Christ. The Mormons began setting up competing businesses where they settled, including an attempted usurpation of the lucrative trade with Fort Leavenworth, just over the Kansas border. By 1838, the Mormon population in Missouri was 10,000; by comparison, Caldwell County's southern neighbor, Carroll, had only 1,800 residents. Amid increasing tensions, Mormons began a secret society, called the Danites, dedicated to protecting their settlements and headquartered in Far West.[555]

---

553 LeSueur, 9, 10, 11.
554 LeSueur, 17.
555 LeSueur, 25, 29, 35.

7. The Christian Prince

When Mormons settled a new town called DeWitt in Carroll County in 1838, emotions quickly boiled over; the citizens of Carroll voted to expel the Mormons and went to the town to demand they leave, but were rebuffed. That summer, a mob of one hundred men "rode into DeWitt and shot up the town, taking prisoners and threatening the Mormon inhabitants." In response, a "steady stream" of Mormons moved into the town to solidify its defense.[556] Due to the religious significance of Adam-ondi-Ahman, Mormons heavily settled Daviess County and quickly became the dominant voting block. Rumors swirled that the local Whigs were planning violence to prevent Mormons from going to voting locations, putting Mormons in Daviess on edge. On August 6, in the small town of Galleton, after a vitriolic stump speech from the Whig candidate for the state legislature, in which he called Mormons "horse thieves, liars, counterfeiters, and dupes," a longtime resident of the county, Dick Weldon, assaulted a local Mormon shoemaker named Samuel Brown. When the Danite signal for distress was given, a full riot broke out, with Mormons and "Gentiles" fighting with "whips, clubs, rocks, and knives." The next day, Joseph Smith led over one hundred Danites from Far West to Daviess County and threatened a judge whom he accused of anti-Mormon activities; in response, Smith was arrested but later released on bail. These types of engagements spread to most other counties with Mormon settlements, with both sides regularly taking part in vigilante violence.[557]

On August 30, Governor Lilburn W. Boggs ordered 2,800 state troops to stand at the ready. A week and a half later, Circuit Court Judge Austin King ordered state militia general David Atchison to raise four hundred troops to quell violence in Daviess, while, at the same time, vigilantes in Carroll postponed their attack on DeWitt to assist their compatriots in that county. Atchison was able to stop the violence in Daviess by September 20, and the Carroll vigilantes returned home, determined to expel the Mormons from DeWitt. By the beginning of October, the situation had so heavily devolved that vigilantes attacked and burned the home and barn of a settler and were preparing a full scale siege of the town. Governor Boggs attempted to

---
556 LeSueur, 55–58.
557 LeSueur, 60–62, 67–89.

intervene with militia, but the anti-Mormon sentiment of the troops was so significant that their commanding general, Hiram Parks, was forced to pull his men back to keep them from joining the vigilantes. On October 11, the Mormons in DeWitt surrendered, most of them fleeing to Far West.[558] On the orders of Smith, the Danites and other Mormons attacked multiple towns in Daviess County, "driving settlers from their homes, plundering, and burning."[559] As LeSueur describes their mindset:

> The desperate crimes committed by the Mormon soldiers can be attributed to several factors. Their militant activities and the belligerent speeches of their leaders during the summer and fall of 1838 had been leading them on a course of increasing lawlessness and violence. Pent-up hostility and frustration, fostered by years of persecution, lay waiting to explode.[560]

The overwhelming Mormon force drove most non-Mormons out of Daviess, and the attackers felt confident that God was behind them. Referencing Deuteronomy 32:30, one member of the party later wrote, "I thought that one Danite could chase a thousand Gentiles, and two could put ten thousand to flight."[561] Militia generals refused to involve their troops, knowing that they would act no better than the vigilantes. General Atchison informed the governor that vigilantes on both sides were acting like "madmen" and "committing numerous crimes and outrages." He said that he would not call upon his troops because they would simply join the non-Mormon side of the fighting.[562]

Mormons regularly excommunicated those who questioned Smith's actions and, on October 24, two former "apostles" signed affidavits describing the continued militant intent of Mormon leadership and their secret Danite society. Under the (reliable) assumption that the Mormons intended to continue their campaign, an openly anti-Mormon captain under

---

558 LeSueur, 88, 90–112.
559 LeSueur, 112, 120–21.
560 LeSueur, 121.
561 LeSueur, 126–27.
562 LeSueur, 129.

7. The Christian Prince

General Parks, Samuel Bogart, set camp with his troops at Crooked River, just south of the Caldwell County line, and prepared to march on the main Mormon settlement of Far West.[563]

A scout reported to Mormon leadership in Far West that Captain Bogart and his men had crossed the river and were threatening to attack the town. Bogart was known by the Mormons as someone who "was as lawless, if not more so, and as mobocratic as the worst of the mob." His men were among those who had sided with the vigilantes in Carroll County, requiring General Parks to withdraw; Parks reportedly later tried to have him discharged from the militia. The Mormons sent a spy party, but Bogart's men captured three of them; according to those who escaped, the Missourians had threatened to kill the prisoners in the morning.[564]

Fifty volunteers were authorized by a Caldwell County judge to act as militia and placed under the command of Captain David W. Patten, a Danite and "apostle" known as "Captain Fearnot." The party rode to Crooked River in an attempt to free the spies. At 3:00 AM, they dismounted and marched towards Bogart's location, and when they were within a mile, one of Bogart's sentries ordered them to halt. Thinking he heard a gun shot, the sentry fired on the Mormons, hitting militiaman Patrick O'Banion, and then retreated with his fellow sentry back to the camp. Bogart's men, hearing the commotion, scrambled from their tents and formed a battle line; at daybreak, the Mormons attacked.[565]

Initially, the battle was not going well for the Mormons because they had attacked from an open field while the Missourians had taken cover behind trees; in a desperate attempt to recover the situation, Patten ordered a charge. The Mormons, shouting "God and Liberty," drew their swords and ran directly into Bogart's line. His men panicked and tried to escape across the river, many appealing, "We are brethren," to no avail. One Mormon participant later remarked that "many a mobber was there baptised with out faith or repentance under the messingers of lead sent by the bretheren." Another claimed he had seen an angel's hand holding back

---

563 LeSueur, 130, 134–37.
564 LeSueur, 132, 138.
565 LeSueur, 138–40.

the arm of a Missourian as the Mormons slashed him with their swords. Message of the defeat quickly made its way throughout Missouri; initial reports stated that the entire company had been massacred, but the actual number was ten dead. Nine Mormons laid wounded and Patrick O'Banion died of his wound the next night.[566] On October 27, Governor Boggs received news of Crooked River and issued an order to General John B. Clark, which contained the following:

> I have received… information of the most appalling character, which entirely changes the face of things, and places the Mormons in the attitude of an open and avowed defiance of the laws, and of having made war upon the people of this state. Your orders are, therefore, to hasten your operation with all possible speed. **The Mormons must be treated as enemies, and must be exterminated or driven from the state if necessary** for the public peace – their outrages are beyond all description. (emphasis mine)[567]

The Mormon settlement of Haun's Mill, at the eastern edge of Caldwell County, normally housed ten to fifteen families, but another twenty emigrant Mormon families had arrived after the disturbances had started and were living out of their wagons. Though state militia under General Parks was near the settlement, a temporary treaty had been signed; Mormons had set up a guard, but were not expecting an attack. They were going about their daily tasks when two hundred soldiers emerged from the woods, one hundred yards away. Without a word spoken, the Missouri troops raised their guns and indiscriminately fired on men, women, and children. It is possible they had received Governor Boggs's recent "extermination order" and took it literally.[568]

Fifteen men and three boys ran to the blacksmith shop, which was a predetermined defensive position; while the boys hid under the bellows the men fired upon the troops, providing cover for other settlers to escape. The

---

566 LeSueur, 140–43.
567 LeSueur, 151–52.
568 LeSueur, 162–65.

7. The Christian Prince

men were unable to hold off the advance and most were killed, one by one. Eventually, the order to flee was given, but most were shot while retreating. A sixty-two year old Mormon, Thomas McBride, surrendered to the Missourians, but Jacob Rogers, a ferry operator from Daviess, took the defenseless old man's loaded weapon and shot him in the chest. Inside the blacksmith shop, ten year old Sardius Smith remained under the bellows while his father lay mortally wounded near him. Though the boy begged for his life, William Reynolds of Livingston County shot him point-blank in the head, blowing the top of his skull clean off. Reynolds reportedly later said, "Nits will make lice, and if he had lived he would have become a Mormon."[569]

One day after the massacre at Haun's mill, when peace terms were refused by Missourians, Joseph Smith and other Mormon and Danite leaders surrendered themselves to the militia to face trial. After the Mormons were disarmed, soldiers ransacked their homes; one resident later said that the Missourians would enter homes at night, wake Mormons up with cocked guns, saying they were searching for weapons, but would instead take whatever they pleased. Roving bands of armed brigands were seen "strolling up and down Caldwell county" plundering houses, driving off farm animals, and "leaving the poor Mormons in a starving and naked condition." Soldiers reportedly shot farm animals for sport, jesting that they were "Mormons running away on all fours." There were at least two credible eyewitness accounts of attempted rape. One month after the surrender, the Mormons in Far West were called to the town square and forced, one by one, to deed over their land to the state to pay back the expenses for the war. One Missourian was overheard saying, "Joe Smith could not make the Saints consecrate, but we can make them consecrate."[570]

State legal proceedings only looked into Mormon offenses, and "regardless of who was at fault or who broke the law, it was Mormon leaders who were jailed, and Mormons who were forced to abandon their homes." There was never a single inquiry into Haun's Mill, and a motion for an investigation into the full conflict by the state legislature was

---

569 LeSueur, 166–67.
570 LeSueur, 169–73, 180–81, 183, 232.

quashed. Though Governor Boggs admitted that there were wrongs committed by non-Mormons, he whitewashed them by saying "they must be attributed to the excited nature of the contest of the parties and not to any desire on the part of our constituted authorities to willfully or cruelly oppress them." Mormons were still hounded throughout the state; Captain Bogart and his company continued "hunting the Danites" who participated in Crooked River.[571]

By January 1839, realizing that the legislature would not act to protect them, the Mormons prepared to leave. Most who still had property traded it for land in Illinois, where they had chosen to settle. Those who did not have equipment for the move were forced to sell their land to cover expenses and were usually heavily taken advantage of. As LeSueur writes:

> But those who needed cash and equipment accepted the low offers, and many Mormons reported trading their farms for a wagon and team of cattle. The expulsion of the Saints, Reed Peck wrote after their departure, opened "a field for speculators who now reap the advantages of labor done by the banished Mormons."[572]

Nancy Hammer, whose husband was killed at Haun's Mill, had only a blind horse and a small wagon to move her six children the one hundred miles to Illinois in the cold of winter. Her son John later wrote:

> Into this small wagon we placed our clothes, bedding, some corn meal and what scanty provisions we could muster, and started out into the cold and frost to travel on foot, to eat and sleep by the wayside with the canopy of heaven for a covering… When night approached we would hunt for a log or fallen tree and if lucky enough to find one we would build fires by the sides of it… Our family, as well as many others, were almost barefooted and some had to wrap their feet in cloths in order to keep them from freezing and protect them from the sharp points of the frozen ground. This, at best, was very imperfect protection and often the blood from our feet marked the frozen earth… There was scarcely a day while we

---

571 LeSueur, 195, 216, 228, 230, 231, 253.
572 LeSueur, 239.

were on the road that it did not either snow or rain. The nights and mornings were very cold.[573]

LeSueur notes that "Religious prejudice played an important role in shaping the participants' perceptions and actions during the disturbances." One Missourian belligerent's daughter reminisced of how her father's religious views drove his actions, saying, "Father believed the Bible, particularly where it said smite the Philistines, and he figured the Philistines was a misprint for the Mormons and he believed it was his religious duty to smite them… He was a great hand to practice what he preached so he helped exterminate quite a considerable few of them."[574]

Joseph Smith escaped from prison (most believe the guard was bribed) and met with his followers in Nauvoo, Illinois. Five years later, he again found himself accused of treason and riot. While sitting in a cell in Carthage, Illinois, an anti-Mormon mob broke into the jail and shot him to death.[575]

I have no faith that a Christian Nationalist revolutionary movement or government would do any better than the Mormons and Missourians. We are the same sinful people they were less than two hundred years ago; as much as we like to see ourselves as rational beings, we are driven far more by emotion than reason. It beggars belief that self-described Christian Nationalists, some of the most belligerent people in "Christian" discourse, who dedicate their public personas to defining enemies, who unashamedly belittle and mock their ideological opponents, who advocate for *preemptive* violent revolution when they still live in a comfort and peace that the majority of the world envies, would suddenly gain a sense of decorum and restraint when tensions *escalate*.

A civilly enforced blasphemy law will implicitly label whole swaths of people *the other*. Would those who see themselves as literal "soldiers of

---

573 LeSueur, 239–40.
574 LeSueur, 246–47.
575 LeSueur, 261–62.

Christ" be able to restrain themselves and treat *the other* with respect, or will they do what *everyone else* in history has done when given institutional power and told that another group of human beings is *the other*, and become dedicated persecutors who commit horrendous atrocities? Recall that Wolfe wants to "unashamedly and confidently assert Christian supremacy over the land," believes that non-Christians have made Christians suffer the "indignity of perpetual humiliation" and wants the Christian Prince to "suppress the enemies of God."[576] Could he maintain the relative docility of the monster he would bring to life, or will someone years from now again write of how "a misconceived devotion to God carried the conflict beyond the control of its participants"?

VI. The King and Kingdom of God

> There is, I admit, a natural fittingness to Christian nationalism and the prince as the "head of the Church." But granting the prince this title would be, in my view, an abuse of power and constitute the usurpation of Christ's kingship over the church.[577]

In some ways, I commend Wolfe for looking to separate civil and ecclesial power as proper *temporal* and *spiritual* kingdoms, but, as with blasphemy law, his application is the same type of academic theory that will fall to pieces when confronted with actual human behavior. One can look to Northern European countries and their centuries of attempts to have similar polity that ultimately wound up liberalizing the church, to the point that most have little in common with what their founders envisioned. Five hundred years ago, the Anglican church supported the execution of recalcitrant Catholics; by a century and a half ago, a significant portion of ministers denied the divinity of Christ[578]; in February of 2023, the Anglican General Synod voted to bless same-sex unions.[579] This is not to endorse any

---

576 Wolfe, *The Case for Christian Nationalism*, 217, 241, 323.
577 Wolfe, 300.
578 See: W.H. Fremantle from *Introduction: The Great Renewal, II. Definition*.
579 Harriet Sherwood, "Church of England Votes in Favour of Blessings for Same-Sex Unions," *The Guardian*, February 9, 2023, sec. World news,

7. The Christian Prince

of these positions, or to make a liberal/conservative distinction, but it shows how churches will often be changed by their culture over time. Even worse, a state-church is not only shaped by the culture of its nation but by the political maneuvering of the people in civil power. Of course, independent denominations can be subverted over time as well, but one of the key reasons American Christians continue to be more conservative than their European counterparts is the lack of an official state religion. Having no official state-church, especially in a majority Christian nation, allows people to dedicate themselves to Christ – it allows them to actually be good citizens of the *spiritual kingdom* without the worry of lowering their social status within a Christian society that is at odds with their beliefs.

We know that, in Wolfe's full vision, women and non-Christians will not have the right to decide how they are governed; what other religious preclusion would he impose on the people? For example, would someone not in the state-church be allowed to hold public office at all levels? Within several generations, the power structure of the civil and ecclesial institutions would inevitably become commingled; in *theocratic Caesarism*, what would prevent the Christian Prince's extended family and their allies from attaining a majority stake not just in the halls of civil government but also in the state Presbyterian General Assembly? Who would oppose them attaining that dual-power when the head of their family already wields the civil sword of a "totality of national action" and *suppresses* anyone he deems the "enemy of God"?

> The visible kingdom of Christ, though extending to things external and temporal, does not destroy or abrogate what is earthly.[580]

It is again worth noting the poor theology that states that Christ, Lord of all creation, who conquered death itself, does not possess the power to "abrogate what is earthly." The definition of a miracle is God working an act of creation, altering or *abrogating* something functioning in its expected

---

https://www.theguardian.com/world/2023/feb/09/church-of-england-votes-in-favour-of-blessings-for-same-sex-unions.
580 Wolfe, *The Case for Christian Nationalism*, 305.

earthly manner. There is a deep irony in that Wolfe will, in the next chapter, argue for violently abrogating the earthly authority of heavenly-appointed government when it meets his subjective definition of *tyrannical*. It would seem that Christ cannot abrogate what is earthly, but Stephen Wolfe can.

Wolfe next gives a description of the *visible church* as "a Christian people's life around sacred things."[581] This statement, as well as most in this section on Two Kingdoms Theology, are in line with Calvin's view, but this distinction of the *visible church*, which necessitates an *invisible church*, is at direct odds with Baptist theology. In the Baptist view, since all baptized members of the church have made a profession of faith, there is *technically* no distinction between the visible and invisible church (though they recognize that not all in the church are true believers). This lack of distinction has been noted by several Baptist theologians, including Scott Aniol, Professor of Pastoral Theology at Grace Bible Theological Seminary, who made the statement on Twitter that "Baptists and Christendom are inherently incompatible." Wolfe's response was to claim that this would mean "Baptists and political atheism are compatible," which Aniol rightly rejected as a false dichotomy.[582] As previously mentioned, conservative Christian Americans who adhere to credobaptism exponentially outnumber those who adhere to paedobaptism and the visible/invisible distinction.

Moving on to the difference between the mediation of Christ and the Prince, Wolfe says, "Christ as mediator, as he relates to his mediatorial office, **lacks civil power**" (emphasis mine). As above, the Christology of Wolfe is highly flawed; Christ is God and God ordains civil power. Even though He holds multiple offices (Prophet, Priest, King), how can One who ordains civil power *lack* civil power? Wolfe then claims that the Christian prince "can direct the church to a great extent" in matters tangential to the church and that he "exercises his power *for* the kingdom – on things

---

581 Wolfe, 308–9.
582 https://twitter.com/ScottAniol/status/1643006399985639425
    Scott Aniol: "Baptists and Christendom are inherently incompatible."
    Stephen Wolfe: "So, Baptists and political atheism are compatible."
    Scott Aniol: "Absolutely a falsity to claim that CN and political atheism are the only options."

7. The Christian Prince

extrinsic but necessary and supplemental to the advancement of that kingdom." This extrinsic power includes the extremely vague category of "defensive power about ecclesial matters," taken from Turretin.[583]

What would prevent a *theocratic Caesar* from taking the same path as Ukrainian President Volodymyr Zelenskyy? In 2022 he declared the Ukrainian Orthodox Church to be infiltrated with Russian agents and had cathedrals and monasteries raided, presenting "photos of children's bibles, prayer books, old liturgical books, archival collections of newspapers and magazines featuring the words 'Russian,' and Christmas or Easter sermons of the Russian Church patriarch" as supposed evidence.[584] In March of 2023, Metropolitan Pavel, the abbot of a Kyiv monastery, was placed under house arrest after allegedly cursing Zelenskyy.[585] What, or who, would stop the Christian prince from using such charges to neutralize any ecclesial authorities that stood in the way of his political ambitions? If Wolfe thinks this is beyond a human being who is adorned with such power that he sees himself as "an image of Christ to his people"[586] he is terribly naive.

> A husband does not ordinarily fulfill the duties of his wife, but he procures what is necessary for her to perform those duties, establishes the conditions for her to perform them well, approves her good performance, and **corrects her when she performs her duty poorly**. (emphasis mine)[587]

Wolfe shows his *patriarchalist* view of marriage, where assessment of performance and spousal correction appears to be a one-way street. He then compares this arrangement to a restaurant owner's relationship to his chef

---

583 Wolfe, *The Case for Christian Nationalism*, 310, 311.
584 Yevhen Herman, "Zelensky vs. the Ukrainian Orthodox Church," The American Conservative, January 25, 2023, https://www.theamericanconservative.com/zelensky-vs-the-ukrainian-orthodox-church/.
585 "Ukraine Places Priest Under House Arrest For Allegedly Justifying Russian Aggression Days After He Cursed Zelensky," The Daily Wire, April 1, 2023, https://www.dailywire.com/news/ukraine-places-priest-under-house-arrest-for-allegedly-justifying-russian-aggression-days-after-he-cursed-zelensky.
586 Wolfe, *The Case for Christian Nationalism*, 309.
587 Wolfe, 312.

employee, which is troublesome, on multiple stereotypical levels; Wolfe is providing egalitarians with the type of extreme statement they often use as a biased sample in their arguments. As those who are in a *healthy* complementarian marriage can affirm, one of a wife's greatest values to her husband is correcting *him* when he's about to make an error. Strong complementarian marriages are those of *teamwork* and *mutual respect*. When Wolfe's version of marital hierarchy is applied to the Christian prince's rapport with the church, we get a clear picture of a temporal kingdom that pays lip-service to Two Kingdoms Theology, but does not actually respect the separation of the kingdoms in practice. This is made exceedingly clear several paragraphs later:

> Lastly, [the prince] has the power to call synods in order to resolve doctrinal conflicts and to moderate the proceedings. following the proceedings, he can confirm or deny their theological judgments; and in confirming them, they become the settled doctrine of the land. But he considers the pastors' doctrinal articulations as a father might look to his medically trained son for medical advice. He still retains his superiority.[588]

How is this not the Christian prince acting within the *spiritual kingdom*? Should not the civil magistrate exist wholly to *enforce* the doctrine of the church, and have no hand in shaping it? How can someone supposedly relegated to civil enforcement have *veto power* over theological judgments? Popes consider cardinals' "doctrinal articulations," but hold ultimate power over final decisions in the same way. How does this statement not confirm everything that some of Wolfe's detractors have said about a "Protestant pope"? He goes on to write that pastors' decisions may be good in principle but injudicious in execution, and it is therefore the job of civil leaders to determine application,[589] but this is wholly different from having control over *doctrinal decisions*. Those are absolute standards set apart from how adherence to them will be enforced; *Sola Fide* (by faith alone), in and of itself, has nothing to do with how someone inside or

---

588 Wolfe, 313.
589 Wolfe, 314.

outside of the church should be rebuked if they argue for justification by works. Wolfe writes that ministers can "cast spiritual judgment, admonish, and even excommunicate" the prince,[590] but how would that be possible when he sets the boundaries of official doctrine? Why would he not veto any doctrinal proposal that could later entrap him? Though he accurately described the concept a few pages back, with this subsection Wolfe has sunk his entire claim that he is promoting a Calvinist view of two separate kingdoms.

> National uniformity in sacred ceremonies will certainly contribute to national solidarity. What better way for a people to imagine their Christian community than for all to worship the same way? The question, however, is not whether uniformity is possible, desirable, and ideal. I affirm that it is, and the magistrate ought to strive within the limits of his power to achieve uniformity.[591]

This statement is utterly utopian and totalitarian; Wolfe is not speaking of uniformity of Second Table, societal morals but uniformity of *thought*. He is speaking of using civil power to shape people's understanding of "Christian community" and "worship" into a *uniform worldview*; these are two of the key experiences of and individual's Christian life, that drive how he engages the world on the most base level. Wolfe claims that the Christian prince cannot force people to uphold this worldview, but what of those who, instead of remaining silent and hidden, openly condemn such measures? We can see the pernicious side of such a top-down civil arrangement by looking at how similar dissent was treated in other authoritarian nations. As Priorelli writes of the Spanish and Italian squadrists, "In a comparative perspective, by monopolising the ideal of the fatherland, the *camisas azules* [Spanish blue shirts] and the *camicie nere* [Italian black shirts] conceptualised the image of the anti-national enemy in a very similar way, often dehumanising it for its violence and cowardice."[592] Once the black shirts attained power, they graduated from

---

590 Wolfe, 314.
591 Wolfe, 316.
592 Priorelli, *Italian Fascism and Spanish Falangism in Comparison*, 48.

Antifa-like mob action to utilizing state power in their active suppression of ideological dissent. Similarly, what would happen to anyone who would dare claim that one of the Christian prince's "sacred ceremonies" was not within the will of God? Would they not be cast into an *Emmanuel Goldstein-like* mold by a *Caesar* who believes it his highest duty to center "national solidarity" and "national uniformity" around his personal mediation as an "image of Christ"?

VII. Conclusion

> Though in the meantime we may need to settle for civil leaders who fail to live up to the standards of a Christian prince, we should pray that God would raise up such a leader from among us: one who would suppress the enemies of God and elevate his people; recover a worshiping people; restore masculine prominence in the land and a spirit for dominion; affirm and conserve his people and place, not permitting their dissolution or capture; and inspire a love of one's Christian country. In a word, pray that God would bring about, through a Christian prince, a great renewal.[593]

This final, *language of destiny* appeal, to close the chapter, has so many connotations that it is worth breaking down into its individual parts. Of significant note is that we are told to pray for renewal "through a Christian prince" but not through the work of the Holy Spirit or through a genuine revival. This may seem like a minor oversight to some, but I believe it speaks heavily to Wolfe's worldview; beyond the category of a "worshiping people," there is nothing in this paragraph, or anywhere in the book, thus far, that speaks to genuine Christian *piety* and the believer's utter dependence on the work of God's Spirit in his heart.

Instead, we are given the prince's humanist task of "restor[ing] masculine prominence in the land and a spirit for dominion." There is a palpable resentment in this statement; healthy masculinity is undervalued and pathologized by our society, but there is still absolutely nothing stopping an individual man from confidently living his life with as much

---

593 Wolfe, *The Case for Christian Nationalism*, 323.

masculinity as he wants. Again, complaining about society turned against you, instead of simply going and being the man you want to be, is a *feminine* response that is only heightened by the call for "dominion." This is not a healthy dominion of man over earth and beast, but is inextricably tied to a restoration of "masculine prominence"; it is the unhealthy desire of someone who sees himself as impotent, but wishes he could turn the tables on those whom he disdains.

This revenge motif is further accentuated by the call to "suppress the enemies of God." This is not the goal of the dedicated Christian, firm in his faith and his eschatology, but of the *insecure, wavering Christian* hoarding his *personal peace* and *affluence*, shown in the earthly fear of "dissolution or capture." This demand cannot be rectified with the explicit instructions of Paul:

> Beloved, never avenge yourselves, but leave it to the wrath of God, for it is written, "Vengeance is mine, I will repay, says the Lord." To the contrary, "if your enemy is hungry, feed him; if he is thirsty, give him something to drink; for by so doing you will heap burning coals on his head." Do not be overcome by evil, but overcome evil with good. (Romans 12:19-21)

If we may temporarily "need to settle for civil leaders who fail to live up to the standards of a Christian prince," what would be the eventual circumstances allowing for such a leader to be *raised up by God* in the 21st-century West? How does a leader willing to *suppress* the enemies of God maneuver into a position of power in a world dominated by constitutional republics, populated by an ever-increasing non-Christian majority? As we will see in the next chapter, Wolfe does not expect Western Christians to pray for "a peaceful and quiet life, godly and dignified in every way" (1 Timothy 2:2) while they await their prince; he expects them to install him by force.

8. The Right to Revolution

Introduction

The chapter justifying religious violence begins by quoting 1 Maccabees 3:43: "Let us take the affliction from our people, and let us fight for our nation and our religion," taken from 16th-century Swiss theologian Heinrich Bullinger's translation.[594] Wolfe must refer to a deuterocanonical text for his example of revolution from the people of God, because the inspired word of the New Testament contains no such language; in fact, it contains the *opposite* sort of language:

> For though we walk in the flesh, we are not waging war according to the flesh. For the weapons of our warfare are not of the flesh but have divine power to destroy strongholds. (2 Corinthians 10:3-4)

Also, the book of 1 Maccabees tells of a Jewish rebellion against the Hellenistic reign of Antiochus IV Epiphanes, a foreign conqueror who had desecrated the temple. Modern translations do not have this verse as "fight for our nation and our religion," but "fight for our people and the sanctuary." If anything, our current situation is much more like the book of Jeremiah, where our own people have turned away from God. The example set by the prophet is one of weeping and pleading, not of organized rebellion.

Wolfe starts by stating, "The dire situation of Christianity in the West calls for action."[595] Though *dire* is a subjective term, this is still hyperbole; with rare exception in the West, even the most extreme, legalistic Christian sects are allowed to freely practice their faith and blast their beliefs from megaphones in the public square, should they desire; the only significant exception is several European countries, including England and Finland, who have categorized the public promotion of a Biblical sexual ethic as "hate speech." Wolfe is a Presbyterian in North Carolina; as a former Presbyterian in North Carolina myself, I can confirm that, though

---

594 Wolfe, 325.
595 Wolfe, 325.

friendliness towards Christianity is waning in the state, due to an influx of coastal elites, his religious situation is anything but *dire*. The mostly secular area of the state where I lived, the "Triangle" of Raleigh, Durham, and Chapel Hill, is rapidly growing and, through members of my former church, I am told that PCA and OPC churches (among others) are being planted in most of the new suburbs being built. Wolfe's supposed *direness* is the same type of hyperbole that characterizes his offense at the lack of "masculine prominence in the land."

> Today, the civil sphere is given a subordinate status in Christian thought, shut off from cognizance of eternal things, and we are conditioned to believe this is normal and good.[596]

This, again, is an entirely subjective and hyperbolic statement. The *civil sphere* has to be one of the *most* discussed topics from the contemporary pulpit, among both liberals and conservatives. What I believe Wolfe takes umbrage with is a lack of pastors directing their congregations to "assert Christian supremacy over the land."[597] As discussed above, his position is in the extreme minority when compared to the vast majority of conservative American Christians, who follow the Baptist tradition and its near-ubiquitous philosophy of separation of church and state, which was well established before our nation was founded. This is not a modern *conditioning*, but a longstanding worldview that he happens to disagree with.

Wolfe then laments that, "Open blasphemy in our public square is shrugged off as 'to be expected' or part of the world's 'brokenness.'"[598] It bears repeating 2 Timothy 2:24-26, which instructs the Christian in his task of "patiently enduring evil," which would include public blasphemy:

> And the Lord's servant must not be quarrelsome but kind to everyone, able to teach, patiently enduring evil, correcting his opponents with gentleness. God may perhaps grant them

---

596 Wolfe, 325–26.
597 Wolfe, 241.
598 Wolfe, 326.

8. The Right to Revolution

repentance leading to a knowledge of the truth, and they may come to their senses and escape from the snare of the devil, after being captured by him to do his will.

The introduction to the chapter is ended with a *language of destiny* appeal for all out religious war, in our time:

> But we do not have to live like this. And no matter how insistent our evangelical leaders are to the contrary, the Christian religion does not suppress or "critique" that fighting human spirit calling Christians to "hazard the loss of a limb for their religion, magistrates, wives, children, and all of their possessions," as Bullinger said. Here I will justify violent revolution.[599]

Throughout this chapter, I will make the case that such an endeavor would not only be Scripturally and morally unsound, at this juncture, but tactically ludicrous from a military standpoint. I will use my experience as a combat veteran and former Airborne Infantry Sergeant in the United States Army's 82nd Airborne Division to make the latter case. I will do my best to describe the horrors of war to a mostly civilian audience that often gets their notions of combat from Hollywood. In this vein, the first question that must be asked is, *What military experience does Stephen Wolfe have, since he is advocating for religious war?*

Wolfe graduated from West Point in 2008 and spent four and a half years as a Chemical, Biological, Radiological and Nuclear officer in the Army (commonly referred to as CBRN or, in my time, NBC). This is a non-combat position that can be concerned with anything from testing the battlefield for effects of non-conventional weapons to managing the inventory of chemical protection, such as gas masks – I am slightly more familiar with the job than most former infantrymen, because my roommate at Fort Bragg was our company's "NBC guy".

Most likely, Wolfe had very little combat training beyond some West Point activities and Officer Candidate School, which is the commissioned version of basic training. While all soldiers partake in training exercises,

---

599 Wolfe, 326.

there is a chasm of difference between the daily tasks and training of non-combat and combat soldiers; the latter are perpetually training for actual combat, because *that is their job*. Wolfe was stationed at Schofield Barracks, Hawaii, and Fort Campbell, Kentucky, where the 25th and 101st infantry divisions are stationed, respectively, but there is no sign, either through his resume or in his description of his military time later in the book, that he has any combat experience.

This is not to diminish his, or anyone's, service record; someone who is willing to serve their nation should be commended for such. But it must be noted that Wolfe likely has never seen the battlefield and probably has no more than a light book-knowledge of subjects that would be essential to an insurgency in the West, such as *infantry rifle platoon and squad tactics* and *military operations on urbanized terrain*. Speaking from personal experience, it is far more difficult to advocate for deadly violence on our shores when one knows what it is like to kick in a door and have no idea whether an enemy combatant or a frightened child is on the other side.

In Afghanistan, my company was tasked with clearing a village where it was believed a Taliban operator was holed up. After landing in Chinook helicopters in the poppy fields on the outskirts, we began to clear the mud huts that made up the village. I was one of the company radio operators on this deployment, and was sent with a platoon to clear a far-off section of the settlement. After securing the area and finding a weapons cache, which included everything from Chinese rockets to 19th-century Lee-Enfield rifles left by the British, the platoon sergeant told me to head to the rendezvous point by myself. I knew this was a bad idea; you are to *never* go anywhere by yourself, but he very much outranked me (I was a private first class). I started to walk back the way we came in when he pointed in another direction and yelled at me, "No, dumbass, that way!" I was fairly sure that this was not the way, but, again, he outranked me.

I was correct and, after crossing through a wadi (ravine), I found myself alone in an uncleared portion of the village. I did my best to stay calm and avoid the huts while getting back to my company as quickly as possible. I

8. The Right to Revolution

had little choice but to pass within thirty yards of a hut the size of a small cabin and, as I walked backwards while facing it, somebody popped out from behind it. I immediately raised my rifle, put the red-dot on target, and released the safety. It was a small boy. His mother, in full burka, came out a few seconds later and started screaming at me; though I did not know a word of what she said, I knew she was pleading with me to not shoot her child. I slowly backed away, with my rifle at the ready, and regrouped with my company. I have many times thanked God that I did not reflexively pull the trigger.

This is what revolution in our nation would mean for our children.

I. Definition and Explication

> As a "forcible reclamation of civil power," revolution uses force as the instrument to unseat civil rulers… The manner of unseating can be the ruler's acquiescence or flight, effectively unseating himself, or by direct physical capture. Both modes of unseating could be "bloodless" or non-violent, though that is less likely in the latter case.[600]

The only notion more unrealistic than the possibility of a bloodless revolution or "national divorce" in today's United States is that the common people could muster a large enough force to violently unseat civil rulers. As Stanley Milgram concluded in his famous 1963 experiment, two-thirds of people will go along with nearly any destructive action that a person in a position of authority tells them to do.[601] Our military is commanded by bureaucrats loyal to the "regime," "oligarchy," "military-industrial complex," "global American empire," or whatever other term one thinks best describes the Washington power-structure. The average Apache helicopter pilot, under the orders of such bureaucrats, will have no issue

---

600 Wolfe, 326–27.
601 Stanley Milgram, "Behavioral Study of Obedience.," *The Journal of Abnormal and Social Psychology* 67, no. 4 (October 1963): 371–78, https://doi.org/10.1037/h0040525.

using his M230 30mm chain-fed machine gun to turn an American insurgent into a pile of goo from a mile away (the weapon is accurate up 1500 meters and controlled by computers). The maximum effective range of the custom AR-15s that most militiamen go to the woods and play soldier with is 500 meters (but not in their hands). In Deh Rahwood, Afghanistan, while several kilometers away from a battle, I saw an AC-130H Spectre plane light up an entire square kilometer of land with infrared light. It was so high up that it looked like a spotlight from heaven, and it took out multiple targets with its chain-fed cannons. This was only visible through night-vision goggles; the enemy never even knew they were spotted. It was repugnant when President Joe Biden said of his political adversaries, "If you need to work about taking on the federal government, you need some F-15s. You don't need an AR-15,"[602] but he was telling the truth.

> The agents of force must be "the people," for the act of revolution rescinds the people's consent and aims to reclaim civil power for their good.[603]

Amplifying the ridiculousness of the notion of religious revolution is the fact that the overwhelming majority of Americans are not ready to put their lives on the line for any right-wing movement, let alone *theocratic Caesarism*. Wolfe would find himself in an extreme minority, even within the Protestant church. The 2022 Ligonier Ministries State of Theology survey concluded that 58% of self-described evangelicals believe that God accepts the worship of all religions, and 44% do not even believe in the divinity of Christ.[604] Though half of Americans believe there will soon be a civil war,[605] the majority want nothing to do with it; any revolution would

---

602 Louis Casiano, "Biden Takes Swipe at Second Amendment Supporters: 'You Need F-15s' to Take on the Federal Government," Text.Article, Fox News (Fox News, January 16, 2023), https://www.foxnews.com/politics/biden-swipe-second-amendment-supporters-you-need-f15-take-on-federal-government.
603 Wolfe, *The Case for Christian Nationalism*, 327.
604 The State of Theology, https://thestateoftheology.com.
605 Wintemute et al., "Views of American Democracy and Society and Support for Political Violence."

8. The Right to Revolution

be waged by an extremely small minority. The best hope that Wolfe and his compatriots have would be to join a greater right-wing insurgency and politic their way into a position of power or negotiate their way into an arrangement for their own micro-nation after the war, but this is still a pipe dream. The right-wing side of the Spanish Civil War was waged mainly by monarchist generals who had the loyalty of many troops and the monetary and military assistance of Germany and Italy, but it still took them three years of horrific, atrocity-filled war to overcome the Soviet-backed republican forces. There are very few, if any, generals in the United States military who would be willing to break ranks; as bureaucrats who wage wars from tactical operations centers, they would also not command the type of loyalty from their troops that Franco did with his Legionnaires, whom he had personally taken into battle.[606] The only real option that a Christian nationalist "revolution" would have would be to carry on a small-scale guerrilla insurgency, also known as a terror campaign.

One morning, in the spring of 2004, I was woken up by the largest explosive concussion I had ever felt, larger than when mortars and rockets had impacted near me. I was in my top bunk in a tent that held my platoon of roughly thirty men at Camp Anaconda, the largest air base in Iraq, just outside of the city of Balad. It was one of the most bombarded bases in the country during this time, and we were getting mortared multiple times a day, so it took quite a bit to startle me as much as that explosion did. Nobody had any clue what had just happened, but we put on our body armor and ran into the makeshift bunker dug into the ground just outside of the tent. We quickly learned, over the radio, that a car bomb had been detonated at the main entrance to the base; that was nearly three miles away.

As luck would have it, my squad was that day's quick reaction force, which meant that we were on twenty-four hour duty to immediately respond to any emergency situation. After calling in on the radio, we were directed to use another gate and drive around to the crossroads, three-

---

606 Preston, *Franco*, 144–70.

quarters of a mile past the main entrance, and pull guard until the area could be cleared. Afterwards, we were attached to FBI units and told that we were to assist them in searching for evidence of how the bomb was constructed. The scene of the explosion was awe-inducing. The vehicle that had been detonated was packed with so much C4 that the engine block had been blown roughly two hundred yards. Multiple shipping trucks had been mangled and bent in half, like plastic toys melted by fire, and the entire area was still smoking. But that was, by far, not the worst of it.

Body parts were everywhere. I was handed a pair of latex gloves and told to start going through the wreckage and to show anything I thought of interest to an agent. Along with the mangled and broken pieces of vehicles and possessions, I had to pick up and move countless bones stripped of most of their flesh by the explosion (mostly vertebrae) looking for ball bearings, wires, and electronics boards, all while perpetually standing in, and sinking my hands into, an inch-deep puddle of blood mixed with motor fluid that rested at the base of each vehicle. There was an entire half of a bloody human rib cage laying on the side of the road, charred and dusted with gravel; my first thought was that it looked like what the Flintstones are handed in the intro to the cartoon. To this day, I will not eat ribs, and for years I could not even sit at a table with someone else eating them.

I was not rummaging through the ancient remains of an archaeological site; these were the body parts of people who, just hours ago, had left their homes, their families, and their children to come to our base to perform benign tasks, such as delivering supplies and performing manual labor. These were human beings, made in the image of God and of boundless worth, with loved ones still waiting for them at home, who had just been brutally murdered for political effect. Not a single American had been killed by the explosion and only a few, American-trained, Iraqi soldiers. I was told that day that over twenty civilians were murdered; the lucky ones were those who were instantly disintegrated by the blast.

This is what guerrilla insurgency in our nation would mean for our loved ones.

8. The Right to Revolution

II. Statement of the Question

> A Christian people share particular norms, customs, blood, etc., which are not easily forced upon them.[607]

Wolfe has spent much of his book, especially in chapter 5, attempting to make the case that a "Christian people" can be made up of those who have had "Christian culture" forced on them. On top of this, he made the case that it is good for society to have churches full of people pretending to believe, rather than openly disbelieving. This sentence does not logically comport with that main theme of his book. Secondly, it must be noted that he has injected "blood" into what makes up a "Christian people." This should be rejected outright by members of the *universal church*.

> Nor is the question whether a group of Christians, dwelling in a non-Christian nation under *non*-tyrannical conditions, may revolt... non-Christian rulers still have true civil power, and resisting them is resisting God... The question is whether a Christian people, being under tyrannical conditions, may conduct revolution to establish a Christian commonwealth...[608]

As previously mentioned, the belief that Christians can revolt against tyrannical rulers is out of step with Calvin and other reformers and does not meet the bounds of his appeals to "Reformed tradition." Again, considering that Wolfe uses Calvin as his most cited exegetical source, he must provide his own exegesis to counter this assertion. He will attempt to somewhat do so with Romans 13 in the sixth section of this chapter, so I will save my full rebuttal for then. Something Wolfe also fails to mention is that conducting this type of war against a subjectively "tyrannical" government requires looking at everyone in your nation who does not agree with you as a potential mortal enemy.

---

607 Wolfe, *The Case for Christian Nationalism*, 328.
608 Wolfe, 328.

III. Just Revolution

> God's law is thereby mediated through the judgment and promulgation of appointed human magistrates, effectively making these judgments ordinances of God. For this reason alone, they bind the conscience: they are derivative of God and hence (mediately speaking) God's judgments. When a legitimate ruler uses civil power to command what is just and the people disobey this command, they are disobeying God himself...[609]

Like "tyrannical," the term "legitimate ruler" is entirely subjective and is of no help in justifying revolution. Since 2016, the United States has been in an ideological struggle between two increasingly polarized sides, both of whom have openly declared the other's elected President "illegitimate." As of right now, every American is allowed to worship how he pleases, speak his thoughts freely, and exude as much "masculine prominence" as he wishes. The overwhelming majority of human beings who have previously lived and died would choose our conditions over theirs in a heartbeat. That Wolfe will attempt to make a case that our civil leaders are illegitimate, because they, like the Romans when the New Testament was written, enact laws that are at moral odds with Christianity, is a sign of – to reuse the military terminology – *a lack of intestinal fortitude.*

This is not, in any way, to claim that Christians should retreat from the civil sphere, but the statement, "Thus, civil authority extends only to what is for our good,"[610] is simply not inline with Scripture or the Reformed tradition. As shown previously, Calvin believed that "The power of a tyrant must indeed be endured, even by men of courage."[611] The hard-line notion that any command one finds unjust does not bind the conscience[612] is a recipe for disaster. Only civil commands that directly violate God's commandments are not conscience binding on the believer. For example, a

---

609 Wolfe, 329.
610 Wolfe, 329.
611 John Calvin, Commentary on Isaiah, [on Isaiah 3:12].
612 Wolfe, *The Case for Christian Nationalism*, 330.

8. The Right to Revolution

Christian who concealed carries a pistol is conscience bound to obey the laws of states that ban concealed carry, even if he considers them in violation of his constitutional rights, because God does not explicitly bind our consciences in the matter.

> The child ought to obey his father within the scope of fatherly order. But if the father were to lose his mind and seek to murder his son, the son is free to resist, seize, and incapacitate his father.[613]

Wolfe's distinction between the authority of person versus office shows its brokenness, in that the father/son analogy must be taken to the utmost extremes before it makes sense within the context of revolution. I have not seen any roving bands of deputized death squads going about the country, murdering dissidents; that would be the civil government equivalent to this analogy. What Wolfe argues for is violent resistance from the child, because his father is verbally pressuring him to do something immoral, but not physically forcing him. There are issues that Christians should be alarmed about, such as the postmodern left's obsession with irreversible "gender-affirming" procedures for minors, but that issue is still very much a legislative battle, and there are plenty of peaceful options remaining on the table for opponents. As with the introduction to this chapter, Wolfe's position is one of absolute hyperbole.

The analogy of lawful and unlawful orders within the military is not applicable either, because the bounds of lawful orders are not individually subjective, they are *explicitly codified in military law* and agreed to by soldiers when they raise their hand and give the oath of enlistment. Should the Uniform Code of Military Justice be updated by military leadership, or the United States sign a new treaty, any order a superior gives within those updated bounds is still lawful, regardless of whether "tyrants" are in the chain of command that updated the law. A soldier does not have the right to disobey such an order simply because he finds it "unjust." I once had to obey an order I found utterly despicable.

---

613 Wolfe, 331.

I was the foremost American guard at the same checkpoint in Iraq where a car bomb had previously been detonated. In front of me was a quarter-mile long line of cars waiting to come into the base, one by one; a vehicle would first be inspected by an Iraqi Civil Defense Corps soldier, pass by a trailer with a bomb scanning x-ray, and then go through my position, where I would direct them into an area where the vehicle would again be inspected by someone in my platoon. My job was mainly to be the first-line contact for an Iraqi soldier, should he find something suspicious.

One of the soldiers came to me and, through the interpreter, informed me that there was a man in line, with two very ill children, looking for medical assistance. I radioed for our platoon medic and he went out to the car, about fifty yards from my position, with the Iraqi soldier and the interpreter. A few minutes later they came back with the father, and the medic told me that the children likely had advanced spinal meningitis and would soon die if they were not immediately given antibiotics. I told the father, through the interpreter, that we would help them. The thought did not even cross my mind that not helping was a possibility. This is simply what we did in Afghanistan; our forward operating bases served as de facto hospitals for the local town, and the Balad, Iraq, civilian hospital was barely functioning. The man thanked me profusely and I told him, "This is what we're here for."

I got on the radio and notified the base's tactical operations center that we would be sending the car to the sizable medical facility on base (this was the biggest air base in country and they surely had the necessary medicine). I was immediately told to hold on that decision; we stood there for what seemed like an eternity until I heard back on the radio that I was to tell the man to leave. I double checked with command, and reminded them that there were *two dying children* and I was speaking to their father. We could have at least had some oral antibiotics brought to the father at the gate and given those children a chance. They were unsympathetic and repeated the order. I had to look that man in the face and take back my

8. The Right to Revolution

promise to him, both of us knowing that it meant his children would die. We both cried. *God, forgive me.*

It was a lawful order.

———

Wolfe gives a definition of the varying types of resistance, but admits that the chapter is oriented towards violent overthrow of civil leaders.[614] He then moves into a definition of what, in his mind, constitutes *tyrannical rule*:

> *A tyrant is any civil ruler whose actions significantly undermine the conditions in which man achieves his true humanity or, as I've called it, the complete good.*[615]

As with other statements in this chapter, this definition is purely subjective. Could one conduct a survey, asking people what the "complete good" is, and get the same answer from any two people? Would one not get the exact same result when asking what would "undermine the conditions" of fulfilling "true humanity"? The vagueness and emotional appeal of this statement serves Wolfe's revolutionary ends. It also bears repeating that the "complete good" is his version of the traditional fascist concept of the nation's *full self-realization*. Immediately following this, he describes the supposed behaviors of a tyrant, including that he is "mammish." This is most likely a derivative of the word *mammy*, which he previously used in the plural, in chapter 7.[616] Urban Dictionary has an alternate definition of "someone who is an extreme retard and is very young and has no friends at all,"[617] but this does not make sense as his context, considering the preceding adjective of "smothering" fits the *mammy* stereotype. As before, I must conclude that he uses this word with full understanding of its racist connotations.

———

614 Wolfe, 332.
615 Wolfe, 333.
616 Wolfe, 288.
617 https://www.urbandictionary.com/define.php?term=mammish

> A tyrant in effect is one who, though having the appearance of civil authority, is but a man ordering fellow men to great evil. His injustice is worthy of a higher type of resistance, for it concerns the whole of civil life; it is not merely an injustice here or there.[618]

By these bounds, the United States is not under tyrannical rule. We are not yet being ordered to commit great evil, we are merely *pressured to affirm evil*. We are completely free to reject this proposition and form our own social and civil networks; conservative Christians are still allowed to be elected to public office and enact legislation that is at direct odds with things we believe are evil. Let us compare this to what being a Christian in an *actual* tyrannical government looks like.

In 1948, Bulgarian Baptist minister Haralan Popov was denounced by the communists as a capitalist spy, along with most other Protestant ministers in the country. He would spend the next thirteen years in prisons and gulags while his wife and children suffered as social outcasts until they were allowed to leave the country. In his book, *Tortured for His Faith*, Popov described the first night of his interrogation:

> On 5th August, under the 'death diet' I was put into solitary confinement and subjected to a twenty-four-hour-a-day, non-stop interrogation. I had three interrogators, each one working an eight hour shift. This allowed them to keep up the physical and psychological torture twenty-four hours a day. This solitary confinement cell had one very unusual feature. The wall was shiny white, painted with a white high gloss enamel paint. I was ordered to stand facing the glaring white wall at a distance of eight inches and to keep my eyes open – wide open. My interrogator began to shout -
>
> 'You must not move one inch!'
> 'You must not close your eyes for one moment!'
> 'You must not shift your weight!'
> 'You must not move a muscle!'

---

618 Wolfe, *The Case for Christian Nationalism*, 334.

8. The Right to Revolution

'You must not... You must not...' on and on he ranted as I stood at the wall. After only a few moments, my eyes burned as though hot irons were in them. At eight inches I was so close to the glaring white enameled wall that my eyes couldn't focus. I suggest that my readers try this for only a moment. One's eyes rebel. They fight to close or to focus and they can't. It is terribly painful and yet when I merely blinked, my interrogator struck me across the side of my face.

The pain in my eyes became unbearable. 'Tell me about your spy activities!' shouted the interrogator.[619]

We are not living under benign rule; for example, the Biden administration has arrested pro-life protesters, such as activist Mark Houck, and attempted to railroad them for process crimes. But the justice system is still functioning well enough that he was acquitted.[620] He was not put on a starvation diet and tortured until he would denounce himself, like Popov was. We are nowhere near being under the type of tyrannical government where violent revolution by Christians could *perhaps* be justified. Again, to hold such a position, as a Christian, is to telegraph one's *lack of intestinal fortitude* and, ultimately, a *lack of trust in God's sovereignty and providence*.

Wolfe then cites Aquinas and Althusius's justification of the dissolution of tyrannical rule. He does not cite Scripture, because it does not explicitly condone such actions, and it must be noted that neither Aquinas nor Althusius forthrightly justifies *violent* rebellion in the provided quotes.[621] The latter is also of great note, because the analogy of the "incurable cruelty" of a husband towards his wife is the very situation that Wolfe attacked Russell Moore over in chapter 5, for citing it as an undesirable

---

619 Haralan Popov, *Tortured for His Faith*, 2nd ed. (London: Lakeland, 1971), 24.
620 Louis Casiano, "Pennsylvania Jury Acquits Pro-Life Activist Mark Houck on Charges of Obstructing Abortion Clinic Access," Text.Article, Fox News (Fox News, January 30, 2023), https://www.foxnews.com/us/pennsylvania-jury-acquits-pro-life-activist-mark-houck-charges-obstructing-abortion-clinic-access.
621 Wolfe, *The Case for Christian Nationalism*, 335–36.

effect of cultural Christianity (in that women felt a cultural pressure to not leave abusive husbands).

Three justifications for violence are then given; I will address them individually:

- The nation is indeed a corporate individual, but *a Christian individual is still primarily bound by the word of God*. The New Testament could not be clearer that we are not to engage in proactive violence, even under tyrannical rule (2 Corinthians 10:3-6, 1 Peter 2:20-25, 1 Peter 3:13-20, 1 Peter 4:12-19, Matthew 26:52-54, Romans 12:19, Titus 3:1-7) and there are no New Testament verses to directly counter this interpretation.
- There is no situation in which a *majority* of citizens peacefully gather to demand the removal of a civil leader where either a) the leader realizes the hopelessness of his situation and peacefully abdicates his position, or b) the leader uses military or police power to violently suppress the peaceful majority, making any proceeding violence from the majority *reactive*, instead of *proactive*. There is no Christian justification for consciously firing the first shot. Wolfe's dilemma is that *he is not in the majority* and, therefore, could not bring about *reactive conditions*.
- "If a man aggresses against a nation, doing it harm, then the nation can respond as a nation to end the aggression" *through peaceful, legal means*. That would be how a dissenting strong majority would remove an individual tyrant. Wolfe again is attempting to paint his extreme minority as somehow embodying the will of a whole nation.

This attempt to justify violent revolution by Christians is paper-thin, unscriptural, and sophomoric. It should be outright rejected by Bible-believing Christians.

IV. Conditions for Revolution

The title of the first subsection, *Revolution for True Religion*, is antithetical to the entire purpose of the spiritual kingdom and is borderline blasphemous. Paul, in his letter to the Philippians, demonstrates the true

8. The Right to Revolution

heart of our faith, that "Greater love has no one than this, that someone lay down his life for his friends" (John 15:13):

> Do all things without grumbling or disputing, that you may be blameless and innocent, children of God without blemish in the midst of a crooked and twisted generation, among whom you shine as lights in the world, holding fast to the word of life, so that in the day of Christ I may be proud that I did not run in vain or labor in vain. Even if I am to be poured out as a drink offering upon the sacrificial offering of your faith, I am glad and rejoice with you all. Likewise you also should be glad and rejoice with me. (Philippians 2:14-18)

Wolfe does not celebrate this type of peaceful, sacrificial love, in which Paul was imitating the love of Christ for his sheep (1 Corinthians 11:1). He would rather *someone else die* so he can find his "true religion." He believes that a tyrant is one who has "denied man the space to exercise his highest gift and tyrannized over the soul."[622] But, in order to accept this, one would have to believe that Paul, while shackled in a Roman jail awaiting execution, was not able to exercise his "highest gift" and was not able to find his "complete humanity." There are few other false concepts about the Christian's walk with Christ that deserve more condemnation.

His next claim that "violence can be used to secure [Christ's kingdom] indirectly and outwardly"[623] flies in the face of God's statement that His "power is made perfect in weakness" (2 Corinthians 12:9). To "preserve [the church] by means of arms" is a circumstantial byproduct of the Second Table task to preserve innocent life, not a proactive, First Table task of preserving doctrine by force. That is not what Christ did and, therefore, it is not what we are to do.

> With our minds enmeshed in the secularist norm, we confidently think that pleading for religious exemptions before secularist

---

[622] Wolfe, 338.
[623] Wolfe, 339.

overlords is the timeless politics of Jesus. How convenient for us that we happen to live in secularist times.[624]

It is a rare occurrence that I completely agree with Wolfe; his definition of this problematic mindset among Western Christians is entirely accurate. His solution, to take up arms in order to bring about a government that throws the Western Liberalism baby out with the bathwater, could not be more wrong, though.

In November of 2021 I learned that the company I was working for was instituting the federal contractor version of the vaccine mandate. This mandate had no testing option, meaning that employees must either disclose their medical status to the company and the government, file for a religious exemption, or be laid off. COVID hysteria was at a fever pitch during this period. Leftist thought-leader and activist Noam Chomsky was calling for the unvaccinated to be separated from society and basic services,[625] and being lauded for it by MSNBC's Mehdi Hasan[626], and the Prime Minister of New Zealand, Jacinda Ardern, admitted on camera that she was looking to create a two-tier society.[627] I understood the totalitarian ends of what governments around the world were attempting to implement; when it had already been proven that the vaccine did not stop transmission,[628] I also perceived the mandate as a secular, "religion of science" loyalty test, no different in principle than when Nebuchadnezzar

---

624 Wolfe, 341.
625 Paul Bois, "Noam Chomsky: Unvaccinated Should Be 'Isolated' from Society," Breitbart, October 25, 2021, https://www.breitbart.com/politics/2021/10/25/noam-chomsky-unvaccinated-should-be-isolated-from-society/.
626 https://www.washingtonexaminer.com/author/becket-adams, "MSNBC Host Agrees: Unvaccinated Should Be Denied Access to Basic Goods and Services," Washington Examiner, October 26, 2021, https://www.washingtonexaminer.com/opinion/msnbc-host-agrees-unvaccinated-should-be-denied-access-to-basic-goods-and-services.
627 *Jacinda Ardern Admits New Zealand Will Become a Two-Tier Society between Vaccinated and Unvaccinated*, 2021, https://www.independent.co.uk/tv/news/jacinda-ardern-admits-new-zealand-will-become-a-twotier-society-between-vaccinated-and-unvaccinated-b2179915.html.

8. The Right to Revolution

demanded all of the state officials bow to his idol (Daniel 3). Knowing the moral ramifications of filing for a religious exemption and, by proxy, condoning the stripping of rights of consent from non-religious people, I refused and chose to lose my job. I politely let my manager know exactly why I was refusing the mandate, telling him, "Due to my Christian convictions, I cannot condone turning conscientious objectors into a pariah class." He understood, let me know how sad he was to see me go, and told me I was welcome to come back, if things changed.

At this time, there was no sign that any of the government mandates would be overruled, and many companies in my field were implementing mandates of their own volition. I truly thought the career I had spent a decade and a half building was over and that I may have been relegating my family to poverty. It seemed that almost every job in the software industry required proof of vaccination; most job postings were clear about having such a requirement, and the majority of the interviews I landed ended abruptly or awkwardly when I answered the first question of why I was looking for a new job – I had resolved not to obfuscate, not only because it was the ethical thing to do, but because any company that hired me might implement a mandate later on. My wife and I were making contingency plans on how we would work in the gig economy (as long as that was viable) and do odd jobs to keep a roof over our head and feed our children; even entry-level, manual labor jobs in our very politically left city required compliance and, with no job, we had no stable way to move away. It was a very frightening time and, in the privacy of my home office, I regularly cried out to God. *But I knew in my heart that I was doing the right thing and being faithful to Him.*

I had not bothered to call recruiters, because most of the jobs offered through them are for companies with at least one federal contract. A little over a week into my search, the recruiter who had placed me at the company I was leaving unexpectedly called me and asked what had happened. I told him the truth and he answered, "I understand. Let's get you a new job." I had an offer within a few days; I am still at that company

---

628 "Covid: Double Vaccinated Can Still Spread Virus at Home," *BBC News*, October 28, 2021, sec. Health, https://www.bbc.com/news/health-59077036.

and it is one of the best places I have ever worked. Now that the majority of America has left COVID hysteria behind, it can be easy to forget how precarious our national situation was in the fall and winter of 2021, and how draconian, ill-conceived, and long-lasting the policies were; the Biden administration did not announce the lifting of the federal vaccine mandates until May 1, 2023.[629] That I found a new job may seem like a minor thing to most, but I cannot think of that situation, and how faithful God was to me after I made a Spirit-driven decision that put me in a very insecure position, and not instantly well up.

If there is anything I hope to impart to the reader it is that *God is faithful to his people when they forthrightly and peacefully stand up for the truth of the gospel*, even tangentially, as I did. He is a good and gracious God who will not abandon us, especially if we trust in Him above our own abilities.

> [Our spiritual forefathers] were not habitually trained to retreat to universality, to justify all their claims of public life by making *the other* the chief beneficiary or to make the object of policy *all* people without discrimination.[630]

The mask slips a little further off of Wolfe with this statement; he explicitly calls people in disagreement with his system of religion and government "the other" and admits his would be a state of *proactive discrimination*. "The other" he refers to is not just the non-religious or practitioners of false religion, but anyone who is not onboard with a paedobaptist state-church and *theocratic Caesarism*, even should they be devoted Protestant Christians. Many true disciples of Jesus Christ would

---

629 Catherine Lucey and Sabrina Siddiqui, "U.S. Covid Vaccine Mandates to End May 11 for Federal Workers, Others," *Wall Street Journal*, May 1, 2023, sec. Politics, https://www.wsj.com/articles/u-s-covid-vaccine-mandates-to-end-may-11-for-federal-workers-international-air-travelers-f8f60668.
630 Wolfe, *The Case for Christian Nationalism*, 342.

8. The Right to Revolution

find themselves with the proverbial boot on their neck under such a government.

The other in this statement is surely the *ethnic other*, as well. In a June 2023 article for *American Reformer* entitled *The Virtue of Hospitality*, Wolfe wrote, "Nations generate a sort of surplus that is reserved for hospitality. But there is a limit that is determined by two stress factors: the degree of cultural difference and the numbers received. Both can place unhealthy stresses on the nation. This limit has nothing to do with bad guests; it is a matter of difference and numbers."[631] The parable of the Good Samaritan (Luke 10:25-37) rebukes this sentiment, in that *cultural difference* is not to be a factor in *Christian hospitality*, even on the national level.

Following this, he moves to naming and attacking the common enemy of all forms of right-wing authoritarian-nationalism (most especially fascism), what he calls "totalizing liberal regimes."[632] He incorrectly identifies the watering down of the faith as a recent, secularist tactic when, in reality, Machen decried this phenomena a century ago in *Christianity and Liberalism*. There will always be an antinomian pressure put upon Christians by the world; to use it as an excuse for extreme political measures is a point of broken eschatology. Wolfe's claim of a "retreat to universality" and his statement that, under liberalism, "Every square inch is secularist, unless granted by an exception by the state," is no different in principle than Primo de Rivera's view that, "Liberalism is, on one hand, the regime without faith, the regime that hands over everything, even the essentials of the country's destiny, to free discussion."[633] The only significant difference between Wolfe's view on liberalism and that of Primo de Rivera is that one attempts to utilize a Reformed "Christian heritage" while the other appealed to Spanish and Catholic heritage as an excuse for crushing classical liberals who would dissent from the preferred authoritarian ends.

---

631 Stephen Wolfe, "The Virtue of Hospitality | Stephen Wolfe," *American Reformer* (blog), June 28, 2023, https://americanreformer.org/2023/06/the-virtue-of-hospitality/.
632 Wolfe, *The Case for Christian Nationalism*, 342–43.
633 Greger, *Jose Antonio Primo de Rivera*, 85.

> The regime also works to channel religion to support it. This is evident in the rise of what I call the "regime evangelical" – the evangelical arm of the ruling class that Christianizes regime narratives and talking points, feigning as insiders in the evangelical camp in order to shape Christian godliness and "witness" from within.[634]

Wolfe makes the very valid point that there is often an attempt from government interests to co-opt the church. In 20th-century communist nations, this was far more overt than in the capitalist West; as shown with Popov, secret police would arrest pastors as traitors and replace them with men loyal to the party who would preach communist propaganda from behind the pulpit. In the United States, there has long been an open door for Democratic politicians to promote their political agenda at theologically liberal churches and, slightly less frequently, for Republicans to do the same at conservative churches. A newer phenomenon has emerged recently: formerly staunch conservatives have inched their way towards promoting socially liberal policies and now lambaste the conservative church as being too fundamentalist for doing nothing more than holding to the same traditional doctrine that the critic used to promote himself. No two people have become the targets of conservative ire along these lines more than Russell Moore and David French.

Despite the truth of Wolfe's statement, there is an incredible irony within it: *The core purpose of his book is to define and promote a regime that would push and enforce a particular Christianized narrative.* His complaint constitutes a genetic logical fallacy, in that he implicitly expects the reader to consider his "Christianized regime narrative" better than his opponents,' though he will not exegete to make that case.

His next claim, that "Christian Americans should see themselves as under a sort of occupation," is true, but only in that this is the case for every Christian who has ever lived. Christ sits at the right hand of God (Hebrews 10:12), who is enthroned over all His creation, but we live in a world that still has a "god" in Satan (2 Corinthians 4:4). This world is not

---

634 Wolfe, *The Case for Christian Nationalism*, 343.

8. The Right to Revolution

the Christian's home, and we will, in some sense, be perpetually *under occupation* until we are with Christ. It is fine to lament this, but to advocate for the violent overthrow of a "ruling class" that one sees as "hostile to your Christian town, to your Christian people, and to your Christian heritage"[635] is wholly opposite to the message of the New Testament. That Wolfe can advocate for such in a published book without secret police kicking in his door and dragging him away proves that he is not living under the type of oppressive regime he attempts to portray the United States as.

> Another question is whether a Christian people, constituting a *minority* of the population under a civil government, can revolt against a tyranny directed at them and, after successfully revolting, establish over *all* of the population a Christian commonwealth. The issue here centers on whether a Christian minority can establish a political state over the whole without the positive consent of the whole. I affirm that they can. The reason is that although civil administration is fundamentally natural, human, and universal, it was always for the people of God.[636]

Take a minute to reread and ingest this statement, because herein exists the core motivation for Wolfe's book. This is the position of someone who places far more emphasis on his earthly treasure than his heavenly; this is further exemplified by his statement to end the section, that it is "tyrannical" to undermine his view of "ethno-cultural" particularity (which has been proven to be more *ethno* than *cultural*) and that this justifies revolution. The notion that a Christian people, existing in the significant minority, should violently overthrow their government and "assert Christian supremacy"[637] over an unwilling populace is *directly antithetical* to everything the Son of God and His Apostles taught. I have previously given a wide selection of verses to prove this point, but the New Testament, as a whole, boldly proclaims that *this is not the way of the disciple.* Wolfe

---

635 Wolfe, 344.
636 Wolfe, 345–46.
637 Wolfe, 241.

does not exegete to make his case because he *cannot* exegete to make his case. He will soon *eisegete* Romans 13.

Wolfe is so unwarrantably confident in his interpretation of Christianity and "true justice" that he next justifies fully "disregard[ing] the withholding of consent by non-Christians." Like most who make this case, he equivocates Second Table enforcement of the Sixth Commandment to punishing thoughtcrime, under the guise of "the highest good."[638] He then again makes the same categorical error as other Christian Nationalists, such as Andrew Torba and Andrew Isker,[639] of extending man's dominion over earth and beast to dominion over other human beings. Again, take a minute to ingest that notion, that simply being a disciple of Jesus Christ would give you *dominion* over another image bearer. How do people act when they believe an innate superiority gives them dominion over other human beings?

My first time "outside the wire" was in Gardez, Afghanistan. After arriving at Kandahar, my company was split by platoons and sent to forward operating bases around the country. I was put into a custom-formed platoon to be headed by our company's executive officer (second in command), whom I was attached to as his radio operator. We were sent to the FOB a few miles outside of Gardez, a town populated by roughly ten thousand people who had no electricity or running water. The only people in the area who possessed anything resembling modern conveniences were us and the local warlord, who had recently won a tense standoff with a rival, and who occupied a 19th-century British fort on the opposite end of the town. His men would occasionally take pot shots at us with an old Soviet recoilless rifle (low-caliber artillery). I once had to cut a call home on our satellite phone short, because I heard a round from the fort whiz past my head as I stood on the roof for better reception. The remoteness,

---

638 Wolfe, 346.
639 Authors of *Christian Nationalism: A Biblical Guide for Taking Dominion and Discipling Nations.*

8. The Right to Revolution

primitiveness, and persistent air of hostility in Gardez was like stepping back in time.

Our mission was to protect a civil affairs team that was working to win hearts and minds within the town. Roughly two weeks into my time there, I was told I would be manning the SAW machine gun atop a Humvee as we accompanied the team on their check-ins with their contacts. The best way I can describe Gardez in 2003 is that it looked nearly identical to the depiction of the streets of Cairo in *Raiders of the Lost Ark*, but with the addition that every man could legally carry an AK-47 – something that obviously put us on constant alert while we were driving through town.

Our first stop was at the storefront of a local merchant, on a narrow, walled street, which presented several security concerns. We parked outside the store and my squad members exited the Humvees while I remained atop. I lit a cigarette while we pulled guard. Almost immediately, two boys, no more than eleven years old, came up to me to ask me for a smoke; I refused, but gave them some candy I had brought along. We were engaged in friendly pantomiming with each other when I spotted a man wearing a plain, matching, olive-green wool suit and cap walking down the street towards us, with his hands behind his back. The suit was not of interest to me, because I had, even in the brief drive to this store, already noted that a large portion of Afghan civilians wore leftover Soviet military clothes. The man did not appear a threat, so I merely kept an eye on him as he approached while I continued to engage the children.

The man walked right up to my Humvee, revealed a one foot long piece of rubber hose that he had been holding behind his back, and proceeded to beat the boys with such mercilessness that he was lacerating them. The beating was so intense that I believed he might kill them; I charged my weapon and was about to take him out when my sergeant ran at me, yelling, "Callens! Don't shoot! That's a police officer!" The commotion caused the man to pause, giving the children the opportunity to run away, screaming in intense pain. He and I locked eyes and then he calmly walked away, with the hose back behind his back.

Without school, young boys roam the streets of towns like Gardez during the day. They are treated no better by locals than wild dogs. I saw people keep piles of sizable stones on their front porch and throw them with full force at any child who got too close. The police officer was merely administering the dominant cultural hierarchy – he was *enforcing his dominion*. I have little doubt that this type of everyday violence is what would eventually happen to non-Christians under Wolfe's revolutionary government.

V. Lesser Magistrates

> People can justly act apart from a lesser magistrate or an established interposing body. That is, they can act for themselves outside any higher earthly authority. But their actions are limited and cannot properly be called acts of the people.[640]

By this principle, if the majority of the people, none of whom are magistrates, gather a preponderant force, it *would not* be an "act of the people," but if a minority of the citizenry recruited a magistrate then it *would* be an "act of the people." This can only make sense to someone seeking to justify a revolution by a minority. Secondly, what level magistrate is required for such legitimacy? In our nation, would you need an elected federal official or a general, or would a city councilman meet the requirement? Wolfe makes no effort to specify what level of responsibility must be held by the intervening magistrate to constitute a *legitimate* revolution.

He then uses the Continental Congress as an example of a lesser magistrate, but it does not suffice for making the case of just revolution by the minority. The Continental Congress was the official representation of the people from all British coastal colonies south of Nova Scotia and lobbied for the majority of British subjects in North America. *All of them voted to secede.* Overall, this section does little to nothing to clarify "the efficient cause of revolution." The lack of specifics on the lesser magistrate leaves more questions than answers. The notion of "the people's concrete

---

640 Wolfe, *The Case for Christian Nationalism*, 349.

8. The Right to Revolution

actions of force, directed as a whole by the interposing authority"[641] requires more than three vague paragraphs over two pages to be at all convincing. Who is this director? What are his minimum qualifications? If this is meant to be the initial position of the Christian Prince, it only makes him more analogous to *el Caudillo* or *il Duce*.

VI. Romans 13

> Paul instructs us to "be subject unto the higher powers." These powers are "ordained of God... for good" (vv. 1, 4). The scope of power permits civil rulers to be "not a terror to good works, but to the evil" (v. 3). Subjection to this power is "for conscience sake" (v. 5), meaning that God binds the conscience through the command of civil rulers. It follows from the text that since the powers ordained of God are only for good, no power ordained of God can command what is evil, and thus no evil command is conscience-binding, for only God can bind the conscience, whether immediately or mediately. A magistrate that is a terror to good works acts outside his authority. With regard to those specific unjust commands, he ought to be resisted. This is not controversial, for we should "obey God rather than men" (Acts 5:29).[642]

Before we break down this attempt at exegesis it is worth asking the question, *why now?* We are 350 pages into a book that has almost exclusively used selected quotes from Catholic and Reformed scholars to make its theological claims. Why would Wolfe now choose to do his own exegesis for Romans 13? Perhaps he believes the importance of this chapter of Scripture requires his extra attention, but, due to his avoidance of the views of the Reformers in this section, I believe it more likely that he knows the *exegetical tradition of the 16th and 17th-century* overwhelmingly disagrees with his position. He is in a bind, because he cannot advocate for revolution without addressing the one chapter of the

---

641 Wolfe, 349.
642 Wolfe, 350.

New Testament that even many nominal Christians know is about submission to governmental authority. Calvin, in his commentary on verse 1, could not be clearer in his absolute disagreement with the basis of Wolfe's argument:

> And it seems indeed to me, that the Apostle intended by this word to take away the frivolous curiosity of men, who are wont often to inquire by what right they who rule have obtained their authority; but it ought to be enough for us, that they *do rule*; for they have not ascended by their own power into this high station, but have been placed there by the Lord's hand. And by mentioning *every soul*, he removes every exception, lest any one should claim an immunity from the common duty of obedience.[643]

Matthew Henry's commentary, written at the turn of the 18th century, concurs:

> The grace of the gospel teaches us submission and quiet, where pride and the carnal mind only see causes for murmuring and discontent. Whatever the persons in authority over us themselves may be, yet the just power they have, must be submitted to and obeyed. In the general course of human affairs, rulers are not a terror to honest, quiet, and good subjects, but to evil-doers. Such is the power of sin and corruption, that many will be kept back from crimes only by the fear of punishment. Thou hast the benefit of the government, therefore do what thou canst to preserve it, and nothing to disturb it.[644]

The Geneva Study Bible, the most common study aid of the 17th-century Reformed world, binds the conscience in this matter:

> The conclusion: we must obey the magistrate, not only for fear of punishment, but much more because (although the magistrate has

---

643 John Calvin, Commentary on Romans, [on Romans 13:1].
644 Matthew Henry, Commentary on Romans, [on Romans 13:1-7].

8. The Right to Revolution

no power over the conscience of man, yet seeing he is God's minister) he cannot be resisted by any good conscience.[645]

It is also of note that Wolfe selectively quotes the verses that he references. Given that there have already been several instances of selective quotes of Calvin, which conspicuously omitted ideas contradictory to his theory, let us examine the referenced verses in their entirety. I will use the King James Version, from which Wolfe quotes:

> Let every soul be subject unto the higher powers. For there is no power but of God: the powers that be are ordained of God. [2] Whosoever therefore resisteth the power, resisteth the ordinance of God: and they that resist shall receive to themselves damnation. [3] For rulers are not a terror to good works, but to the evil. Wilt thou then not be afraid of the power? do that which is good, and thou shalt have praise of the same: [4] For he is the minister of God to thee for good. But if thou do that which is evil, be afraid; for he beareth not the sword in vain: for he is the minister of God, a revenger to execute wrath upon him that doeth evil. [5] Wherefore ye must needs be subject, not only for wrath, but also for conscience sake. (Romans 13:1-5 KJV)

Immediately we can see that Wolfe omits some exceedingly important context, namely that *no power exists but of God* (v. 1). This very much includes governmental powers we find tyrannical. God ordained that Babylon would take Israel into captivity for seventy years in order that they would eventually turn their hearts back to Him (Jeremiah 25:8-11). Placing His chosen people under siege, captivity, and imposed rule *was an act of His love*. The core problem with Wolfe's conclusion is that it is based upon an assumption that the church, even his particular denomination, deserves the reins of society and not God's judgment instead.

Anyone who resists the higher powers, none of which exist but by God's providence, resists His ordinance and *will receive damnation* (v. 2). This full statement warrants far more pause than we are led to believe

---

645 Geneva Study Bible, 1560, [on Romans 13:5].

through Wolfe's selections. As Calvin wrote, "And by judgment, I understand not only the punishment which is inflicted by the magistrate, as though he had only said, that they would be justly punished who resisted authority; but also the vengeance of God, however it may at length be executed: for he teaches us in general what end awaits those who contend with God."[646] How many young Christian men would be willing to sign on to revolution in our time if they truly understood that they risk falling under the *vengeance of God* for doing so?

Even with so much civil strife in the modern West, we live in a climate of comfort and peace that nearly every human being that came before us would envy. We face immense challenges, such as the rise in mass shootings, the explosion of homelessness and crime in our cities, and the degradation of Christian ethics in seemingly every facet of our society. Still, the daily experience of the overwhelming majority of Christians in the West is of governments that "are not a terror to good works, but to the evil" (v. 3). We are currently allowed to live lives of piety and social peace – many of our brothers and sisters far moreso than their parents and grandparents could. The expectation of the average Western citizen is that the magistrates they personally interact with "in the general course of human affairs," as Henry put it, will by and large *properly fulfill their duty* (v. 4); otherwise, society would have already collapsed. We can rightfully have significant disagreements with how our nation is being governed, and there will always be individual injustices, but we still very much "needs be subject... for conscience's sake" (v. 5).

> Paul's silence with regard to revolution is easily explained by the fact that commanding it at the time would have been absurd.[647]

The remainder of the section expands upon his eisegetical base and is not worth addressing, save for this attempt by Wolfe to inject his own intent into the inspired word of God. One must ask Wolfe if he really believes that God intended for most of the New Testament to contain

---

646 John Calvin, Commentary on Romans, [on Romans 13:2].
647 Wolfe, *The Case for Christian Nationalism*, 351.

8. The Right to Revolution

instructions for disciples to be peacemakers to the point of accepting violent attacks in peace (1 Peter 2:20-25), but that He intentionally did not inspire a description of justified revolution, in order that it could be inferred by a political theorist, two millennia later.

As mentioned above, it is unlikely that Wolfe has spent time at a forward operating base in a combat zone and therefore probably does not have first-hand experience with day-to-day life in a war-torn country. I hope that he reads this book and, in particular, the story I am about to tell; perhaps it will cause him to rethink bringing such horrible things to those whom he loves most.

Deh Rahwood, Afghanistan, is a sixty minute helicopter ride north of Kandahar. I was stationed at the forward operating base there for the last month and a half of my time in country. The town is situated on the eastern side of the Helmand River, Afghanistan's largest, and our base was on the opposite side, looking down upon the town. We were stationed there with a Special Forces team and, since there were no hospitals in Deh Rahwood, their officer medic acted as the town's primary doctor.

Being that I was the radio operator, my schedule was different than the majority of the men in my platoon. I often walked around the base, doing my personal chores at odd hours while others were pulling guard, on patrol, or sleeping, so I regularly wound up being pulled in as an assistant when locals came to us with medical needs. Mostly I assisted with minor injuries; one instance that stands out is when I held a child's head while an infected tooth was pulled with a locking wrench, because we lacked proper dental tools. There was also a regular cadence of more serious injuries.

The locals fought and killed each other far more than they attempted to kill us. One time, while walking to the chow hall, I was called to a huge commotion at our gate; an older man and his nephew had been shot with an AK-47. The older man's wounds were severe but recoverable. The nephew, who appeared to be in his twenties, had been shot through the femur, severing it, and another round had gone through his lung, causing a sucking chest wound. I was told to stabilize the broken leg as we transferred him to a stretcher, but the break was so clean that there was nothing I could do; his thigh was like jello in my hands and he screamed in agony as he bled all over me. We transferred him to the medical building and I assisted as we put a tourniquet on his leg; I helped my platoon's medic as he cut open the side of the chest down into the lung, stuck a finger in the hole to keep it open, and shoved a tube in to drain the fluid building up and suffocating the man. We placed both men on a medical helicopter to Kandahar; I do not know if the younger man lived. I was told that they were shot by someone who believed the uncle had stolen a watermelon. This was, by far, not the worst thing I saw in Deh Rahwood.

One night, as I was sitting by the radio in the room next to my quarters with several other men, someone ran in and said, "Anyone with type O blood needs to go to the medical building right now. A local's been shot." I asked, "Positive or negative?" He did not know and I did not ask any more questions; I grabbed my weapon and briskly walked to the building. As I approached, there was an Afghan family of about six people, men and women, huddled together outside the door, hugging each other and sobbing loudly. I trepidatiously went inside.

On the table was a boy, no more than twelve, who had been shot point-blank in the face with a shotgun. His entire jaw was gone; where it was supposed to be attached was nothing but mangled flesh that looked like a pile of hamburger meat. Hanging out of his open throat, his tongue rested upon his neck, like a dog panting. He was fully conscious. I do not know if this really happened, but I cannot remember this moment without envisioning the boy keeping his head still and following me with his eyes as I walked in. I remained in the room for a brief time, long enough to be told that I did not have the right blood type and that the boy had merely been shot for being in the wrong place at the wrong time. The room was already full of men working to save him, so I left and went back to the radio.

I was haunted by this moment for years, thinking about it every day. Twenty years later, I still can rarely think about it without crying. I had walked away from God at this point in my life, but He had not walked away from me. In that moment, He gave me an understanding of general

8. The Right to Revolution

revelation that still drives me to this day – a thought that I could not get out of my mind, no matter how hard I tried. It had such a persistent effect on me, and I so often wrestled with its truth that, at one point, I decided to move into a Buddhist monastery to become a monk so that I could escape its ramifications. Extreme Buddhist praxis offered no solution and, within weeks, I was disabused of the religion I had devotedly practiced for several years. I moved back home, built a career, met my wife, and started a family. Living as an atheist, and then as an agnostic, I was able to function as a fairly normal and balanced member of secular society while retaining this understanding. But the only thing that gave me the actual peace I so desperately sought was the forgiveness of God, through the finished work of His Son, Jesus Christ, on the cross.

In that moment in Deh Rahwood, standing in front of a mutilated child, I immediately saw – in an undeniable, supernatural way deep in my soul – that, given the right providential circumstances, I was perfectly capable of hurting that child in the same way. What I did not understand at the time was that I was shown the naked truth of sin and my own total depravity. I know the ultimate evil men are capable of, because I deeply understand that the same evil exists in me too.

I know what horrors we will allow ourselves to commit if we drive our nation into a civil war of guerrilla insurgency.

VII. Conclusion

> Many want me to end with a word of caution, perhaps to reassure everyone that these are academic conclusions, that they are not serious. Instead, I'll say this: it is to our shame that we sheepishly tolerate assaults against our Christian heritage, merely sighing or tweeting performative outrage over public blasphemy, impiety, irreverence, and perversity. We are dead inside, lacking the spirit to drive away the open mockery of God and to claim what is ours in Christ. We are gripped by a slavish devotion to our secularist

captors. But we do not have to be like this. We have the power and right to act. Let us train the will and cultivate our resolve.[648]

The chapter on revolution ends with yet another, over the top, *language of destiny* appeal to emotion, one that has a new insidiousness, in that it is a genuine call to arms, right here and now. Wolfe will expand upon these ideas in the epilogue, which reads more like a manifesto than a summation of his theory, but, for now, let us work through these current revolutionary statements individually.

What "assaults against our Christian heritage" are Western Christians "sheepishly tolerat[ing]"? Our nation is growing increasingly divided over a clash between absolute, Judeo-Christian ethics and secular relativism. At the forefront of each flash-point – abortion, queer- and gender-theory, criminal justice – are conservative Christians legislatively fighting for the traditional position. These people are also ideologically and financially supported by other conservative Christians. Perhaps what Wolfe takes umbrage with is that, with legal means still much at their disposal, American Christians are overwhelmingly not interested in resorting to violence over "blasphemy, impiety, irreverence, and perversity."

The phrase "claim what is ours in Christ" is borderline heretical. *We have the right to claim nothing.* We are all condemnable sinners who have been given the precious gift of salvation, through Another's work, and have been *explicitly instructed* to actively seek lives of complete humility (Philippians 2:3). It would seem that Wolfe is unsatisfied with our Lord's prerequisite of seeking to be last, should we want to eventually hold claim to any *true* reward (Matthew 20:16).

The concept of his audience being awakened to their "slavish devotion to secular captors" would be comical if he did not genuinely believe it; seeing your fellow countrymen and elected representatives as *evil captors* to be violently overthrown is dangerously unhealthy. Again, next to nothing is preventing Wolfe from living his life wholly as he sees fit and worshiping God in the manner he believes is most beneficial – a privilege that many of our brothers and sisters are still being murdered over. But this

---

648 Wolfe, 352.

is not enough for Wolfe; he wants more; he wants *power over other human beings*, including, as we will see in the next chapter, the ability to execute those with whom he disagrees. God help us if he, or another believer in his theory, should ever get his hands on the reins of society.

9. Liberty of Conscience

I. Statement of the Question

> Asking [about liberty of conscience] is fair and expected, since I have called for public institutions and culture to be Christian. But, in most cases, these questions arise from serious confusion about classical Protestant political theology and from ignorance on how Protestants justified civil action for true religion.[649]

Immediately at the outset of the chapter on liberty of conscience we are presented with an appeal to authority/tradition logical fallacy. What the *fallible men* of the reformation thought about liberty of conscience should only have an advisory influence when determining the *morality* of the subject. Again, to order society solely based upon one's interpretation of their opinions, instead of directly exegeting the infallible word of God (what amounts to a game of telephone with Scripture), is to abandon the very principle of *Sola Scriptura* that those men risked their lives for. *We must start with Scripture.*

It bears repeating that the reformation-era view that "civil magistrates protect and support true religion and suppress false religion"[650] – a view that was far from uniform, even between the different Swiss city-states – has more in common with the medieval Roman Catholic tradition than the earliest Christian government. As shown, the first Christian Emperor of Rome, Constantine, decreed that all citizens and subjects should be allowed to practice their varying religions in peace. This was the milieu in which one of the church's most revered thinkers, Augustine of Hippo, was converted from Manichaeism to Christianity, seven decades later.

Wolfe next claims that those who, "for centuries," have disagreed with his preferred conclusion on liberty of conscience have "improperly state[d] the question" and "asserted a *non sequitur*"[651]; could it instead be that they simply drew a different boundary around what constitutes *immorally*

---

649 Wolfe, 353–54.
650 Wolfe, 354.
651 Wolfe, 354–55.

suppressing thought? This type of unnecessary straw-manning of his opponent has become characteristic of his rhetoric and is a sign of the weakness of his own position. Regardless of how one spins it, suppressing "liberty of conscience" and/or "liberty of tongue and practice" is prosecuting *thoughtcrime*.

The subsection on *internal religion* can be best summed up as, "You can disagree with me about religion, but you better not say so," which is an absolutely totalitarian position. A larger genetic logical fallacy than the one presented in this subsection cannot be made; take any body of thought other than religion and apply it to Wolfe's statement that "… the civil government must ensure that truth is taught and that harmful false teaching is restrained…"[652] Is it the government's responsibility to determine "truth" and utilize state-violence to prevent "harmful false teaching" on finance, medicine, art, literature, humanities, or foreign and domestic policy, to name a few subjects? Wolfe's premise requires the unprovable assumption that his definition of "Christian" is, in every aspect he wishes to enforce, the objectively correct and most beneficial one; otherwise his government would immediately be in violation of the Third Commandment. Furthermore, what constitutes *harmful?* What are the boundaries of such ideological restraint? Later in the chapter, Wolfe will answer these questions in a way that a majority of Western Christians would find abhorrent.

> External religion includes professions of faith (vocal or written), ceremonies of worship, teaching, etc. These are outward and visible and can affect others, and so external religion belongs to the kind of things that external authorities can regulate.[653]

Often when people make this point, as shown earlier with William Wolfe,[654] the example given is of ritualistic human sacrifice, a crime that can be prosecuted as a Second Table violation of the Sixth Commandment without outlawing public profession of the false religion itself. I believe

---

652 Wolfe, 356–57.
653 Wolfe, 358.
654 https://web.archive.org/web/20230208134949

9. Liberty of Conscience

this is because most Westerners, especially Americans, have accepted freedom of speech as non-negotiable. Most of those arguing for active suppression of false religion, consciously or not, know that a direct case for First Table enforcement, such as the previous example of outlawing Hindu temples, would be rejected outright by the average Christian. Stephen Wolfe, to his credit, does not bother with such obfuscation and will soon make the argument that *words are violence*, demonstrating the horseshoe theory of postmodern "wokeism" and Christian Nationalism.

> Suppressing false religion is a *means*, not an end in itself. Thus, the question is not whether the suppression of external false religion by civil government is a good in itself or ought to be pursued for its own sake;[655]

Whether or not the ends of "true religion" is a "good in of itself" is a wholly separate question from whether *suppressive means* are morally justifiable. I am flabbergasted that Wolfe, with a straight face, would seemingly make such a blatant argument for *ends justifying means*; the brunt of his argument in the next section will be that utilizing suppressive means will produce the desired ends of "best outward conditions." Later in the chapter such means will be expanded to include the execution of "arch-heretics" and proselytizers of false religion, with no exegetical justification that his ends are better than the *uniformity of ideology* desired by atheistic communists. As he nears the end of the explication of his theory, its totalitarian aspects become increasingly apparent.

Wolfe closes out this section with the statement that his is a "classical" view of liberty of conscience, in direct contradiction to the "modern" view. This is yet another genetic logical fallacy, in that "classical" is not inherently better than "modern." Also, *classical thought goes beyond 16th-century Northern Europe; if classical is better, Constantine, and his view of religious freedom, is *more classical* than Zwingli.

---

655 Wolfe, *The Case for Christian Nationalism*, 358.

II. Principle

> Those in the denial camp typically affirm that civil government ought to regulate outward religious actions that cause public harm. But they limit public harm to *physical* harm.[656]

This is a major categorical error and straw-manning of his opposition, in that a physical crime, when prosecuted, is wholly separated from its religious motivation. Human sacrifice is prosecuted as a murder, not a *religious murder*, just as sexual abuse by a pastor is prosecuted in the same manner as when it is perpetrated by a public school teacher. Thus, "outward religious actions" are not being regulated in the Baptist model of liberty of conscience. Instead, crimes against other human beings that are illegal for everyone are not given *religious exemption*.

> I will grant here that civil authorities should not prosecute crimes solely against God, as if civil punishment right [sic] wrongs committed against him. But the assumption that external false religion does not harm souls is clearly false.[657]

If someone burglarizes your home and steals your valuables, a *quantifiable amount* of financial harm has been done to you, and you are required to state that amount in the police report. If someone assaults you, there is a quantifiable amount of physical harm done, often measured by medical costs and recovery time. In civil suits resulting from injury, professional and emotional harm is specifically measured by how the physical damage prevented someone from working or functioning normally. How do you quantify the damage done to souls from hearing false ideas?

One might point to the Second Table offense of *vulgarity* as an example. We consider it damaging for unwilling persons, especially children, to be exposed to expressions of debauchery, but that is because

---
656 Wolfe, 360.
657 Wolfe, 360.

those expressions represent quantifiable acts of physical abuse that we use as a benchmark. How is the damage from simply hearing false religious ideas quantifiable in the same way? Some would point to the judgment that faces all who do not place their faith in Christ, but is that a quantifiable earthly damage of the same type by which all other civil judgments are determined? How much can one exact justice along those lines before *he* sins (Romans 12:19)? Even crimes that we prosecute for their *potential* to cause harm, such as public drunkenness, have distinctly quantifiable consequences that are immediate in effect. What is the backstop for a line of thinking that equates publicly expressed thought with physical crime? According to Wolfe, it stops or proceeds by his own arbitrary determination:

> (1) Any outward action that has the potential to cause harm to others is rightfully subject to civil restraint or punishment (in principle).
> (2) External false religion has the potential to cause harm to others. Therefore, (3) external false religion is rightfully subject to civil restraint or punishment.[658]

Could there be any looser and less legally justifiable definition for a thoughtcrime than "the potential to cause harm"? Wolfe engages in a shell game, claiming that "belief itself is neither the ground of the civil action nor the object of the action."[659] But *spoken belief* is indeed his grounds for punishment, for it is the action that "has the potential to cause harm." External circumstances may inform the *level* of potential harm, when punishment is meted, but it is still the actual act of expressing belief that would be punished.

> As for the minor premise, there is no question that those who actively and outwardly espouse damnable error can lead people astray, especially when they have skill and personality.[660]

---

658 Wolfe, 361.
659 Wolfe, 361.
660 Wolfe, 362.

Take a minute to appreciate the irony that this sentence was written by the same man who bases his entire political theory on a wildly unsound imagining of prelapsarian earth and of our post-fall nature, built upon no exegesis of his own, that was roundly rejected by nearly every theologian who reviewed his book. For example, Andrew T. Walker, a professor of ethics and public theology at Southern Baptist Theological Seminary wrote:

> He points to what the world must have been like in Genesis 1 and 2 had they continued without the fall. But the argument about the natural principles in Genesis 1 go beyond what the text allows. "Duty" denotes the idea of authority to command such outcomes. But, again, the most that Wolfe does is make inferences from an unfallen Adam to the role of government today. He fails entirely to give sufficient attention to the Bible's creation-fall-redemption-restoration storyline and assumes we can simply repristinate Eden without calling attention to the developing saga of the covenants and what they require for government's calling. Wolfe seems to think that the world of Genesis 1-2 is the world that contemporary governments are called to resurrect. This notion, however, ignores massively the fall and the calling of government within a fallen era, as detailed in the Noahic Covenant in Genesis 9.[661]

The last person qualified to discuss punishing "damnable [theological] error" is someone who is guilty of it himself and who, as Walker points out, fails to even properly incorporate the four points of the gospel into his expressed worldview.

Wolfe gives three justifications for what he sees as the civil magistrate's ability to have "cognizance of what would be good for the soul,"[662] which is an argument that none refute; *cognizance* does not automatically transfer to *authority*. For example, the President of the United States likely knows that eating McDonald's every day is detrimental to a citizen's long-term

---

661 Andrew T. Walker, "Book Review: The Case for Christian Nationalism, by Stephen Wolfe," 9Marks, accessed May 16, 2023, https://www.9marks.org/article/a-baptist-engagement-with-the-case-for-christian-nationalism/.
662 Wolfe, *The Case for Christian Nationalism*, 362–64.

9. Liberty of Conscience

health. Does that mean he has the right to limit Americans to two Big Macs a month? I will address how Wolfe's three examples of cognizance similarly do not transfer over to authority.

His first point is that a civil magistrate can "order outward things in the interest of mental health," but magistrates are usually intentionally limited in their reach with such measures. Most often, preventative mental health actions are limited to people who present a physical threat to themselves or others. Therefore, this point actually works *against* Wolfe's argument for limiting impious speech and *for* the position of restricting only physical harm. Next he attempts to equate the Second Table to the First, writing, "So, at least with regard to natural religion, the magistrate can have principled cognizance of true and false religion as captured in the First Table of God's law. The Second Table-onlyists are thus refuted." No such thing has happened; that he would attempt such an argument is laughable, because the Baptist view of liberty of conscience in no way denies that the magistrate can have a *cognizance* of the First Table. The argument is whether he has the Scriptural directive to *enforce it*. The last argument he gives is that because any man can know true religion, the magistrate is not excluded from such knowledge. This is obviously true, but also has no bearing on whether the magistrate has the right to impress such knowledge on other citizens.

Further arguments for "supernatural knowledge" are then given, most of which have the same issue as the previous three.[663] I will address the details of each of these briefly:

- Though Scripture is indeed "a possession of the people of God", civil rulers are not always "installed by and from the people of God." As shown in Romans 13, civil rulers are always "instituted by God," even if they may be tyrannical towards the people of God. A majority Christian nation can, and likely would, elect Christian civil magistrates, but if that magistrate based his actions on Scripture, he would leave blasphemers in peace, as all Christians are instructed to do.

---

663 Wolfe, 364–69.

- We do not "elevate the magistrate's abilities in unaided reason," nor would we "downgrad[e] his abilities in theology," for *ability* and *authority* are not the same thing. Who would argue that when someone is elected to public office their unaided reason becomes elevated? Are officials not simply given more responsibility to exercise with their existing reason?
- Though, because of special revelation, the civil magistrate can know the Triune God, this has nothing to do with whether he has the authority to use state-violence to force such orthodoxy of practice in others.
- The notion that earthly civil government has a natural function of "ordering the people to their supernatural end" is a self-referential argument, based upon earlier statements in the book that have already been refuted.[664]
- There is no Scriptural basis for the claim that, "The magistrate is the first among the people of God who sit under the instituted teaching ministry that they have constituted." As far as the *spiritual kingdom* is concerned, the magistrate is of equal standing to all other non-ordained members.
- Wolfe repeats his faulty assertion of a Scriptural precedent for the Christian family carrying over to the civil magistrate[665], making the ridiculous claim that, "To deny the possibility of a Christian magistrate entails denying the possibility of a Christian father." This statement is hyperbolic and authoritarian in nature, in that it argues for a singular *father-figure* to rule over the nation.

Wolfe yet again mixes the *temporal* and *spiritual* kingdoms by claiming that ministers "pronounce *positive* judgments" and that civil rulers "legislate a *negative*" omitting the negative judgment in First Table matters exercised by the spiritual kingdom through *church discipline*. Overall, his epistemological argument is based upon false equivalence, self-reference, and a highly assumptive interpretation of natural law.

---

664 See chapter 2, *Redeemed Nations*.
665 See chapter 4, *Perfecting the Nation*, section III, *Objections*.

9. Liberty of Conscience

> The accusation that restraining and punishing heresy will produce hypocrisy goes back at least to the 16th century... The principle is, *all have the right to express outwardly what they affirm inwardly*. If they don't have this right, then they are forced into hypocrisy, as the claim goes... But this is arbitrary. Criminalizing sins of the Second Table – such as murder, adultery, theft and defaming character - also makes men hypocrites. One might inwardly want to murder his enemy and even believe sincerely that killing him would be just, but the fear of civil punishment might lead him to act like a friend.[666]

We are yet again presented with a false equivalence, in that the act of murder has the most *quantifiable amount* of harm, and the strictest definition of causation, of all crimes. We can absolutely know when it has been committed, because there will be a dead body, and we can categorize the level of intent of the perpetrator based upon predefined standards for premeditation. By contrast, the amount of "harm" caused to a "victim" who heard a false religious idea is entirely arbitrary. I have little doubt that, in Wolfe's vision for *theocratic Caesarism*, the right to express outwardly what one affirms inwardly would be strictly limited in far more subjects than just doctrinal matters. After all, the Christian Prince "mediates divine rule"[667] and is a little-G *god* with veto power over doctrinal decisions. Why would Wolfe not see public questioning of the prince's actions and authority as condemnable religious dissent worthy of civil punishment?

> To avoid [the above conclusion on hypocrisy], one would have to claim that the sins of the First Table and those of the Second Table are different.[668]

Wolfe either does not understand his opposition's interpretation of Scripture at all, or he is deliberately straw-manning them again. Under the New Covenant, the Christian is given instructions to leave those who revile God in peace (1 Peter 2:20-25), which has nothing to do with the *moral*

---

666 Wolfe, *The Case for Christian Nationalism*, 369.
667 Wolfe, 290.
668 Wolfe, 370.

implications of the First Table versus the Second. This position is similar to how all foods are now clean and how circumcision is no longer required – the Epistles provide new rules on how believers are to deal with blasphemy and heresy. The question at hand is whether there is an *exception* to this instruction allowed for an explicitly Christian government. As I argued previously, a Christian government is a *collective Christian* and is bound by all of the same commandments as individual Christians.

> It is true that whenever Christ himself is not at work, your **[i.e., the magistrate's]** work, your service and your power touching the gospel only makes men hypocrites… (emphasis mine)[669]

Through a literal *injection* of the civil magistrate into the Berner Synodus, a document meant to settle clerical disputes, and that was primarily concerned with pastoral directives, Wolfe is once again playing fast and loose with Reformed thought. Perhaps he is counting on his audience to not know, and to not investigate, the purpose of the document he is quoting and through which he is unwarrantably applying rules meant for the *eternal* kingdom to the *temporal*. He then closes the subsection on hypocrisy by repeating the false notion that utilizing state-violence in the punishment of thoughtcrime is not an attempt to alter the "inward man". His eisegetical usage of 1 Timothy 2:2 to justify arbitrary governmental restraint of "outward expressions of false religion"[670] is especially egregious, in that the "quiet and peaceable life" Paul instructed Timothy to pray for was one that was *free from government interference in the church.*

I have sufficiently demonstrated that Wolfe has not "sufficiently demonstrated the truth of [his] principle."[671] There are so many leaps of logic, selective quotations, and false statements of his opposition's position that this section fails, on every front, to make the case for the magistrate's right to violently suppress religious dissent.

---

669 Wolfe, 370–71.
670 Wolfe, 372.
671 Wolfe, 372.

III. Prudence

> As Althusius points out, suppressing false religion to the degree that the commonwealth itself is threatened may violate the very end of such suppression, for the false religionists may overthrow the state and attack the church.[672]

With this sentence the notion that a Christian nation, adhering to Wolfe's model, could naturally and peaceably come to be in our generation, and likely more, is completely sunk. This is why he must promote violent revolution to achieve it, but the revolutionary overthrow of a majority secular government negates any notion of *prudence* he would attempt to put forth. He later specifies the highly limited boundaries of his tolerance, when he writes, "The point here is that *Protestant* magistrates ruling a *Protestant* people have principled flexibility when faced with religious diversity" (emphasis mine). Given everything he has written, thus far, it must be assumed that he would outlaw the practice of all non-Protestant religion, including Catholicism. Imagine the atrocities that would have to take place to enforce such a policy in the modern West.

Thus there is little need to parse out the minutiae of his "prudence" in enforcing orthodoxy, because it is no real prudence at all. The discussion of what may or may not be "secondary matters"[673] among Protestants means nothing in the post-Christian West; Wolfe would have to banish or execute the majority of people in any locale before he could begin to worry about such matters. This is more sociopathy than political theory. That he later chastises secular governments for "mak[ing] politics a sort of religion – into an abstract, transcendental vision of the good, which is forcibly immanentized into earthy life"[674] is the peak of self-unawareness.

Wolfe would replace "the moral insanity of our time" with his own brand, one where a single man, his Christian Prince, would be the final word on what doctrinal beliefs are acceptable to hold. He would form an

---

672 Wolfe, 373.
673 Wolfe, 377–79.
674 Wolfe, 379.

army of the "soldiers of Christ", who would likely be tasked with the violent suppression of false religion (and "unacceptable" doctrine), at the very least banishing its adherents and, as we will see later in this chapter, executing those who refuse to relent in proselytizing. His nation would, in every way, live up to the left-wing pejorative of a "Christian Taliban". Scripture has instructions for those of us who fully understand his call to action, and have the means to resist:

> If you faint in the day of adversity,
> your strength is small.
> Rescue those who are being taken away to death;
> hold back those who are stumbling to the slaughter.
> If you say, "Behold, we did not know this,"
> does not he who weighs the heart perceive it?
> Does not he who keeps watch over your soul know it,
> and will he not repay man according to his work?
> (Proverbs 24:10-12)

There are very few things in this world that would cause me to advocate for, and personally return to, proactive violence. Stephen Wolfe and his compatriots attempting violent revolution to enact his vision would be one of them.

Wolfe uses Aaron Renn's framework of *positive/neutral/negative worlds* to make the case that current Reformed thinking on public engagement is mostly based upon treatises written during the period where being a Christian was seen as a culturally neutral stance.[675] Though this is a reasonable starting point, he quickly jumps to an unnatural conclusion, writing, "Now that we're in the negative world, political theology is predictably moving in neo-Anabaptist directions in an attempt to recover neutrality by neutralizing true religion as a threat to the secularist establishment."[676] Much of contemporary political theology, including Renn's, advocates for Christians to form their own economic and social structures within the greater, secular society. Their position is not one of

---

675 Wolfe, 379–80.
676 Wolfe, 381.

retreat, but one of creating formidable *alternatives* that are in the world but not of it; this is hardly a "neo-Anabaptist" position. Ironically, seeking to form your own micro-nation, where outward expressions of religion are judged and regulated by societal authorities, is far more traditionally Anabaptist.

Though Renn has previously taken a non-aggressive approach to cultural engagement (at least compared to Wolfe), in 2022 he co-founded an online journal, *American Reformer*, with several people who are known for championing Christian Nationalism and/or authoritarian worldviews, including Josh Abbotoy, Nate Fischer, and Timon Cline. On May 22, 2023, Abbotoy tweeted, "Basically, America is going to need a Protestant Franco."[677] The next day, Cline described Charles Haywood's "positively glowing" review of Franco – where he claimed that accounts of Franco's mass murders are exaggerated[678] – as a "Good piece!"[679] Cline has written positively of Wolfe's vision of theocratic Caesarism in *American Reformer*, with an essay entitled *Hail Caesar?*[680]

> Experience over the last decades has made evident that there are two options: Christian nationalism or pagan nationalism. The totality of national action will be either *Christian*, and thus ordered to the complete good, or *pagan*...[681]

The false dichotomy of the authoritarian proposition is once again presented. Our descent into open postmodernism as a state-sanctioned, secular religion is less than a half-century old and, despite this, America is still generally known worldwide as a beacon of freedom, prosperity, and hope. We need not wholly upend our society, in either direction, to solve our current predicament. Wolfe's insistence that the only option to combat paganism is that "Christians should assert the godly direction" of Christian

---

677 https://twitter.com/Byzness/status/166085191442941132
678 Haywood, "On Francisco Franco • The Worthy House."
679 https://twitter.com/tlloydcline/status/1661105005774921729
680 Timon Cline, "Hail Caesar? | Timon Cline," *American Reformer* (blog), December 8, 2022, https://americanreformer.org/2022/12/hail-caesar/.
681 Wolfe, *The Case for Christian Nationalism*, 381.

Nationalism does not pass the slightest muster of critical reasoning. In his assessment, we must bring about a "great renewal" of the benefits of previous Christian culture in the West. He believes the "early American republic" had it right (except for the First Amendment[682]), yet this culture also worked well enough in the 20th-century Bible Belt that Russell Moore should be chastised for taking any issue with it. He claims the way to bring about this renewal is to wage violent revolution to place an autocratic ruler over the nation and allow him to use the "totality of national action" – a concept that fits in the mold of Italian fascism – to actively suppress all non-Protestant religion.

What Wolfe presents is the *same authoritarian policies* of state-enforced orthodox thought advocated for in growing numbers on the secular left, with the key difference being that his orthodoxy is "Christian". He confirms this when he writes, "Furthermore, the left is correct that disagreement in public discourse must be bounded within an acceptable range of acceptable opinion."[683] In this, Wolfe affirms the *Horseshoe Theory*, that the far-left and far-right have more in common with each other than the majority of society. To consciously choose either "Christian nationalism or pagan nationalism" is to place yourself in ideological and, eventually, physical chains.

> Another holdover from the neutral world is the argument that religious liberty or a neutral or "contestable" public square will allow the space for the best argument to win... As a result, the left now effectively excludes conservatives from positions of influence and power... But most intellectual conservatives today, naively proclaiming their commitment to principle, continue the same

---

[682] On Twitter, Wolfe will often refer to the First Amendment's restriction of Congress alone in determining a state religion, and discuss how multiple states initially had official churches (https://twitter.com/PerfInjust/status/1661733228682592256). This is true, but no state went as far in their restriction of religion as he is proposing, and he would not allow regional magistrates under the prince to choose other religions, so the point is mute.

[683] Wolfe, *The Case for Christian Nationalism*, 383.

9. Liberty of Conscience

losing struggle for "viewpoint diversity." Most on the left have little interest in it and so conservatives continue to lose.[684]

It is undoubtedly true that the political left is more concerned with attaining power than seeking objective truth. Likewise, Wolfe shows that he is far more concerned with earthly power than Christian ethics, when he writes, "But let's give the left some credit: They are acting according to good principles."[685] These supposedly *good principles* of seeking worldly power for the attainment of an earthly "complete good" are, in fact, directly contradictory to the instructions of Scripture. As Paul wrote to Timothy, regaling how he was *literally* pushed out of the public square, the Christian is expected to receive such a response from the world and to maintain *patience* and *love* in their conduct.

> You, however, have followed my teaching, my conduct, my aim in life, my faith, my patience, my love, my steadfastness, my persecutions and sufferings that happened to me at Antioch, at Iconium, and at Lystra – which persecutions I endured; yet from them all the Lord rescued me. Indeed, all who desire to live a godly life in Christ Jesus will be persecuted, while evil people and impostors will go on from bad to worse, deceiving and being deceived. (2 Timothy 3:10-13)

Wolfe next moves to complaining about the "controlled opposition" of "conservatives on the 'center-right'" who play a part in assisting the left to shape "the acceptable range of opinion today". He quickly takes this observation in a further conspiratorial direction, writing, "The American regime is tolerant of a few regime-faithful 'center-right' Christian pundits who are anti-abortion, because they know that being anti-abortion is necessary to operate as an insider among conservative Christians, and being an insider allows them to critique 'their own' from secularist publications on behalf of the regime."[686] He will expand upon his

---

684 Wolfe, 382–83.
685 Wolfe, 383.
686 Wolfe, 383–84.

ideological foil of the "globalist American empire" in the epilogue; for now it is worth noting that he provides no evidence for his claims that men like Russell Moore and David French, whom he would most certainly place within this category, are *controlled opposition* and not simply genuine Christians who hold a different opinion than him.

> Christian nationalism does not deny the good of viewpoint diversity. But, as with the American regime, the acceptable range ought to be bounded by principles of inclusion and exclusion... Christian nationalism will exclude at least the following from acceptable opinion and action: (1) political atheism, (2) subversion of public Christianity, (3) opposition to Christian morality, (4) heretical teaching, and (5) the political and social influence of non-Christian religion and its adherence.[687]

Once again, we are presented with a genetic logical fallacy; every one of these vague points has a wide variance of definitions within orthodox Protestant Christianity, leaving us to trust that Wolfe's personal definition of what does and does not constitute proper "Christianity" is good, in and of itself. Why is Presbyterianism the best choice, other than that is the church Wolfe belongs to? Secondly, this list can be easily modified to fit any form of totalitarianism:

> Communism will exclude at least the following from acceptable opinion and action (1) political theology, (2) subversion of party activities, (3) opposition to revolutionary principles, (4) industrialist propaganda, and (5) the political and social influence of capitalism and its adherence.

Wolfe closes this section by confirming that his goal is to use the same power he believes the left is abusing, against them.[688] Again, the Apostle Paul directly rebukes such notions:

---

687 Wolfe, 384–85.
688 Wolfe, 386.

> Do not be overcome by evil, but overcome evil with good. (Romans 12:21)

IV. Specific Groups

> This section applies my discussion of principle and prudence to specific groups, namely, heretics, non-Christians, dissenting Christians, and conforming Christians.[689]

As he gets to brass tacks, what Wolfe describes as "prudence" will likely not seem as such to most Western Christians. He advocates for a range of actions, from the "active suppression" of "fellow Christians" who dissent from the doctrine of the state-church, to the execution of recalcitrant "arch-heretics" and proselytizers of false religion. The dryness of his description of sin and punishment gives this section a clinical air, but the actual application of his "principle" would be bloody atrocity. I will not attempt to directly argue what is or is not heresy, nor will I argue what is or is not "the Reformed tradition". Instead, I will focus on the practical outcomes of using state-violence to suppress religious dissent in the 21st-century West. It will become quickly clear that such actions would almost assuredly result in multiple Second Table violations, meaning that the revolutionary movement, its hypothetical nation, and its leaders would be guilty of condemnable sin themselves.

> Arch-heretics are publicly persistent in their damnable error and actively seek to convince others of this error to subvert the established church, to denounce its ministers, or to instigate rebellion against magistrates. For this reasons [sic], they can be justly put to death...
>
> This is not to say that capital punishment is the necessary, sole or desired punishment. Banishment and long-term imprisonment may suffice as well...

---

[689] Wolfe, 386.

> Those who do not profess Christianity and yet actively proselytize their non-Christian religion or belief system or actively seek to refute the Christian religion are subject to the same principles outlined above.[690]

The lowest category of punishment would be meted out to those whom he calls "conforming Christians" who commit "sins of commission and sins of omission", including punishing those who do not attend church.[691] He again plays a shell game with civil punishment, by writing, "In other words, the magistrate punishes for the violation not of failing to worship itself but because the failure to attend violates a fundamental norm of Christian civil community." It is hard to believe that such regulations would allow for non-state-sanctioned forms of Christianity to function in peace within such a nation. For example, what would happen to Catholics, who profess to be Christian but who would refuse to attend a state-sanctioned church?

One out of every five Americans identifies as Catholic, over fifty times the amount that belong to the Presbyterian Church in America.[692] Let us temporarily put aside the ridiculous notion that an orthodox, "pan-Protestant" order in the West can be achieved above the objections and resistance of the overwhelming, non-Protestant majority. Mississippi, the state with the lowest percentage of Catholics (4%), still has roughly a quarter of a million practitioners. There is nowhere in the modern United States where Wolfe and his compatriots could bring about his preferred government without having to violently suppress Catholics. As shown with the 1838 Mormon war in Missouri, it is highly unlikely that such an embedded population would peacefully deport themselves. The same can be said of Pentecostals, who outnumber all orthodox Presbyterians by over four to one. Many Charismatics still claim someone is not truly saved until they demonstrate the gift of tongues, something that would likely constitute a heresy in Wolfe's nation.

---

690 Wolfe, 391, 392.
691 Wolfe, 395–96.
692 "Religious Landscape Study."

9. Liberty of Conscience

Perhaps he would concede this point, and allow Catholics and Charismatics to peacefully practice their religion, as long as they did not evangelize. What of Seventh Day Adventists and Jehovah's Witnesses who would refuse a Sunday Sabbath? What of those same Jehovah's Witnesses, as well as Mormons, who would likely refuse to cease their evangelization efforts and would qualify as both *arch-heretics* and *active proselytizers of non-Christian religion*? What would Wolfe do to an entire population of recalcitrant non-Christians? Would he kick them off their land and mass banish them (a violation of the Eighth Commandment)? What if they refused? Would he send the "soldiers of Christ" to violently remove them (a violation of the Sixth Commandment)? He would likely reject these questions as hyperbolic, pointing to his statement on the "status of non-Christians", where he writes, "Since civil society is a human institution, it must guarantee equal protection and due process with regard to human things with all people. That is, it must guarantee justice and secure natural rights."[693] But this is a negated principle in a nation where to publicly disagree with the state religion is to "subvert the established church" and be marked for civil punishment. In order to guarantee religious minorities' natural rights, Wolfe's nation would need to do the near-impossible and be the very first in human history to explicitly create an *underclass of conscience* that is not actively oppressed by the in-group. This is especially unlikely, considering he immediately contradicts his guarantee of natural rights by stating that "non-Christians are more limited in [exercising rights] due to their rejection of Christianity."[694]

There is simply no way that such a government could come into being in the 21st-century West without immense atrocity being committed. Even in the most Christianized areas of the West, *orthodox* Protestant Christians are in the minority, before one even stratifies for those who would sign on to Wolfe's vision. Hypothetically speaking, if the United States military was not a factor (a failed state scenario), even to form a micro-nation, he and his compatriots would need to violently expel a significant portion of any locale's population; this would likely be the majority of residents, for

---

693 Wolfe, *The Case for Christian Nationalism*, 392.
694 Wolfe, 392.

what city in the modern West has a majority population interested in instating a state-church, let alone an orthodox Presbyterian one? Yet he will end the book with a call to action to organize Christian Nationalist movements on the local level. I believe this impracticality makes his philosophy *more dangerous*, because, when combined with his call for revolution, those who sign on will become increasingly interested in guerrilla activities when their low numbers result in little to no conventional political progress. That they believe unrepentant pagans deserve execution will only exacerbate the problem.

V. Conclusion

> I will stress for the last time that the central point of this chapter is an outline of principles, not a blueprint for action. This follows my principle throughout this work, that each people-group must decide for themselves how they will govern and arrange themselves.[695]

I do not see how this statement be taken seriously by anyone who has gotten to this point in the book. This is a good place to again list the core principles Wolfe has laid out, thus far:

- An ideal government would, in a "totality of action", prioritize nation over individual. A hierarchical structure is of inherent greater worth than egalitarian arrangements and, based on natural variances within humans, a natural aristocracy arises. From this will come "a man who can wield formal civil power to great effect and shape the public imagination by means of charisma, gravitas, and personality." This man will need to weigh "unpleasant trade-offs" and have the "fortitude to enact and enforce the greatest good, despite unfortunate costs involved" by "shun[ning] the moralism that limits action". This Christian Prince, by wielding the *totality of action*, would "restore masculine prominence in the land" and "suppress the enemies of God," up to and including

---

[695] Wolfe, 396.

executing non-Christians who refuse to cease publicly professing their religion.[696]

- Preferring to live with those genetically similar to you (and, downstream from that, culturally similar) is "natural and good", not "a product of the fall", and grace "affirms and completes it"; "much good would result in the world if we all preferred our own", and though some intermarriage is acceptable, "blood-ties" are integral to "ethno-genesis", and "a 'community of blood' is crucial to ethnicity." The "in-group/out-group distinction" is a prelapsarian good that "preserves cultural distinctives", and "differences in food sources, climate, and other factors" also produce, on the macro, ethnic level, a natural variance in which some people groups are objectively "more beautiful, and all ways better disposed". Recognizing this "instinct to socialize and dwell with [ethnically] similar people" is wrongly "understood as evil or pathological" by the West.[697]
- Though the West has been multi-ethnic for generations, "perhaps in some cases amicable ethnic separation along political lines is mutually desired," because people of different ethnic groups, including ethnically differing Christians, "cannot have a life together that goes beyond mutual alliance," nor attain the "complete good". To achieve this *complete good*, a "forcible reclamation of civil power," also known as violent religious revolution, is justifiable, because "a Christian people share particular norms, customs, blood, etc., which are not easily forced upon them." Christians are only allowed to revolt when under "tyrannical" government, defined as a civil authority "ordering fellow men to great evil", which, by the endorsement of revolution here and now, must include the current United States government, who are our "secularist captors".[698]

There are few, if any, "principles" in Wolfe's theory worth integrating into a genuinely Christian "blueprint for action". His theory is more

---

696 Wolfe, 13, 16, 31, 68, 72–73, 90, 139–40, 323, 392.
697 Wolfe, 23, 25, 65, 67, 117–18, 142, 145.
698 Wolfe, 149, 151, 326, 328, 334, 352.

Nietzschean authoritarian ethno-nationalism than *Scriptural* Christian political theory.

10. The Foundation of American Freedom

I. Introduction

> Does the American political tradition permit a Christian self-conception, Christian governments, and church establishments? One popular narrative is that the American founding was anti-establishment and secularist and reflects the influence of "Enlightenment philosophy." How can we get Christian nationalism out of that? But that narrative is false, as this chapter shows.[699]

As he has regularly done throughout the book, Wolfe chooses the opposition most easy to counter. He is correct that America's founders were not dominated by secularism, though their thinking was most definitely influenced by the philosophy of the Enlightenment; the Declaration of Independence's "Life, Liberty and the pursuit of Happiness", taken from John Locke's "life, liberty and property," serves as a prominent example. As is most often the case with history, the story of religious influence in the founding of the United States is multi-faceted and not dominated by wholly positive or negative influences. Throughout this chapter I will give examples of colonial and early-Union history that will provide a more holistic and nuanced view of the role of religious toleration, or lack thereof, in the nation's founding. As for where that toleration has led us, though Wolfe avoids the question, "Is America now a Christian nation?"[700], theologian Francis Schaeffer answered it in his 1969 book, *Death in the City*:

> And so too in the days of Jeremiah we find that the Jews had turned away from the true fulfillment. However, these ancient Jews were not nearly as bad off as the modern man of our own post-Christian world. They turned to false gods, but at least they

---
699 Wolfe, 398.
700 Wolfe, 399.

still knew something was there. In a similar way the Greeks built their culture. Of course their gods were inadequate, so that, for example, Plato never found what to do with his absolutes because his gods weren't big enough, and the Greek writers didn't know what to do with the Fates because the gods were not great enough to always control them. But at least they knew something was there. It's only our foolish generation (and I am using "foolish" in the same sense it has in Romans 1) that lives in a universe which is purely material, everything being reduced to mass, energy, and motion. Thus we find that the Jews left the true God for false gods, just as the Greeks, the Romans, etc., had false gods, but they were not as far from the truth as our generation. Our generation has nobody home in the universe, nobody at all.[701]

Contemporary America is far from being a Christian nation, though it used to be, at least in a general sense. As noted earlier with the popular, Reformation-era Swiss proverb, "If you act like a sheep, you'll be eaten by a wolf," modern Christians often hold a nostalgic view of a *mass orthodoxy* among people of former "Christian nations" that rarely comports with reality. The notion that, through human effort, American Christians can "drive away the open mockery of God and to claim what is [theirs] in Christ"[702] is laughable. The truth is that there are far more people in the United States willing to fight a war *against* imposing a state-church, and all that comes with it, than *for* it.

Wolfe states that the founders' opposing positions on establishment of state religion "rely on standard positions in historic, classical Protestantism" and that the majority "affirmed some form of establishment at the colony-state level."[703] This is historically accurate, as many states instituted religious restrictions on public office well into the 19th century, unchallenged by the federal government. The 1778 Constitution of South

---

701 Francis A. Schaeffer, *Death in the City* (Wheaton, Ill: Crossway Books, 2002), 42–43.
702 Wolfe, *The Case for Christian Nationalism*, 352.
703 Wolfe, 400.

Carolina even made Protestantism the official state religion, which was not changed until after the civil war:

> That all persons and religious societies who acknowledge that there is one God, and a future state of rewards and punishments, and that God is publicly to be worshipped, shall be freely tolerated. The Christian Protestant religion shall be deemed, and is hereby constituted and declared to be, the established religion of this State. That all denominations of Christian Protestants in this State, demeaning themselves peaceably and faithfully, shall enjoy equal religious and civil privileges.[704]

In this chapter, I will give examples of how this allowance for discriminatory religious practices by states bred an environment of animosity, particularly between Protestants and Catholics, which led to multiple acts of religious violence (such as the aforementioned 1834 mob arson of the Ursuline convent) some of which turned murderous. The story of early "Protestant America" is anything but one of ubiquitous "prudence and resolve."

II. Puritan New England and Free Expression

> In every famous incident in which New England authorities "persecuted" dissenters – Roger Williams, Antinomians, Quakers, and Baptists – the authorities claimed to have good civil grounds to suppress the expression of dissenting religious belief… In their accounts of these events, New England authorities denied that they conducted persecution; rather, they suppressed those who (in their minds) disturbed the peace of the church and the state.[705]

"In their minds" is the operative phrase in this statement, for it was varying, subjective interpretations of Protestant Christian doctrine that led

---

704 "Constitution of South Carolina - March 19, 1778," Text (Washington, DC : Government Printing Office, 1909, December 18, 1998), https://avalon.law.yale.edu/18th_century/sc02.asp.
705 Wolfe, *The Case for Christian Nationalism*, 402–3.

to events that were either *justified suppression* or *unwarranted persecution*. Should a Presbyterian state-church be instated today, would the vocal protestations of Baptists be considered *disturbing the peace*? Wolfe references minister and theologian John Cotton's account of how "some" Antinomians and Baptists were allowed to attend state Congregationalist churches (while omitting what the conditions of this arrangement were), and how Presbyterians were allowed to have their own congregations. But Cotton's writings were in defense of the Massachusetts colony's expulsion of Roger Williams and other dissenters; he is far from an objective observer of the matter. What Wolfe *completely ignores* in this section is how *Catholics* were treated in colonial America. Here are some notable events:

- A law banning Jesuits entry into Massachusetts was passed in 1647, and the 1691 colonial charter of New England stated that "no Jesuit or spiritual or ecclesiastical person ordained by the authority of the Pope or See of Rome was allowed within the colony."[706]
- In both England and colonial America, those denounced as Catholics could have their property and entire estates confiscated.[707]
- In 1649, Maryland passed the Toleration Act, designed to protect the Catholics in the colony, which was specifically chartered under the Catholic Lord Baltimore, from the majority of Protestant settlers. The Protestants ultimately gained control of the legislature in 1654, expelled Baltimore from the colony, banned the mass, and passed a new act, which stated "none who profess to exercise the Popish religion, commonly known by the name of Roman Catholic religion, can be protected in this province." By the 1740s, Maryland law held that priests who evangelized were to be declared guilty of treason and made subject to the common penalties for that offense.[708]

---

706 Williams, *Shadow of the Pope*, 24, 26.
707 Williams, 14.
708 Williams, 26; Billington, *The Protestant Crusade,1800-1860*, 6, 11.

10. The Foundation of American Freedom

- In 1696 the New Hampshire legislature passed an order requiring all inhabitants to take an oath against the Pope and the doctrines of the Catholic religion.[709]
- When Georgia was first chartered, an inspector was appointed to make sure that no Catholics immigrated.[710]
- In the colonies, Guy Fawkes day was made Pope Day and an effigy of the Pope was commonly burned. This tradition lasted through the revolutionary era, and was publicly denounced by George Washington.[711]
- In Virginia, where the official church was Anglican, rumors that Catholics were allying themselves with natives "to cut the throats of the Protestants" resulted in the legislature passing a law preventing Catholics from settling in large groups. A law passed in 1641 required all priests to leave Virginia's borders on being warned by the governor.[712]
- In New York, Catholic Thomas Dongan was appointed governor by King James II. His policy of toleration attracted many Catholics seeking to escape persecution elsewhere, but caused resentment and alarm among Protestant settlers. When the king was deposed in the Glorious Revolution of 1688, New Yorkers seized the opportunity, removed Dongan, and replaced him with Jacob Leisler, who quickly outlawed Catholics from "places of trust" and ordered the arrest of "refuted Papists." A decade later, the colony required that all Catholics be disarmed under threat of imprisonment. In 1741, when a fort and several houses were burned down, a man suspected of being a priest was lynched.[713]

Wolfe next makes a case that religious strife in 17th-century New England was primarily the fault of credobaptists for not recognizing the infant baptism of their Congregationalist neighbors. There is a leap of logic required for this conclusion, namely the assumption of a *requirement* for an official state-church; the Puritans, in their desire to have a theocracy,

---
709 Billington, *The Protestant Crusade,1800-1860*, 9.
710 Billington, 10.
711 Williams, *Shadow of the Pope*, 36.
712 Billington, *The Protestant Crusade,1800-1860*, 7, 10.
713 Billington, 8, 14.

greatly contributed to the climate in which dissent over baptism could become an existential crisis. As professor of history and humanities at Boyce College Cory D. Higdon describes the political environment of colonial Massachusetts:

> The links between church and state exacerbated their political and social conditions. Controversy after controversy besieged the colony, pitting orthodox Christians against other orthodox Christians, which was complicated further by the power of magistrates to intervene in religious disputes. Political elections became doctrinal contests, and to the victor went the spoils. Even orthodox Christians found themselves banished, or worse. Moreover, within a generation, the colony had to alter its theology of baptism and eventually the Lord's Supper because second-generation colonists were not repenting or providing evidence of regeneration.[714]

Wolfe notes that these disputes "follow[ed] a familiar pattern" of disagreement over whether persecution or justified suppression had taken place. A quote by Samuel Willard used to bolster the paedobaptist side reveals an incongruity in Wolfe's framing, for Willard referred to his opposition as "Anabaptists," as did his compatriot, Increase Mather.[715]

Anabaptists were known throughout Europe for shunning civil government, believing that Christians could not serve as magistrates, swear oaths, or hold private property; they were regarded as having wrongly transferred the government of the *spiritual kingdom* into the *temporal*.[716] They were not well liked, to put it mildly. As previously mentioned, Calvin referred to them as "frantic and barbarous men... furiously endeavoring to overturn the order established by God."[717] This is not who the Massachusetts Baptists were – most formed their own similar civil

---

714 Cory D. Higdon, "No, You Don't Want a State Church," WORLD, June 15, 2023, https://wng.org/opinions/no-you-dont-want-a-state-church-1686830793.
715 Wolfe, *The Case for Christian Nationalism*, 406–7, 408.
716 Tuininga, *Calvin's Political Theology and the Public Engagement of the Church*, 170–71.
717 Calvin, *Institutes of the Christian Religion*, sec. 4.20.1.

10. The Foundation of American Freedom

governments where they resettled – but that Willard refers to them as such is telling of how he viewed them. Wolfe's use of two extended quotes from the paedobaptists in defense of their position, and only a single, highly edited quote from a credobaptist, limited to charges of "molestation," sans details, is emblematic of the one-sided perspective of this section.

> The Mathers had come to believe, as with much of New England apparently, that the Baptists were no longer (or never had been) a threat to New England civil and ecclesiastical order...
>
> We can conclude that it was not the Enlightenment, Lockean philosophy or Baptist theological arguments that convinced Cotton and Increase Mather that a pan-Protestant political order was possible;[718]

We are presented with no evidence that "Baptist theological arguments" had no effect in convincing Cotton and Increase Mather that Baptists could live in peace with Congregationalists. In fact, it seems highly unlikely that Baptists' self-defense of their theological positions would play no part in the Mathers' change in stance on their Baptist neighbors over several decades. Wolfe's surety is pure conjecture. We can also unequivocally say that Enlightenment, Lockean philosophy had a notable effect on the American nation's founding, roughly six decades later.

Wolfe also confirms that his "pan-Protestant political order" would likely include "forbid[ding] 'papists' and atheists,"[719] which I have argued would be nearly impossible to achieve without committing atrocity. Likewise, the Massachusetts colony did not reach its Protestant peace without committing atrocity, for in 1692, one-third of Salem's six hundred residents were accused of witchcraft and nineteen executed. Increase Mather's book *An Essay for the Recording of Illustrious Providences* is considered by some historians to have helped contribute to the hysteria, although Mather himself was instrumental in ending the witch trials.[720]

---

718 Wolfe, *The Case for Christian Nationalism*, 411.
719 Wolfe, 410–11.

III. Religious Liberty in the Founding Era

Wolfe begins this section with the sweeping statement that "The founders were unanimous in the belief that religion is necessary for civic morals and public happiness."[721] This is a highly reductionist and dubious framing; one of the most influential founders, especially in the realm of civil law, Thomas Jefferson, was an outspoken materialist who outright rejected Christ as presented in Scripture as well as Protestantism's core tenets of *Sola Fide* and *Sola Gratia*. In an 1820 letter to William Short, the former American ambassador to Spain (and his former private secretary), in which he enclosed a syllabus on the *Philosophy of Jesus*, he wrote:

> But while this Syllabus is meant to place the character of Jesus in it's true and high light, as no imposter himself, but a great Reformer of the Hebrew code of religion, it is not to be understood that I am with him in all his doctrines. I am a Materialist; he takes the side of spiritualism: he preaches the efficacy of repentance towards forgiveness of sin, I require a counterpoise of good works to redeem it Etc. Etc. it is the innocence of his character, the purity & sublimity of his moral precepts, the eloquence of his inculcations, the beauty of the apologues in which he conveys them, that I so much admire; sometimes indeed needing indulgence to Eastern hyperbolism. my eulogies too may be founded on a postulate which all may not be ready to grant. among the sayings & discourses imputed to him by his biographers, I find many passages of fine imagination, correct morality, and of the most lovely benevolence: and others again of so much ignorance, so much absurdity, so much untruth, charlatanism, and imposture, as to pronounce it impossible that such contradictions should have proceeded from the same being. I separate therefore the gold from the dross; restore to him the former, & leave the latter to the stupidity of some, and roguery of others of his disciples. of this band of dupes and impostors, Paul was the great Coryphaeus, and first corrupter of the doctrines of Jesus. these palpable

---

720 "Increase Mather | Biography, Sermons, & Salem | Britannica," August 19, 2022, https://www.britannica.com/biography/Increase-Mather.
721 Wolfe, *The Case for Christian Nationalism*, 412.

interpolations and falsifications of his doctrines led me to try to sift them apart. I found the work obvious and easy, and that his part composed the most beautiful morsel of morality which has been given to us by man. the Syllabus is therefore of his doctrines, not all of mine. I read them as I do those of other ancient and modern moralists, with a mixture of approbation and dissent.[722]

This type of questionable framing from Wolfe continues in the next subsection on the political thought of John Witherspoon, the only active clergyman to sign the Declaration of Independence. He provides selective quotes from Witherspoon and then attempts to frame them through his previous statements on "prudence." The problem is that the quotes, even when highly edited, read far more like an endorsement for a modern Baptist view of *liberty of conscience* than for even a prudent *theocratic Caesarism*. For example, he quotes Witherspoon:

> [We] ought in general to guard against persecution on a religion account as much as possible because such as hold absurd tenets are seldom dangerous. Perhaps they are never dangerous, but when they are oppressed. Papists are tolerated in Holland without danger to liberty.[723]

He then writes, "Witherspoon has not denied that civil governments can, in principle, withhold toleration from subversive sects. Rather, he denies that withholding toleration is effective, since subversion is often its consequence."[724] Yet Wolfe has previously set the limit of his toleration at publicly expressed heretical thought that "cause[s] public harm, both to the body and the soul," and has stated that "the civil government must ensure that truth is taught and that harmful false teaching is restrained."[725] Let us compare this with the sentences in Witherspoon's lecture leading up to the portion that Wolfe selectively quoted:

---

722 Thomas Jefferson, "Letter to William Short, 13 April 1820" (University of Virginia Press, n.d.), http://founders.archives.gov/documents/Jefferson/03-15-02-0505.
723 Wolfe, *The Case for Christian Nationalism*, 416.
724 Wolfe, 416.
725 Wolfe, 31, 357.

> It is commonly said, however, that in case any sect holds tenets subversive of society, and **inconsistent with the rights of others**, that they ought not to be tolerated. On this footing Popery is not tolerated in Great Britain; because they profess entire subjection to a foreign power, the fee of Rome; and therefore **must be in opposition to the proper interest of their own state**; and because **violence or persecution for religion is a part of their religion**, which **makes their prosperity threaten ruin to others**, as well as the principle imputed to them, which they deny, That **faith is not to be kept with heretics**. But, **however just this may be in a way of reasoning**, we ought in general to guard against persecution on a religious account as much as possible because such as hold absurd tenets are seldom dangerous. Perhaps they are never dangerous, but when they are oppressed. Papists are tolerated in Holland, without danger to liberty. **And though not properly tolerated**, they are now connived at in Britain. (emphasis mine)[726]

In the full paragraph, Witherspoon states that it is not inaccurate to believe that Catholics meet *all of the qualifications* Wolfe sets for a heretical group to be of damage to the *body and soul* of the citizens of a Protestant nation; but Witherspoon then affirms that nations should "guard against persecution" of these heretical groups "as much as possible" because they are usually not dangerous *until they are actively suppressed*. In essence, he makes the case that restricting a vocal religious minority, in the ways proposed by Wolfe in chapter 9, leads to inter-religious violence. Half a century after his death, Witherspoon's theory would be proven correct in two murderous riots between Protestants and Catholics in the city of Philadelphia.

As with most larger Northern cities, the Industrial Revolution had brought an influx of immigrant labor to Philadelphia, mostly Irish, who

---

726 John Witherspoon, *The Works of John Witherspoon: Containing Essays, Sermons, &c., on Important Subjects ... Together with His Lectures on Moral Philosophy Eloquence and Divinity, His Speeches in the American Congress, and Many Other Valuable Pieces, Never Before Published in This Country* (J. Ogle, 1815), 120.

settled into culturally homogeneous suburbs. By 1844, tensions between the Irish and "natives" had reached a boiling point, at one point breaking out into an open-air mob brawl during the spring elections.[727] At this time, American "No-Popery" was at its height; the bestselling book *The Awful Disclosures of Maria Monk*, published in 1835, told an entirely fabricated tale of concubine nuns, locked away in convents and forced to watch as the offspring of their forced liaisons with priests were baptized, murdered and thrown into a pit in the basement immediately after birth.[728] After the book's release, Monk's claims were disproved; multiple men, including one of her staunchest supporters, Colonel W.L. Stone, toured the convent in Montreal at the center of her stories, and all returned reporting that the building and its occupants were wholly different than her descriptions.[729] By 1838, she had moved to Philadelphia with a male traveling companion and gave birth to her second child out of wedlock (the first she claimed to have been fathered by a priest), and most of her supporters abandoned her. Despite this, her book continued to be exceedingly popular among anti-Catholic Nativists, including Philadelphia's American Protestant Association. The book retained its popularity and was regularly cited as factual by influential anti-Catholic lecturers in the South as late as the 1910s.[730]

Until quite recently, American Protestants were overwhelmingly in favor of public education. A key factor in this stance was that the Bible was taught and prayer practiced in most public schools well into the 20th century. Many, if not most, American *Catholics* did not share that sentiment, because the Bible used was the King James Version and, through it, Protestant theology was both implicitly and explicitly taught. This was the case in Philadelphia, causing the city's bishop, Francis Kenrick, to petition the Board of Controllers of the public schools in 1842

---

727 Billington, *The Protestant Crusade,1800-1860*, 220.
728 Maria Monk, *Awful Disclosures of Maria Monk and the Startling Mysteries of a Convent Exposed!* (Philadelphia: T.B. Peterson, 1850), 129–30, https://archive.org/details/in.ernet.dli.2015.68174.
729 Billington, *The Protestant Crusade,1800-1860*, 221; Williams, *Shadow of the Pope*, 71.
730 Barnes, *Anti-Catholicism in Arkansas*, 21, 27.

to have Catholic children be taught with a version of the Bible selected by their parents and to allow them to be excused from other religious instruction. The board assented to the request, to the great consternation of the American Protestant Association and other Nativists. Billington writes of their response:

> Pamphleteers and the local religious press were unrestrained in their condemnation of the Controllers' action and demanded that Protestants throw every obstacle in the path of Catholics who sought to introduce un-Christian education. "The interference of foreign prelates," wrote one author, "and of a foreign ecclesiastical power, should perish at our threshold. Let a grave be sunk, then, over which even the great Papal hierarch himself cannot step." This challenge was accepted without question by a large part of the population. When a school board member of the [Irish Catholic] suburb of Kensington tried to stop Bible reading in a local school, a mass meeting was held to demand his resignation. A similar public gathering was staged in Independence Square, Philadelphia, on March 11, 1844, where a large audience heard speeches against Catholicism and resolved:
>
>> That the present crisis demands that without distinction of party, sect, or profession, every man who loves his country, his Bible, and his God, is bound by all lawful and honorable means to resist every attempt to banish the Bible from our public institutions.[731]

Though Bishop Kenrick attempted to cool the situation by writing a second letter to the Controllers confirming that he did not wish to banish the Bible, but only allow Catholic children to use their own version, tensions continued to mount. It is not surprising that the Nativists would not take the bishop at his word, for national news was made two years prior when a priest in New York burned King James Bibles handed to Catholics by Protestant Bible societies, often fronts for Nativist organizations.[732]

---

731 Billington, *The Protestant Crusade,1800-1860*, 221–22.
732 Amanda Beyer-Purvis, "The Philadelphia Bible Riots of 1844: Contest Over the Rights of Citizens," *Pennsylvania History: A Journal of Mid-Atlantic Studies* 83,

10. The Foundation of American Freedom

On the morning of May 6, the local Nativist paper, the *Native American*, printed that a meeting of "American Republicans" would be held in the heart of Kensington that afternoon. Billington notes that this "would naturally attract rowdies from the lower classes." Several thousand Nativists showed up to the corner of Master and Second streets and marched towards their meeting place of the Market House. As they were beginning to enter, shots rang out and one of the marchers, George Shiffler, was mortally wounded. As they carried the dying man into the building, a mob of Irish broke through and forced the Nativists to retreat.[733] The next day, the *Native American* compared the violence to the 1572 massacre of Huguenot Protestants in Paris:

> Another St. Barthomomew's day is begun on the streets of Philadelphia. The bloody hand of the Pope has stretched itself forth to our destruction. We now call on our fellow-citizens, who regard free institutions, whether they be native or adopted, to arm. Our liberties are now to be fought for; – let us not be slack in our preparations.[734]

After meeting at the State House yard and adopting a resolution that charged Catholics with attempting to remove the Bible from schools, a Nativist mob marched back into Kensington and began damaging homes. They were confronted by an equally riotous and armed mob of Irish Catholics and a full-scale conflict broke out; by nightfall, over thirty Irish homes were burned to the ground. The next day, the mob had grown to such ferocity that entire blocks of homes were set ablaze, and the militia, which had ended the fighting the night before, was powerless to stop the resumed violence. Much like black business owners in Los Angeles did during in the 1992 riots, Protestants placed signs on their doors declaring that they were "Native Americans" in the hope of saving their property from the torch.[735]

---

no. 3 (2016): 366–93, https://doi.org/10.5325/pennhistory.83.3.0366.
733 Billington, *The Protestant Crusade,1800-1860*, 221–22.
734 Billington, 225.
735 Billington, 225.

Next, the Nativist mob set their sights on Saint Michael's church, for rumor had it that arms were stored within. After finding no weapons, but setting the church ablaze anyway, they moved to Saint Augustine's church with similar intent. The mayor, who instead of rushing to the scene at the outset had been busy celebrating his daughter's birthday, made it to Saint Augustine's just in time to address the mob. He told them that the building had no arms and that he had the key, but this only assured the mob that they were free to break in. Having been given word that the militia would not intervene, they burned down that church, as well. Approximately fourteen people were killed during the course of the riot.[736]

The mob was so extreme in its actions that even the *Native American* wrote, "No terms that we can use are able to express the deep reprobation that we feel for this iniquitous proceeding; this wanton and uncalled for desecration of the Christian altar." Though the majority of violence ceased after several days, smaller groups continued to destroy Catholic property and the bishop, fearing violence, closed churches that Sunday. What peace there was to be had was short lived. On July 4, Nativists organized a procession of carriages containing the widows and children of those on their side who had been killed; seventy thousand people escorted them through the streets of Philadelphia. The reinvigoration of emotions resulted in a second riot, the next day.[737]

Rumor was that weapons were now being stored in the Church of Saint Philip de Neri in the suburb of Southwark; the sheriff arrived before the mob, who demanded an investigation. This time, the rumor was true, and over eighty guns and a supply of ammunition were found, but the investigators kept this knowledge to themselves and dispersed the crowd. News leaked the next morning, and a multi-day standoff, with several breakout skirmishes, took place over the next few days. At one point, the mob procured a cannon and fired it at the Irish militiamen guarding the door of the church. By the time peace was restored, at least thirteen people

---

736 Billington, 226; Beyer-Purvis, "The Philadelphia Bible Riots of 1844," 366–67.
737 Billington, *The Protestant Crusade,1800-1860*, 226–27.

10. The Foundation of American Freedom

had been killed and over fifty wounded.[738] There was little self-reflection and no accountability for the violence. As Billington writes:

> Although Philadelphia publicly mourned its dead and openly deplored its period of carnage, many even among the more substantial citizens were secretly exultant. Quaker merchants, who spoke indignantly of the outrage in public, returned to their shops to express the sincere belief that "the Papists deserve all this and much more," and, "It were well if every Popish church in the world were leveled with the ground." Official inquiries reflected this same spirit of intolerance. A city investigating committee laid the blame for the riots entirely on the Irish who had broken up a peaceful procession of American citizens.[739]

Catholics are no longer a religious minority in the United States; in fact, they far outnumber the members of any single Protestant denomination and are only slightly exceeded in number by the broad category of "Evangelical Protestant." But roughly one out of every one hundred and forty Americans are Hindu, nearly one out of a hundred are Muslim, and one out of sixty-two are Mormon.[740] These people are not going away, and, as with the Irish Catholics of Kensington, they would likely not accept their Protestant neighbors forcing their religion onto their children, let alone a whole system of "theocratic Caesarism." Even Wolfe's most "tolerant" and "prudent" version of Christian Nationalism would almost assuredly result in tensions boiling over as they did in Philadelphia in 1844.

Wolfe points to the 1780 Constitution of Massachusetts as an "example of both full toleration and establishment," but, as was previously shown with the arrest of Father Cheverus (the future Bishop of Boston) in 1800 for nothing more than marrying a Catholic couple[741], "toleration" was strictly limited to Protestants. This anti-Catholic attitude lasted through the

---

738 Billington, 228–29; Williams, *Shadow of the Pope*, 76.
739 Billington, *The Protestant Crusade,1800-1860*, 230.
740 "Religious Landscape Study."
741 See chapter 1, *Perfecting the Nation*, section I., *The Christian Nation*.

first half of the 19th century in Massachusetts and often resulted in mob violence; as late as 1854, a Catholic church in Dorchester was dynamited by Protestant Nativists.[742] In these cases, Protestants were the ones violating what Wolfe calls the "common elements" of religious law put forth by "pro-establishment voices":

> ... (1) the necessity of organized religion for public happiness and civil order, (2) the effectiveness of religious establishment to provide religious instruction throughout society, (3) a provision stating that toleration is condition on peaceful assembly and support for the civil government, and (4) that civil government should suppress violation of natural religion, such as blasphemy and impiety, and prevent one sect from harming another.[743]

Rarely were these principles, in the law of Massachusetts or elsewhere, applied towards perpetrators of Nativist violence, let alone the incendiary rhetoric that encouraged it. Often it was bombastic, anti-Catholic *Protestant ministers*, such as the main instigator of the Ursuline convent arson of 1834, Lymann Beecher, who violated the conditions of peaceful assembly and prevention of "one sect from harming another."[744] Wolfe's statement that "inner beliefs accompany or produce *outer* or external expressions... As such, they can clash or conflict with others' activities"[745] is an easily abused principle – those who once riled mobs into riotous action against "Papists who owe no allegiance but to Rome," based their convictions on similar notions. Wolfe's regular use of this premise is a reminder that non-Protestants, let alone non-Christians, would be forced to keep their heads down and their mouths shut under his government, lest they be considered a threat to "public happiness" and/or "public safety" and face state-sponsored violent suppression. This is again made clear in his criticism of James Madison's *Memorial and Remonstrance against Religious Assessments*.

---

742 Williams, *Shadow of the Pope*, 84.
743 Wolfe, *The Case for Christian Nationalism*, 418.
744 Williams, *Shadow of the Pope*, 65.
745 Wolfe, *The Case for Christian Nationalism*, 421.

10. The Foundation of American Freedom

> ... Madison writes that "[r]eligion then of every man must be left to the conviction and conscience of every man, and it is the right of every man to exercise it as these may dictate... It is [an] unalienable [right] because the opinions of men... cannot follow the dictates of other men."... He then says that legislatures lack "jurisdiction" over religious belief, having "limited" authority. But, without logical justification, Madison extends the restriction of civil jurisdiction over the inner man to the outward man. In so doing, he not only fails to make the crucial and classical inward/outward distinction, but he is also led into a practical absurdity: that people have a right to outwardly express all inward religious beliefs, even when they are publicly harmful.[746]

As he has done multiple times before, Wolfe very selectively quotes Madison, failing to address passages from *Memorial and Remonstrance* that make convincing counterarguments to his preferred form of theocratic government. Here are some of those very pertinent rebukes from Madison, which speak to the *public harm* of state-enforced religion:

> True it is, that no other rule exists, by which any question which may divide a Society, can be ultimately determined, but the will of the majority; but it is also true that the majority may trespass on the rights of the minority...
>
> The preservation of a free Government requires not merely, that the metes and bounds which separate each department of power be invariably maintained; but more especially that neither of them be suffered to overleap the great Barrier which defends the rights of the people. The Rulers who are guilty of such an encroachment, exceed the commission from which they derive their authority, and are Tyrants. The People who submit to it are governed by laws made neither by themselves nor by an authority derived from them, and are slaves...
>
> Who does not see that the same authority which can establish Christianity, in exclusion of all other Religions, may establish with

---

746 Wolfe, 422–23.

> the same ease any particular sect of Christians, in exclusion of all other Sects? that the same authority which can force a citizen to contribute three pence only of his property for the support of any one establishment, may force him to conform to any other establishment in all cases whatsoever?...
>
> Because experience witnesseth that ecclesiastical establishments, instead of maintaining the purity and efficacy of Religion, have had a contrary operation. During almost fifteen centuries has the legal establishment of Christianity been on trial. What have been its fruits? More or less in all places, pride and indolence in the Clergy, ignorance and servility in the laity, in both, superstition, bigotry and persecution...
>
> Compare the number of those who have as yet received [the light of Christianity] with the number still remaining under the dominion of false Religions; and how small is the former! Does the policy of the Bill tend to lessen the disproportion? No; it at once discourages those who are strangers to the light of revelation from coming into the Region of it; and countenances by example the nations who continue in darkness, in shutting out those who might convey it to them.[747]

Wolfe's limited defense against Madison's *Memorial* is an appeal to tradition and genetic logical fallacy; he states that Madison does not adhere to the "classical inward/outward distinction," as if *classical* is automatically *better*. He also writes, "Mark Hall states that he 'could find no record of any civic leader being influenced by, or appealing to, Madison's *Memorial* prior to the ratification of the Bill of Rights [in 1939].'"[748] This argument is unbelievably fallacious, because the man who wrote most of the Bill of Rights and who is most credited with its passing is *James Madison*. It was written and passed by Congress four years after the *Memorial and Remonstrance,* and first ratified two years later; clearly

---

747 James Madison, "Amendment I (Religion): James Madison, Memorial and Remonstrance against Religious Assessments," June 20, 1785, https://press-pubs.uchicago.edu/founders/documents/amendI_religions43.html.

748 Wolfe, *The Case for Christian Nationalism,* 424.

10. The Foundation of American Freedom

Madison's views on religious liberty played an integral role in the first ten amendments to the Constitution and, consequentially, had a significant effect on common views regarding the proper limits of government power in the new American republic.

Wolfe relies almost exclusively upon Mark David Hall's *Did America Have a Christian Founding?* to make his argument that Madison was not as integral to the drafting of the First Amendment as most historians claim.[749] Though Hall, in the selected quotes, does not mention George Washington, Wolfe references him twice in this chapter as someone who disagreed with Madison "on the role of government in religion." Washington's religious beliefs are a subject of great debate among historians. Wolfe evokes him as an endorser of church establishment, but his personal practice was less than exemplary; though he attended Anglican churches, he was never confirmed. One can technically champion the establishment of a state religion while not devoutly practicing that religion, but, as with Jefferson, Washington's personal practice again brings into question Wolfe's claim of the founders' supposed *unanimity* regarding the role of religion in society. Joseph Waligore notes that Englishmen and Americans "who ridiculed Christianity often went to church because it was their social duty,"[750] suggesting the founders likely held an assortment of beliefs that are not easily compartmentalized. He writes of Washington:

> Until his early forties, he went to church on average only once a month. The other three Sundays of the month, he transacted business, visited relatives, traveled, or even went fox hunting. When he was in the public eye right before and during the Revolutionary War, his church attendance increased to two to three times a month. When he was president, and very much in the public eye, he attended church almost every Sunday. After he resigned the presidency and returned to Mount Vernon, he went back to going to church only once a month…

---

749 Wolfe, 425–26.
750 Joseph Waligore, *The Spirituality of the English and American Deists: How God Became Good* (Rowman & Littlefield, 2023), 174.

> Washington's habit of not taking communion when he was president was very much noted by his congregation and the church's assistant minister, D. James Abercrombie. Instead of partaking in communion, Washington would leave the church early... Abercrombie then lamented during one mass about "the unhappy tendency of the example of those dignified by age and position turning their backs upon the celebration of the Lord's Supper." Washington knew this remark was aimed at him, but rather than taking communion, he stopped going to church on days when communion was given. Abercrombie later said about Washington's refusal to take communion: "I cannot consider any man as a real Christian who uniformly disregards an ordinance so solemnly enjoined by the divine Author of our holy religion, and considered as a channel of divine grace."[751]

Wolfe is correct in his assertion that the First Amendment was meant to only curtail the establishment of religion on the federal level, and that multiple members of Congress supported establishment at the state level. But their reasons for prohibiting a federal endorsement of Protestant Christianity were the same as Madison's convictions at the state level, namely "the same authority which can establish Christianity, in exclusion of all other Religions, may establish with the same ease any particular sect of Christians," and a governmental authority that has such power ultimately has the power to force the citizenry "to conform to any other establishment in all cases whatsoever." Citing political scientist Vincent Phillip Muñoz, Wolfe affirms that Anti-Federalists feared "the new Congress would impose one form of church-state relations throughout the nation."[752]

Even if one concedes that a near-homogeneity of religious belief in some states allowed for peaceful establishment at that level – though the history of inter-religious violence in the 19th century brings that into question – there is no place in the *modern* United States that would meet this criteria. This is why Wolfe's theory requires a call for revolution and continued violent suppression of religious dissent, because there is no other practical way to form a geological boundary of religious homogeneity. The

---

751 Waligore, 173, 174.
752 Wolfe, *The Case for Christian Nationalism*, 426–27.

concerns around federal establishment in the 18th century have become hyper-local concerns in our time, unless one resolves to force his agnostic neighbors from their land and mass banish them at the end of a gun.

> We should not overemphasize the "founding" of the American founding, as if every consideration used to construct the federal government is generally applicable, reflecting some universal arrangement for *all* governments. In other words, despite the fact that the Constitution lacks Christian language, we cannot forget that the American people in the founding era and early American republic were Protestant Christians, animated by religious concerns, who viewed themselves as a Christian people and relied on Protestant principles and biblical argumentation.[753]

While this statement is correct on the surface level, there is no such thing as a national self-conception devoid of *some negative effects*. Wolfe has failed, at every point in this chapter, to give even passing mention to a downside, opting to paint 17th and 18th-century American Protestant views of civil government in a wholly positive light. This does not hold up to scrutiny; many colonists who settled the region of New England were members of Protestant sects who left their home country to escape persecution from other Protestants, yet they mostly formed governments that emulated the one they left, but for *their* sect of Protestantism being made the established church.

IV. Conclusion

The notion that the United States is, or has previously been, a "Christian nation" is a longstanding belief in American Evangelicalism, and has much truth to it. The overwhelming majority of Americans during the Revolutionary era identified as Protestant Christians and, even today, slightly over half self-identify as Christian (though that does not mean what it used to). Be that as it may, the rose-tinted view of a bygone age of a great, peaceful, Protestant America is nostalgic at best, and downright historically illiterate at worst.

---

753 Wolfe, 429.

Anti-Catholicism reached its pinnacle in New England in the 1850s, with the rise of the Know Nothing party, which swept the 1854 elections for the Massachusetts legislature on their promise to defend Protestantism against the rise of Catholicism in the Commonwealth and beyond. Known for their belligerent behavior towards all who opposed them, the Massachusetts Know Nothings committed one of their more notorious actions the following year. After passing a bill allowing a select committee to inspect all manner of Catholic institutions (on the premise that they were secret dens of evil), a committee of seven, plus an unofficial thirteen more, trounced through Holy Cross college in Worcester, harassing students and nuns while they turned the building over, looking for evidence of debauchery and vice. Though they found nothing, the group afterwards threw themselves a party, complete with a prostitute for entertainment, and charged the entire affair to the state.[754]

At that time, mob violence against Catholics was still not an uncommon occurrence throughout the nation and was not limited to attacks on church infrastructure. Williams describes how a Papal nuncio, who was making a tour of the United States before heading to his post in South America, was received in Cincinnati, Ohio:

> On Christmas Day, 1853, an attempt was made on the life of [Archbishop] Bedini by a mob six hundred strong who marched upon the Bishop Purcell residence where he was staying, 'armed with clubs, swords, knives, and pistols and carrying torches with which they meant to set fire to the cathedral and ropes with which they intended to hang the Nuncio.' The police, having been apprised of the criminal purpose of the demonstration, rushed upon the mob, and arrested some fifty of the rioters. A number of shots were fired and numerous persons wounded.[755]

After the quick national demise of the Know Nothings in the mid-1850s, anti-Catholicism retreated to its previous residence in various Nativist "Protestant associations," but it would see a sharp resurgence in

---

754 Billington, *The Protestant Crusade,1800-1860*, 414–15.
755 Williams, *Shadow of the Pope*, 82–83.

the early-20th century, particularly in the South and Midwest; by the 1920s anti-Catholic activism was led by the Ku Klux Klan, most active in those regions. The sparse remaining records of the second era of that secretive organization show that not only were Protestant ministers active participants, but they were often high-ranking leaders. From one of the few surviving Klan membership lists, it is known that the rolls of Klan No. 108 of Monticello, Arkansas contained thirteen Protestant ministers, and its Exalted Cyclops was the pastor of the town's Methodist Church.[756] The first imperial commander of the Women of the Ku Klux Klan, Lula Markwell, was previously president and treasurer of the Women's Christian Temperance Union in Arkansas for twenty years.[757] Otis Spurgeon, who made a name for himself nationwide as a particularly vitriolic anti-Catholic lecturer and debater – he was once driven outside of Denver, beaten, and left naked by members of the Knights of Columbus after a speech – was pastor of First Baptist Church in Poplar Bluff, Missouri, until he resigned to be the Exalted Cyclops of Missouri Klan No. 48.[758]

In 1928, when Catholic Democrat Al Smith ran for president, the Southern Baptist Convention passed a resolution against voting Catholics into public office.[759] The Missionary Baptist Association in Arkansas adopted a more strongly worded resolution, which stated, "We recommend that the members of the Churches of this Association, the pastors and the missionaries use their utmost influence as citizens against the political encroachments of the Papacy... And in order to preserve our religious and civil liberties let us preach, pray, teach and work against our common enemy at all times and places."[760] From behind the pulpit, many pastors attacked Smith for his religion, including head of the Anti-Smith Democrats, Bishop James Cannon, Jr. of the Methodist Episcopal Church, South, and avowed Klan member Reverend C.C. Crawford of Fourth Christian Church in St. Louis. Reverend Dr. M.F. Ham, pastor of First Baptist Church of Oklahoma City, said from behind the pulpit, "If you vote

---

756 Barnes, *Anti-Catholicism in Arkansas*, 94.
757 Barnes, 123.
758 Barnes, 50, 171.
759 Barnes, 141; Williams, *Shadow of the Pope*, 195.
760 Barnes, *Anti-Catholicism in Arkansas*, 166.

for Al Smith you're voting against Christ and you'll all be damned." On August 30, 1928, the *Western Recorder*, published by the Baptist State Board of Missions for Kentucky, reprinted an article from the Arkansas Baptist State Convention's fiercely anti-Catholic paper, the *Baptist Advance*, entitled A Roman Catholic Throne in the White House. Earlier that year, the *Baptist Advance* ran an article from Dr. Selsus Estol Tull, pastor of First Baptist Church of Pine Bluff, Arkansas, in which he wrote, "It is impossible for Catholicism to synchronize with American ideals. Every Catholic owes his first allegiance to the Pope. He therefore can not become a true American."[761]

During the presidential election of 1960, when Democrats successfully ran Catholic John F. Kennedy, the SBC again passed a resolution against voting for Catholics. W.O. Vaught Jr., then Vice President of the SBC and later Bill Clinton's pastor while he was Governor of Arkansas, officially opposed Kennedy from behind the pulpit, declaring Catholicism and communism to be the two most deadly threats to freedom in the world.[762]

There has never been a time in the four-century history of America where a state church was established *and* religious minorities were treated equitably by the majority. Even after the states revoked or effectively ignored their established religions, fervent anti-Catholic animosity remained a strong force in the nation. At its height in the 1920s, the Klan had five million members, nearly one out of every ten adult American men.[763] We are the same fallen people they were. Should a group of Christians, led by a call to violently "drive away the open mockery of God and to claim what is [theirs] in Christ" and "unashamedly and confidently assert Christian supremacy over the land,"[764] actually achieve their goals, it is difficult to believe that those who do not adhere to the tenets of Christianity, or even to official national doctrine, would be treated with the

---

761 Williams, *Shadow of the Pope*, 193–94, 196–97, 200, 208; Barnes, *Anti-Catholicism in Arkansas*, 140.
762 Barnes, *Anti-Catholicism in Arkansas*, 181, 182.
763 US Census Bureau, "1920 Census: Volume 3. Population, Composition and Characteristics of the Population by States," Census.gov, 1920, https://www.census.gov/library/publications/1922/dec/vol-03-population.html.
764 Wolfe, *The Case for Christian Nationalism*, 241, 352.

full dignity that should be afforded all human beings, made in the image of God.

Epilogue: Now What?

Introduction

Having finished the explication of his authoritarian- and ethnonationalist political theory, attempting to frame it as a modern day recovery of *Two-Kingdoms Theology* and *Puritan theocracy*, Wolfe closes his book with a manifesto on the state of America and the next steps he believes are required of those who have been convinced of his worldview. His language becomes looser and more bombastic in this chapter; Wolfe will name the "globalist American empire," run by a "gynocracy," as the primary foil of Christian Nationalism. For those not convinced of his theory, this chapter will read as fairly *wild-eyed*, while, for those who are bought in, it will be a rallying cry delivered in the *language of destiny*.

> But this book is not an action-plan. It is a justification of Christian nationalism, and we are early in recovering the movement. Every movement needs its intellectuals, pamphleteers, strategists, organizers, and foot soldiers. This book belongs in the first category, and perhaps in the future I can contribute in other ways. Let each have his role.[765]

Wolfe conspicuously identifies himself as an *intellectual force* in the burgeoning Christian Nationalist movement; most movements like the one he is looking to spearhead begin with books of philosophy or political theory that are dismissed as *fringe* by mainstream thought leaders. In 1917, Giovanni Gentile was a professor of history and philosophy at the University of Rome, whose writings claiming fascism as the inevitable endpoint of the national unification of Italy, known as the Risorgimento (resurgence), were considered fringe by many Italian politicians and intellectuals. Five years later, he was Benito Mussolini's Minister of Public Education, inculcating fascism into the curricula of an entire generation of his countrymen. His later writings for the party would become "one of the

---

[765] Wolfe, 433–34.

most important and publicised ideological rationalisations of the Fascist phenomenon."[766]

Though the way Wolfe addresses his concerns in this chapter may come across to moderates as hyperbolic, it should not be flippantly dismissed. A growing number of young American men are becoming frustrated with a society that values them less than it did their fathers and grandfathers, and which increasingly utilizes economic pressure to maintain ideological conformity. It is common for discontented young men to externalize their angst and to seek out philosophies that offer a sense of belonging and meaning; Wolfe's offer is attractive to many disillusioned, young Christian men of *Western European descent*.

I. The New America

> The Christian nationalist project is not "conservative." Post-WWII conservatism is inadequate for our situation. I have no interest in conserving the liberalism of the 1980s or 1990s or the militaristic adventure-imperialism of the "compassionate" conservatives of the 2000s… [O]ur institutions are not only captured by the left; they have become fundamentally oriented against us. The conservative cannot fathom this. He is an institution man, the sort who lined up against Donald Trump to "protect the institutions."[767]

I must agree with Wolfe about the "adventure-imperialism" of George W. Bush and his associates – how can I not, having been sent halfway around the world to kill people over a lie about weapons of mass destruction? Our institutions most certainly are captured by a bureaucracy that overwhelmingly leans left, and the organs of the state are increasingly turned against those who would question its authority; one need only look at how the vaccine-hesitant were treated in 2021 to see how far the state is willing to go to enforce compliance. But Wolfe's "conservative" is not the average self-identifying *American conservative;* it is the small number of beltway insiders and their champions in legacy media who do not want to

---
766 Morgan, *Italian Fascism*, 79.
767 Wolfe, *The Case for Christian Nationalism*, 434.

rock the boat of the military-industrial complex for fear of losing meal-tickets, perks, and kickbacks. The average center-right American is as fed up with Washington as Wolfe is, but painting the entirety of the center-right as tools of the state is a common, politically expedient talking point of authoritarian rightists. Primo de Rivera who, like Wolfe, sought to replace his dysfunctional liberal democratic government with an authoritarian state, also made the *regime conservative* his ideological scapegoat:

> How often have you heard men of the Right say: "We live in a new age, we must set up a strong state, we must harmonize capital and labor, we have to seek a corporative form of existence? I assure you that none of all that means a thing, it is all mere windbaggery... So that when they talk of harmonizing capital and labor, what is meant is to go on nourishing an insignificant privileged minority upon the exertions of all..."[768]

The truth is that, despite the self-serving machinations of the political class, the day-to-day life of most Americans is very much worth conserving; we still have our *life, liberty,* and *property*. We are still allowed to worship God as we please and publicly associate with whomever we want without fear of civil repercussions, something that Wolfe would want to rescind. We are free to choose our education and professions. Can our Christian brothers and sisters in nations like China and Iran say the same? We face serious societal challenges, but the notion that the average American is under a dire threat that requires the abandonment of "conservatism" for radical action is simply not true. We still very much have recourse within the constitutional system, and there is no *Christian* justification for abandoning that approach until it has been fully cut off.

> Thus, we are past the time of "conservative principles." People conserve what they know and love. How can you love institutions that hate you? Why would you want to "conserve" them? The

---

[768] Greger, *Jose Antonio Primo de Rivera*, 112.

solution is renewal, not conservation. What we need is the *instauratio magna*, the Great Renewal.[769]

The word *renewal* is a highly inaccurate euphemism, because what Wolfe actually advocates for is the *violent overthrow* of these institutions, a secession from the United States, and the instantiation of a new nation governed by *theocratic Caesarism*. Those who would be caught on the other side of his proposed actions would see this more as *retrogradation* and *persecution* than *renewal*. He is not praying for a loving God to move His Spirit and begin a Third Great Awakening; he is calling for angry men to start an American *Risorgimento*.

> Thus, the narrative of America as embodied in our institutions today is relentlessly hostile to Old America. That means that New America is relentlessly hostile toward *you*. Every step is overcoming *you*. Ask yourself, "What sort of villain does each event of progress have in common?" The straight white male. That is the chief out-group of New America, the embodiment of regression and oppression.[770]

This is true; the New America is relentlessly hostile to the average white male Christian. *So what?* "For what have I to do with judging outsiders?" (1 Corinthians 5:12) If you are active in your local church, and your church family shares your values, how much of your daily life is actually altered by this hostility? Do you *have to* consume mainstream media? Do you *have to* buy products from companies that promote values antithetical to yours? Do you *have to* participate in public celebrations of worldviews hostile to orthodox Christianity? When we have brothers and sisters around the world dying for the faith, is *your* faith in Christ so weak that you are more willing to get violent than to peacefully lose a job?

Perhaps the only area in which our nation's descent into postmodernism persistently breaks through the insulation of Christian community is public schools. But if there is any call-to-action to be made to Christian men in a

---
769 Wolfe, *The Case for Christian Nationalism*, 435.
770 Wolfe, 436.

Epilogue: Now What?

post-Christian nation, it is to make the necessary sacrifices to allow for your children to be raised within, and instructed in accordance with, Christian values. Most American Christian families, if they accepted downsizing to a more modest lifestyle, or returned to the pre-WWII norm of multi-generational homes, could afford to either homeschool, co-op, or send their children to a private Christian school. What stops many of them – and what drives much of Wolfe's own angst over not possessing the supposed "complete good" – is worship of *personal peace* and *affluence*. What prevents most American Christians from attaining their idealized lifestyle is not the "New America," but their own idolatry. How weak is the "faith" of men willing to kill others in a religious revolution before first attempting every personal sacrifice available?

It is worth recounting that, in chapter 3, Wolfe wrote that "Most leftwing social movements exploit Western universality and Western guilt, leveraging the bizarre tendency of Western man to out-group himself."[771] Before writing *The Case for Christian Nationalism*, he put this same sentiment in an explicitly white context, in his review of Jake Meador's book, writing, "Meador – a white male – can 'prove' his assertions only by out-grouping himself and by speaking ill of his civilization."[772] Here, again, we see that Wolfe's concern is not the betterment of a generic "Western Man," but of *white men*. This chapter's rallying cry is specifically directed at his "Western European male audience,"[773] and its proclamations should be viewed as yet another affirmation that, despite the obfuscation, his "ethnicity" is more genetic than cultural.

> The conservative's patriotic history is also fundamentally a story of progress. It goes something like this: The US was founded on principles of equality, freedom and individual rights, though we didn't live up to them. But a promise was made by them, and over time through civil war, labor struggles, immigration, fighting fascists, more immigration, more noble foreign wars, civil rights

---

771 Wolfe, 170.
772 Wolfe, "An Unhelpful Review of "What Are Christians For?"
773 Wolfe, *The Case for Christian Nationalism*, 119.

for blacks, gay rights, more immigration, and so on it was finally realized.[774]

Wolfe, like all Protestant Nativists before him, believes that immigrants are the primary threat to the peace and stability of his homeland, so much so that he mentions them three times in one sentence. This sentiment resonates with a large portion of Americans; two out of five respondents to a 2022 survey on the condition of American society strongly agreed with the statement that, "in America, native-born white people are being replaced by immigrants."[775] It is important to make a distinction between those who want to curtail illegal immigration and those who want to prevent nearly anyone from legally immigrating, but the latter camp, to which Wolfe assuredly belongs, is far larger than most Americans realize.

Wolfe commits yet another genetic logical fallacy by framing *progress* as fundamentally bad (or good, in his opposition's view). The Civil War ended chattel slavery, 20th-century labor struggles curtailed child labor, fighting fascists ended the Holocaust, and civil rights are a legal recognition of the imago Dei. There are legitimate directions in which conservative Christians may not want to see their nations progress, but the work of the Holy Spirit in your life as a believer results in a *progressive sanctification* that should, more and more, cause you to "do justice, and to love kindness, and to walk humbly with your God" (Micah 6:8). In postmillennial and amillennial eschatologies, and even somewhat in the premillennial, the natural result of the Great Commission should be a *progressive* growth of these qualities in the world. Wolfe would have us deny our brothers and sisters in Christ access to a society of justice and mercy if they are not of the *preferred ethnicity*.

> But what was the reward for your blood, sweat, and tears? To be called "racists" by the Squad, to be denounced as the source of all bad social outcomes, and to be passed over by the incompetent and

---

774 Wolfe, 436.
775 Wintemute et al., "Views of American Democracy and Society and Support for Political Violence."

Epilogue: Now What?

> neurotic. You fought the fascists abroad and then at home only became the fascists of the New America.[776]

Wolfe's complaints about the current state of conservative American men are effeminate and childish. *Our* generation did not fight fascists abroad, we were born into the most peaceful and materially wealthy nation the earth has ever seen. We entered the world an entire generation, or more, after our grandparents and great-grandparents put their lives on the line to stop the last group of authoritarians who attempted to order their nations around "a common *volksgeist*."[777] Sacrificing "blood, sweat, and tears" while being reviled by secularists and pagans is exactly what we are called to do as Christians (Matthew 5:11, Luke 6:22, 1 Peter 2:21-23). It is unbecoming of Christian men to whine about such a state of affairs; we are to embrace the joy we have in Christ and literally bless those who curse us, so much so they they would be put to shame for their slander (Romans 12:14, Titus 2:7-8). This is the exact opposite of the actions Wolfe advocates for.

> To be a good American – committed to one's national story – one has to be progressively inclusive. This rhetoric has worked time and time again, and it will work again.[778]

What takes more bravery, to revile and threaten those who would have you affirm beliefs counter to the Law of God or to stand firm and say, "I will not do what you say, nor will I hurt you"? Wolfe is correct that the military has been ideologically captured; I will advise my children against enlisting, because it is true that they would be sent to fight endless wars for the monetary gain of a bureaucracy that shuns traditional mores. Patriotic young Americans are indeed being "duped into fighting for causes that harm them."[779] But the Christian answer to our countrymen being persuaded by *progressive rhetoric* is to boldly proclaim the gospel, not to

---

776 Wolfe, *The Case for Christian Nationalism*, 347.
777 Wolfe, 139.
778 Wolfe, 438.
779 Wolfe, 438.

throw a collective tantrum. "For the weapons of our warfare are not of the flesh but have divine power to destroy strongholds" (2 Corinthians 10:4).

> You fight the fascists abroad only to be called a fascist at home. You fight Communists far from home to be spit on by Communists at home. It is invade the world, invite the world.[780]

Wolfe next delivers a lengthy, vitriolic diatribe on the new "American way of life," in which you, the conservative American, are *oh so good*, while those on the other side are *oh so bad*. He must be reminded of the core, Christian principles that "Christ Jesus came into the world to save sinners, of whom I am the foremost" (1 Timothy 1:15), and that "you, the judge, practice the very same things" (Romans 2:1). A man whose political theory is centered around using violent revolution to invert his nation from one that recognizes the inalienable rights of the individual to a "redundant web of obligation that orders everything ultimately to the national good"[781] has no room to complain about being "called a fascist at home," for that is the textbook definition of *fascism*.

> Those who oppose the [globalist American empire] will be will be deemed "right-wing extremists" and marked for elimination. When it is too late, however, Ukrainians of the older sort – after waking from a drunken slumber induced by GAE consumption – will learn that they chose not a new identity but a sort of liberal soft occupation…
>
> America is just as much under the GAE as countries like Ukraine.[782]

Wolfe paints the forces of globalization, which in reality are far too international to be labeled an "American empire," as a nearly-unstoppable leviathan. There is much to be concerned about the *soft-totalitarianism* that has swept across the West in the last decade. There is hardly anyone who

---

780 Wolfe, 439.
781 Wolfe, 13.
782 Wolfe, 441.

does not, to some degree, self-censor out of fear of economic repercussions should they be seen as expressing ideas contrary to the three centuries of conclusions derived from Jean-Jacques Rousseau's statement that man is *naturally good*. There is a real threat from the left, just as there was a real communist threat in Italy in the early 1920s and Spain in the 1930s. But, like Gentile and Primo de Rivera, Wolfe would have you believe that the solution to repressive leftism is an *equally repressive rightism*. This is the *false dichotomy of the authoritarian proposition*. Thankfully, Christians are not governed by the dictates of worldly politics, but by the commandments of Scripture. Again, through what has perhaps become the Scriptural theme of this anti-Christian Nationalist rebuttal, Paul give us a clear direction for how to react to ideological belligerence, from either side:

> And the Lord's servant must not be quarrelsome but kind to everyone, able to teach, patiently enduring evil, correcting his opponents with gentleness. God may perhaps grant them repentance leading to a knowledge of the truth, and they may come to their senses and escape from the snare of the devil, after being captured by him to do his will. (2 Timothy 2:24-26)

The "liberal internationalists" that Wolfe names as the enemy are essentially no different than the enemy of early-20th-century rightist authoritarians, the "international banker," which often took on a Jewish stereotype. He further delves into a paranoiac variant of this worldview when he writes, "The fact that they look and sound like us does not mean they are of us."[783] This is the same thing most die-hard communists would tell others about "capitalists," or a cult leader about "suppressive persons."

> Why are large corporations, the entertainment media, academic institutions, educational institutions, social media companies, and other powerful entities so interested in sexualizing and injecting gender questioning among kids five to eight years old?...

---

783 Wolfe, 442.

They want child warriors. Kids with gender confusion is to the GAE what a child with an AK-47 is to third-world warlords. They fight their battles and lose their souls, but they also pledge life-long loyalty.[784]

It is absolutely true that the recent injection of Queer Theory into elementary education is an attempt at ideological subversion, though most who push it are not *cynically* looking to indoctrinate children, as Wolfe alludes to. Our nation is polarized on nearly every front, but none more so than the ultimate Rousseauian endpoint, complete and utter sexual liberation. Over several generations, our universities – and hence our most educated citizens – have been convinced of the *sexual revolution* of Wilhelm Reich, the *utopia of Eros* of Herbert Marcuse, and the *purposeful transgression* of Michel Foucault. This includes those among the world's most wealthy who, along with sexual liberation, push their own transhumanist agenda in search of immortality through technology. All around us, our fellow human beings are futilely attempting to achieve an escape velocity from the *death* and *despair* that are a result of the fall. Using the French philosopher Albert Camus, Schaeffer expertly explained both the humanist's despair and the Christian response; it is worth quoting him at length.

> Consider further Camus in *The Plague*. Nothing is better for understanding modern man's dilemma. Modern man asks, "Where does justice come from? How can I move?" Camus says, "You can't. You're really damned." The more you feel the tension of injustices, the more your damnation as modern man and the modern rationalist increases... And poor Camus died with this dilemma upon him. He never solved it.
>
> In contrast, of course, you have the magnificent account in the Bible. Jesus Christ who is God and claims to be God in the full Trinitarian sense stands in front of the tomb of Lazarus. As he stands in front of the tomb, he is angry. The Greek makes that plain. As Jesus stands there in his anger, we may notice something.

---

784 Wolfe, 442.

Epilogue: Now What?

> The Christ who claims to be God can be angry at the result of the Fall and the abnormal event which he now faces *without being angry at himself.*
>
> It is titanic. Suddenly I can fight the injustice knowing I am not fighting what is good. It is not true that what is is right. I can fight injustice knowing there is a reason to fight injustice. Because God does not love everything, because he has a character, I can fight injustice without fighting God.[785]

Jesus wept for the death of Lazarus, who was a sinful man, just as we are (John 11:35). The Christian can be angry about the results of the fall without damning those fully mired in its results, even when they are attempting to indoctrinate our children into a Marcusian worldview. We have been purposefully given the example of forgiving those who would go as far as to murder us (Luke 23:34, Acts 7:59-60), therefore we have no moral excuse to respond differently. We can use our still functioning system to advocate for Christian values, most especially the protection of children, without hating our opposition. If you truly *love your neighbor as you love yourself*, you will be far more concerned with exhibiting and sharing the love of Christ, as an example to your enemy, than you will be with actively suppressing his hatred of God.

> Facebook and Instagram explicitly allowed calls for violence against Russians on their platforms.
>
> Any promising Christian nationalist movement would face the same degree of opposition. The GAE will see no difference between Putin's Russia and any Christian nationalist movement. To them, we're like the Taliban of the West.[786]

Why would Wolfe dedicate an entire chapter to justifying violent revolution, yet take umbrage with the notion that his GAE opposition

---

[785] Francis A. Schaeffer, *The Church at the End of the 20th Century* (Downers Grove, Ill: Inter-Varsity Press, 1970), 24.
[786] Wolfe, *The Case for Christian Nationalism*, 444.

would frame American Christian Nationalism in the same light as Russia or the Taliban? What other response would be expected towards a movement that openly seeks to upend the constitutional system via civil war? He goes on, writing, "Christians [sic] nationalists threaten liberalism; they see us as regressive and authoritarian." As has been proven, Wolfe's Christian Nationalism does not only *appear* authoritarian (and not only to liberals), its core tenets are genuinely inline with rightist authoritarian political theory of the early 20th century. One cannot argue for execution of individuals for publicly expressed wrongthink without giving the appearance of being *regressive and authoritarian*.

With zero self-awareness, Wolfe next evokes the "Two Minutes Hate" from George Orwell's 1984, likening it to pro-Ukraine propaganda, somehow missing the fact that he has spent the last six pages building his own Emmanuel Goldstein of the *globalist American Empire*.

> The bulk of late-modern Western man sits on his couch watching Fox News or CNN (it doesn't matter which) enmeshed in the Breaking News, as if watching the latest Marvel movie…
>
> It is only a matter of time before Christian nationalists become the villains in the next imagined reality, and our fellow believers, who are just as enmeshed in this world as their secularist neighbors, will join in the Two Minute Hate. But let us remain free in mind, be the true liberals. The mind is its own place.[787]

The truth is that very few Americans are aware that a "Reformed" Christian Nationalist political theory exists. What little coverage the mainstream media gives "Christian Nationalism" is focused on the Donald Trump supporting non-denominational movement led by people like former General Michael Flynn and Sean Feucht, a former worship leader at the highly charismatic and prosperity gospel-preaching Bethel Church. Perhaps the most mainstream secular outlet to take serious notice of Wolfe's book is *Reason*. In contrast to those from pastors and theologians, Paul Matzko's review for the outlet spent little time on doctrinal claims of

---

787 Wolfe, 446.

prelapsarian earth and focused more on how those claims feed an authoritarian and ethno-nationalist political theory:

> ... Wolfe has composed a segregationist political theology. If ethnic differences are the natural order of things and if the natural order is good, he reasons, then those differences should dictate the bounds of an ethnically homogenous Christian nation. Wolfe denies that he is making a white nationalist argument, partly on the grounds that he has nonwhite friends and partly because "the designation 'white' is tactically unuseful." But black friends or not, if you wanted to inject a sacralized white supremacy into the conservative mainstream, this book would be a primer on dog whistling past that particular graveyard.[788]

Matzko was so struck by the ethno-nationalism in Wolfe's theory that he wrote a separate, supplemental blog post on his personal Substack, entitled *A (White) Wolfe in Sheep's Clothing*.[789] In it he reveals that the quotation of Sam Francis, which opens the first chapter of *The Case for Christian Nationalism*, is from an article published by VDARE, a website dedicated to anti-immigration policy and particularly known for its regular publication of articles by avowed white nationalists. Matzko correctly concludes, "At this point, Wolfe's sheepskin is so threadbare as to be a disguise for only the most gullible sheep in the herd."

Whatever mainstream attention this particular variant of self-described *Christian Nationalism* receives, it would be hard to mischaracterize it, because it genuinely lives up to the fears of the most dedicated MSNBC watcher. Wolfe's public utterances, such as, "White evangelicals are the lone bulwark against moral insanity in America,"[790] a statement so rife with ethnocentrism that his publisher felt compelled to publicly denounce it,[791]

---

788 Paul Matzko, "Beware the 'Christian Prince,'" *Reason.Com* (blog), May 13, 2023, https://reason.com/2023/05/13/beware-the-christian-prince/.

789 Paul Matzko, "A (White) Wolfe in Sheep's Clothing," Substack newsletter, *Matzko Minute* (blog), May 16, 2023, https://matzko.substack.com/p/a-white-wolfe-in-sheeps-clothing.

790 https://twitter.com/PerfInjust/status/1647931701773860865

791 Canon Press: "To be clear, this is dumb." https://twitter.com/canonpress/status/1648067653645516800

meets all the parameters of "White Christian Nationalism," a moniker increasingly pushed by the liberal-wing of anti-Christian Nationalist authors. Again, anyone who calls for violent revolution in America to instate an ethnically homogeneous, theocratic monarchy has no room to complain about being portrayed as an extremist.

> Some political theorists fear that modern liberalism, by pathologizing any way of life besides the last man, offers no outlet for what Francis Fukuyama called "megalothymia" - viz., striving for superiority, the passion for a higher life.[792]

It is incredible that Wolfe would write two whole subsections about man's desire for a purposeful life without once mentioning the only *true* life available through Christ Jesus. This exposes the rot at the heart of his theory – nobody can properly take the commandment "If anyone would come after me, let him deny himself and take up his cross daily and follow me" (Luke 9:23) *figuratively* until he is has first accepted it *literally*. Through the course of his book, it has become obvious that Wolfe is far more concerned with his earthly well-being than his heavenly treasure, and seeks to convince other disaffected men to do the same at the cost of genuine, focused dedication to Christ. The Christian nationalist call-to-action does not speak of Christ's "Greater love has no one than this, that someone lay down his life for his friends" (John 15:13); it instead attempts to Christianize George Patton's "No dumb bastard ever won a war by going out and dying for his country. He won it by making some other dumb bastard die for his country."

II. Gynocracy

> We live under a gynocracy – a rule by women. This may not be apparent on the surface, since men still run many things. But the

---

792 Wolfe, *The Case for Christian Nationalism*, 441.

governing virtues of America are feminine vices, associated with certain feminine virtues, such as empathy, fairness, and equality.[793]

God's qualities include empathy, fairness, and equality, all of which we men are instructed to heavily promote. Here are verses from Scripture proving that these are qualities men are to proactively work into their behavior:

Empathy
For because he himself has suffered when tempted, he is able to help those who are being tempted. (Hebrews 2:18)

Bear one another's burdens, and so fulfill the law of Christ. (Galatians 6:2)

Fairness
To know wisdom and instruction, to understand words of insight, to receive instruction in wise dealing, in righteousness, justice, and equity; (Proverbs 1:2-3)

Masters, treat your bondservants justly and fairly, knowing that you also have a Master in heaven. (Colossians 4:1)

Equality
There is neither Jew nor Greek, there is neither slave nor free, there is no male and female, for you are all one in Christ Jesus. (Galatians 3:28)

The rich and the poor meet together; the Lord is the Maker of them all. (Proverbs 22:2)

Wolfe attempts to make the case that "men can succeed only if they are effeminate or female-adjacent," because the *gynocracy*[794] has now subjected society to "credentialism... risk-aversion, and strict rules of

---

793 Stephen Wolfe, "Classical Reformed Theonomy," The London Lyceum, July 4, 2022, 448, https://www.thelondonlyceum.com/classical-reformed-theonomy/.
794 Taken from Aristotle and Calvin's *gunaikokratia*, the government of women.

conduct that disincentivize masculine, competitive expression."[795] I have some sympathy for him when it comes to this; in order to attain a PhD in political theory he has spent a significant portion of his life in academia, which, more than any other institution, has been feminized. It is likely very difficult for him to find meaningful work in his field of study without capitulating to a leftist worldview that is as equally belligerent as his own. It is perhaps near impossible after publishing his book.

But the average American male, though he is subjected to marketing and propaganda made by people funneled through the higher-education system, is not *forced* to become effeminate in order to succeed. He is only forced to alter his behavior if he wishes to succeed in fields that have become primarily led by women – just as a woman has always been forced to alter *her* behavior to succeed in fields dominated by men. The last thing that anyone who spent five minutes with me would accuse me of is being effeminate – I can be a hard-nosed male to a fault – yet I have built a successful career and have worked for multiple household name companies in the software field, an industry that Wolfe assuredly associates with the *gynocracy*. That is not to say I have not seen a significant increase in left-wing activism being normalized in the space, but I know many masculine conservative Christians who continue to succeed in white-collar careers.

> But the feminine natural instinct for third-party power makes women prone, especially when having institutional power, to subject *everything* to rules and credentials that equalize the sexes and even favor women. Thus, feminized spaces tend to subject all actions to procedure and process, and all grievance, no matter how slight, is delivered to the authorities whose job it is to act on the grievance.[796]

Wolfe fails at a root-cause analysis of the issue at hand, for bureaucracies that enforce ideological orthodoxy existed far before third-wave feminism and women's liberation. There were already a myriad of taboo opinions within bureaucratic spaces well before a majority of women

---

795 Wolfe, *The Case for Christian Nationalism*, 448.
796 Wolfe, 449.

participated in the workforce. What he sees as the "gynocracy" is the effect of women joining *existing bureaucracies* and, over time, adding new, more feminine orthodoxies to enforce, along with new sub-bureaucracies to do the enforcing. Though he incorrectly targets women as the sole cause, he is correct that much of current society "pathologizes masculinity"; it does not, however, make "'successful' men essentially panderers to women and subjected to processes that hinder their ability to succeed in ways most natural to men."[797] This was already a factor in the cubicle-laden world of white-collar corporate work decades ago, and there has always been a difference in the type of male personality that leads to success in the C-Suite versus the construction site.

Therein lies the irony of this subsection, for the persistent complaining about an ubiquitous, oppressive force keeping men from "succeeding" unless they emasculate themselves is the very type of argument Wolfe would categorize as *feminine hyperbole*, should it be pushed by his opposition. Flipping Wolfe's perspective to the stereotype of an angry feminist ranting about the *patriarchy* leaves the spirit of the message intact. I have yet to meet a single man exhibiting *healthy Biblical masculinity* that has been held back in his life, on account of that masculinity. I would suggest Wolfe worry about his own public behavior, and the atrocious things he advocates for, before he complains about *society* holding him back.

It is true that "Feminine empathy is good in itself, but its virtues arise only when constrained,"[798] but this true of all virtues, regardless of whether one classifies them as masculine or feminine. We are again presented with naked irony because the case can be easily made that Wolfe's own worldview is one of unrestrained virtues gone awry; can that not describe a philosophy that takes "masculine virtues" so far that the relationship between husband and wife is compared to a restaurateur and his chef employee?[799]

---

797 Wolfe, 450.
798 Wolfe, 450.
799 Wolfe, 312.

> Take the bizarre celebration of obesity today. It makes little sense apart from unconstrained feminine empathy. Or what about hoards of mainly single, able bodied men from patriarchal nations who have migrated to Western borders? The West lets them all in and then has to conceal the spike in sexual assaults, and women will only quietly acknowledge their fear of going out in public…
>
> The most insane and damaging sociological trends of our modern society are female-driven.[800]

In classic authoritarian fashion, Wolfe takes a hard-line framing of social issues that the average citizen may be concerned about and names an *enemy* driving the social ill. Imagine someone criticizing COVID policies of 2020 through 2022, but instead of directly naming the specific bureaucracies responsible they claimed that these wrongs were *scientist-driven*. Was COVID policy not also *politician-driven* and *corporate-driven*? Was it not also fueled by *existential dread* within the general populace? Likewise, there are multiple factors, both direct and indirect, in the issues he names. As with the GAE, Wolfe is again hypocritically engaging in his own *Two Minutes Hate*, this time towards women.

Wolfe next writes of a flamboyantly gay officer, lauded by his female compatriots, but despised by straight males, writing, "If the formation were exclusively male and they were not constrained by higher administration, the men would find ways to rid themselves of this officer."[801] I was in a male-only occupational specialty before *Don't Ask, Don't Tell* was repealed, but I can affirm that most soldiers have the same contempt for those who have a chip on their shoulder about their own masculinity and who overcompensate with aggressive, stereotypical "masculine" behavior. These men often fall into the category of a *Blue Falcon*, someone who undercuts others to his own advantage. Wolfe will next accuse women of regularly doing this in professional settings.

---

800 Wolfe, 450–51.
801 Wolfe, 451.

> But many men hesitate to fully integrate women in high-level discourse, because they suspect that inclusion will heavily gender the discourse... The fear is that women will take disagreement personally and frame the disagreement as an oppressor silencing the oppressed.[802]

It must be noted that, based upon his resume, Wolfe has never worked in the private corporate sector; since leaving the Army, he has spent his time exclusively in academia. Therefore, because he presents no evidence to substantiate this claim, it must be considered highly subjective and biased, perhaps even completely made up; this section reads more like a description of online, activist, or cable news discourse than everyday interactions in the real world. I have spent over fifteen years in the white-collar corporate space and have a considerable amount of experience with executive meetings run by both men and women. In all that time, I have only seen one woman, a mid-level employee with no subordinates, play the "oppressed" card; she got nowhere with the complaint because it had no merit. I have never seen a female executive even remotely suggest she was currently held back by her male colleagues – the notion would be ridiculous for the multiple VP- and C-level women I have worked under. I also have never heard a male manager or executive complain about female managers or executives in this manner. In my experience, "high-level discourse" in the upper echelons of American companies, beyond the trappings of the idolatry of career, has a very healthy, egalitarian nature.

Wolfe ends the section with a call to build a society ruled by masculinity, but what he offers is not masculine at all, it is a *beta-male's imaginary ideal of a proto-masculine order*. Women are not adversaries to be conquered and contained, they are fully human and of equal worth as men. A truly *complementarian* masculinity allows women to offer *their* complimentary talents to any sphere, whether the home, the workforce, or government. Scripture restricts the specific office of church overseer to men (1 Timothy 3:1-7), but it takes no issue with female leadership in broader society (Acts 16:14-15). Ultimately, Wolfe's argument against the

---

802 Wolfe, 452.

"gynocracy" is one of weakness, because he must believe that his own innate masculine ability is not strong enough to succeed in female-led systems.

III. Universalism

> We often have to act against our psychological inclinations; we have to run from cognitive comforts and from the embrace of modern society; we have to retrain the mind by the strength of will. We might *feel*, for example that it is wrong for public space to be exclusively Christian, but it still ought to be. Remember that most of our spiritual forefathers had the opposite feeling. We must overcome ourselves.[803]

Wolfe's theory is meant to be a *Christian* nationalism and, more so, *Reformed* Christian nationalism. In all of his discourse on the need to overcome our "psychological inclinations" towards what we feel is wrong, there is not a single mention of the work of the Holy Spirit in the believer's heart and mind; there is no mention of prayer; there is no mention of testing one's ideas against Scripture; there is no mention of the discipleship and discipline of elder Christians. In essence, there is no actual *Christian practice*, only a Christianized Nietzschean "will to power."

> In every case, the manner [evangelicals] go about addressing some topic is determined by ruling-class sentiment towards that topic. This is true even when we address fellow Christians. Thus, "good faith" discussions between Christians about same-sex attraction look very different from the unequivocal denunciation of anything with a semblance of "kinism".[804]

One need only look at "Christian Twitter" in June to know the claim that evangelicals overwhelmingly have "good faith" discussions about same-sex attraction and transgenderism is demonstrably false. Secondly,

---

803 Wolfe, 455.
804 Wolfe, 456.

there is a key distinction between interacting with someone who is engaged in self-destructive behavior and someone whose destructiveness is aimed at others. There is a difference between the way the average evangelical interacts with someone who sees themselves as transgender versus someone who argues that parents who do not "affirm their transgender child" should lose custody, just as there is a difference between how someone engages a suicidal person versus someone arguing for euthanasia of the mentally ill. At its base level, "kinism," which is Christian insider-lingo for the very type of ethno-nationalism Wolfe promotes in his book,[805] seeks to label ethnically different human beings *the other*, and should be countered accordingly.

> Christians must overcome a psycho-rhetorical hurdle and affirm the dangerous thought that their political vision has no room for the secularist elite... Free yourselves from their enslavement... There is no credibility we can establish with them. Unavoidably, we are threats to their regime.[806]

Genuine Christians are a threat to no one; only the good news of Jesus Christ is a "threat" to the secular world. As shown in chapter 8, a Christian Nationalist movement poses no serious ideological or physical risk to the American establishment; the lack of mainstream coverage of anything other than January 6 rioters and MAGA grifters as "Christian Nationalists" proves that. What Wolfe's movement is a threat to is *conservative Churches*. While our Christian thought-leaders spend the vast majority of their time decrying *wokeism*, a movement that nearly every conservative Christian rejects before it walks in the door of their church, many Christians afraid of the shifting cultural landscape are turning towards the prospect of authoritarian measures. Now is the time to address this burgeoning threat, while its particulars are still being debated by its proponents; it will be much more difficult to counter should the American

---

805 Wolfe's podcast co-host, Thomas Achord, who was revealed to have had anonymous, white nationalist Twitter and Facebook accounts, co-authored a kinist book, entitled *Who Is My Neighbor?: An Anthology In Natural Relations*.
806 Wolfe, *The Case for Christian Nationalism*, 456.

political situation continue to devolve and conservative Christians become more desperate to retain *personal peace* and *affluence*.

> You denounce this; you disclaim that; you distance yourself from [insert the uncouth]; you love your country, but you're not a fascist; you disagree with homosexuality, but you're not a homophobe; you're patriotic but recognize our "checkered" national history; you're not woke, but "God hates racism"… Okay, we get it. You're not a baddie.[807]

Let us break down these juxtapositions, some of which are quite odd:

- *You love your country, but you're not a fascist*: Who but the most bought-in MAGA Republicans, the kind that antagonistically wear the red hat into spaces where they know it may not be welcome, have been called a *fascist* simply for expressing their fondness for America? Perhaps some in overwhelmingly leftist cities, like Portland or San Francisco, have been unfairly called a fascist for being overtly patriotic, but this is a wholly foreign experience in most of the United States.
- *You disagree with homosexuality, but you're not a homophobe*: If you disagree with homosexuality so much that you're unwilling to be around homosexuals without perpetually deriding or preaching to them, then they rightfully take issue with your behavior. I have seen this situation play out multiple times, where a Christian has a particular discomfort with homosexuality or transgederism that sucks the air out of a room and makes everyone uncomfortable. If you genuinely care about exuding the love of Christ, you will not shy away from friendly associations with any unbeliever, even if their behavior disconcerts you, within reason (1 Corinthians 5:9-10). You will take care to let people know that your convictions do not render them unwelcome, and this will be reflected in your public and private words.
- *You're patriotic but recognize our "checkered" history*: Wolfe recognizes the checkered history of "adventure-imperialism" that killed

---

807 Wolfe, 457.

up to one million Iraqis, so what issue does he take here? The most likely conclusion is that the type of "checkered" history he wishes to overlook are subjects like slavery, race relations, and the treatment of Native Americans. This issue could not be more falsely pushed into a binary; are there any other aspects of American history that require more mature, nuanced discussion, and where deliberate dismissal is a good sign that someone harbors ethnic prejudice?

- *You're not woke, but "God hates racism"*: The only people who will accuse you of being woke for opposing racism are *people pushing racist beliefs*. This one is an outlier, because the other three are supposed accusations from the left. Here Wolfe overplays his hand and reveals that rightists like him play the same dialectical games as leftists.

Wolfe affirms the Hegelian dialectic[808] is in being used, when he writes, "We're playing a rhetorical game, one that is rigged against us. Don't play the game."[809] But his solution, a purposeful leaning into combative rhetoric, is an incredibly stupid move when faced with an unfair dialectical *thesis*; it is playing right into your opposition's hands, because you are only offering an extreme *antithesis*. You must openly acknowledge that the other person is posing a thesis and *refuse synthesis*. This works both with leftists and rightists who play dialectical games, including Wolfe. For example, on June 23, 2023, he tweeted:

> A type of antifascism is the true faith of the conservative. They genuinely believe all sorts of anti-socialist things. But they deeply *feel* their rejection of [right-wing] ideas. They drop everything by habit to eradicate them, and their confident, emotional denunciation is euphoric.[810]

---

808 Put simply, the dialectic is the process by which one party poses a *thesis*, another counters with an *antithesis*, and the two eventually compromise with *synthesis*. This is often abused by people who deliberately push an exaggerated political thesis, much in the same way people "anchor high" in business, starting with a deliberately high price with the goal of forcing the other party to believe they are negotiating down to a fair deal, when they are actually agreeing to the full price.
809 Wolfe, *The Case for Christian Nationalism*, 457.
810 https://twitter.com/PerfInjust/status/1672241397745823745

I could, as Wolfe warns against, attempt to disprove his thesis by claiming that I am a "real conservative" who equally hates communism, but this would only weaken my own position. I could do as he suggests and ignore his statement and lean into my hatred of fascism (which is considerable), but that would only confirm his thesis. Instead the answer is to acknowledge that Wolfe is playing the exact same dialectical game he decries from the left. This correctly frames *his* statement as deliberate exaggeration, and allows me to next "walk away from the table" by stating the truth that I will not have synthesis with such a person.

> The Western mind has a universalizing tendency. The root of this tendency seems to be our emphasis on the human over the ethnic. Try to imagine how you would view the world if you had no comprehension of the concept "human", no universalizing concept of man. One ethnicity to another would be as dogs are to cats.[811]

The only reviewer I have found that mentioned this statement is Neil Shenvi, who quoted it, with only the clarification that Wolfe "definitely affirms that there is only one human species," during his live-tweeting while reading Wolfe's book.[812] I am not shocked that Wolfe wrote it, but I am amazed that so few theologians and Christian journalists who had supposedly read his book and wrote about it failed to mention, let alone condemn, the many plain-as-day, traditional ethno-nationalist arguments in it. It was six months after the release of the book, after Christian news organizations had mostly forgotten about it, that Reason, a secular outlet, finally published an article covering what is in plain sight.[813] This does not give me much confidence in American Christian intelligentsia.[814]

---

811 Wolfe, *The Case for Christian Nationalism*, 457.
812 https://twitter.com/NeilShenvi/status/1593617235037212677
813 Matzko, "Beware the 'Christian Prince.'"
814 Once notable exception is G3 Ministries' Virgil Walker, who wrote an article in April 2023, entitled *The Dangerous Intersection of Christian Nationalism and Ethnocentrism*, https://g3min.org/the-dangerous-intersection-of-christian-nationalism-and-ethnocentrism/.

Epilogue: Now What?

In Deh Rahwood, Afghanistan, I had extensive opportunities to work directly with locals who did daily work around our forward operating base. These were the exact type of tribal people whom Wolfe claims are irreconcilably different from us; they had never been exposed to "Western" values, they had no choice but to be Muslim, and they viewed themselves not as Afghans, but as members of one of several local clans. I spent extended time with different subgroups of these people, everyone from a group of young boys who did odd jobs around our forward operating base (one of whom suffered from a rapid-aging condition), to old men still able to work construction projects. Two of my favorites were a six-and-a-half-foot tall, muscle-bound gentle giant with a gloriously long beard whom we called Taliban Ted, and our hardworking and honest foreman, Lalam – *scorpion* in the local dialect, given for the tattoo of one on his forearm. Beyond the language barrier when we didn't have an interpreter around, my interactions with these people were no different than with anyone else. During down time we would take meals together and discuss all manner of things, through the interpreter. At no point did I ever get the sense that, at an innate and irreconcilable level, these men were any different than me.

Wolfe is partially correct in that there are aspects of Afghan tribal culture that *are* irreconcilable with Christian culture, most notably bacha bazi (*boy play*), the practice of feminizing and prostituting young boys, which was socially acceptable and popular among some of the men. At multiple bases, I had to make it clear up front that the early-teenage boys who worked there were off limits and several times had to very forcefully remind them when one would touch or try to kiss a boy; none of the men who did not practice bacha bazi were interested in stopping the others.

Every Western Christian has ancestors who engaged in equally abhorrent cultural practices. Even God's chosen people turned from him and sacrificed their children to the Baals (Jeremiah 19:4-5). In the non-Christian worldview, these evils can be seen as irredeemable cultural sins, and a case for societal sequestration can perhaps be made, but this is exactly the type of sin the heart-change of the Holy Spirit rectifies in believers. To purposefully exclude other Christians on the basis of ethnicity, as Wolfe argues for, is to deny the Holy Spirit's ability to bring the universal church of Jesus Christ together in holy communion. Those who focus on "Western ethnicities" may desire to "view the world more through an ethnic frame,"[815] but the Christian is *commanded* to view the world through the frame of the sacrificial love of Jesus Christ (1 Corinthians 11:1, 1 John 2:4-6, Ephesians 5:1-2). You cannot view the world through this frame, *you cannot imitate Christ*, if you insist on treating other ethnicities, most especially *Christians* of other ethnicities, as *the other*.

IV. Dominion

> The chief end of men is not protecting women... But the man is given the mission from God and the woman is made his helper, and his mission is not directed at the woman but outside himself – to the world. The woman is an object of protection because she is integral to the mission, not because she is the mission or the chief agent of that mission.[816]

The chief end of men is *to glorify God and enjoy Him forever*.[817] This does not depend on Wolfe's worldly, self-centered definition of *taking dominion*, to "inscribe one's will into a piece of dirt, to stand at its boundaries and with resolve say mine to both fellow man and the world."[818] Peter emphatically instructs us, "But let none of you suffer as a murderer or a thief or an evildoer or as a meddler. Yet if anyone suffers as a Christian, let him not be ashamed, but let him glorify God in that name" (1 Peter 4:15-16). Wolfe would have us banish proselytizers of false religion and usurp their property, and even potentially kill them; he would have us upend our God ordained liberal democracy by waging violent religious

---

815 Wolfe, *The Case for Christian Nationalism*, 459.
816 Wolfe, 459.
817 *The Westminster Confession of Faith and Catechisms*, WSC Q. 1.
818 Wolfe, *The Case for Christian Nationalism*, 462.

Epilogue: Now What?

revolution to instate a theocratic monarchy. The one thing he does not entreat us to do is *peaceably suffer as Christians*.

Wolfe devotes the next three subsections to promoting a "rugged austerity" among Christian nationalists through homesteading and similar practices. He complains that others deride this as "LARPing, or live action role playing – that one's anti-modernity is superficial, imaginary, and made possible by modernity itself."[819] Learning skills such as gardening, tending livestock, canning your own goods, and maintaining a home without full reliance on modern consumerist infrastructure is commendable. But, much like the idolatry of "manliness" or the worship of classical art and architecture, it is strange to frame homesteading as part of a *Christian Nationalist aesthetic*. When one goes beyond learning and adopting new, beneficial activities and perspectives and declares them markers of self-identification, he is trying on identities, like a teenager deciding he is now a "metal head" or "goth." That is what makes it LARPing.

> If you are a white, heterosexual, cis-gendered male, then the world will not offer you any favors. Indeed, your career advancement depends on sacrificing your self-respect by praising and pandering to your inferiors who rule over you.[820]

Again, by his resume, Wolfe does not have first-hand experience in the day-to-day life of white-collar corporate work. There has most certainly been a sharp increase in the broadcasting of left-wing politics in the workplace, and to counter such official company opinions will not endear you to management and will most likely cost you professionally, but active "praising and pandering" is only required in the most malignantly political companies that most conservative Christians would likely not choose to work at in the first place. Outside of deep-blue cities, most "socially conscious" companies are not at all like this, and "white, heterosexual, cis-gendered male" Christians currently do just fine in them as long as they are nice people who do good work. What one cannot do is be a vocally

---

819 Wolfe, 460–63.
820 Wolfe, 464.

belligerent patriarchalist lamenting the *psycho-sexual ethno-masochism* of "Western Man" inside the modern American office. This is not a new development; it has not been acceptable for decades. After all, what manager would put up with a subordinate who considers him an *inferior* only placed in his position as a "diversity hire"?

> There is certainly an unhealthy individualism, either the fake expressivist variety or the libertarian version that denies pre-political ties and unchosen bonds... The collectivist fear of individualism is that it isolates man from man or sets people in destructive opposition. But this falsely assumes that individuals pursuing mastery cannot spontaneously generate hierarchy. In such hierarchies, skills are synchronized under authority for a common mission.[821]

While Wolfe derides the left-wing form of collectivism, given what else he has written about naturally occurring aristocratic hierarchies, *corporate synchronization* of varying levels of ability in labor would likely not be a pure meritocracy under his system. Though he does not explicitly state it here, he already promoted the ultimate top-down ends of his nation when he stated that Christian Nationalism creates a "redundant web of obligation that orders **everything** ultimately to the national good" (emphasis mine).[822] Given these national obligations, corporate hierarchies would likely function closer to the authoritarian economic model of *National Syndicalism*, the belief that individual productivity is best ordered by a series of hierarchical organizations that funnel into top-down state control. Can it be believed that, under theocratic Caesearism, one could ascend to the status of *mid-level synchronizer of labor for the common mission* without being a member of good standing in the state church, much like some nations require major business owners to be members of the ruling party?

---

821 Wolfe, 465.
822 Wolfe, 13.

Epilogue: Now What?

> No one is a man among men, but a person among persons; and your standing among others is not because of something you've achieved but simply by virtue of the fact of existence, or by being superior at congratulating everyone for their existence or empathizing with another's "trauma."[823]

The amount of hyperbolic social grievance expressed through this section is no better than what one is likely to hear about "capitalist imperialism" at a Democratic Socialists of America convention. We still live in a world that requires goods and services for human sustenance, and those goods and services are provided by skilled labor, not by "congratulating everyone." How many people have read Wolfe's book and agree with this premise because they are actually forced to "empathize with another's 'trauma'" as a regular work task? This type of extreme framing of, and overreaction to, leftist excess does not solve the issue; it only creates an equally excessive rightist counter-option. Both sides straw-man and feed off of each other, further polarizing and escalating tensions until a breaking point is reached.

Wolfe's definition of the *American dream* as "each person's striving can attain him a respectable place among fellow Americans" and "recognition as a man among men"[824] is quite inaccurate. The dream has always been primarily economic, in that one's striving eventually moves him up one rung in the economic ladder, allowing his children to start life in a slightly better station, moving themselves up another rung, and so on. This is still happening, especially within immigrant communities; it is anything but "degrading and futile in most areas of the economy," and most Americans do not work for "woke corporations" that require they adopt ideologies of "self-loathing and self-incrimination."[825] These companies exist, and conservative Christians must be be increasingly judicious about evangelizing in the workplace (perhaps rightly), but Wolfe is exaggerating the issue to engender an emotional knee-jerk reaction from the reader. Only a Christian brought to an unnecessary fight-or-flight state by persistently

---
823 Wolfe, 466.
824 Wolfe, 466.
825 Wolfe, 467.

ingesting this type of hyperbole can be convinced to "reject the talk of 'universal dignity,'"[826] a core Christian principle grounded upon the existence of God's image in every human being.

> The need for a connection of people and place is natural and good. The Gospel did not "critique" or eliminate this. We should seek out forms of living that make that life possible.[827]

Before a Christian of *Western European descent* moved to a location where he could find a supposedly greater sense of connection of people and place, I would ask him whether he has taken the time to get to know his current neighbors. Has he spent time with the Arab Muslim family next door, and do they know him as their *friendly* and *kind* neighbor, or does he avoid them because they are ethnically and religiously different? Does he talk to the married gay couple across the street, and do they know him as the conservative Christian who obviously disagrees with their lifestyle, but who still exudes the love of Christ in their interactions, or is he the "bigot" who looks down his nose at them? Does he actually make an attempt to *live the gospel*, or is he more interested in retreating to a place of comfort, while ironically calling others *Anabaptists*?

> Christian nationalism, in light of grace, is most natural to the Christian human being. Thus the precursor to any Christian nationalism is a people intentionally seeking their natural good according to man's nature.[828]

The message that Christians are to primarily seek their own material good as their most natural and beneficial path is directly antithetical to the gospel. "Let no one seek his own good, but the good of his neighbor" (1 Corinthians 10:24). To reject this as a key directive is to reject the commandment of Christ, when he said, "If anyone would be first, he must be last of all and servant of all" (Mark 9:35). Christian Nationalist political

---

826 Wolfe, 467.
827 Wolfe, 468.
828 Wolfe, 469.

theory takes the self-serving actions of the world and wraps them in a fake pietism that speaks to the Western Christian's fear of life as a minority in a post-Christian nation.

> Christian nationalism should have a strong and austere aesthetic... we ought to be men of power and endurance. We cannot achieve our goals with such a flabby aesthetic and under the control of modern nutrition. Sneering at this aesthetic vision, which I fully expect to happen, is pure cope. Grace does not destroy T-levels...[829]

As opposed to the goal of good health or even just looking more attractive, the hyper-focus on physiological aesthetic as a *social marker* has long been a common theme in Nietzschean white nationalist online circles, where anonymous account holders often share pictures of themselves from the rear in bodybuilding poses like the *back double biceps* while hiding their face. It is strange that Wolfe would speak in similar terms as them in his *Christian* Nationalist theory, even to go as far as to use childish Internet lingo such as "pure cope." In November of 2022, only a week before Thomas Achord was exposed as holding explicitly white nationalist beliefs, he and Wolfe interviewed an anonymous white nationalist author, "Raw Egg Nationalist," on their podcast.[830] His book, *The Eggs Benedict Option*, a tongue-in-cheek play on Rod Dreher's *The Benedict Option*, is published by the white nationalist book publisher Antelope Hill, along with his magazine, *Man's World*. Raw Egg Nationalist is very much obsessed with aesthetics, most especially physical conditioning, often using homoerotic images of bodybuilders in his branding and social media.[831] It is difficult to

---

829 Wolfe, 469–70.
830 Stephen Wolfe on Twitter: "I can't remember if I tweeted this. We interviewed Raw Egg Nationalist... Check it out."
https://twitter.com/PerfInjust/status/1594809643460599809
831 Raw Egg Nationalist on Twitter: "A TESTOSTERONE MASTER THREAD. Here's a master thread of threads and posts about testosterone. You're sure to find something interesting in here, so make sure you bookmark this. In no particular order."
In the tweet is a picture of a naked man standing on a rock, with his legs and arms spread wide open, with a red light machine barely covering his genitals and with

believe that Wolfe would similarly speak of these types of aesthetics of male physique as a Christian Nationalist social marker without full knowledge of its common use among ethno-nationalist online accounts like Raw Egg Nationalist.

> For too long, we have looked to fiery political sermons to satisfy our concerns over the "culture"… This exaggerates things a bit, but still Christians have treated Sunday as their weekly political meeting. It should be no such thing, and practically speaking turning it into a political church hinders Christian political movements. We must form civil associations outside ecclesiastical sphere, and without pastoral leadership.[832]

I agree with Wolfe that politics should not be the primary messaging from behind the pulpit and that political churches hinder Christian political movements – but they also hinder individual Christian growth. The prevalence of political sermons in churches is one reason so many conservative American Christians have joined the world in equating political opinions with moral action, to the point where some now argue that Christians who vote for Democrats should face church discipline. Is there a more undeserved sense of moral superiority than believing you are a good person because you hold the "correct" opinions and vote for the "right" candidates?

Christian political movements should live outside the direct supervision of the church, but Christians themselves should not. Many of the core arguments of Wolfe's theory, if promoted within all but the most reactionary churches in America, would be considered discipline-worthy sins: for example, the belief that variance in "climate" produces differences in beauty and personal traits among people groups, that Christians should seek to live with people who are ethnically similar to them, and that ethnically differing Christians cannot live a fully beneficial life together.[833]

---

his face blurred.
https://twitter.com/Babygravy9/status/1652310463345033216

832 Wolfe, *The Case for Christian Nationalism*, 470–71.
833 Wolfe, 23, 67, 117–18, 142, 149, 151.

Epilogue: Now What?

The local church and its pastor serve as a guard against such extremist ideology among Christians through the processes of discipleship and discipline.

> Producing numbers [by having more babies] will not make a people, especially when the secularists actively try to steal them from us. Having babies is only one part of a greater project. Let us not be passive in things we can accomplish now.[834]

Wolfe rightly chides the popular notion of having children for the purpose of sending them into the world as little missionaries. Sending your children to secular high schools and colleges is more likely to make them like the world than the other way around. He is also correct that Christian parents should take more personal responsibility and be less passive in "things we can accomplish," but his obsession with political victory undercuts the most important goal, *to preach Christ crucified*. If Christians spend their lives hyper-focused on political victories for an imagined better future position for their tribe, what makes them any different than their secularist liberal opposition, but for the claim to be "doing God's will"? What makes this any different from the prosperity preacher who also claims he has devoted his life to giving Christians access to God's material blessings?

The section is ended with an appeal to read "old books, especially the epics – Homer and Virgil."[835] Wolfe could not more telegraph how little he is concerned with genuine Christian ethics than to only name pagan Greek and Roman authors when discussing classic writings for "morally formative education." What of Augustine of Hippo, John Bunyan, Martin Luther, John Calvin, John Owen, Jonathan Edwards, J.C. Ryle, Charles Spurgeon, and C.S. Lewis? *What of the Bible?* How could any dedicated Christian take the diatribes in this chapter seriously when Wolfe is so little concerned with the actual tenets and implications of the faith?

---

834 Wolfe, 471.
835 Wolfe, 471–73.

V. America is Not Lost

Reprising his subjective determination that "No unjust federal law is an ordinance of God, and so it is not backed by a power of God," Wolfe calls on state governors to "recall their duties to God and fight against injustices of the federal government."[836] As shown in chapter 9, Christians are to obey governmental authority as long as it does not instruct us to disobey the commandments of God. Wolfe does not elaborate on how state governors would fight the federal government, but, given that he dedicated a chapter to justifying revolution, and that he believes individual American states have the right to become theocracies, everything up to and including seceding from the Union would likely be on the table. Contrast this with how many of our Chinese brothers and sisters, under the yoke of a far more repressive government, view their situation and their greater responsibility to God's word. Wang Yi is pastor of an illegal Chinese "house church," who is currently serving a nine-year sentence for "inciting subversion of state power and illegal business operations," the set of charges thrown at him for refusing to join the official state "Christian" church, the Three-Self Patriotic Movement. He writes of how the church and its people are to seek peaceful obedience to the law of the land, even when tyrannical governments do not follow their own law, as long as the law's commands do not directly contradict the higher "constitutional power" of God's Law. This would also apply to state governors, who are "deputies of God" and bound by the same moral commandments.

> But here is the more important question: Is the Chinese government illegal? We should honestly and courageously respond: yes. For sixty years, this country has continuously trampled upon its own constitution and laws regarding religious freedom. Whether it is church worship, freedom of assembly, doctrine, religious property, the sacraments, missions, seminary training, pastor ordination, publishing, children's Sunday school, charity work, and so on, the government uses illegal, autocratic,

---

836 Wolfe, 473.

Epilogue: Now What?

and barbarous methods to oppress the church and the children of Christ in China...

"Aren't house churches illegal?" If the constitution is "the king" of the modern state, if the Chinese government claims that its power comes from the Chinese constitution and that it must comply with the constitution, I must honestly answer that for sixty years the house churches are the perfect model for submitting to the king and following the constitution. The church follows the constitution up to a point, even though all government officials have chosen to defy it, imprisoning those who do not violate the constitution with them. Still, the church continues to act "according to law" by upholding the constitutional right to worship God and preach the gospel just as before. And because we must abide by a higher "constitutional power," we dare not comply with the unconstitutional actions of the religious administrative system.[837]

How many devoted Christian pastors and churches would find themselves in the same position under *theocratic Caesarism*, forced to make a decision of whether to obey their interpretation of God's word or face civil punishment for refusing the direct influence of the state church? How weak of a people are American Christians if many of us are ready to forgo the directives of Romans 13 (or eisegete our way around them), because the majority of our countrymen no longer share our religious convictions? I have far more respect for a man who is willing to peaceably suffer for the gospel than one who looks to pick up a rifle and "defend" his praxis. Wolfe writes of local Christian Nationalist movements taking root in the United States, though "the GAE has captured" it nationally.[838] But there are few, if any, cities in America with a majority of orthodox Protestant citizens, let alone a majority of people who would be willing to put up with belligerent wannabe theocrats. I am greatly concerned, as our nation continues to polarize and, save a movement of the Spirit, Christianity continues to lose social influence, that those who sign on to

---

837 Yi Wang, "Chinese Christians' Costly Allegiance," Plough, March 14, 2023, https://www.plough.com/en/topics/faith/witness/chinese-christians-costly-allegiance2.

838 Wolfe, *The Case for Christian Nationalism*, 474.

Christian Nationalist visions like Wolfe's will increasingly come to the conclusion that violence is the only pathway out.

> Many claims in this book will worry many American conservative Christians. I've said that political governments can suppress false religion, establish a church, even require people to attend church. I also wrote about a "Christian prince," which is not the sort of political title one would find in America. I will not walk back those arguments;[839]

Wolfe has made far more than these arguments. He has argued for a "totality of national action" that completely inverts the liberal democratic order of *the state for the individual* into the *individual for the state*, the textbook definition of fascism. He has argued for using organized violence to "assert Christian supremacy" over non-Christians and to deny their right of consent of the governed. He has argued for executing people for unrepentant public wrongthink. He has argued that seeking ethnic homogeneity is a prelapsarian good, and that Christians of different ethnic groups are incapable of jointly finding the "complete good" in this life.

To this I only have one response: *anathema*.

---

839 Wolfe, 475.

Afterword

The Case for Christian Nationalism is not a Christian book. It is a book of traditionally secular, authoritarian, and ethno-nationalist political theory resting atop a strange, unscriptural hypothesis of prelapsarian man, validated through a loose "natural law" that serves as a faux-Christian justification for whatever the author finds most expedient, and wrapped in a cloak of Calvin's Two-Kingdoms theology, all to launder abhorrent views to a Christian audience. In many ways, it has been successful in its task. The average Christian intellectual gatekeeper, someone who has dedicated their education and profession to the topic of theology, likely does not know the sometimes esoteric tenets of rightist authoritarianism that are littered throughout the book, and most missed them in their reviews. In addition, the growing polarization of Western society has made many conservative Christians more friendly, or at least more charitable, towards bombastic rhetoric around ethnicity. Christian intelligentsia seems much more comfortable in discourses on church history and doctrine than new, supposedly "Christian" political theories. Within Reformed circles, many seem far more interested in challenging leftist excess outside of the church, something that will receive near universal praise from their colleagues, than to position themselves against Canon Press, who goes as far as to sell *The Case for Christian Nationalism* t-shirts, and, by proxy, Douglas Wilson, who wields notable influence within conservative Reformed thought-leadership.

Self-described *Christian Nationalism* is still in the formative, philosophical phase. Though Wolfe is the only author to provide a complete political theory, his is not the only definition of "Christian Nationalism" gaining traction. There are several overlapping camps who are friendly with each other, but who promote different visions. Stephen Wolfe promotes a more traditional, Nativist ethno-nationalism online and is most prominently joined by William Wolfe who, in his fervent disgust for "multiculturalism," regularly makes antagonistic comments about other ethnicities, including comparing a multicultural worship service to rape gangs.[840] Andrew Torba and Andrew Isker promote a Christian Nationalism that is more defined by open disdain for Jews than any other group. Beyond Torba's history of antisemitic comments on social media, their book, *Christian Nationalism: A Biblical Guide for Taking Dominion and Discipling Nations*, is less than seventy sparsely-filled pages long but dedicates an entire chapter to denouncing Talmudic Judaism. Isker has also claimed that a policy of Christian Nationalism should be to "oppose demographic replacement of the majority ethnic group in America."[841] A political and theological declaration, entitled *The Statement on Christian Nationalism and the Gospel*, was authored by anti-abortion activist James Silberman and pastor Dusty Deevers and was edited by several consistently belligerent and absolutist online Christian Nationalism proponents, including William Wolfe and pastor Joel Webbon.[842] It is a brief document that bills itself as a set of broad "governing principles" and affirmations, based upon very conservative Reformed Baptist theology, yet it contains no practical proposals for enacting those principles in the now overwhelmingly secular American system. Despite this, most of its authors and editors have expressed resentment that Christian Nationalism opponents have not given it the same level of attention as Stephen Wolfe's nearly five-hundred page, detailed treatise. They also seemingly expect their statement to be judged solely on its stated "principles" and not by the

---

840 Ben Marsh on Twitter: "Today's service had singing and prayer in three languages, sometimes simultaneously, prayer for the sick and for sin. Sermon from the Word. Ended with chapati, NC bbq, goat choma, fried plantains, beans and rice, peanut curry, peach cobbler, sweet tea. Multiculturalism [for the win]!"
William Wolfe: "Is this 'multiculturalism for the win?'"
Linked in the tweet is the Wikipedia entry for the Rotherham child sexual exploitation scandal.
https://twitter.com/William_E_Wolfe/status/1642601619572379648

841 Andrew Isker on Twitter: "An unstated part of the Christian Nationalism debate: is the intentional demographic replacement of the core ethnic group in America a good thing or a bad thing. If you oppose demographic replacement of the majority ethnic group in America, many Christian leaders will accuse you of sinning! Not good!"
https://twitter.com/BonifaceOption/status/1653179541777465345

842 James Silberman and Dusty Deevers, "The Statement on Christian Nationalism & the Gospel," CN & the Gospel, May 23, 2023,
https://www.statementonchristiannationalism.com.

Afterword

individual policies its authors and editors have promoted, such as Webbon's patriarchalism that includes the belief that a husband has the right to dictate what his wife can and cannot read, which received considerable online push-back.[843]

Regardless of how it may appear, it would be a mistake to consider this movement and its various camps as unserious and not very dangerous. Nearly every authoritarian movement of the 20th century, while in its formative phase, was regarded as a small fringe that did not need to be taken seriously. Secondly, one can consider authoritarian Christian Nationalism to be fringe enough that it will never gain traction within the broader American system while being keenly aware that it is a growing movement within the conservative church; besides, should Christians not be far more concerned with the health of the church than that of the government? Young Christian men who have spent their formative years fighting the "meme war" have taken its worldviews and tactics and are applying them to "Christian" political discourse. There is little that I have seen from Christian Nationalists, in the way of authoritarian and ethno-nationalist talking points, that I have not previously seen in vitriolic Internet forums like *4chan*, *The Donald*, and Torba's *Gab*. Wolfe, Torba, and Isker even use this lingo in their books: *pure cope, mammies, doomers,* etc. As long as theologians and pastors continue, by and large, to ignore this growing issue, more and more young Christian men who are often treated as dangerous extremists by mainstream media for publicly holding to conservative Christian social mores will come to the same conclusion as Christian Nationalism proponent Rett Copple, who wrote in response to the July 2023 French riots, "We are all France unless enough of us have settled in our hearts that it is time to be called 'racist.'"[844]

Wolfe's book speaks to a materially-obsessed American Christian church, specifically those who have spent their lives in the comfort of

---

843 Joel Webbon in a video recording of a sermon, describing how his wife was reading a book on paedobaptism: "There are certain books that I've just had to say, 'Hey, I don't know if this is a bad book, but I don't have time to read it, and so you're not going to read it either.'"
https://twitter.com/AndrewNWoodard/status/1678944596674375680

844 https://twitter.com/RettCopple/status/1674982912284868611

cultural Christianity and relative wealth and who are deathly afraid of either of those going away. Wolfe is correct that there is a perniciousness to the post-war consensus, not that it, as he wrote, "permitted Roman Catholics and Jews to have equal standing" and "transformed the country demographically and morally,"[845] but that it gave American Christians an inflated sense of worldly belonging. Only in the material abundance of post-war America could the *prosperity gospel* be born and, though middle of the bell-curve theology has long rejected its false tenets on the surface, many individual Christians have let its key value proposition into their hearts: that dedicating oneself to God is to be guaranteed a comfortable and materially abundant life. Now that conservative American Christians, within a few generations, have become a distinct minority, this false promise has been laid bare, leaving many feeling helpless and threatened. Wolfe does what all authoritarian theorists before him have done; he attempts to capitalize upon his audience's fear of losing social station to convince them that he and his ilk must be given top-down control of the nation in order to wrest society from *the other* and restore the *proper social order*.

That is not the gospel of Jesus Christ.

The victory over death was won by the Son of God on the cross roughly two millennia ago. He does not require our assistance to bring about His eternal, physical Kingdom. One day, in real space and time, He will return to judge the living and the dead. There is a gamble those promoting Christian Nationalism are taking: if God truly wants His people to physically suppress His enemies and to use state violence to assert the

---

845 Stephen Wolfe on Twitter: "Postwar conservatism was, in a way, a replacement movement opposed to the old American political tradition of Anglo-Protestantism, by insisting on the exclusive and simplistic *universalism* of the Founding, which permitted Roman Catholics and Jews to have equal standing in a country that deemed them, in a social sense at least, outsiders. But this unleashed the very universalism that has transformed this country demographically and morally. It is why they have no answer to our current crisis. It is why we no longer have a country."
https://twitter.com/PerfInjust/status/1671525126767091712

Afterword

supremacy of orthodox Protestant doctrine in the West, then those who obey would likely be received as extremely good and faithful servants. But if they are wrong in this assessment, and grievously take the name of God in vain, just like the prosperity gospel preaching, faith-healing televangelist, they risk being told, "I never knew you; depart from me, you workers of lawlessness" (Matthew 7:23). There is one thing I am certain of, that no man who abandons worldly gain, and who dedicates his life to peacefully preaching Christ crucified to a fallen world, will risk hearing those words.

Download the e-book for free at *christiannationalismnotes.com*

Printed in Great Britain
by Amazon